EUROPEAN MANAGEMENT GUIDES
General editor: Pete Burgess

Recruitment, Training and Development

Incomes Data Services

Institute of Personnel and Development

Phototypeset by The Comp-Room, Aylesbury
and printed in Great Britain by
Short Run Press, Exeter

British Library Cataloguing in Publication Data
A catalogue record for this book is available
from the British Library

ISBN 0 85292 648 0

The views expressed in this book are the
contributors' own, and may not necessarily
reflect those of the IPD.

**INSTITUTE OF PERSONNEL
AND DEVELOPMENT**

IPD House, Camp Road, London SW19 4UX
Tel: 0181 971 9000   Fax: 0181 263 3333
Registered office as above. Registered Charity No. 1038333
A company limited by guarantee. Registered in England No. 2931892

Contents

General Introduction

European Management Guides

The internationalisation of businesses within the European Union (EU), the creation of new corporate entities as a result of mergers and acquisitions across national boundaries, and the complexities of meshing cultures and practices – often accompanied by painful rationalisation – continue unabated in the 1990s. The management of the human resource dimension to these processes continues to pose fresh challenges to personnel practitioners, especially those confronted with international personnel issues for the first time.

The programme to realise a Single European Market by 1993 triggered a new raft of European-level legislative proposals intended to complement the commercial and economic aspects of European integration with a 'social dimension'. Although influential, and occasionally decisive, in a number of areas of employment regulation, EU legislation has left the diverse institutional structures of the member states largely untouched. Substantial differences in cultures, institutions, law and practice will persist for the foreseeable future, tempered more by broader economic exigencies than by legislative intervention from the European Commission. Indeed, the philosophy behind the 1993 Treaty on the European Union (the Maastricht Treaty) and the European Commission's more recent approach to employment policy is that greater scope should be left to negotiation and local implementation rather than monolithic prescription from Brussels.

Understanding and working with national diversity will therefore continue to be vital for personnel or line managers entrusted with European responsibilities. Although professional advice is indispensable when approaching a European venture or major personnel decision, access to basic and structured information can help in shaping the agenda for decisions – as well as saving precious time and money. The European Management Guides series aims to meet this need for accessible and comprehensive information on employment in the major economies of Western Europe. The second edition of the series, researched and written by Incomes Data Services Ltd (IDS) and published by the Institute of Personnel and Development (IPD), consists of three volumes covering:

- contracts and terms and conditions of employment
- industrial relations and collective bargaining
- recruitment, training and development.

European Management Guides are based on research carried out by the International Department of IDS using original national sources: this embraces the business press, specialist publications (including those from employer associations, trade unions, and personnel management organisations), legislation, collective agreements, and material on policy and practice supplied by companies and consultants, including extensive and regular face-to-face interviews with specialists and practitioners. The main sources, including published secondary material, are listed at the end of each country chapter.

Each volume presents information on a country-by-country basis, structured to allow easy comparative reference. Appendices detail local organisations that can provide further help and information. However, European Management Guides are not intended as a substitute for expert advice tailored to an individual situation and provided in the context of a professional relationship. Every effort has been made to ensure that the information contained in them is accurate and relevant. The publishers and authors offer them to readers on the understanding that neither organisation seeks to take the place of a lawyer or a consultant.

Incomes Data Services

Incomes Data Services has monitored employment developments in Europe since 1974. IDS's International Service publishes:

- *IDS Employment Europe*, a monthly subscription journal on pay and employment law and practice in member states of the European Union. Each issue includes news on pay, collective bargaining and legal developments in EU member states, a Country Profile drawing together trends and developments in the economy, pay, employment law, labour costs and executive remuneration for an individual country, together with regular supplements on European Union-level legislation and issues, with features, and regular statistics on pay trends and prices.
- *IDS International Documents,* comprising two series of in-depth reference sources on an individual country basis covering i) Pay and Conditions, ii) Recruitment and Dismissal. Updated regularly, each series provides both context and detail in these crucial areas of personnel management.

For more details contact: IDS Subscriptions, 77 Bastwick Street, London EC1V 3TT (tel: 0171 250 3434, fax: 0171 608 0949).

Acknowledgements

European Management Guides are researched and written by the staff and contributors of the International Department of Incomes Data Services Ltd, London. Individual country chapters were prepared by Matthew Bell, Angela Bowring, Pete Burgess, Mike Cannell, Fintan Hourihan, Sally Marullo, Tony Morgan, David Shonfield, Steve Steadman, George Tsogas, Marion Weißkirchen, and Caroline Welch. The series editor is Pete Burgess. The authors would like to thank the many individuals, companies and organisations who helped in the research for their time and co-operation, and in particular Fernando Tempera (Lisbon), Peter Forster (Roy C. Hitchman, Zurich), Dikran H. Katsikian (Hansar Excel, Athens), and Danae Salepoula-Weber (ALBA, Athens); the staff of the publishing department of the Institute of Personnel and Development, for their patient and scrupulous editorial input; and the national committees of the IPD for their support and advice.

Introduction

Recruitment, Training and Development

Recruitment, Training and Development is the third volume of the new three-volume series of IDS/IPD European Management Guides. It sets out to provide detail and context for 14 European Union (EU) member states on the following:

- the labour market, participation rates, education and skill levels
- statutory requirements and codes of practice on recruitment
- using flexible alternatives – part-timers, fixed-term contracts and agency workers – to permanent employment
- recruitment routes, selection methods and sex equality
- the education system and vocational training
- management education and continuing training
- useful addresses and reference sources.

In particular, it aims to offer a starting-point for those looking at recruitment across Europe as practitioners by outlining the background to the educational and vocational qualifications of potential (and existing) employees.

The changing recruitment context of the 1990s

Compared with the first edition of the IDS/IPD European Management Guide covering recruitment (published in 1990), the recruitment context in Europe has been characterised by a number of marked changes. We summarise some of the main trends below.

Whatever happened to the `demographic time bomb'?

The end of the 1980s boom and the onset of a phase of recession and, at best, muted growth in most EU countries in the early to mid-1990s was paralleled by a corresponding shift from short-term skill shortages, laced with anxieties about longer-term reductions in the supply of qualified younger workers because of the 'demographic time bomb', to persistent and high levels of unemployment, especially among semi-skilled and unskilled workers.

The quantitative expansion of higher education also eased employer worries about serious shortages of graduates: in many countries, the impending shortages of the late1980s have turned into a glut. However, as we note below, this very expansion has raised new problems of selectivity for graduate recruiters: the universal cry of employers throughout Europe is that many graduates lack the very skills – social and communicative competence, and a commitment to careers – that they were thought to embody. Moreover, the glut in overall graduate output co-exists with emerging shortages in a number of specialist subjects – especially engineering and electronics, capable multi-media specialists, and accountancy. In part this is attributable to the 'counter-cyclical' character of subject selection by undergraduates. For example, the recession in German manufacturing industry in 1993/4 blunted the enthusiasm of young people for training in mechanical engineering, with a switch into law and business management – subjects favoured by the growing consultancy sector. Rising manufactured exports and a contraction in the supply of graduate engineers have now enhanced the recruitment prospects of this reduced cohort.

The 'demographic time bomb' has not gone away: the populations of Germany and Italy are set to shrink over the next 30 years, and every European country will see an adverse shift in the relationship between the economically active population and the retired. Rather, the demographic problem has been shifted primarily to those responsible for designing social security systems – and ultimately to the working populations of the future. None the less, the prospect of longer working lives and more career changes within those working lives will mean that offering life-long learning opportunities, continuing training and enhanced employability will remain central policy concerns for the education and training community, both in public roles and in personnel management.

Higher education expands – but UK goes against the grain

The first half of the 1990s saw a continuing expansion of higher education, particularly marked in the UK, Spain and France. In mainland Europe, and especially in Austria, Germany, Switzerland and Portugal, much of the prospective expansion of higher education will be taking place in non-university, more vocationally oriented institutions (*Fachhochschulen* or 'polytechnics') which either give a vocational twist to academic learning or seek to broaden the education of those choosing higher vocational education after school. At any event, the graduates of these institutions are regarded as highly employable, and are often preferred to university graduates by many employers who value the practical and social dimension to the work experience which is an integral part of such students' education.

Although university reform is on the agenda in a number of countries, large tracts of higher education in mainland Europe still suffer under the burden of – virtually – open enrolment, overcrowded facilities, overstretched faculties, and lack of direction: drop-out rates continue to be very high, and the pressures on these systems can only increase in the short run as more and more young people turn away from initial vocational training and pursue the right to enter tertiary education.

The UK is exhibiting some contradictory trends, converging in some respects with the rest of Europe but moving away in others. First and foremost, the rapid expansion of higher education in Britain has run in parallel with the abolition in 1992 of the differences between universities and the former polytechnics (now dubbed the 'new universities'). In contrast, as noted above, in much of Europe the expansion of tertiary education is taking place primarily through non-university institutions with an overtly vocational approach, shorter courses than their national university degrees (although often still longer than a UK first degree), and work placements as a standard component. In Germany, for example, the university authorities have indicated a target of 40 per cent of all students to be in polytechnics by 2010, compared with 12 per cent in 1995. Although many of the 'new' UK universities will continue to be marked by their polytechnic legacy, with an emphasis on modular and vocationally oriented curricula and a local focus, other countries have taken the view that their future needs will be best served by a distinctive 'brand' of institution.

At the same time, more and more UK universities will undoubtedly draw closer to the practices of Continental European higher education. The expansion of higher education has seen a substantial rise in drop-out rates as enrolment opportunities have been expanded and direct financial support for students reduced. The need for greater parental support, combined with enrolment of mature students, could also lead to a fundamental lifestyle change for British undergraduates, increasing numbers living at or near home – much more in line with their Continental counterparts.

Whether this localisation will change the current broad hierarchy of institutions and graduate recruitment practices towards the prevalent pattern in Europe remains to be seen. However, the development of close links between businesses and local universities, with greater targeting of recruitment onto known faculties and responsiveness of curricula towards regional business needs, could be beneficial and cost-effective for employers, especially for smaller firms that need graduates to develop their businesses but cannot afford to embark on expensive national campaigns.

The changing legal framework for recruitment

Although the UK continues to stand out as offering probably the most unregulated route into employment, the 1990s have seen a number of changes in statutory recruitment procedures and the legal environment in several EU countries. The placement monopoly enjoyed by the public employment service has been abolished in Germany and Spain, for example, and the conditions under which employment agencies operate – for temporary and permanent positions – have been eased in many EU member states, although statutory restrictions on how employers may use temps remain widely in force. Only Italy and Greece retain a formal ban on temporary work agencies, although the extensive informal economies operating in both countries do allow employers other options when looking to meet short-term needs. Moreover, there is an emerging consensus in both countries that their economies might benefit from a legalisation of agencies without detriment to employees. Draft legislation has been in existence for some time in Italy, and the Greek trade unions are reported as no longer opposed in principle to a relaxation of the law.

Recruitment procedures have been markedly simplified in Italy, which has one of the most notoriously difficult systems to navigate, and there are efforts to shift the public employment service there from one essentially designed to monitor and control recruitment activity to one that seeks to match jobseekers with prospective employers. Although often overwhelmed by rising unemployment, other public employment services have been trying to improve their image and efficiency.

Where employment agencies have been recently legalised, such as in Austria and Germany, they account as yet for only a tiny proportion of placements; this may change should the economic outlook improve and should they succeed in building a positive image with prospective applicants and personnel departments.

The lack of statutory prescription in British recruitment procedures is offset to some degree – certainly in companies that seek to follow accepted standards of best practice – by a body of case-law and institutional support in the area of sex and, in particular, race discrimination which has had an impact on the recruitment process far beyond that seen in most other EU member states.

Despite the public difficulties associated with word-of-mouth and family based recruitment in the UK, it remains a prime route of entry into employment in many EU countries, and is the predominant method in Southern Europe.

European Union training initiatives

Under the Treaty of Rome (article 118), the European Commission is entrusted with the task of promoting co-operation between member states in the areas of basic and advanced vocational training. Article 128 also requires the Council of Ministers to lay down general principles for implementing a 'common vocational training policy' whose role is to contribute to the 'harmonious development of . . . national economies and the common market'. The European Social Fund, established under article 123 of the Rome treaty, makes funds available for measures intended to promote geographical and occupational mobility, and specifically for vocational retraining.

The organisation responsible for Commission activities on training is the Education, Training and Youth Directorate, DG XXII, although activities conducted under the European Social Fund come under the Employment, Industrial Relations and Social Affairs Directorate, DG V.

Research and co-ordination of information-gathering on education and training are carried out by a separate agency, the European Centre for the Development of Vocational Training (CEDEFOP), based in Thessalonika in Greece. Although it is independent of the Commission it co-operates extensively with DG XXII, because one of its tasks is to provide technical and scientific support for the Commission in developing and implementing its vocational training policy. It may be that this role will be expanded in the future and that CEDEFOP will become more proactive. Among CEDEFOP's publications are monographs describing the vocational training systems in EU member states.

EU efforts in the field of vocational education and training currently centre on the following areas:

- mutual recognition of professional qualifications
- comparability of vocational qualifications
- the Leonardo da Vinci programme, which focuses on sustaining quality and supporting innovation in vocational training through trans-national projects
- support for training in individual member states through the European Social Fund and the ESF's ADAPT initiative.

With the exception of grants and contributions to training schemes through the Social Fund, most of these programmes have been aimed at improving the mobility of labour rather than shaping or harmonising national training programmes. Moreover, whereas the programme for the mutual recognition of professional qualifications has culminated in directives imposing obligations on member states, such activities as have taken place in the field of vocational qualifications are intended to provide information; for example, there is no requirement on an employer recruiting workers to accept a vocational qualification awarded in another EU country as equivalent to a national qualification.

Mutual recognition of professional qualifications

The EU has adopted two broad approaches in seeking to enhance the free movement of professionally qualified people within the Union. They are termed the 'sectoral approach' and the 'general approach'.

The sectoral approach represented the first method by which the then Community sought to guarantee free movement. Under it the Community compared the education and training of individual professions in each member state, then attempted to harmonise them across the entire Community. Member states must restrict entry to the selected professions to individuals with a qualification that meets the harmonised standard. Any individual holding such a qualification is entitled to have it recognised in other member states. The outcome has been a series of directives for specific professions; at present, they cover doctors, vets, midwives, pharmacists and general practitioners. Architects have been subject to a slightly different approach, under which member states are required to recognise any architectural qualification of degree standard provided it covers the fields set out in the directive and lasts for a specified minimum duration. This approach has been protracted and complex: 17 years were required to agree the directive on architects, for example.

In 1985 the Commission moved to a broader procedure, under which qualifications covering all 'regulated professions' would be recognised by all member states in fields requiring at least three years' university-level education (or the equivalent). In the UK, the term 'regulated profession' includes those directly regulated by the State but more commonly by professional bodies operating under royal charter. The professions covered include accountants, chartered engineers, barristers and solicitors, teachers, and state-registered professions supplementary to medicine such as physiotherapy and chiropody. The approach was embodied in Directive 89/48/EEC, adopted by the Council of Ministers in December 1988 with implementation from January 1991. The provisions of the directive apply in Norway, Iceland, and Liechtenstein as well as in the 15 member states of the EU. Most countries have now implemented the directive into their national laws, but there are still a few professions in some countries where implementation remains incomplete.

The system operates through the regulating bodies, which are required to examine qualifications and accept applications subject to a number of safeguards. First, if the length of training received by an individual in one member state is shorter than in the country they wish to work in, the regulating body can ask for evidence of up to four years' experience as a fully qualified professional. Secondly, if there are differences in the content of curricula, incoming professionals can either take an examination to verify their ability or undergo a period of up to three years' supervised practice. However, in occupations involving a detailed knowledge of national law the member state can impose a procedure. In the UK the regulations implementing the directive are the responsibility of the Department of Trade and Industry (see below).

In June 1994, when Directive 92/51/EEC came into effect, this approach was extended to regulated occupations, admission to which requires a qualification (diploma, certificate) obtained after one to three years' study. In the UK, this would embrace a number of occupations accredited as National Vocational Qualifications (SVQs in Scotland) at Levels 3 and 4.

Comparability of vocational qualifications

In contrast to EU initiatives in the field of professional qualifications, there is no requirement on member states to provide for mutual recognition of vocational qualifications. However, between 1985 and 1992 the Commission, through CEDEFOP (in consultation with employers' organisations, trade unions and training organisations), prepared information aimed at enhancing workers' freedom of movement by enabling them, and prospective employers, to gauge the status of qualifications for a range of skilled jobs, grouped by sector.

Nineteen industrial and commercial sectors, and 209 occupations within them, were selected for examination. The results were published in the then EC's

Official Journal around the end of 1992, each time as a separate publication. For each job description, the procedure examines the title (and in some cases the level) of the qualification (in the original language and in translation), the institutions providing training and the organisations awarding the qualification.

It should be emphasised that by now much of this information is out-dated (for example, it would not have taken account of much of the development of N/SVQs in the UK) and is by no means comprehensive. There are no plans for a similar exercise in the future, or for mutual recognition of vocational qualifications (as opposed to professional qualifications).

However, in its 1996 White Paper, *Teaching and learning: towards the learning society*, the Commission noted that all European countries were attempting to identify key skills and the best ways of acquiring, assessing and certifying them. It therefore proposed to set up a European system to compare and disseminate such definitions, methods and practices. This would involve pinpointing a number of well-defined areas of knowledge of a general or more specialised nature (mathematics, information technology, accountancy, finance, management etc), devising validation systems for each of them, and introducing new, more flexible ways of acknowledging skills. The aim would be to complement formal qualification systems – on a voluntary basis – and to 'awaken a new thirst for education in those not wishing or unable to learn in a conventional teaching setting'.

About 1 per cent of the EU's workforce do not work in their home country and, arguably, need a means of demonstrating their skills in other countries. 'Personal skills cards' would therefore be provided to allow individuals to have their knowledge recognised as and when it was acquired, and a European Skills Accreditation System would be set up covering technical and vocational skills, based on a co-operative venture involving higher education establishments, vocational sectors, chambers of commerce, employers and trade unions.

At the time of writing (February 1997) a pilot project based on assessment via the Internet using multiple choice questions was about to begin. The reason for the choice of computer-based testing is that it would make the assessment totally objective, whereas other methods would be administratively cumbersome. However, UK employers have expressed reservations about the approach proposed by the Commission, pointing out that it is contrary to the way N/SVQs have developed: N/SVQs are about whether people can do particular jobs rather than measuring their knowledge. Moreover, there is a danger that such computer-based assessments could be either so general that they reveal virtually nothing or so complex that they would be difficult to understand.

The German central employers association, the BDA, has also objected that the use of British benchmarks is disadvantageous to German vocational qualifications. The BDA argues that a completed German apprenticeship should be worth more than Level 3, given the period of time and intensity of study or training under the German dual system.

Leonardo da Vinci programme

Commonly known as Leonardo, this (together with ADAPT – see below) replaced the previous Comett, Euroform, Eurotecnet, Force and Petra programmes, all of which expired at the end of 1994. Leonardo will run until 1999.

The programme aims to support and sustain quality and innovation in member states' vocational training systems. Activities include:

- trans-national pilot projects concerned with the content and delivery of initial and continuing vocational training, vocational guidance, transfer of technologies, university-business co-operation, promoting equal opportunities for men and women in training, and development of language skills
- trans-national exchanges and placements for young trainees and workers, higher education students, graduates and those who deliver training
- surveys and analyses and the exchange of comparable data
- support for a European network of national organising bodies.

The measures are grouped into three strands, each with an overall focus:

Strand I supports the improvement of vocational training systems and arrangements in the member states through trans-national pilot projects and transnational exchanges and placements.

Strand II supports the improvement of training actions aimed at companies and employees (including university/enterprise co-operation) through trans-national pilot projects and trans-national exchanges and placements.

Strand III supports the development of language skills, knowledge and dissemination of innovation through:

- trans-national pilot projects to improve language skills
- trans-national exchanges between enterprises and language training institutions
- 'multiplier-effect' projects to disseminate the outcomes of pilot projects
- trans-national exchanges for decision-makers
- trans-national surveys and analyses
- exchanges of comparable data on training in the member states.

Financing

The overall budget for the programme is 620 million ECU. Trans-national pilot projects can attract funding to cover 75 per cent of costs, to a maximum of 100,000 ECU per year. Projects can last up to three years, except for 'multipliereffect' projects, which will have a maximum duration of two years.

Trans-national exchanges and placements will attract up to a maximum of 5,000 ECU for each participant on each placement. Only placements and exchanges lasting for the maximum duration set down in each category will qualify for the maximum grant.

Surveys, research and information activities will attract funding to cover between 50 per cent and 100 per cent of costs.

Eligibility and participating countries

Any organisation involved with vocational training is eligible to apply for funding. In the UK this includes, for example, Training and Enterprise Councils (TECs) and Local Enterprise Companies (LECs), industry training organisations, lead bodies, businesses, private training companies, trade unions, voluntary bodies, professional organisations, and further and higher education institutions.

Applications will be ineligible if they involve partners from fewer than three participating countries (except Strand I placements and exchanges and Strand III language projects which may involve partners from only two member states). Participating countries are the 15 member states of the EU plus the EFTA states of the European Economic Area (Iceland, Liechtenstein and Norway).

In 1996 the following countries outside the EU and EFTA were added: Bulgaria, Cyprus, the Czech Republic, Estonia, Hungary, Latvia, Malta, Poland, Rumania, Slovakia and Slovenia. However, any partners from the above-mentioned countries can only be added to partnerships that already fulfil all the criteria: in other words, the partnership must be trans-national and consist of at least three partners from three different EU or EFTA countries. The European Commission could not in 1996 fund any activities from these Eastern European or Mediterranean countries, so partners from these states had to pay the costs of their participation out of their own funds. At the time of writing, this situation was under review.

Maximising chances of success

The selection process is highly competitive: in 1995, although the standard of UK bids was generally regarded as high and the UK had the second highest number of projects in the Community, only one in six of the proposed UK-led projects succeeded in getting funding.

The Department for Education and Employment (DfEE) advises that key elements of successful bids include:

- the added value from the trans-national dimension
- developing 'business' links and opportunities or networks
- developing better products
- development of individuals' competences
- sharing experience and expertise.

Particular types of partner need to be considered. Those especially encouraged are:

- partnerships combining previous experience of Community programmes with the fresh approach of partners new to European training programmes
- proposals aimed at sharing innovative practice with less developed regions
- proposals that are employer-led or have significant employer input
- partnerships bringing together different types of organisations – for example, employers and training providers.

Proposals should involve more than one partner within the UK and should strengthen domestic partnerships. Thus, educational bodies and other training organisations are advised by the DfEE to involve employers and employer-led organisations in their project proposals. Partnerships might be local, involving for example an employer with a TEC, LEC or local educational institution; or sectoral, perhaps involving an Industry Training Organisation (ITO) with other bodies; or a combination of local and sectoral.

Management arrangements should demonstrate that the partners can respond quickly to the inevitable changes to plans and priorities that will occur during the course of any project; and, above all, that there are detailed criteria in place for monitoring and evaluating project activities.

Where the project involves placements or exchanges, and where the linguistic proficiency of the participants is inadequate, provision must be made for the linguistic and cultural preparation of the trainees.

Proposals in all areas need to specify their objectives and expected outcomes. In particular, they must demonstrate how they will support member states' training policies and objectives. Guidance on the criteria, both for the UK and the Community, is published annually but for the UK it is likely that key factors and priorities for the foreseeable future will include, for example, whether:

- the project is likely to contribute to achieving one of the National Targets for Education and Training
- it is concerned with training people for competence-based vocational qualifications such as N/SVQs
- one of the organisations involved is committed to or has achieved the Investors in People standard
- it seeks to meet the needs of those disadvantaged in the labour market, especially young people
- there is an involvement with the Business Links programme.

Additional information that might be included in proposals might be how they promote equal opportunities or innovative forms of training or how they focus on industrial change.

A key factor in successful applications is the proposed arrangements for dissemination and transfer of results. These should be proactive and include, for example, plans to exploit the products developed and to transfer the good practice more widely. Applications should say a good deal about dissemination. Moreover, dissemination activity is recommended to start early in the life of projects; this has proved a valuable way of testing the intended outputs.

Submitting applications

Calls for proposals are usually issued annually towards the end of February, with a deadline for the submission of applications around the end of May. The relatively short time-scale between call and deadline means that would-be applicants are advised to have their proposals and potential partners fairly well worked out by the time the call is issued. The DfEE runs annual conferences to advise would-be applicants and to help them find partners from other member states.

Applications may be assessed by people who, although having a broad knowledge of training policies and initiatives, may not be experts in particular specialist areas or have English as their first language. Proposals should therefore be detailed, clear, concise and free from jargon.

European Social Fund

The European Social Fund (ESF) is one of the three Structural Funds established under the Treaty of Rome to strengthen the economic and social cohesion of the Union (the other two cover regional development and agriculture). It aims to help improve employment opportunities by providing financial support for the running costs of vocational training schemes and job creation measures. Funds have played a central role in developing training and public employment institutions in Portugal and Greece, as the national chapters below illustrate.

Measures under the ESF address the following priority objectives:

Objective 1 – to improve the development of regions that are currently underdeveloped. (In the UK, these are Northern Ireland, Merseyside, and the Highlands and Islands. Funds in Northern Ireland are administered by the Northern Ireland Office, and in the Highlands and Islands by the Scottish Office.)

Objective 2 – to regenerate designated areas affected by industrial decline. (In Great Britain, these are West Midlands, East Midlands, Yorkshire and Humberside, North West England, Stoke on Trent, Burton on Trent, West Cumbria, Barrow, North East England, industrial South Wales, East and West Scotland, East London and the Lea Valley, Thanet and Plymouth.)

Objective 3 – to combat long-term unemployment and assist young people into work; to help those liable to exclusion from the labour market; and to promote equal opportunities between men and women. This objective operates throughout

Great Britain outside the Objective 1 areas.

Objective 4 – to facilitate the occupational integration of young people (not applicable in the UK).

Objective 5a – to speed up the adjustment of agricultural structures, and

Objective 5b – to promote the development of rural areas. This is the rural equivalent of Objective 1. In Great Britain, the areas are Devon, Cornwall and West Somerset, Dumfries and Galloway, rural Wales, the Northern Uplands, East Anglia, the English Marches, Lincolnshire, Derbyshire, Derbyshire and Staffordshire, the Borders, rural Stirling/Upper Tayside, North and West Grampian.

The ESF operates under the principle of partnership between the relevant national authority, the European Commission and the organisations running projects, which are represented on committees and working groups and which have a say in the monitoring of objectives. Current partners include TECs, LECs, further and higher education institutions, local authorities, voluntary organisations and industry training organisations.

Type of assistance

The Fund will contribute towards the operational running costs of projects by matching amounts provided by public authorities up to a maximum of 45 per cent (higher in Objective 1 areas – up to a maximum of 75 per cent).

Eligibility

Any recognised organisation that runs eligible training schemes or employment measures can apply for ESF support, as long as it is supported financially by a public authority such as a local authority, central government, TEC or LEC. Individuals cannot apply for ESF support.

All schemes must fall within the broad areas of vocational training, retraining, job creation (including self-employment opportunities) or vocational guidance and counselling.

Priorities for ESF assistance in Objective 2 areas are principally assistance for the development of small and medium-sized enterprises, improving the image and attractiveness of the region, tourism, and support for research and development.

Applications to the Fund in the UK must be submitted through the DfEE, which provides application forms as well as guidance on eligibility and presentation. The DfEE supports annual conferences around April aimed at helping potential bidders maximise their chances of success and find partners.

The ADAPT programme

ADAPT is the European Social Fund Initiative designed to help European employers and workers anticipate industrial change and deal with its effects. Unlike the initiatives described above, ADAPT operates nationwide.

The UK is the largest recipient of Community funds for ADAPT, with a total Community contribution of 286.60 MECU and a total budget, including the UK government contribution, of 620.30 MECU in the period of life of the programme between 1995 and 1999.

ADAPT has links with Leonardo, but whereas Leonardo is concerned with the quality and the structure of training and qualifications across the whole workforce, ADAPT concerns itself with employment retention and creation. In this, training is important but other measures such as forecasting and the development of support structures also form an integral part.

Specifically, ADAPT's aims are:

- to help accelerate the adaptation of the workforce to industrial change
- to increase competitiveness in industry, services and commerce
- to prevent unemployment by developing the workforce through improving qualifications and their internal and external flexibility, and ensuring greater occupational flexibility
- to anticipate and accelerate the development of new jobs and new activities, particularly labour-intensive ones.

The rationale behind ADAPT is that since 1980 the European economies have been performing worse than both the United States and Japan in terms of levels of unemployment and the creation of new jobs. Most new European jobs are created by small to medium-sized enterprises (SMEs), which make up more than 90 per cent of European companies but which carry out less training than their larger counterparts. They also frequently lack local support which could help them develop further and faster, and retain and consolidate existing jobs. In the UK in particular, the focus of resources is very much on SMEs (defined as those employing up to 250 people), given the continuing decline of jobs in large companies and the growth of jobs in SMEs, especially those which employ fewer than 50 people.

Unlike Leonardo, calls for which are issued annually, calls for ADAPT projects are issued less regularly. Projects typically run for periods of two or three years.

The principles behind ADAPT

All ADAPT projects must have at least three trans-national partners in other member states to enable them to benefit from each others' experience and ideas and, above all, to ensure that the experience gained is shared as widely as possible. They must also be innovative in some way – in their content, in the way in which they are executed, in the types or combination of partners involved, or in their final products. A key consideration in the selection of projects is how their outcomes could lead to new developments in some aspect of labour market policy. They should contribute locally, and therefore combine the largest possible range of local labour market organisations and companies, and have a multiplier effect, in that they should not only help the organisations involved locally to develop policies and strategies to forecast and cope with industrial change, but also affect policy and practice at all levels by being recorded and evaluated and made publicly available.

Funding

ADAPT will fund up to 45 per cent of the eligible running costs of projects (not capital costs), except in some Objective 1 areas, such as Merseyside and Highlands and Islands in the UK, where the ESF will fund up to 50 per cent. The remainder of the funding must come from public and private sources. Projects must have a minimum of 25 per cent public match funding and 20 per cent private match funding.

ADAPT target groups

Different member states have slightly varying emphases, but in Great Britain ADAPT targets three groups either directly or through training or informing agents of change (such as trainers or managers) who will go on to influence the ultimate beneficiary groups:

- employees of SMEs threatened with redundancy due to industrial change
- former employees who have lost their jobs as a result of restructuring
- workers who have involuntarily moved to part-time work and have the potential to be employed in newly created jobs after retraining.

Preference is given to projects involving firms with fewer than 50 employees; direct training measures are restricted to the latter group.

ADAPT measures

ADAPT measures are directed at preserving and stabilising existing jobs, at supporting the creation of new jobs, and at the movement of workers vulnerable to the effects of change into new occupations and forms of work.
  Four measures exist to serve these objectives:

- training, counselling and guidance activities, improving companies' expertise and capacity to produce business and training plans, developing training for new skills and qualifications, improving guidance systems, and giving special emphasis to improved training for SMEs and entrepreneurs

- forecasting, networking and the creation of new employment opportunities, involving the creation of sectoral and regional networks to analyse labour market trends, training and co-operation related to new fields of economic activity
- the adaptation of support structures and systems, including intercompany co-operation on research and technology transfer, training of trainers to adapt workers to industrial change, and regional, interregional and trans-national co-operation between companies
- information, dissemination and awareness activities such as databases on employment, interregional and trans-national dissemination of best practice, studies on industrial change, and awareness-raising activities.

Projects carried out under ADAPT might include, for example, inter-company responses to skill and training needs, training for new qualifications and skills, development of databases on employment, training and economic information, or training and support for prospective entrepreneurs.

Private companies may not initiate ADAPT projects. This must be done by bodies with at least an element of public funding. In the UK this includes TECs, LECs, Business Links, ITOs, local authorities, government departments, and universities and colleges. Organisations other than these wishing to run an ADAPT project should contact one of the above. Advice can be obtained from several sources in Britain and Northern Ireland (see below). It is strongly advised that if the applicant organisation is not a TEC or LEC, advice should be sought from the local TEC or LEC, given their important role in developing local strategies for employment and training.

Selection

The selection process is competitive, based on the quality of the applications, the extent to which they innovate in line with national policy, and the depth of the trans-national links.

In addition, preference is given to projects that demonstrate partnership by involving a number of firms, enable employees to obtain competence-based qualifications (especially those at N/SVQ Level 3 and above), aim to retrain workers from occupational areas traditionally occupied by men or women to higher-level skill areas in which their sex has previously been underrepresented, and are complementary to activity under the mainstream ESF Objectives (see above), other Community Initiatives, and other European programmes such as Leonardo.

The Employment Initiative

The Employment Initiative is a further Community Programme of the European

Social Fund which will operate until the end of 1999. It targets groups that face specific difficulties in the employment market and has three interrelated strands:

- NOW, aimed at women
- HORIZON, which targets disadvantaged social groups such as the disabled, refugees and drug addicts
- YOUTHSTART, which seeks to improve youth training and employment opportunities, especially for those with little or no basic qualifications who are marginalised from mainstream training and employment options.

Like the other schemes described above, all projects under the Employment Initiative must have a trans-national dimension – that is, operate in close co-operation and partnership with at least one other project financed by the Initiative in another member state. They should be innovative, experimenting with new ideas and approaches; a key consideration in selection is how the outcomes of projects could lead to new developments in some aspect of labour market policy. Projects should be grassroots-based, as experience shows that the bottom-up approach is the most effective way of meeting the needs of target groups. They should involve a wide range of local individuals and organisations to combine knowledge and experience and as with other Community programmes, they should have a multiplier effect to enable their results to be exploited by others than those who have been directly involved.

Other programmes

There are other EU programmes in the area of education and training and development worth a brief mention here because readers may see references to them elsewhere.

Socrates is the educational equivalent of the Leonardo da Vinci programme. Sub-divisions of it cover higher education (Erasmus); school education (Comenius); language learning (Lingua); and study visits for educational decision-makers (Arion).

The European Training Foundation is an autonomous agency of the EU, based in Turin, Italy. It co-ordinates and supports all EU activities in the field of post-compulsory education as part of the Phare and Tacis programmes for economic restructuring in the 24 partner countries in Central and Eastern Europe and Central Asia. Phare covers those former Communist countries in Europe other than those of the ex-Soviet Union (but including the Baltic republics), while Tacis covers those Eastern European and Central Asian states which formerly comprised the Soviet Union. Tempus is the EU's instrument for the development and restructuring of higher education in the Phare and Tacis partner countries.

Organisations

European Commission
Directorate General XXII
Education, Training and Youth
Rue da Loi 200
B-1049 Brussels
Belgium
Tel. +32 2 299 11 11
Fax +32 2 295 57 04
Internet http://www.cec.lu/
en/comm/dg22/dg22.html

CEDEFOP
Marinou Antipa 12
GR-57001 Thessalonika
Greece
Postal address
P.O.B. 27 - Finikas
GR-55012 Thessalonika
Greece
Tel. +30 31 49 01 11
Fax +30 31 49 01 02

Liaison office in Brussels
20 Avenue d'Auderghem
Postbox 327
B-1040 Brussels
Belgium
Tel./Fax +32 2 230 58 24

On professional qualifications
Department of Trade and Industry
Trade Policy and Europe Directorate
Kingsgate House
Victoria Street
London SW1E 6SW
Tel. +44 171 215 4648
Fax +44 171 215 4489

On vocational qualications
Department for Education and
Employment
Qualifications and Standards Branch
Moorfoot
Sheffield S1 4PQ
Tel. 0114 259 4151
Fax 0114 259 4475

EUROPEAN SOCIAL FUND,
ADAPT AND THE EMPLOYMENT
INITIATIVE
European Commission
Directorate General V
Employment, Industrial Relations and
Social Affairs
Rue da Loi 200
B-1049 Brussels
Belgium
Tel. +32 2 295 63 58
Fax +32 2 295 97 70
Internet http://www.cec.lu/
en/comm/dg5/dg5.html

EUROPS
2/3 Place du Luxembourg
B-1040 Brussels
Tel. +32 2 511 15 10
Fax +32 2 511 19 60

EUROPS, the European Office for
Programme Support, assists the
European Commission in the
implementation of the ADAPT
programme.

1

Austria

The regulation of the Austrian labour market is characterised by a strong role for the social partners as well as a number of specialised authorities. Employer and employee organisations, for example, have statutory tasks in supervising the accreditation of occupations within the system of vocational training, as well as a broader role in administering a number of welfare institutions. Some deregulation has begun to take place. In the labour market field, the state employment service has been privatised and the state monopoly on job placement abolished. However, practitioners comment that the lifting of bureaucratic regulations is proving a slow and cumbersome process.

The labour market

Despite economic growth in 1995/6, employment levels have been falling, with concern about the export of jobs to low-wage areas – especially Eastern Europe. In 1995 the labour force stood at 3,265,100 out of a total population of 7.6 million. The overall labour force participation rate has remained broadly constant, at 66–67 per cent, for the past 20 years. This stability conceals a slight fall-off in the male participation rate, and a rise in the female participation rate from 47 per cent to 56 per cent between 1973 and 1994 (compared with the UK's 1994 rate of 61 per cent). Low participation rates for older persons reflect strong incentives for taking early retirement. Indeed, only 8 per cent of men and 17 per cent of women stay in work until the statutory retirement age of 65 for men or 60 for women.

Over the last 20 years the proportion of the workforce employed in the public sector has risen from 17 per cent to 21 per cent, the majority working in local administration. In the light of the budget crisis the government now envisages more drastic measures to cut public spending, including job cuts and a recruitment ban in the public sector.

Unemployment has, however, remained fairly low by international standards – a fact often attributed to a deliberate anti-cyclical macro-economic approach and co-ordinated wage bargaining. On national measures it stood at 5.8 per cent in September 1996 (or 4.1 per cent on Eurostat figures). Unemployment is not expected to fall, as rationalisation in industry and services continues and the size of the working population grows due to immigration.

Work permits and papers

Citizens from member states of the European Economic Area are not required to have a work permit. However, the labour market for non-EEA citizens is quite tightly regulated, with admission requirements set by the official employment service, the AMS (see below). Employers must obtain official permission to employ a non-EEA citizen (*Beschäftigungsbewilligung*), unless the individual concerned already has a general work permit (*Arbeitserlaubnis*). Authorisation to employ a foreign worker is granted at regional level, and is limited to a specific job and geographical area. Work permits, which are applied for by the employee, are less restrictive, although the authorities can set limits on the sector or trade if there are specific labour market problems: they are granted for at most two years.

In order to ensure that foreign workers are employed on the same terms and conditions as EEA citizens and Austrian nationals, employers must notify the regional office of the AMS within three days of employing a foreign worker, indicating their pay and conditions; the notification must be countersigned by the employee.

Work permits can be extended provided the individual's circumstances and any other relevant factors have remained unchanged, or if the employee has been employed in accordance with the legal requirements for the previous 18 months.

In contrast to individual employer authorisation and a work permit, possession of a certificate of exemption (*Befreiungsschein*) allows a foreign worker to be employed without restrictions. Such a certificate is applied for by the employee and will be granted if they can demonstrate at least five years of employment in the previous eight years. The certificate is issued for a period of five years.

Personnel planning

Since the abolition of the state placement monopoly there has been no need to inform the authorities about vacancies, but, as noted above, there are notification requirements in the case of employing non-EEA citizens.

Workforce consultation   Works councils (*Betriebsräte*), which may be elected by the workforce in establishments with at least five permanent employees, have to be informed before a post is advertised and again when it is being filled. However, works councils cannot block a management decision.

Works councils have a number of participation and consultation rights at various stages in the recruitment process. During the phase of personnel planning, works councils have a right to be informed. Employers must provide information to the works council once they have decided on the number of proposed new employees and their area of activity. Employers must also meet works councils' requests for information, where appropriate. However, works councils have no powers as far as the individual hiring process is concerned.

Works councils must be informed of all new hirings, including the area of activity, grade, pay, and the length of any probationary period – and in sufficient time to allow employee representatives to ensure that the hiring corresponds with the relevant statutory and agreed provisions.

Employers must also inform works councils about the use of temporary agency employees. In particular, works councils can require the employer to inform them about how long such employees will be used, and their payment. Contraventions of employee information and consultation rights are punishable.

Using part-timers and temps

Part-time work   Part-time work is defined as any weekly working hours which are lower than the standard working week provided for either by law or by any applicable collective agreement. The duration and organisation of any part-time work, and the conditions under which either can be altered, must be specified in the individual contract of employment, unless this is already regulated by a workplace collective agreement.

Since 1993, legislation has been in force which gives part-time staff the same employment rights pro rata to full-timers. In addition, when changes are proposed to their working time schedules, sufficient notice must be given, and the consent of the employee obtained.

Fixed-term contracts   Fixed-term contracts may be agreed under a number of statutory provisions, some of which are general in character while others regulate particular occupations. In principle, a fixed-term contract may be limited either by setting a specific date or the attainment of a pre-determined objective. However, some collective agreements, which may apply throughout an industry, allow fixed-term contracts to be concluded only when a starting and finishing date is agreed. In general, if an employee carries on working beyond the agreed period, the contract will be deemed to have become permanent. The law does not require a particular reason to be cited when a fixed-term contract is agreed. However, case law does demand economic or social reasons to justify any succession of fixed-term contracts, which must be demonstrated on each individual occasion. An automatic succession of fixed-term contracts, so-called *Kettenarbeitsverträge*, will be null and void as far as the fixed duration element is concerned and the contract will be deemed to be permanent. (For termination provisions, see below).

Agency employment   Temporary work agencies are permitted and agency employment is regulated by the 1988 Law on Temporary Employment (*Arbeitnehmerüberlassungsgesetz*). This statute also covers situations in which employers temporarily make their employees available to a third party under exceptional circumstances, rather than as a commercial business. Temporary workers are permanent employees of the agency, not of the client company, and are protected by a number of statutory proscriptions which are intended to shield the employee from the business risks entered into by their employer: these include a ban on their income being linked to the length of assignments with a client company, a ban on fixed-term contracts – unless there is a material reason – and a ban on any provision which prevents the employee taking up a full-time job with a client.

Agency employees are subject to most of the collective or customary provisions applying in the client company (for example, as regards working time), but not necessarily on pay. There is also a collective agreement for the sector setting out minimum terms and conditions. In many cases temporary staff may prove to be cheaper to use than permanent employees, as rates paid by the agencies tend to be the minimum in the collective agreement, and this is likely to be below contractual pay in a client company, which will include company-level supplements.

Anti-discrimination provisions

Sex equality

The law on equal treatment between men and women at work (*Das Gesetz über die Gleichbehandlung von Frau und Mann im Arbeitsleben*) prohibits direct discrimination in the field of recruitment, pay, and benefits, initial and continuing vocational training, promotion, other terms and conditions of employment, and termination. There is no requirement to introduce equal opportunities schemes to encourage the employment or promotion of women in the private sector. However, targets for the recruitment of women are rarely met and women remain in a minority at supervisory and managerial levels.

The law forbids employers from advertising specifically for men or for women, unless a particular sex is an indispensable prerequisite. The dictates of German grammar mean, however, that an impression of which sex is preferred can be indicated, while nominally complying with the law. For example: 'Sekretärin gesucht (Männer dürfen sich auch bewerben)' – that is, '(Female) secretary sought (men may also apply)'.

Women's night-work is still illegal in Austria, and this needs to be brought into line with EU directives, as clarified by ECJ rulings. This is currently being discussed by the social partners.

Disabled workers

By law, employers with at least 25 employees must employ one person with disabilities for every 25 employees – that is, 4 per cent. This may be lowered to 2 per cent in certain industries or regions. Employers who fail to meet this quota must pay a sum in compensation. Conversely, employers who employ more than the minimum quota are entitled to a financial premium.

Job creation incentives

The lion's share of the official employment service budget – over 70 per cent – is devoted to active labour market policies, including the initial training and continued training of the unemployed.

Companies that employ from special groups of unemployed people, such as the handicapped, the long-term unemployed, the young, older people, and women with children, can benefit from wage subsidies of up to 66 per cent of gross pay for up to a year. The exact amount of subsidy and the length of contract are negotiable.

Under the 'Espora' programme, which has been running since 1993, an employment agency run under the auspices of the official employment service AMS (see below) will provide temporary employees, with the employer having the option to keep the employee on permanently once the contract expires; this happens in about half the temporary contracts arranged.

Many employers find existing employment-creating measures insignificant and the incentives negligible. This seems to be particularly true in the case of taking on older employees, who are automatically entitled to seniority pay when recruited and are hence very expensive in additional labour costs. AMS incentives would not compensate for this.

Finding the applicant

The principle of *Aufstieg vor Einstieg* – promotion before recruitment – highlights the fact that jobs are normally filled internally, if possible, before resorting to external recruitment.

Employers use the official employment service (see below) almost solely to recruit blue-collar workers. The main means for finding white-collar and skilled blue-collar workers is newspaper advertisements, as well as making use of any pool of speculative applications. Top executive positions are rarely advertised and about half of them are filled via recommendation or direct approach, either by the employer or through a headhunter. Placement services must provide their services free of charge to applicants and operate in an impartial and unbiased fashion.

Application documents

The CV is very similar to the German layout, although somewhat less detailed – which some employers find easier to handle. Often an interview may be arranged over the telephone, in which case the applicant will send a CV together with some references. Only at this second stage would candidates be expected to submit a full 'German style' application dossier; this would include photocopies of all diplomas, work certificates, professional references and all documents of potential interest to the recruiting company. These documents are usually kept by the employer and not returned as a matter of course.

Employers prefer CVs to be fairly short, of the order of one to two pages. The CV is typed and generally not accompanied by a photograph unless otherwise specified. Some senior managers' CVs are written in English: some senior managers will also not release their CV until having met a headhunter. Information is normally given in chronological order, and the CV is sometimes signed. Civil status would be expected to include not just the candidate's name, age, and existence of spouse or children but also the profession of parents. Education will often be listed from primary school onwards including secondary school up to *Matura* (equivalent to A-levels), university education received – specifying the time taken and marks awarded.

References given by previous employers, or employment certificates (*Arbeitszeugnis*), are of considerable importance for established managers. These are not only mentioned in the CV but are actually included with the application documents. Certificates are not only given to all employees on leaving employment but also where employees change their manager, even if this does not entail leaving the company. Certificates must not contain remarks which might be detrimental to the employee's future employment prospects. As in Germany, there is coded language in which superficially favourable observations by previous employers can carry a deeper, less enthusiastic message about the employee's worth.

Application forms   Application forms which go beyond collecting basic data on individuals and their qualifications require the agreement of works councils: care is also needed to ensure that, even where the works council has given its assent, questions do not violate the personal privacy of candidates. This includes asking about pregnancy, membership of political parties, trade unions or religious affiliation.

Application letter   The application letter constitutes the first of the application documents, unless an interview has been fixed by telephone. The application letter can be either handwritten or typed. The norm is that the letter is handwritten and the CV typed. The letter is usually short (a page to a page and a half) and is expected to be formal in style.

Placement services

The state placement system   Reform of the Austrian public employment service came into force on 1 July 1994. The Labour Market Service Act (*Arbeitsmarktservice-Gesetz*) provided for the establishment of an independent institution, in the form of a public corporation, responsible for labour market administration, including placement and employment measures. The old employment service was therefore effectively removed from direct ministerial responsibility. At the same time private employment agencies were allowed to enter the placement market for all sections of the labour market, having previously been available only to executives and artists.

The new official employment service (*Arbeitsmarktservice*, AMS) is made up of a central administration, plus nine directorates at constituent state (*Land*) level and 108 regional offices. The central administration is responsible for setting broad guidelines on targets and a general framework for intervention, and co-ordinating and monitoring the implementation of policy. The *Land* directorates decide which labour market measures should be used to achieve set targets, allowing them a great deal of autonomy in determining the main focus of intervention and budgetary allocations. The implementation of labour market policy is the responsibility of regional directorates.

The broad aims of the AMS, as defined by law, are the maintenance of social standards and the achievement of full employment. This is to be achieved through the provision of measures targeted in particular at disadvantaged groups in the labour market.

The old employment service had been the subject of increasing criticism, in particular from employers who complained that placement services did now meet their needs. Moreover, the old authority had been overburdened with tasks that at best were only indirectly linked to the labour market – tasks mostly now assigned to other organisations. Previously the AMS had been under the exclusive control of the Ministry of Labour and Social Affairs. Under the new arrangements, the trade unions and employers have been integrated into the supervisory board of the service. The popularity of the service both with employers and job seekers has increased since the reorganisation.

AMS is financed by employer and employee contributions of 3 per cent of gross salary each, which go to the Finance Ministry: this in turn allocates a share to the AMS in the annual budget.

As well as placement, the AMS also manages the system of unemployment insurance and vocational counselling, mostly aimed at young people.

Registration with the AMS is compulsory for all individuals who want to claim unemployment benefit. This has maintained its image with employers as essentially a repository of poorly qualified job seekers, encouraging them to turn to private providers for skilled staff. However, the AMS remains reasonably popular: employers use it for filling just over 40 per cent of all vacancies on average – 65 per cent of unskilled vacancies, 25 per cent of skilled but only 8 per cent of managerial staff.

Only 20 per cent of employees found their job either through public or private placement services. The most important routes remain information from relatives or friends, which accounted for a third of all recruitment, and making unsolicited applications, which accounted for just over a quarter.

AMS advertises vacancies in newspapers and via an on-line computer system accessible from AMS branches, in vocational advice centres, some shopping centres and even selected airports.' Applicants can then make contact with the employer directly or via the AMS depending on the employer's preference. The AMS also publishes regional journals with adverts of job seekers which are automatically sent to bigger companies.

A new measure is the use of 250 AMS staff, freed up by the computerisation of unemployment benefit administration, to establish contacts with companies to identify vacancies. This is partly the result of AMS losing its monopoly, which has prompted it to become more active in some areas.

Any employer who wants to use AMS must register the vacancy, and also inform the AMS if the vacancy has been filled. AMS can offer some pre-selection of candidates by interview before sending them to companies. Vacancies advertised through AMS are, on average, filled within 44 days.

Recruitment agencies   Until 1994 recruitment agencies were not allowed to place candidates in permanent employment, as this was the monopoly of the state placement service. They were, however, allowed to find candidates for companies provided they acted merely as consultants. Since 1994 agencies may place people of all qualifications. However, only very few qualify under the law, and even fewer actually practise it. The main deterrent seems to be the certification requirements for organisations and individuals, including examinations for those running and those working in a recruitment agency. Local offices of the Labour Ministry also have a right to scrutinise the books of employment agencies.

Partly as a result of this, by March 1995 there were only 16 agencies licensed to place managerial personnel, 31 agencies dealt with the placement of artists, and only 5 had applied for a licence to run general placement services on a commercial basis. Of these only 14 or 15 are thought to be actively in business. Very few executive recruitment consultants took up the option of becoming broader placement agencies.

Only 936 placements were made by private agencies in 1995 – they were described by one company as irrelevant – and these were mostly highly skilled and managerial staff already in employment, but seeking to change jobs.

The law stipulates that private placement services have to be free of charge to job seekers. Fees to employers vary and are on average between one and three months' salary, but some agencies may work on a flat-fee basis. Some also offer guarantees under which the agent undertakes to replace an unsatisfactory employee free of charge or reimburse the fee.

Placement must be confined to vacancies, the requirements for which can be detailed. A job seeker can pursue a case for damages if the agency makes false or misleading statements about vacancies.

Executive recruitment consultants

The activities of executive recruitment consultants in Austria have been boosted by the strategic position of the country as a gateway to Eastern Europe. GKR

Neumann, the largest recruitment firm operating in the Austrian market, has also built itself into the largest search consultant for the whole of Central and Eastern Europe. A number of other international consultants use Austria as their main base for conducting cross-border searches in Eastern Europe.

The profession of personnel consultant is regulated by statute, and individuals who wish to practise in the field must obtain a licence (*Konzession*) which is awarded after examination by the Federal Chamber of Trade and Industry, the statutory body for employer representation. It is illegal to set up a consultancy without such a licence, although some individuals might do so. Approximately 2,000 people hold the BWK consultant's licence, but not all practise.

There are an estimated 25–30 consultancies in Austria. Most of these function exclusively at regional level and only few cover the whole of Austria or are internationally orientated. The major operators at this level are GKR Neumann, Amrop, Egon Zehnder and Wieringer-Oberhuber, which is part of the INESA network.

Most executive recruitment consultants use a mixture of search and selection, even for quite senior posts, especially where potential candidates might be outside the immediate sector in which the employer operates. However, some companies which deal only in top management positions will confine themselves to direct approach only. Adverts have to be placed via an agency that has to hold a special licence to operate.

Consultants use a mixture of fixed and percentage fees, and there is no formal requirement to charge fixed fees. The going rate on a percentage basis is 33 per cent of gross annual earnings for the post, plus expenses.

Direct recruitment

Approaching candidates directly in the Austrian system still happens to a great extent through co-opting. Austria's civil society is composed of numerous clubs and networks which provide rich opportunities for recruiting outside of familiar circles. This system is able to work because of the small size of the country; however, it militates against using objective criteria to fill a post.

Recruitment media

Advertising

There are two main newspaper vehicles for advertising for senior managers: the conservative *Die Presse* and the liberal *Der Standard*. Another paper, the *Kurier*, carries more adverts for middle managers. The majority of adverts are placed by recruitment consultants.

The text of adverts aimed at the Austrian market is in a traditional style. Only adverts aimed towards Eastern European countries, and especially Hungary, tend to be less formal. Adverts usually include a description of the post and the profile corresponding to the criteria and competence required. It is usually stressed particularly that applications are to be made in writing.

Local newspapers are often the first choice for more routine positions, reflecting the fairly low level of employee mobility.

Internet advertising

Recruitment via the Internet is not yet highly developed, and there are no specific Austrian on-line job exchanges. Some computer companies and the Giro-Credit bank advertise their vacancies on their web pages. The Austrian telecommunications organisation, Telecom, has a jobs section on its home page which steers Web navigators through to companies using its server to advertise vacancies.

Selection methods

Interviews

Interviews are usually conducted in a very structured way and cover all aspects of the job on offer as well as the candidate's education, professional experience, reasons for changing jobs and expectations. Questions impinging on the candidate's personal life and affiliations should be avoided. Great emphasis is currently placed on good personal presentation and communication skills, as well as the ability to work in teams.

Aptitude tests

Aptitude tests are not common and are used only in situations of mass recruitment, such as filling apprenticeship places, trainee programmes or for posts where a great number of people are likely to apply. In these cases, assessment centres may be used. Larger companies tend to make use of a broader range of tests, including personality tests, intelligence tests, attitude tests, concentration tests and mathematical aptitude tests. These may be coupled with specific tests according to the profession involved (IT, management, etc) or to meet certain requirements (eg, foreign languages).

Graphology

Graphology is little used. Firms that do use it are either branches of French companies or family businesses.

Privacy

Computer-based management and personnel information systems require the permission of works councils. Personal data must be kept secure and all employees, including works council members, are required to keep such data confidential. Employee data must be deleted from such systems after employment is terminated, unless the employer can demonstrate a legitimate need for retaining it.

Medical examinations

Where the law designates particular activities as potentially dangerous for certain employees the employer must confine any questions on the employee's health to the issue of their suitability for the post in question, and not seek to obtain specific information about illnesses from which the employee may suffer. Medical examinations may be required in certain occupations, especially in the case of young persons.

Military service

Military service is obligatory for men in Austria. Its duration is normally eight months, which some people extend to one year to obtain access to higher military ranks – although these are not particularly valued in the course of recruitment. Potential conscripts can also opt for civilian service (*Zivildienst*) in place of military service: this lasts for 11 months.

Appointment

Appointment formalities

New employees must be given a written contract of employment. If the employee was placed via the AMS state employment service the latter has to be informed of the recruitment. Employers must register new employees with the social security authorities.

There is no statutory formula for handling rejection of unsuccessful applicants. However, as with offers of employment, rejections tend to be in writing.

Education and training

Secondary education

Compulsory education in Austria is predominantly provided by public institutions (there are a few independent denominational schools) and comprises nine years of schooling. As a rule, children start school at 6 years of age, attending primary school (*Volksschule*) for four years. Special schools (*Sonderschule*) exist for children with disabilities or learning problems. On completion of the fourth primary year there is a choice between a four-year secondary modern school (*Hauptschule*) – the majority choice outside large cities – and the four-year first stage of higher general secondary school (*allgemeinbildende höhere Schule*, AHS).

Choices must again be made prior to enrolment in the ninth year. A substantial proportion of the pupils in this age bracket, mainly those from the *Hauptschule*, opt for a pre-vocational year (*polytechnischer Lehrgang*), which becomes their last year of compulsory full-time schooling before entering apprenticeship training. The primary, special, secondary modern schools and the pre-vocational year are referred to as general compulsory schools (*allgemeinbildende Pflichtschulen*).

There is an alternative route to vocational qualifications which can be taken from the ninth year onwards: this is via intermediate and higher technical and vocational colleges (*berufsbildende mittlere Schulen*, BMS and *berufsbildende höhere Schulen*, BHS) or intermediate and higher teacher training colleges (*lehrerbildende mittlere und höhere Schulen*), which train kindergarten teachers. These colleges offer programmes of up to five years and, on completion, award qualifications equivalent to those gained in the 'dual' system of vocational training (see below). The technical and vocational programmes train students for skilled industrial, commercial, business and agricultural occupations, and all higher programmes that terminate in final matriculation examinations (*Reifeprüfung*, *Matura*) qualify for university and most non-university tertiary admission.

Second-stage programmes of upper secondary education (*AHS-Oberstufe*) last four years and take pupils from the higher first stage who, in practice, remain on the same premises. There are three main types: *Gymnasium*, *Realgymnasium*, and *wirtschaftskundliches Realgymnasium*, which specialises in business. The *Realgymnasium* can also exist as a separate second-stage institution (*Oberstufenrealgymnasium*), designed as a special programme for main general secondary school leavers. All AHS-programmes culminate in the matriculation examination (*Matura*).

About 70 per cent of all 12- to 14-year-olds go to a *Hauptschule*. However, the popularity of compulsory schools and vocational training has been falling over the past decade or so, with increasing numbers of young people pursuing the *Matura*, which enables them to enter university. About 31,000 people pass the *Matura* each year, of which some 20,000 enrol with universities; however, less than half of these actually obtain an academic qualification.

Schools are financed by the Federal and *Land* authorities, and companies finance the work-experience part of training. Higher and vocational education is financed and administered centrally by the Federal government, which also finances the national curriculum.

The Education Ministry is responsible for vocational schools, while the company-based part of training is under the overall responsibility of the Federal Chamber of Trade and Industry (*Bundeswirtschaftskammer*), the statutory body representing employer interests, in conjunction with the Labour Ministry.

Overall, 16 per cent of young people go into vocational training via the five-year vocational training higher schools (BHS), 13 per cent pursue their *Matura* in a general higher school (AHS), 8 per cent go into a three- or four-year vocational intermediate school (BMS), and 41 per cent go into the dual system of apprentice training (*Lehre*).

Although one great strength of the Austrian system lies in the fact that only 2 per cent of young people do not pursue education and training after compulsory education, 20 per cent subsequently fail to gain a qualification after three years of further education or training. The drop-out rate at schools has been increasing significantly, particularly in the big cities such as Vienna. The number of those dropping out of education after the ninth obligatory school year has also increased markedly.

Tertiary education

Universities   University education is open to all candidates who have successfully completed their secondary studies at a higher general or higher technical and vocational institution (AHS or BHS), that is, acquired the *Matura*. For adults without this formal qualification, an alternative route is offered by a set of preparatory courses and a special examination (*Studienberechtigungsprüfung*) leading to university admission in a particular field of study.

Most courses offered at universities are degree courses which are completed by a final diploma examination after submission of a thesis (*Diplomstudien*). The first degree in the Austrian system is either a master's degree (*Magister/Magistra*) or diploma (*Diplom*). A course in medicine leads to a doctor's degree. In the case of continuing and adult education, there are also non-degree courses (*Kurzstudien*) and vocationally oriented courses at post-secondary level (*Hochschulkurse*). Students who have successfully completed a non-degree course may continue in the corresponding degree course. Students with a master's degree may enrol in postgraduate studies either for a doctorate (*Doktoratsstudien*) or in continuation courses (*Aufbaustudien*). The minimum length of all the study courses is defined by law: a *Diplom* requires between four and five years, a course in medicine six years, doctoral studies between one and two years in addition. Duration of non-degree courses is between two-and-a-half and three years. A longer duration of study, however, is usual, and most students study for six to eight years for their first degree. Drop-out rates are quite high, and as much as 30 per cent in business and economics. Most undergraduates start their studies when they are 20 to 22, and are at least 26 to 28 years old when they graduate.

While the number of students enrolling at university for the first time has been ranging between 21,000 and 22,000 over the last ten years, this is expected to increase significantly. In 1994/5 the number of women enrolling exceeded that of men for the first time. Many graduates – especially in the social and political sciences – head for the public sector, but this is about to change with recruitment curbs in public services, and graduates are now looking increasingly towards private business.

Current debates on reforming higher education have centred on the issue of whether private universities should be allowed, and whether study fees should be introduced. Ministers have indicated that the current ban on private universities will be lifted.

Polytechnics   Polytechnics (*Fachhochschulen*) are a new development, first established in the academic year 1994/5. The *Fachhochschule* offers a combination of economic and technical training and represents Austria's attempt to introduce a third level of education located between vocational schools and universities, and more closely attuned to the needs of business.

As with their namesakes in Germany, *Fachhochschulen* offer an alternative to universities with shorter and often more practical courses, some of which include a placement semester. The minimum duration of the courses is three years plus the placement period, and they culminate in a degree.

Their establishment was sparked off by the EU's recognition of shorter academic courses. Entry requirements are a *Matura* from an AHS or BHS, or a vocational qualification obtained from a vocational school or apprenticeship. Due to the limited number of places, individual institutions are pursuing selective admission policies. In 1994/5 77 per cent of FH students were men, and technical subjects dominated.

The increasing popularity of FH studies among both students and employers – who frequently complain about university graduates' lack of work experience – is mainly due to their shorter courses and higher practical content. Some companies sponsor special courses financially.

The FH model has also been designed to increase the amount of lateral mobility within the education system. Although the FH model is explicitly designed to produce practitioners, provisions have been made for graduates of FH to enter into doctoral programmes at universities after the completion of additional university course work.

The introduction of *Fachhochschulen* also represents the abandonment of the monopoly that the Austrian Federal government has had on higher education to date. FH operations will be overseen, accredited and periodically reviewed by an independent agency of 16 experts (*Fachhochschulrat*), appointed for three-year terms by the Minister for Science and Research. Furthermore, provinces, municipalities, professional chambers and private organisations may now establish and operate post-secondary educational institutions, provided they meet the formal and quality criteria established by the law.

FH courses are offered in 16 locations offering a choice of 20 courses. About 1,200 students are currently studying, although this number is expected to increase to 10,000 by the year 2000. Polytechnic students enjoy status equal to university students and are entitled to the same grants and benefits.

Other institutions   The main areas of education and training in non-university tertiary education are teacher training colleges and colleges for training social workers.

Graduate recruitment

One of the main sources of university-trained managers is the business university (*Wirtschaftsuniversität*) in Vienna, which trains 2,000 graduates each year. Other universities of the same type in Linz and Graz are very small. Courses are on average six-and-a-half years. However, only 40 per cent of students bring their studies to a successful conclusion – reflecting the high overall drop-out rates. Degrees in business administration awarded by universities are not MBAs.

Approaching students on campus directly is not yet systematically practised, and advertising by employers in the quality press (see above) is the main way in which graduates are found. Recruitment fairs, information exchanges on campuses and personal contacts with professors recommending students also constitute important recruitment routes. Students also undertake their own advertising to make themselves known to prospective employers.

The majority of students will complete their courses in Austria rather than abroad. Some may go on to to do an MBA in Switzerland. Work placements organised by the AESTE for engineers and technicians, and by AIESEC for commerce and managers, open more possibilities. (AIESEC also organises campus recruitment events.) Exchanges are conducted with Germany, Switzerland, Great Britain and the US. The Business University at Vienna, for example, has a network of agreements with schools and universities abroad.

Most students at foreign universities study at postgraduate level, but this is still rare and the proportion of students studying abroad is much lower than in other European countries, although integration into the European Union may change this. Postgraduate European study courses and programmes including several languages are becoming more popular. Only 10 per cent of Austrians are university graduates, and the majority of these are employed in the public sector. Academic unemployment is very low.

Starting salaries for business graduates are between AS 308,000 to AS 406,000 gross per annum (£18–24,000). Languages and work experience abroad are becoming more and more essential.

Vocational training

The most significant recent development in vocational training has been the reduction in the availability of apprenticeship places. One of the reasons for this is the steady marginalisation of training in the 'dual system', which combines on-the-job training and theoretical education, by special vocational schools. The higher vocational schools (BHS) offer a five-year training programme (age 14 to 19) in which placements are increasingly integrated. The main reasons for a company to continue providing apprenticeship places seem to be either the need for specialists which it wants to train and keep, or a desire to have access to cheap – 'apprentices' – labour. Moreover, most young people aim for more than an apprenticeship and pursue either a higher vocational course or try to obtain their *Matura*.

The Chamber of Trade (*Wirtschaftskammer*) has started a campaign to win back young people's interest in apprenticeships. However, there is statistical evidence that people with an apprenticeship have a higher rate of unemployment compared with higher qualifications, particularly in administrative and commercial jobs.

The drop in apprenticeship places is particularly marked in industry: places are more plentiful for hairdressing, shop assistants etc.

Initial vocational training

Apprenticeship   The Austrian apprenticeship system resembles the German one, in that it is a dual system which combines attendance at a vocational school with in-company training. Completion of compulsory general education (ie nine years of schooling) is a precondition. Attendance at vocational school is compulsory for all apprentices throughout their term of apprenticeship (two to four years) and is on a block- or day-release basis. Training at work is given by qualified instructors and takes place according to a national syllabus. The process culminates in a final formal examination (*Lehrabschlußprüfung*) which, if passed, grants the trainee a vocational or craft qualification.

Employees are required by law to retain apprentices for a period of four months after completion of their training (*Behaltepflicht*): this is extended to six months in some collective agreements.

So far the number of those with *Matura* embarking on an apprenticeship is insignificant in Austria compared to Germany, where a considerable number of people with the equivalent qualification, the *Abitur*, choose an apprenticeship. The trade unions are also not in favour of *Maturanten* entering into apprenticeship training as it is felt that they crowd out others with lesser qualifications. A specific apprenticeship programme for graduates was set up in 1987 offering those holding a *Matura* a practice-oriented alternative to university education, and allowing them to take a shortened apprenticeship.

In order to be allowed to train people, companies must have properly equipped facilities, and employ as trainers individuals who must have obtained a higher vocational qualification – the *Meisterprüfung* – in the training of apprentices.

While the number of apprenticeship places made available by companies is falling, statistics published by the Federal Chamber of Labour (*Arbeiterkammer*), the statutory body for employee representation, in 1995 confirm that the number of young people taking up apprenticeships is also on the decrease. Since 1979 the numbers have dropped by just over 40 per cent. The proportion of non-Austrian nationals taking apprenticeships now accounts for over a quarter of all places, reflecting the drift away from apprenticeships by young Austrians who are increasingly pursuing university entrance.

The number of companies offering apprenticeships is also declining, and half the total of 5,700 firms that participate in the system take on only one apprentice; apprenticeships are increasingly concentrated in a few sectors. The quality of training varies dramatically, from very basic levels to award-winning standards. A third of apprentices stated in a 1995 Chamber of Labour survey that they were treated badly by their employers, often having to do work not related to their profession and having to work overtime. Both apprentices and instructors have been calling for quality control measures, so far without success.

The fact that the number of apprentices has been dropping continuously for more than 10 years led to moves to reform the vocational training system in 1994, aimed at increasing the flexibility of the system and raising standards. This involved more theoretical training in the vocational schools, a stronger emphasis on the German language, and communication and foreign languages. However, many of these reforms were subsequently dismantled only months after implementation, mainly due to pressure from employers' federations which opposed the increase in vocational school hours, and demanded guarantees to maintain the current training time at company level – a position heavily criticised by the Austrian trade union federation (ÖGB), which pointed out that the undoing of the reforms meant that key innovations, such as teaching computerised accountancy and communication, would be lost. At the time of writing, discussions were in progress on broader reform of the whole system.

Employers have argued that the main reason for the drastic drop in the offer of apprenticeship places is that it is very expensive to maintain the infrastructure to train apprentices and pay them, and that their obligation to retain apprentices after qualification is too onerous. Moreover, apprentices are not allowed to do overtime or nightwork, which is particularly problematic in the catering industry. It is also illegal to make an apprentice carry out tasks outside their specified training and work-experience requirements.

Sixty per cent of girls are doing apprenticeships in the traditional professions such as hairdresser and shop assistant. To open up more opportunities in this field AMS encourages companies to offer training for girls in 'unclassical' professions by paying them a subsidy of AS 4,000 (£235). This is also available for those offering retraining for adults.

Until now there have been formal limits on what occupation an individual may pursue after they have completed an apprenticeship. Following calls for more flexibility, consideration is being given to the idea of making initial training broader and more flexible to raise the versatility of trainees.

Duties of the employer Apprentices are employed in accordance with a formal apprenticeship training agreement and are protected by employment and social security law. The training agreement between the training company and the apprentice is the basis of vocational education and training in the dual system. It must be in writing and must detail the name of the apprenticeship trade, the duration of apprenticeship, pay, particulars about the training company, and any training or education measures to be undertaken off the employer's premises. Employers must release the apprentice for the purpose of attending part-time vocational school.

Payment of apprentices   The apprentice's remuneration must be in accordance with the Vocational Training Act and must be adapted to local customary salaries or to similar apprenticeship trades. In general, the level of payment is negotiated between the employers' associations and the trade unions. However, the apprenticeship training agreement is not tied to the agreed minimum, and may exceed it. Remuneration increases annually; in the last year of apprenticeship pay generally amounts to 80 per cent of the fixed average income of a qualified person. For example, in 1994 an apprentice bricklayer in the construction industry earned AS 7,136 in the first, AS 10,695 in the second, AS 14,263 in the third and AS 16,052 (£419–£944) in the fourth year of training.

Training for those returning to the labour market   State help is available from the official employment service to help women returners to the labour market. This includes help with child care costs, vocational guidance and courses for women.

The AMS also has its own consultancy wing to assist unemployed people who want to start their own business. During the initial setting-up period individuals can continue to receive unemployment benefit, and loans on favourable terms are also available.

Continuing training

Adult education and continuing training are not regulated by the state, and attendance at courses is financed either by individuals seeking to improve their qualifications or by employers. There is a culture of continuing training, particularly in larger companies.

A variety of institutions offer courses. The most popular ones are the following.

The BFI (*Berufsförderungsinstitut*) is run by the Chamber of Labour and the Austrian Trades Union Confederation. It is largely self-financing, and is in competition with the employers' equivalent, WIFI (*Wirtschaftsförderungsinstitut*), established by the Federal Chamber of Trade. Both depend on finance for courses commissioned by the official employment service, AMS. Eighty per cent of BFI's turnover is accounted for by courses for the AMS. However, WIFI is financially more independent of AMS, but is subsidised by the Chamber of Trade: 80 per cent of its turnover is earned by courses offered on the training market. WIFI also offers a consultancy service, and is the market leader in quality training for small and medium-sized companies.

Competition also comes from adult education schools and private language and computer schools.

WIFI and BFI courses are more expensive than adult education classes, but also offer a wider range of subjects and qualifications, including those formally accredited by the state. BFI also runs its own schools for obtaining a vocational *Matura*, which takes about four to five years.

About a third of the BFI's activities are intensive courses of a year which lead to qualification as a craft worker: these are aimed at people of at least 21 years of age, and are partly financed by the AMS, which also selects the participants. The courses are very popular, with a high success rate. The BFI also offers careers guidance and work-experience courses of two to four months on behalf of the AMS.

Despite growing competition, adult education schools are still very popular, especially for those wanting to catch up with missed school qualifications. About half a million people attend courses each year.

Further training   About 11 per cent of Austrians take advantage of further vocational training each year. These are mainly people with higher education and income. According to a WIFI study, three-quarters of those participating in further training courses in 1994 took the initiative to do so themselves, compared to 59 per cent in 1988. Over the same period encouragement from employers to take up further training has diminished considerably: 16 per cent of people took up further training on the recommendation of their company (26 per cent in 1988), 9 per cent were sent by their company (12 per cent in 1988) and 8 per cent went encouraged by others (11 per cent 1988).

The government is planning a campaign to promote life-long learning which will be particularly aimed at unskilled workers. This will also involve taking certain elements out of school curricula and integrating them into further training.

Employee time-off rights

Employees do not have any statutory rights to training leave. If further training is indispensable to the employee's tasks, the employer will almost invariably grant time off on full pay and meet the costs of the course. In some circumstances, they can insist that employees attend courses. If further training is merely 'desirable' (*betriebserwünscht*), usually meaning that the employee would like to do it but there is no immediate need, a compromise solution on leave and costs is usually found.

Managerial and supervisory training

Further training is an important element in personnel development in Austria, particularly for executives. Most companies consider internal seminars as the most effective way to train their executive staff. MBA programmes, however, are considered to be too expensive and time consuming to be paid for by the company and is normally viewed as best taken immediately after graduation.

WIFI, which normally specialises primarily in vocational training (see above) has recently set up a new training programme for executives. Its aim is to offer practice-related courses in work organisation, corporate planning, and quality management for middle and top managers.

Consultation on training

Industry level The Minister for Economic Affairs is responsible for the apprenticeship system. The basic legal provisions are laid down in the Vocational Training Act of 1969, which has been amended several times since. It is a peculiarity of the Austrian system that the regulations for each apprenticeship trade are designed and issued as an ordinance by the Minister for Economic Affairs, but only after the receipt of an expert opinion from the social partners channelled through the Federal Advisory Board on Apprenticeship (*Bundes-berufsausbildungsbeirat*). The members of the latter are appointed by the Minister for Economic Affairs on the proposal of the social partners. Matters such as appeals on apprenticeship matters – including the withdrawal of a company's training authorisation – are dealt with at *Land* level.

The implementation of the regulations and supervision of the system is undertaken by the Chambers of Trade. At company level, works councils have a number of consultative rights concerning the planning and implementation of company-based apprenticeship education and training.

Financing

Investment in training Companies provide apprenticeship training voluntarily and at their own expense. The costs of the company-based part of apprenticeship education and training are borne by the employer; the costs of the part-time vocational school are borne by public funds. According to 1994 figures, Austrian companies spend approx AS 24 bn (£1.4 bn) each year on initial vocational training, a large part of which is trainees' remuneration.

Companies are spending increasingly more on further training and it is estimated that Austrian employers invested well over AS 30 bn (£1.75 bn) in job-related training and further training in 1994.

Educational attainment of the population

Level	Percentage of 25–64 age-group
Lower secondary	32
Upper secondary	60
Higher education (non-university)	2
University	6

Source: OECD (1994)

Organisations

Bundesministerium für Arbeit und
Soziales
Stubenring 1
1010 Vienna
Tel. + 43 1 711 00

ÖGB (Österreichischer
Gewerkschaftsbund)
Hohenstaufengasse 10
1010 Vienna
Tel. + 43 1 534 44

AK Kammer für Arbeiter und
Angestellte
Prinz Eugen-Straße 20–22
1041 Vienna
Tel. + 43 1 501 65

Bundeswirtschaftskammer
Wiedner Hauptstr. 63
1045 Vienna
Tel. + 43 1 501 05

AMS (Arbeitsmarktservice)
Treustraße 35–43
1200 Vienna
Tel. + 43 1 33 17 8

BFI (Berufsförderungsinstitut der AK
und des ÖGB)
Kinderspitalgasse 5
1090 Vienna
Tel. + 43 1 408 3501

Media

Die Presse
Parkring 12A
1015 Vienna
Tel. + 43 1 514 140
Fax + 43 1 514 14 368

Der Standard
Herrengasse 1
1010 Vienna
Tel. + 43 1 53 170
Fax + 43 1 53 170 131

Kurier
Lindengasse 48–52
1072 Vienna
Tel. + 43 1 52 1110
Fax + 43 1 52 111 2261

Main sources

Arbeit und Wirtschaft, various issues; Bundeskammer für Arbeiter und Angestellte/ÖGB.

Trend – das österreichische Wirtschaftsmagazin, various issues

ARBEITSMARKTSERVICE. *Geschäftsbericht 1995* (annual report 1995). Arbeitsmarktservice, Vienna, 1996

BRANDEL, FRANZ *et al. Aspekte der Arbeitsmarktintegration von Lehranfängern; Materialien zu Wirtschaft und Gesellschaft.* Kammer für Arbeiter und Angestellte, Vienna, 1994

BUNDESMINISTERIUM FÜR ARBEIT UND SOZIALES. *Forschungsberichte aus Sozial- und Arbeitsmarktpolitik.* Bundesministerium für Arbeit und Soziales, Vienna, 1992

BUNDESMINISTERIUM FÜR WIRTSCHAFTLICHE ANGELEGENHEITEN. *Die Berufsausbildung in der Lehre in Österreich.* Bundesministerium für wirtschaftliche Angelegenheiten, Vienna, 1995

GRUBER, ELKE AND RIBOLITS, ERICH. *Karriere mit Lehre?* Kammer für Arbeiter und Angestellte, Vienna, 1993

KAMMER FÜR ARBEITER UND ANGESTELLTE. *Die Lage der Arbeitnehmer 1995.* Kammer für Arbeiter und Angestellte, Vienna, 1996

LENTSCH, WOLFGANG. *Berufsausbildungsbericht 1995.* Bundesministerium für wirtschaftliche Angelegenheiten, Vienna, 1995

SCHWARZ, WALTER, and LÖSCHNIGG, GÜNTHER. *Arbeitsrecht.* Verlag des österreichischen Gewerkschaftsbundes, Vienna, 1995

STEINER, HANS, AND SPREITZER, HANNES. *Bericht über die soziale Lage 1994.* Bundesministerium für Arbeit und Soziales, Vienna, 1995

2
Belgium

Recruitment in Belgium is complicated by the country's division along linguistic lines, with the further influence of political and religious differences in some circumstances. Over half the population live in Flanders, the northern part of the country which is officially Flemish speaking. About a third live in the southern French-speaking provinces of Wallonia, while 10 per cent reside in the capital Brussels, officially designated as bilingual. A small number of German speakers live in the east of the country.

These divisions mean that, despite its small size, the Belgian labour market is split between French- and Flemish-speaking communities. In the last decade this has been paralleled by the devolution of many formerly national responsibilities to regional and community administrations, culminating in the July 1992 amendment to the Constitution making Belgium officially a federal state of three regions (Wallonia, Flanders and Brussels). This process is set to continue, with the regions, in particular Flanders, clamouring for more autonomy and independent control. There is a certain amount of reluctance to cross the regional divide. The structure of most organisations reflects these divisions and therefore they usually function on a regional rather than a national basis. Similarly, the press finds its readership either exclusively in one region or publishes separate editions in French and Flemish.

By law, companies operating in Belgium must use the language of the region in which they are located for all legal instruments and documentation, including communications with their staff. The Flemish regional executive has defined this further, requiring all individual and collective contracts, oral and written, to be in Flemish, as well as all advertisements placed for positions in Flanders. Non-Belgian recruiters will therefore have to familiarise themselves with the networks that operate in the region where they are based. Most executive employment is in Brussels and many organisations functioning in the area cater for French and Flemish, and frequently also for English speakers.

The labour market

Alongside the formal process of devolution, the move to socio-economic autonomy has developed in the two regions over the past decade. A gulf exists between the north and the south in terms of economic development. The traditional heavy industries in Wallonia bore the brunt of the 1970s and 1980s recessions, which saw a sharp upturn in unemployment in the region and a major

23

restructuring in industry. Newer industries in Flanders, with a higher potential for technical innovation, proved more resistant to these downturns and have shown a higher rate of growth. This situation has complicated the financing of devolution, with Flanders arguing that it would no longer support the loss-making industries of Wallonia. This attitude has arguably hardened during the early 1990s, with the emergence of an extreme right-wing Flemish nationalist party.

Unemployment overall stood at just over 13 per cent in mid-1996. Part-time work has become increasingly common in the 1980s and 1990s, with some 12 per cent of employees working part-time in 1995 (27 per cent of women and 2 per cent of men) compared with about 9 per cent in the early 1980s. The participation rate among women is not particularly high at 36 per cent. The labour market is highly regulated but has considerable scope for flexibility within this framework, notably on the issue of working time – a fact not always understood by outside observers. Nevertheless, many procedures in Belgium are highly bureaucratic and require careful preparation and strict documentation in order not to fall foul of the law or collectively-agreed provisions. Unionisation rates are high at about 65 per cent, and collective agreements cover large swathes of employment terms and conditions for the vast majority of the workforce.

Recruitment

Official requirements

The most important feature of the Belgian recruitment system is the existence of a national collective agreement (CCT No. 38) governing the recruitment and selection of workers which was concluded in 1983 and amended in 1991. Although most elements of the agreement are intended as guidelines, certain parts were made legally binding by royal decree in 1984. These mainly cover reimbursement of expenses, and provision and return of documentation.

By law, organisations which on average employ 20 or more staff must inform the official placement service in their area (or the area in which the vacancy has arisen) if a position has been vacant for three days, or is to be advertised in the press. Employers must give details of the trade or profession (most manual and non-specialist white-collar jobs are classified according to industry systems), the qualifications sought, remuneration and other main terms and conditions.

The service can then check:

- whether the job falls within regulations governing public decency
- whether it is categorised as dangerous or involves handling dangerous substances (where prior medical examination is required)
- location of the job (does it involve home-work?)
- working time schedules (does it involve night-work?)
- whether pay conforms to minimum rates laid down in collective agreements

Work permits

No work permits are required for other EU nationals, who, however, must obtain a residence permit. Foreign nationals require work permits, of which a variety of types exist.

Citizens of other European countries, and those with which Belgium has an agreement (Algeria, Tunisia, Morocco and Turkey), or their employer can apply for a Type A permit which is of indefinite duration and covers all occupations; the main condition is prior residence and employment in Belgium. A Type B permit is restricted to one activity and employer, and is valid for up to two years; it is issued only when no suitable EU nationals are available for work. A Type C permit is issued for specific professions and jobs, including port workers, certain sports and artistic professions, workers in the diamond industry and domestic helpers.

Residence permits are required for all foreign workers in Belgium. These can be obtained from the local town hall of the district in which the employee is resident. They are valid for a minimum of three months and can usually be renewed for a further three months. A permanent residence permit is granted for one year and can be renewed indefinitely.

Workforce consultation

Works councils – which by law must be set up in every private establishment with at least 100 workers – must be consulted on general recruitment policies. They must also be kept informed of any proposals to use part-time or temporary staff, since in some circumstances their approval is required before staff are hired.

Sectoral agreements may give works councils further rights over the use of temporary workers, job creation schemes and induction procedures. For example, the clothing industry agreement provides for consultation on training issues resulting from the introduction of new technologies. In smaller companies where no works council exists these functions are carried out by the health and safety committee, or by the trade union delegation (*délégation syndicale/syndicale afgevaardigte*).

National agreement on recruitment guidelines

A national collective agreement on recruitment and selection was concluded by the tripartite National Labour Council in 1983. Although intended primarily as a series of recommendations and guidelines, some of its clauses were made legally binding in 1984. These cover payment by the employer of any costs related to the selection procedure; provision of written confirmation of the time and date of the interview on request by the applicant, even after it has taken place; return of any documentation submitted by the applicant; and a limitation on the documentation that may be requested by the employer for official or authorised certificates, diplomas and references once the selection procedure has been completed. Failure to comply with these stipulations may incur a fine.

The recommendations within the national collective agreement cannot be legally enforced, but may be transposed into sectoral or company collective agreements, and therefore become binding at industry or company level.

Agreed provisions on job creation

Job creation provisions have become a feature of the national multi-industry framework agreements regularly concluded within the National Labour Council. These usually run for two years, with the most recent covering 1995/6. In view of the rising number of jobless at the time, this agreement contained additional measures, most of which require elaboration in sectoral or company agreements in order to be carried out. A national collective agreement (CCT No. 60) was also signed in the National Labour Council in December 1994 enabling certain legal changes to pave the way for sectorally-agreed provisions. These include early (part-time) retirement options with replacement from an 'at risk' group; work redistribution plans (not frequently used); social security reductions for taking on staff resulting in a net increase in the workforce; career breaks with replacement from the 'at risk' groups; and some training initiatives.

The majority of sectoral agreements signed in 1995 and 1996 have implemented some or all of the above measures and in particular the early retirement option (most often from age 56 with 33 years' service), improved careeer breaks (see below) and encouragement to part-time work or even job sharing. For example, the metal goods trade agreement urges job shares for the over-50s.

In the chemical industry agreement provision is made for a one-off training subsidy (up to BF 150,000 [£3,000] for full-time; BF 100,000 [£2,000] for part-time workers) to be paid by the chemical industry fund for new employees under a social security contribution reduction scheme (see below), as well as for young recruits straight from school; for work placements and recently-qualified trainees from vocational courses run by the fund; and for recruitment of former chemical industry employees made redundant due to restructuring in the industry. In order to qualify, the employee must be recruited on a contract of at least one year. Works councils (or trade union delegations) are charged with monitoring this system. The agreement stipulates that 1,750 hirings will be made in the industry under these terms.

Employment incentives

There is a plethora of schemes intended to encourage employers to take on recruits, particularly from the 'at risk' groups (long-term unemployed, low skilled, ethnic minorities, women) or those on low wages (up to BF 60,840 a month [£1,200] in 1996). The majority of these schemes – at national and regional level – involve some reduction in employer social security charges for newly-recruited employees, varying from complete exemption for a limited period to staged reductions for up to three years in the case of some young people. An element of training may be required from the employer, and in a number of instances the employee has to be recruited on a permanent contract for a minimum length of time (usually one or two years). Under the terms of successive national multi-industry framework agreements signed in the National Labour Council, since 1989 employers have been obliged to contribute a given percentage of their wages bill to a national fund. The percentage is set by the agreement and for 1995/6 equals 0.30 per cent. This is divided up as follows: 0.05 per cent for unemployment intiatives; 0.05 per cent for child care facilities through a national fund; 0.05 per cent (1995 only) for educational leave options; and 0.15 per cent (0.2 per cent in 1996) to be allocated by collective agreement for specific sectoral or company training measures.

Other measures include work placement and youth training schemes (see below). There is often a limit to the number of subsidies available for any one company. Works councils (or trade union delegations) must by law be informed of all recruitment and employment subsidies paid to the company, as well as given an assessment of their impact on overall labour costs and employment figures.

The so-called Maribel subsidy, introduced to help offset the high labour costs of Belgian industry, was recently amended following pressure from the EU Commission because the subsidies were deemed to constitute unfair competition. The original Maribel subsidy was paid out of national funds, and contributed towards employers' costs for new recruits. In 1993 an alternative Maribel was created, with a higher payment for companies in industries deemed to be in 'internationally highly competitive sectors of activity'. This was challenged in late 1995 by the EU Commission on the grounds of unfair competition and in response the higher Maribel subsidy was extended to most sectors of industry in 1996. The level of the subsidy is set at BF 1,875 (£37.50) per quarter per employee in firms of more than 20 employees; BF 3,000 (£60) per quarter for each of the first five blue-collar workers working at least 51 per cent of normal full-time hours, and BF 1,875 (£37.50) for other eligible employees in companies with fewer than 20 employees.

Under the terms of the 1994 multi-industry framework agreement concluded between the social partners at national level, various additional incentives were established; these had to be incorporated into sectoral agreements to become valid. They included reductions in social security contributions of up to BF 37,500 (£750) per quarter for any hirings resulting in a net increase in the workforce and for taking on a long-term unemployed person (over one year), with a 75 per cent reduction on social security charges for one year and a 50 per cent reduction for the second year. Where new recruits have previously been unemployed for over two years, the percentages rise to 100 per cent and 75 per cent respectively. This was taken up by nearly all sectoral agreements (chemicals, metalworking, foodstuffs etc).

In the 1995/6 construction industry agreement there was a stipulation to limit overtime. This is linked to the creation of shift-work teams (*équipes relais*). For each new recruit taken on, three shift-work places may be created, up to a maximum of 20 per cent of the workforce. In the metalworking agreement for 1995/6, all companies with more than five staff had to choose one of the stipulated means of employment measures; these cover (part-time) early retirement, move to part-time working, career break (full or part-time) or training initiatives (with either 2 per cent of working time devoted to training across the board, or an increase of 1 per cent of total working time, the time devoted to training). All these initiatives have to be agreed either within a company collective agreement, with the works council or with the trade union delegation, and the relevant sectoral joint committee has to be informed of the measures taken.

Using part-timers and temps

Part-time employment   Part-time work is increasingly being encouraged, with attached requirements for employers to take on new staff to cover potential shortages. Under 1995 legislation workers have a right (with some limitations) to request a transfer to part-time work with loss of pay. Many sectoral agreements have set out to encourage the use of part-time working in order to stimulate job creation; examples include chemicals, foodstuffs and the national agreement for white-collar staff. Part-time early retirement is also an increasingly popular option, with a national multi-industry framework agreement signed in 1995 by the social partners enabling (part-time) early retirement from age 55 after at least 33 years' service (see above).

Fixed-term contracts and agency employment   Fixed-term or temporary contracts can be concluded only in certain circumstances detailed by statute. These include the temporary replacement of a permanent employee whose contract has been suspended for reasons other than economic necessity or industrial action; during exceptional increases in workload; or for specific and exceptional assignments (such as preparing a conference or acting as secretary to business people on secondment, urgent repair and emergency work). Contracts can be concluded directly between the employer and the employee (*contrat de travail temporaire*) or between the employer and a temping agency (*contrat de travail intérimaire*).

Most temporary replacement contracts can run for up to three months, although in the case of replacement for an employee summarily dismissed this can be six months, and up to two years for replacement of an employee on career break. The employer must normally consult with the trade union delegation prior to employing someone on a temporary replacement contract (except where the replacement is for an employee who has been temporarily suspended). Temporary contracts to cover exceptional workloads may only be requested for a maximum of one month at a time, although they can be renewed repeatedly.

Use of temping agency workers may not in principle exceed six months, although the works council/trade union delegation may authorise the longer use of temping agency workers. A number of collective agreements, notably construction and transport, prohibit the use of agency workers. Any worker supplied via a temping agency must work under the terms and conditions laid down in the collective agreement covering agency workers. This agreement stipulates that agency workers should be given the same pay and other conditions that are standard in the company in which they are temporarily employed. A recent survey found that temping work leads to a permanent job in the user company in 40 per cent of cases, and increasingly graduates and other school-leavers are finding that a temping job can be an important first step into the wider labour market. Temporary workers are most commonly used in large companies (56 per cent) with only 6 per cent of small companies making use of agency workers. They are most often brought in to fill administrative functions such as secretarial work, bookkeeping or as receptionists/telephonists. Manual work for which temping agencies are used includes packing, stacking and production work, as well as cleaning, while more specialised jobs cover, for example, nursing. In 1995 some 280,000 people were working via temping agencies across Belgium.

Discrimination and equal opportunities

Equal treatment is enshrined in the Belgian Constitution, outlawing direct and indirect discrimination. This applies specifically to employment and recruitment procedures and is restated in national agreement No. 38. Gender may be a qualification for selection only in certain job categories defined by royal decree, such as the performing arts and certain health care services. Until recently women were prohibited from doing night-work, but the law is in the process of being changed to comply with EU law. Sex equality does not preclude positive action for women in areas where they are underrepresented. Some employment incentives may relate to such areas of activity (see above).

National collective agreement No. 38 prohibits employers from treating candidates in a discriminatory fashion. No distinction may be made based on personal factors which do not have a bearing on the job or the nature of the business. So discrimination on the grounds of gender, race, marital status, ethnic origin, medical history, trade union membership, political or religious affiliation is prohibited. There is, however, very little case law relating to discrimination during the recruitment and selection procedure. In conjunction with its works council a company may draw up a positive action programme giving targets and specific policies. In any case, part of the annual report to the works council must include an employment report giving details of employees and recruitment by gender.

Finding the applicant

Internal recruitment

Vacancies may be advertised internally prior to being advertised externally. This may be stipulated in a collective agreement, and jobs are usually advertised through a company bulletin board or newsletter. According to a 1995 study carried out by the research organisation HIVA, some 17 per cent of vacancies are filled internally. This is more common among medium-sized firms than in small or very large firms. In Wallonia the use of informal recruitment channels such as internal advertisement or word of mouth is more widespread (with two-thirds of places filled this way) than in Flanders.

Placement services

There are few practical restrictions on which organisation may deal with job placements. However, the official placement service, which has now become a regional responsibility and is dealt with by three organisations, retains a monopoly of placement in the public sector. Otherwise companies are free to use the official service, the myriad private agencies or to advertise directly, as they please. External recruitment to fill vacancies is very much the norm, although tighter labour markets in the late 1980s did encourage companies to put more resources into their in-house training programmes (see below).

Official employment service

As a result of constitutional changes, the latest of which were approved in 1992, the National Employment Office (*Office National de l'Emploi*, ONEm) was restructured and now deals with matters relating to unemployment and the payment of benefits. Job placement as such has been devolved completely to the three regional authorities. The use of official services is more common at the lower skill end of the market, reflecting the fact that none of the regional placement offices has a specialist section dealing with executive recruitment. Opinions on the efficiency of the official services vary, depending on the type of staff sought and the region where the company is based. There seems to be less dissatisfaction with the service in Flanders, where it has been established longer, but in general they are regarded as overly bureaucratic. The official services compete with private agencies, many of which have been operating over several decades and have therefore built up well qualified and experienced pools of labour. However, the official service does have a cost advantage over the private agencies, with some services provided free of charge, and others requiring only nominal fees.

The regional job placement agency for French-speaking Wallonia is FOREm. This agency also has responsibility for French-speaking Brussels and for German speakers in the eastern provinces. It deals with all aspects of job placement and training in the region, and is administered by a joint management committee with responsibility for the day-to-day running of the service. The aims of the service are defined by the Regional Executive Council for Wallonia, and include a wide variety of training, ranging from services for the unemployed to provision of training advisory services to companies.

The VDAB exercises the same functions for Flanders and the Flemish speakers in Brussels. The employment and educational services in Flanders were established in 1984, with their functions further defined in 1988. The VDAB consists of a headquarters, a network of 80 local placement offices and some 20 vocational training centres, as well as an extensive database of employment information. Employers are by law charged a nominal fee. In 1994 some 80,000 jobs were advertised through the VDAB network, of which 63,000 were filled. There is also a separate network of psychological testing centres where, for a fee, employers can arrange for candidates to be tested and job applicants may seek free advice. Use of the official placement service is not a condition for either group wishing to avail themselves of the centres' services.

ORBEm undertakes job placement for all workers in the Brussels region, regardless of their mother tongue.

Employment agencies and personnel consultants

Larger companies are more inclined to be directly involved in recruitment and selection, although even they are increasingly contracting-out parts of these procedures to agencies and consultancies. Small firms in Belgium make extensive use of permanent recruitment agencies (*cabinets de sélection/selektiebureaus*). Private employment agencies are well established and numerous in all parts of the country. There are very few restrictions placed on their activities. They are used principally to find white-collar and executive staff. At the more qualified end of the market are recruitment agencies specialising in graduates and in recruitment by function, such as for sales and marketing staff, PR, secretarial, IT, banking and finance, accountancy and health service staff. Although the employment agencies have a low overall market share they are important in some specific functions and at the top end of the labour market.

Temporary agencies are well developed, although there are more statutory constraints regulating the employment of temporary workers (see above). Temporary employees can also be obtained via the official placement services' agencies, T-Interim, which operate across both regions. In all, the public agencies have 20 per cent of the market, and as they are not required to yield a profit they can offer a cheaper service than the private agencies.

The trade association for temporary agencies, UPEDI, accounts for the vast bulk of the business. UPEDI is a member of CIETT, the European trade association for employment agencies.

The annual publication *Who's recruiting who in Belgium* lists addresses of the main media sources, employment agencies, executive search and selection bureaux and permanent and temporary agencies. The contact addresses are given at the end of this chapter.

Executive search

There are over 100 firms specialising in executive search or selection. By law, firms cannot offer both search and selection, although many large companies have link-ups to provide an all-round service. Agencies may either draft and place press advertisements or pre-select candidates, often using graphological and psychological testing. The vast majority are located in Brussels where over half the country's executive employment is to be found. Most agencies tend to look at job placements for salary levels of BF 2.5 million (£50,000) and above. Fees are usually charged as a percentage of the salary offered for the position; some are fixed, some are success-dependent. A full search service at the top end of the range would normally entail a fee of 30 per cent of annual salary offered. The larger agencies in particular may offer guarantees including resuming the search if the appointed candidate leaves within a given time.

The market is dominated by the major international executive search organisations led by Korn Ferry, Egon Zehnder and Heidrick & Struggles. There is also a trade association of consultants, Ascobel, which includes HR and recruitment consultants.

(Graduate recruitment is dealt with separately after the section on higher education.)

Recruitment methods

The press is widely used directly by employers and by recruitment agencies for advertising jobs at all levels. According to a recent survey carried out by the research group HIVA (*Hoe werven bedrijven in België*), press advertisements are the single most important means of recruitment for Belgian companies, while informal contacts and unsolicited applications are also increasingly important. There are regional differences highlighted in the survey: in Wallonia only 15 per cent of jobs were filled by advertising, while in Brussels it was 35 per cent. Informal channels accounted for two-thirds of job placements in Wallonia, while in Flanders 40 per cent of jobs were filled in this way. Somewhat controversially, the public employment services in both regions were found to overestimate their own influence in job placements: according to the survey, the VDAB filled only 12.5 per cent of vacancies compared with its own claim of 32 per cent, while FOREm had only 7.2 per cent to its name. However, the services were more often used by large companies, in service industries and by non-profit organisations. Employment agencies had a very low market share but were used most frequently for specialist jobs, particularly in commercial and administrative functions.

Some 70 per cent of successful applicants were either school-leavers (23 per cent) or unemployed (48 per cent). New recruits are more frequently put on temporary contracts (33 per cent) compared to the overall percentage of the workforce on such contracts (5 per cent). The most difficult vacancies to fill were in managerial positions, as well as sales staff, IT, engineering and senior administrative posts.

The press

Public authorities must advertise vacancies in the press, and if they are for organisations at a national level both the Flemish and the French press have to be used.

The rules on job advertisements are not particularly rigid. Advertisements must comply with legislation prohibiting discrimination on the grounds of race or sex. Thus advertisements must not specify an applicant's sex (except in categories defined by royal decree) and must make it clear that jobs are open to both sexes. Pay is rarely mentioned in advertisements except by some UK or US multinationals. Employers will often advertise for recruits in a certain age range so that they fit in with the age profile of the company. In addition, the national agreement on recruitment (No. 38) stipulates a minimum level of information that should be contained in an advertisement. This includes:

- details about the company and its business
- details about the nature and location of the job
- minimum requirements for the job and other specifications.

Press advertisements normally invite applications by telephone or by submission of a CV, often specifying a supporting handwritten letter. Companies are prohibited by law from using fictitious job adverts to publicise their own activities.

There is no national newspaper in Belgium. The largest-circulation daily in Flemish is *De Standaard*. It carries job advertisements every day, covering a wide variety of positions, and an executive supplement (*Personeelsgids*) in its weekend issue. The paper has a policy of carrying job adverts in Flemish or English only.

Le Soir serves a similar function for francophone Belgium, with over 2,000 jobs appearing weekly. Over half of these are middle or senior management positions, many of them featuring in the weekend edition. It publishes advertisements in all languages. The *Gazet van Antwerpen* and *La Libre Belgique* are other important dailies.

The local press, including free journals, also carry advertisements for a diversity of jobs, including executive level.

The Roularta media group through its Carrière division organises job columns in a number of its own publications in French and Flemish, including *Trends*, *L'Express*, *Le Vif* and *Industries*. There are some specialist journals such as *La Semaine Informatique* and *Ingenieursblad/Journal des Ingénieurs*. The publishing company Geres runs a monthly bulletin to which readers can take out an annual subscription, giving details of job seekers in specified categories.

The Internet

The public employment service in Flanders, VDAB, has a web page which includes details of the service and vacancies, as well as information on its temporary employment service T-Interim (http://www.vdab.be).

There is a Belgian branch of the recruitment organisation 'Jobs & Careers', with vacancies in all Belgian languages and English (http://www.job-career.be).

The Catholic University of Louvain has a jobs page for helping engineers find placements and employment. Termed CCII-Kot Emploi, it also has links to other employment-related sites in Belgium and the rest of Europe.

Selection procedures

Recruitment documents

Most applications are made initially through submitting a CV with a supporting letter. Media advertisements will often specify a handwritten letter, but photographs are rarely requested. Initial selection is based on the CV, letter and an application form where necessary. Consultants and recruitment agencies often require a standard application form to be completed.

It is customary to take up personal references and this may be done by telephone. Employers do not usually enquire into criminal records, except in highly sensitive posts.

Verification of qualifications and previous employment is standard practice. However, employers are forbidden by law from requesting authorised documentation until the selection procedure has been completed. Although investigations into financial standing are not prohibited by law, they are rarely conducted. Candidates are expected to co-operate in good faith in the selection and to supply all the necessary information.

Selection methods

Graphology tests are widespread, both as a pre-selection procedure and to back up impressions of candidates gained by other means. Psychometric tests are also common, although they are more commonly used for older or more senior candidates in positions of considerable trust. Intelligence and aptitude tests are also standard, with screening procedures usually carried out by a third party even for large organisations.

Once pre-selection has been made, interviews are the most common form of short-listing and selecting candidates. Candidates are usually invited to an interview in writing, and may be requested to bring references with them. The national collective agreement regulates a number of aspects of the interview procedure, notably the requirement to respect privacy in the questions asked.

Assessment centres are being used increasingly for the selection of candidates, especially by large companies. These can involve several days of assessment and all costs must be borne by the employer. The national agreement does state, however, that the selection procedure should be conducted within a reasonable time and if it involves practical tests, they may not last longer than is necessary to establish the candidate's competence.

Privacy

National agreement No. 38 stipulates that employers and other persons involved in the selection procedures should respect the candidates' privacy. This means that information provided by the candidate and that gleaned from tests, and medical examinations must be revealed only to those who require the information. Questions may only be asked of the candidate's private life that are relevant to carrying out the job in question. Thus, questions relating to marriage plans or starting a family would be prohibited. However, this is difficult to enforce, particularly as freedom of contract is an underlying principle and there are few restrictions on what kind of enquiries the employer can make during the period when a decision is being reached.

Medical examinations

Medical examinations may be required prior to conclusion of a contract of employment. Some categories of workers may also be required by law to undergo regular medical examinations once in post. These include:

- employees under 21.
- those in jobs with a risk of occupational disease
- those in jobs involving use of vehicles, cranes or other potentially dangerous machinery
- those handling foodstuffs, for sale or for consumption on company premises
- handicapped employees.

On the recommendation of the company health and safety committee, this list may be extended by the employer.

Offer and rejection

National collective agreement No. 38 states that the employer should inform unsuccessful applicants at the earliest opportunity, in writing. The employer must provide proof of the time and date of any job selection exercise to unsuccessful candidates upon request. Where necessary, this must also give the reasons for rejection. Overqualification for a post is not deemed an adequate reason for rejecting a candidate. Successful applicants should also be informed in writing, although this letter of information does not constitute a contract of employment, and may be made contingent upon the outcome of a medical examination or references.

Military service

Since the early 1990s military service has been effectively suspended. The provision for military service for all males over age 18 is still contained in the statute books, and is still covered by employment legislation. However, virtually no one is called up, although men can still volunteer. In this case they would serve between eight and twelve months.

Education and training

With the division of Belgium into three federal states, responsibility for education as a whole has been devolved to the three linguistic regions (Flemish-speaking Flanders, French-speaking Wallonia and the German-speaking eastern provinces). The national government retains control only over setting compulsory starting and finishing ages for education, minimum standards for achievement of qualifications, and pension arrangements in the education sector. It controls a number of education-related issues requiring provisions in national legislation, such as educational leave, apprenticeships or training initiatives contained in sectoral collective agreements. These come largely under the remit of the national Ministry of Labour and Employment. In Flanders the Ministry has devolved day-to-day management and control to a separate body, *Autonome Raad voor het Gemeenschapsonderwijs* (ARGO), while in Wallonia it remains in the hands of the region's Ministry for Education. The German community is largely supported by the Wallonia authorities. Vocational training has been a regional responsibility since 1980; in Flanders and Flemish-speaking Brussels through the *Vlaamse Dienst voor Arbeidsbemiddeling en Beroepsopleiding* (VDAB); in Wallonia and French-speaking Brussels through the *Office communautaire et régional de la formation professionelle et de l'emploi* (FOREm).

Education system

Under the 1983 Education Act, full-time education is compulsory from the age of 6 to 16 (although many children start pre-school from as young as age 3), and part-time until age 18. In order to qualify for official recognition and state funding, schools must conform to basic legal guidelines regulating curriculum, structure and class size and submit to state inspection. Schools may be privately or publicly run. State education must be non-denominational, while most private education is run along religious (largely Catholic) lines.

No external examinations are carried out in Belgian schools; all certificates, diplomas and other qualifications are issued by the individual school, provided they conform to government standards. In primary schools certificates are issued by teachers, in secondary schools by class councils, and in higher education by boards of examiners. In cases where school standards are found wanting, a warning is issued by the state inspector, and in extreme cases a school's certificates can be derecognised.

Secondary education

Secondary education (*école secondaire/middelbare school*) begins at age 12, after completion of the certificate of basic studies. In looking at secondary education it is important to distinguish between the curricular options on the one hand, and the system (or Type) on the other, which determines the duration and phases (cycles) of education. All secondary education allows pupils to select one of four curricula. The choice is influenced by the child's achievements at primary school, teachers' advice, and assessments that may be made in a pedagogical (PMS) centre. However, ultimately the decision rests with pupils and parents. Most secondary schools offer more than one curriculum, although a few specialise in one option only. The choices are as follows:

- general secondary education (ASO), which is customarily intended as preparation for university education
- technical secondary education (TSO), combining general education and more technical training; this can lead to a profession or to further study
- art education (KSO), which mixes general education with an arts emphasis; this also leads to either a job or further study
- vocational education (BSO), which provides specific vocational preparation for a job. Under some circumstances further education is also an option after an additional year's schooling.

The TSO and BSO courses provide the main system of initial vocational training for technical, skilled and semi-skilled workers (see also below). Certificates awarded at the completion of ASO, TSO and KSO courses (lasting at least six years) allow the student to move into higher education (see below). Certificates are awarded by the schools themselves, but may be validated by external bodies, including the universities themselves.

In Flanders all schools have now adapted to the structure introduced in 1989 of three cycles of two years from age 12 to 16 (*eenheidsstructuur*); in Wallonia and the French-speaking community (as well as the German-speaking community) there remains a mixture of two school structures. Type 1 largely reflects the new Flemish system, Type 2 is the old system of two three-year cycles. However, the vast majority of schools follow the new (Type 1) system, with only 4 per cent of pupils under the old structure.

One of the main differences between the old and the new systems is that under the new structure, the first cycle of two years is common to all four strands of education, allowing for much greater movement from one to the other, whereas the old system follows a separate curriculum depending on the chosen form (general, technical, artistic or vocational – see above).

Selection of one or other of the courses is made after the second year, although some vocational training may also begin after the first year. The courses last six years, with a seventh for BSO students wanting to progress to higher education. Students may leave full-time education at age 16, or at age 15 after completing at least two years of full-time secondary education. They are then required to carry on in part-time training until age 18, and only then will they receive their qualification (part-time education leads to a lower form of qualification). Part-time education is usually offered in conjunction with an apprenticeship or work placement (see below). Theoretical elements are taught either at a centre for alternative education and training (usually attached to a secondary school, and offering 600 periods of 50 minutes each, spread over 20 weeks) or at a training centre recognised by the appropriate regional bodies responsible for training (VDAB or FOREm), in the context of apprenticeships for the self-employed professions. In 1993 a charter was signed by the French-speaking community authorities and employers' association extending the provision for work placements and practical training within the context of part-time education (see below).

Higher education

Higher education comprises university education and non-university higher education. As with secondary education, it is split along linguistic lines. Entry to all forms of higher education requires a certificate of secondary education, with universities usually requiring a minimum standard of proficiency (*diplôme d'aptitude/bekwaamheidsdiploma*). Qualifications are usually awarded by the schools, although there is a central examination board in Wallonia which can also award certificates. There are no entrance examinations as such for higher education, except for some university engineering courses.

Universities   There are six full universities in Belgium divided on linguistic lines; three are Flemish-speaking (Rijksuniversiteit te Gent, Vrije Universiteit Brussel, Katholieke Universiteit te Leuven), and three French-speaking (Université de l'Etat à Liège, Université Libre de Bruxelles, Université Catholique de Louvain). In addition a number of institutions offer a more limited range of university courses such as the Universiteit Antwerpen. Attendance at higher education is relatively high in Belgium, with 32 per cent of all 20–24-year-olds registered on a course of higher education in 1993.

University education consists of three cycles. The first, lasting two to three years, leads to the status of *candidat/kandidaat* – equivalent to a bachelor's degree; the full degree (*licencié/licentie*), regarded as equivalent to a UK master's, is obtained after a further two to three years' study including submission of a thesis. A third cycle of study leads to a doctorate. This entails at least two years' study, but frequently considerably longer (up to five years is the norm).

Non-university higher education This is offered at a variety of institutions generically called HOBU institutes (*Hoger onderwijs buiten de universiteit*). Courses are divided into long and short courses, and there are eight study categories (technical, economic, agricultural, paramedical, social sciences, arts, teaching, and merchant marine). Short courses last two to three years and usually lead to a vocational qualification or diploma in the given subject. These courses are more technically oriented with a considerable practical element. They are available in fields such as nursing, social work or primary school teaching. The long courses, considered much on a par with university education, consist of two cycles of at least two years each. The first cycle is more general, the second leads to greater specialisation. The student is required to submit a project paper after the second cycle. Diploma and degree qualifications vary depending on area of study (these include industrial engineering, architecture, secondary school teaching etc). Successful completion of the second cycle can allow students to move on to a university *licencié* degree, although usually with an additional bridging year. There has been a considerable increase in the number of students attending non-university higher education, particularly on the short courses; in Flanders 65 per cent of non-university students were on a short courses in 1993, in Wallonia it was 68 per cent in the same year.

There are 150 non-university higher education centres in Flanders alone (40 offer long courses, 130 offer short courses, with some offering both). In the French-speaking community a number of reforms, implemented in 1996, aim to bring together a number of colleges offering long or short courses into so-called 'grandes écoles' offering both types of course.

Management education

A number of MBA courses are also offered, for example at the Katholieke Universiteit te Leuven and at the Solvay School, which is part of the Free University of Brussels. Take-up rates in Belgium are still fairly low, reflecting low demand. However, according to some recruitment agencies, the number of companies seeking some sort of formal business qualification has begun to rise in the last couple of years. This is particularly true of 'high flyer' graduate programmes where students are often recruited directly from well respected business schools across Europe.

Graduate recruitment

Employment after graduation is very much determined by the choice of degree subject studied. Nevertheless, there is often a gap between the theoretical knowledge gained and the requirements of companies. Many firms, especially large ones, offer some form of formalised training in the initial stages of graduate employment. Increasingly companies are also looking for graduates with some work experience, and more and more graduates are using temping agency work as a means of gaining a foothold in the labour market. The official placement services (VDAB, FOREm and ORBEm) also offer work experience programmes, including for graduates.

Graduate recruitment fairs and direct contacts with universities and other institutes of higher education are popular ways of recruiting graduates. Campus recruitment takes place between November and March. However, it is still rare for graduates to fix themselves up with a job before graduating. There are few university-run careers advice centres and placement services. Those that do exist tend to be run by former students. Notice boards and bulletins may be used, but increasingly direct company contacts with individual departments or unsolicited applications from students are important means for recruitment. Partly for this reason, companies are keen to advertise in student bulletins and newsletters, and attend recruitment fairs in order to maintain a high profile and sustain a flow of applications.

Advertising by companies seeking graduates tends to be concentrated in the summer. Every Tuesday during the summer months the Flemish daily *De Standaard* runs a jobs column (*Pas afgestudeerd*) devoted to graduate job seekers. Similarly, French newspapers such as *Le Soir* have supplements for graduates. *Intermédiaire*, a weekly appearing in French and Flemish specialising in job advertisements also carries articles on graduate recruitment. The directory *Move Up*, published in two languages, gives information on companies seeking to recruit, as well as types of vacancies and qualifications sought. The introduction to the directory offers advice and examples of CVs, letters of application and other hints for graduates. The 1996 edition also contains some contact addresses and information relating to foreign companies recruiting Belgian nationals, and general recruiters elsewhere in Europe.

According to a survey carried out by the research organisation HIVA in 1995/6, increasingly high qualifications are being demanded from graduates by recruiters. In over 40 per cent of cases, companies were looking for some form of higher education diploma, although in practice one-fifth of successful applicants actually had lower qualification levels than demanded originally.

Vocational education and training

Secondary vocational training is available to those who have completed technical courses (see above) or initial vocational courses (BSO). Full-time compulsory education ends at age 15, but since 1983 part-time education has been required until age 18. The law stipulates that this must be 360 hours of study per year if begun before the student reaches 16; this falls to 240 hours per year for students aged between 16 and 18.

Part-time vocational training can be carried out at secondary schools in parallel with full-time courses; in addition, special vocational training centres also exist. Part-time training may be combined with an apprenticeship (see below), with a work placement or with another form of employment (such as working in a family business).

Apprenticeships

Apprenticeships are relatively limited in Belgium. There are two types of apprenticeship contracts: one for craft workers or self-employed professions (*formation permanente des classes moyennes/leerovereenkomst in de middenstand*); the other for salaried or industrial apprentices (*contrat d'apprentissage industriel/industriele leerovereenkomst*). In practice the industrial apprenticeship is little used, with other types of on-the-job training, work placements and vocational education being more widespread (see below).

An apprenticeship contract for crafts and professions is defined as one which is signed for a fixed term and by which the employer agrees to provide general and vocational training to enable the apprentice to carry out a certain craft or profession, usually in a small to medium-sized business. This is usually through practical and theoretical courses. Such a contract may be signed directly between employer and apprentice (only for those aged under 18) and is most often for unpaid apprentices, eg within a family business, or through a third party (*secrétaire d'apprentissage*). These types of apprenticeships are available for a range of skilled manual and service jobs.

Apprenticeship contracts for crafts or professions are intended for young people aged at least 15 who have completed at least two years of full-time secondary education. Contracts are signed for a minimum of one year and a maximum of three years. However, in the French community this may be extended by up to one year if the apprentice fails to meet the required standard within the allotted period.

Certain conditions are also imposed by law on employers, who must be at least 25 years old (23 years for those with a management qualification) and have six years' experience or a formal qualification of some sort. The employer must ensure that the apprentice undergoes a medical examination at least once a year for those over 18 – twice a year for the under-18s – at the employer's expense. Apprentices have a right to time off in lieu of time spent in training or exams outside their normal hours. Minimum pay rates are laid down by law in the three communities as follows:

	1st year	2nd year	3rd year
Flemish Community	BF 9,000 (£180)	BF 12,000 (£240)	BF 15,000 (£300)
French Community	BF 5,004 (£100)	BF 7,737 (£155)	BF 9,309 (£185)
German Community	BF 5,200(£105)	BF 8,300 (£165)	BF 12,000 (£240)

Higher rates apply for those over 18 in the Flemish community. Minimum rates above the statutory minima may also be stipulated in collective agreements. Training consists of 28 hours per week within the company in the first year, 32 hours in the second and third years, as well as 120 hours of off-the-job theoretical education per year. These types of apprenticeships are still popular, although the numbers did drop in the early and mid-1990s. In 1992 there were over 10,000 in Flanders, some 8,000 in Wallonia, and over 500 in the German-speaking areas.

Industrial apprenticeships are for students aged between 16 and 18 who have completed full-time education but are still required to follow part-time educational courses. Since 1987 these apprenticeships have also been available for 18- to 21-year-olds already in employment or seeking employment. These can last from six months to two years and must include at least 21 hours of training per week. The content and nature of training is laid down by the relevant joint committee (*commission paritaire*) for a sector, and the committee may also stipulate longer apprenticeships for certain professions. The apprentice is paid in accordance with the sectoral minima, pro rata to the hours worked. Works councils monitor all apprenticeship contracts and training schedules. Certificates (*getuigschrift van beroepsbekwaamheid*) are administered and monitored by the educational bodies with the sectoral joint committees. These are joint bodies charged with designing training programmes, organising examinations and setting recognised standards. They may also set the terms and conditions of apprenticeships through collective agreements. On completion of the training, apprentices receive a certificate detailing the period and content of the training programme.

The industrial apprenticeship contract has a probationary period of one to three months. However, these types of apprenticeships are actually not widely used. In part this is because only 15 out of 35 joint committee education bodies are operational, and also due to the low recognition accorded to these qualifications. Work placements and apprenticeships for the self-employed are much more widespread and popular.

Work-training contracts

Work-training contracts (*contracts emploi-formation/overeenkomst werkopleiding*) were introduced in 1987 for new recruits aged between 18 and 25 requiring (further) training. To qualify, these recruits must *not* hold any higher education qualification or a certificate of technical secondary education. On this scheme, the employer is entitled to a reduction in social charges for that recruit for the duration of the contract (one to three years). This type of contract may also be used for young people aged 16 to 18 wanting to undergo training in sectors for which there is no industrial apprenticeship scheme available. The contract must be for at least half normal annual hours and no more than full-time annual hours less the hours devoted to training. Since 1991, legislation has required that training must be provided for at least 240 hours each year. The company works council monitors all work-training contracts, while the joint education bodies, where they exist, have overall sectoral responsibility.

Work placements for young people

Primarily as a means of reducing youth unemployment, a series of work placement options (*stages/groeibanen*) were introduced in the mid-1970s and expanded in the mid-1990s. These are usually aimed at young people under 30, and entitle the employer to some form of reduced social security payments relating to the new recruit. A number of these include a specific training obligation.

Legislation stipulates that firms with a workforce of at least 50 must take on a number of *stagiaires* equal to at least 3 per cent, but no more than 4 per cent, of the workforce. Since 1996, legislation stipulates that half of work placements must be in the form of CPEPs (see below). Companies with fewer than 50 staff need provide no more than three work placements. Exceptions are made for companies in financial difficulties and those that are recruiting from 'at risk' groups. For the purposes of the law certain apprenticeships are considered as work placements. Work placements are made available for the under-30s with no more than six months' work experience or those who have been out of work for at least two of the preceding four years. *Stages*, which may be full or part-time, are either for six months or 26 weeks, and may be extended once by a further six months or 26 weeks. Pay for a *stagiaire* is set at 90 per cent of the agreed pay for the job function carried out. A number of incentives exist to encourage the employer to take on a *stagiaire* permanently, including pay for the first year of full employment at 90 per cent of the agreed rate and a reduction in social security contributions for the second year of employment equal to 10 per cent of gross pay.

Since 1995, young people under 30 with no work experience, and registered as unemployed for at least nine months, may be offered a so-called first job work placement (*contrat de première expérience professionelle*, CPEP). These contracts are for six months, non-renewable, and are paid at the same level as other work placements (90 per cent of the agreed rate for the job function). *Stagiaires* on a part-time CPEP contract may be entitled to continued payment of some benefits up to a maximum of BF 6,000 (£120) per month. In this case the employer may deduct the amount from monthly pay. Other work placement and youth initiatives include the *emploi-tremplin* scheme and the youth employment scheme.

Other company training initiatives

In-house training may be carried out by a company's own training personnel, through facilities offered by the regional training offices (VDAB and FOREm) or through private training agencies. Some advanced vocational training schemes exist for crafts and self-employed professions along similar lines to the work placements. A number of sectors (such as metalworking, chemicals, and textiles) operate their own training centres while smaller companies make use of the centres and training facilities run by the VDAB and FOREm (see below).

According to a study carried out among companies in Belgium in 1991, the average time spent in training per employee was 4.5 days per year. In more than half of the companies surveyed, up to 25 per cent of employees received some form of training, and in just over 13 per cent of firms some 75 per cent of staff underwent training during the year in question. Professional and technical training were the most commonly offered (43 per cent of training time) followed by management training (22 per cent) and language or commercial training (15 per cent). Large companies tend to run more in-house training than small to medium-sized firms, and on-the-job training is most common for manual workers. Few companies – and most often the larger ones – have detailed training policies or programmes; while 30 per cent of companies surveyed had one part-time worker devoted to training supervision and planning.

Workforce consultation on training

Agreed provisions on training may be laid down at national level in multi-industry framework agreements or at sectoral or company level. The latest national agreement was for 1995/6 (see above). Agreed measures include quotas for training, such as in the metal industry agreement which stipulates that 0.5 per cent of working time or 40 hours per year must be spent in training. Details are left to companies to settle with their works councils or trade union delegations. For example, the agreement for garages allows trade union delegations to negotiate annual training schedules and programmes at company level. The general agreement for white-collar employees includes a plan to increase training time off by 1 per cent through schemes set up in consultation with works councils. Limited subsidies are made available from a joint fund for this purpose.

Continuing training in the public sector

Constitutional changes aimed at devolution led to a restructuring of the National Employment Office which used to deal with all training and employment matters, and a shift of its powers to regional and community offices: FOREm and VDAB. Both are administered by joint management committees under the control of executive councils. The VDAB was set up in 1984; FOREm in 1988.

Both are organised along the same lines, operating their own vocational training centres, centres run in co-operation with companies, and general education centres for both secondary and higher vocational education. A considerable amount of the vocational training organised by VDAB and FOREm is carried out at their own training centres, where two types of programme are offered: training for the technical and industrial sectors and training for the service sector. There are over 400 training centres offering technical or industrial courses including for the construction, metalworking, transport, textiles, electronics, and hotel and catering industries. Courses can be for up to 38 hours per week and last for up to one year, but there is also increasing demand for shorter courses. The number of participants on technical courses has declined over the past few years, and there tend to be more job seekers than employees on such courses; in 1994, for example, the Flemish VDAB trained 18,900 job seekers in technical subjects, compared to 8,500 employees. The numbers attending service sector courses have increased. These include IT, secretarial and administration, languages, bookkeeping and management, and tend to be used more for employees than job seekers (1994 VDAB figures: 15,500 job seekers against 21,650 employees).

Although the central courses still account for the vast bulk of training offered by the two regional organisations, both the VDAB and FOREm have noticed increasing demand from companies for in-house training and tailored programmes. Their involvement in in-house company training initiatives ranges from extending official recognition to in-house courses, to paying subsidies to company schemes for employees and creating joint training opportunities with industry. VDAB company-linked initiatives increased from 5,600 in 1992 to 17,400 in 1994, of which just over 40 per cent were carried out in VDAB centres. Companies are required to fund the training offered, and in 1994 income to the VDAB alone from such courses was BF 66.7 million (£1.33 million); these were largely in sectors such as transport and metalworking, but also in general administrative and IT courses.

The VDAB trained over 30,000 employees in its centres in 1994, compared to 22,000 in 1993, as well as over 40,000 unemployed. Of those jobless people completing training courses in 1993, 64 per cent had found employment in the next year.

Management training

A large percentage of managerial employees, particularly those destined for senior management or technical positions in larger organisations, are recruited directly from higher education institutions into graduate trainee positions, depending on qualifications and specialisation. In the case of university graduates, degree subjects for entering business tend to have more direct vocational flavour, although the two-tier process allows for some switching mid-stream.

Training for supervisors and those selected for internal promotion to higher managerial positions is conducted in approved training centres (either private or run by the regional organisations). The public centres also offer management and business training to craftsmen and the self-employed who run small enterprises. A distinction is drawn between business management and skills training, with 128 hours per year required for each. Most courses last for two years, although some are extended to three. Entry requirements vary, but most courses require completion of an apprenticeship or other vocational qualification and/or certain work experience. Over 320 courses are provided, and some 5,400 people undertook management training in the French-speaking community, while 20,000 attended in the Flemish community in 1994. In addition, some commercial companies offer management and business training, but these are largely unregulated, and standards are best assessed by local experts.

Time-off rights

Time-off rights for educational purposes (*congé-éducation payé/betaald educatief verlof*) are granted through a 1985 law applicable to all full-time employees in the private sector. Part-time staff in certain industries may also be eligible (eg in retail and large department stores). The law states that for every hour of the employee's time spent in training, an hour may be taken off work with no loss of pay. Under a 1995 royal decree the amount of paid educational leave was limited to 80 hours per year for general or language courses, and 120 hours per year for vocational courses. Where training is followed during working hours the limits rise to 120 and 180 hours respectively. Prior to the 1995 amendments the limits had been higher, but reductions were made in the light of extended career break provisions (for example, more staff are now entitled to such breaks, which are no longer at the employer's discretion).

The law stipulates the type of courses that entitle the employee to paid leave, and specifies the procedure for applying for such leave. This must be made in writing, with proof of enrolment on a suitable course. Leave may be stopped if the employee does not follow the course properly (for example, if more than 10 per cent of the course is missed), or if the employee carries out other paid employment during the time off. Certain safeguards are provided by law to limit the impact of leave on the operation of the business. Educational leave is monitored by the works council and a company-wide scheduling of educational leave must be agreed with the works council or the trade union delegation (with the individual employees in the case of small firms). In companies of fewer than 20 employees the employer can limit leave to 10 per cent of the workforce; in firms of between 20 and 50 staff, it can be limited to 10 per cent of staff carrying out 'similar tasks' (which are defined in consultation with the works council); in companies of over 100, scheduling and limits are laid down by collective agreement, thereby removing control from the works council.

The employer can claim a number of social security and wage subsidies for paid educational leave, with a ceiling for wage subsidies in 1995/6 of BF 65,000 (£1,300) per month. This is paid from a fund jointly financed by the state and employers, through a 0.04 per cent contribution of the company wages bill.

Skill/competency-based pay

Belgian pay agreements are still very heavily dominated by job categories, with advancement by virtue of promotion, length of service and age. Since the late 1980s some moves have been made towards performance-related pay. These may be individual or team-based, with managerial staff often also judged on company performance, or meeting of targets. However, there is little movement towards skill- and competency-based pay at any level. Some US or UK multi-nationals may have a limited benefit system linked to achievement of certain skills, but these are very rare.

Training for job seekers

Training initiatives for job seekers are broken down into career guidance services, short-term vocational courses and individual training within a company. There is also the possibility of financial assistance for collective retraining in companies engaged in restructuring. Those unemployed and in receipt of benefit are eligible to participate in company training schemes, for which they receive an additional payment from the employer on top of their benefit entitlement. This training lasts from a minimum of one month to a maximum of six months, after which the employer is bound to offer a permanent position.

In Flanders a project established at the end of 1989, and extended throughout the region in 1991, aims at assisting the long-term unemployed back into the labour market: *Weer werk actie* (back to work). It is aimed at bridging the gap between vacancies that are difficult to fill and the large number of long-term unemployed, through retraining or redirection. According to the VDAB, 2,500 of the long-term unemployed completed courses under the project in 1994. Various jobs clubs were also established in the early 1990s in Flanders, providing limited training initiatives under the control of the VDAB. In 1994 some 3,500 job seekers attended job clubs in the region, of which nearly 70 per cent found employment within one year.

A number of collective agreements expand on training initiatives for 'at risk' groups, notably the long-term unemployed, the low-skilled, ethnic minorities, and women in certain activities. For example, the petroleum sector agreement provides technical training for up to 100 long-term or low-skilled unemployed on a one-year full-time contract, with pay at minimum wage levels.

French-speaking community initiatives

In the French-speaking community several initiatives have been set up to assist young people and disadvantaged adults into the labour market. The two most noteworthy are the vocational apprenticeship initiatives (*entreprises d'apprentissage professionel*, EAP) and the integrated development programmes (*actions intégrées de développement*, AID).

The EAP is targeted at people aged between 18 and 25 who have in some way fallen behind in their education and training, or who are disadvantaged and marginalised. The majority are young people who have exhausted their unemployment benefit entitlement and who do not qualify for other vocational training schemes. EAPs offer vocational training based on work in a simulated company context, and they are run on a strictly non-competitive basis. EAPs are authorised and funded by the French-speaking community, with some funding from the European Social Fund. General and vocational training at EAPs lasts up to 18 months, and concentrates primarily on training in building, carpentry, small-scale catering and some farming. Some 40 EAPs are in existence and are dealing with rising numbers of disadvantaged youth: by 1990 they had trained 1,000 and by 1993 the number rose by 6 per cent.

The AID programmes, which have links with the CSC trade union confederation, are in many ways comparable to the EAPs in their target group but are directed at the public sector. There are currently 13 AID projects under way, with some 500 participants. Like the EAPs, they receive their funding from the Wallonia authorities and the ESF.

Other training

A number of training opportunities are provided by and for specific industries: agriculture, army training, training for handicapped workers, government ministries and local authorities. There is also widespread use of adult education classes in the evenings and at weekends (*onderwijs voor sociaale promotie*). This is limited to a maximum of 28 hours per week and is available for a range of subjects, which can be studied up to diploma level in vocational or higher vocational training, or short-type higher education. These courses tend to be very popular, with language training and secondary vocational training courses most sought after. A total of 200,000 people registered to follow such courses in 1992 across the two language communities. Some correspondence courses are also available, with plans to expand the system in Flanders.

Financing the system

Funding for vocational training, as for education in general, is largely the responsibility of the regions. Education budgets are allocated by regional parliaments. In 1994 some BF 175,900 million (£3,500 million) was allocated to the Ministry of Education in Wallonia; while in Flanders the education budget totalled BF 223,000 million (£4,450 million). In both regions almost half of the budget was spent on the provision of secondary education, with the overwhelming part accounted for by labour costs. In Flanders 28 per cent of the secondary education budget was channelled into community education, 13 per cent into subsidised official education and 59 per cent into subsidised private education.

Under the 1995/6 national multi-industry framework agreement, all companies are required to pay a training levy set at 0.15 per cent of the wages bill in 1995 and 0.2 per cent in 1996. This is in addition to funding for employment measures, such as recruitment of at-risk groups, a 0.05 per cent payment for educational leave funds, and 0.05 per cent for child care facilities. Sectoral and company-level agreements may increase the training percentage and detail specific measures to be taken. For example, in the mechanical engineering sector 0.5 per cent of hours are to be devoted to training (with training defined as 'improving a worker's qualifications while responding to the needs of the company'). The metalworking sector recommends 40 hours per worker per year be devoted to training initiatives, and says that an annual plan should be drawn up in conjunction with the trade union delegation. Any training undertaken under the aegis of the sectoral training organisation, Educam, will entitle the worker to paid educational leave and a recognised Educam certification. Companies covered by such additional sectoral measures may be exempt from the nationally-decreed levy, but only if they can prove that an equivalent amount is devoted to training at company level.

In cases where no sectoral or company training initiative is taken to use the 0.15 per cent (0.2 per cent in 1996) for training, an equivalent sum has to be paid into a national fund (*tewerkstellingsfonds*). Approximately BF 4,500 million (£90 million) is raised every year, of which 95 per cent is currently channelled directly into company or sectoral training. Since 1992 a minimum of 0.1 per cent of the wages bill must be paid into the fund in any case, after concerns about how the money was actually being used at company level.

In the metalworking industry – the largest industrial employer, with some 230,000 workers – three broad training schemes are operated with funding from the 0.15/0.2 per cent programme. The first is targeted at apprentices in the industry, granting subsidies to companies that take on apprentices from among the lower qualified or unemployed. These subsidies vary from BF 55,000 to BF 220,000 (£1,100 to £4,400) per apprentice per year. Second, advisers and trainers are provided for a number of regional schemes such as those run by the VDAB for long-term unemployed (see above). Finally, some BF 150 million (£3 million) is allocated to in-house company schemes, with responsibility for specific fund allocations given to six joint industry committees.

The various vocational training courses and apprenticeships are financed through a combination of regional subsidies, grants and employer and/or employee levies. So, for example, the FOREm and VDAB courses receive subsidies from their respective governments and grants from the European Social Fund, as well as contributions levied on companies participating in some of their courses. Part of the collectively agreed wage bill allocations are channelled into VDAB and FOREm initiatives.

Under certain conditions, new companies, and companies undergoing restructuring in Wallonia are entitled to a training subsidy from the regional authorities. New companies must prove they are creating at least five new jobs, and companies under restructuring must guarantee no job losses. Subsidies are granted for training of a technical nature only for between four and 26 weeks, and can be put towards the cost of external training or the payment of in-house instructors.

Educational attainment of the population

Level	Percentage of 25–64 age-group
Lower secondary	51
Upper secondary	27
Higher education (non-university)	12
University	10

Source: OECD (1994)

Organisations

Flemish Ministry of Education
Koningsstraat 71
1000 Brussels
Tel. +32 2 219 9436
Fax +32 2 219 7773

Ministry of Education for the French
Community
Boulevard Pachéco 19
1010 Brussels
Tel. +32 2 210 5511

VDAB
Keizerslaan 11
1000 Brussels
Tel. +32 2 506 1511
Fax +32 2 511 4343

FOREm
Boulevard Tirou
6000 Charleroi
Tel. +32 71 206 111
Fax +32 71 206 799

Ministry of Labour
Rue Belliard 51/53
1040 Brussels
Tel. +32 2 233 4111

UPEDI (Association of temporary
agencies)
Avenue de l'Héliport 21–3
1210 Brussels
Tel. +32 2 203 3803
Fax +32 2 217 4268

FEB/VBO (Belgian employers' federa-
tion)
Rue Ravenstein 4
1000 Brussels
Tel. +32 2 515 0811
Fax +32 2 515 0913

Media

MoveUp Directory
Auguste Reyerslaan 55/8
1030 Brussels
Tel. +32 2 734 9302
Fax +32 2 734 7305

Who's recruiting who in Belgium
HMA
Boulevard Lambertmont 304
1030 Brussels
Tel. +32 2 241 9736
Fax +32 2 245 8534

De Standaard
Gossetlaan 30
1702 Groot-Bijgaarden
Tel. + 32 2 467 2211
Fax + 32 2 466 30 93

Le Soir
112 rue Rotale
1000 Brussels
Tel. + 32 2 225 5555
Fax + 32 2 225 5904

Gazet van Antwerpen
Katwilgweg 2
2050 Antwerp
Tel. + 32 3 210 0210
Fax + 32 3 233 7480

Main sources

Ced. samson. *Commentaire social de poche, 1996/1997*. Diegem, 1996
DENOLF, LIEVEN and DENYS, JAN. *Hoe werven bedrijven in België, 1995*. Hoger Institut voor de Arbeid, Katholieke Universiteit te Leuven, Leuven, 1996
MATTELÉ J. and HORION M. J. *Who's recruiting who in Belgium*, HMA, Brussels, 1995. Contributions and information may be in Flemish, French or English depending on the organisation
CEDEFOP, *Beroepsopleiding in België*. Berlin, 1994

Various sectoral and company collective agreements including metalworking, chemicals, textiles, garages, electricians, and white-collar employees
Annual reports for 1994, VDAB and FOREm

3

Denmark

Employers are able to hire permanent and temporary employees largely free of statutory constraints or notification requirements. Collective agreements and local consultative arrangements may require discussions with employee representatives on broader personnel policy, and white-collar employees are covered by their own statute which imposes some restrictions on the form of contracts which may be adopted.

The state placement monopoly was abolished in 1990, and since then private employment agencies have been free to operate. However, the official employment service still plays the dominant role in placement, and also pursues active labour market measures, including advice to employers.

The labour market

The population of Denmark is just over 3.5 million. The labour force is made up of about 2.8 million people, 2.26 million of whom are classified as wage-earners. By far the largest group of workers (about 908,000) is employed in the public sector. Roughly 445,000 have jobs in manufacturing, with 420,000 employed in retailing, hotels and restaurants, and 270,000 in the financial sector.

In January 1996, 285,000 people were unemployed, equivalent to 10.1 per cent of the workforce. Participation rates are about 89 per cent for men and 79 per cent for women, with the latter the highest figure in the European Union. As is the case in many countries, most female employees work in the public sector – 52 per cent compared to 23 per cent of men.

One of the characteristics of the Nordic labour markets is that they have a high percentage of part-time workers, and Denmark is no exception, with about a quarter of employees working part-time. Roughly 75 per cent of these are women.

Recruitment

Personnel planning

Official notification   Employers have no statutory obligation to report new hirings or resignations/dismissals to the Ministry of Labour, or indeed to any other organisation. This also applies to AF, the state placement system (see below).

Workforce consultation   There are about 3,000 joint workplace 'co-operation committees' in the private sector, established according to the provisions of an agreement between the Danish Federation of Trade Unions (LO) and the Danish Employers' Federation (DA). Such committees may be set up in all companies with 35 or more employees, provided that this is proposed either by the employer or by a majority of employees. The committee is composed of an equal number of members of management and senior executives not eligible for union membership on the one hand, and employees on the other. One of the tasks of the committee is to formulate the company's personnel policy.

Employment incentives   There are as yet no initiatives towards the type of collectively-agreed schemes gaining prominence in some countries, which offer job preservation in return for employee concessions on pay and/or working time.

There are various schemes – targeted at such groups as the long-term unemployed and under-25s, and often training-oriented – which offer employers government subsidies, usually for short-term contracts.

There are no employment incentives which involve the reduction of employer social insurance payments. As the comprehensive social security system is financed through the taxation system, employer social charges are very low – about 2.5 per cent of wages for blue-collar and 4.5 per cent for white-collar employees – and there is therefore little scope for reductions.

Using part-timers and temps

Part-time

Non-standard forms of work are regulated by both laws and collective agreements. White-collar workers are subject to a special law – *Funktionærloven* – which regulates their conditions of employment, and which contains some rules regarding fixed-term employment; these may be supplemented by collective agreements. Rules on part-time and fixed-term blue-collar work are mostly set by collective agreement.

The length of the normal working week is set by collective agreement, and has stood at 37 hours since 1990. Part-time work is not defined in any global sense, but some laws and agreements do offer such definitions. For instance, the provisions on unemployment insurance funds in the Act on Job Placement (*Lov om arbejdsformidling*) define part-time work as being between 15 and 30 hours a week. These limits are also applied by the Industrial Agreement, which covers about 160,000 workers in manufacturing industry and was last renegotiated in 1995. But the collective agreement for shop and office workers, for instance, has no lower hours limit.

Collective agreements often contain sections on part-time work. Provisions vary, but usually entitle part-timers to (pro rata) equal pay. They may also contain strictures on the replacement of full-time staff with part-timers, equal rights to seniority, etc.

Fixed-term contracts

Fixed-term employment is permitted with few restrictions. Although no official figures are published on the number of people employed on such contracts, it is estimated that they make up between 10 and 12 per cent of those in work. This form of employment is most often used in clerical work.

Fixed-term contracts may be limited to a certain period of time or to a certain task. A special term – *midlertidigt arbejde* – is used to describe work lasting less than three months. Where salaried employees are involved, minimum periods of notice may be set by law should either party wish to withdraw during the life of the contract.

Repeated renewals of a fixed-term contract may be viewed as constituting an attempt to evade employment protection legislation, and could lead to the contract being deemed permanent.

Agency employment

Hiring agency employees is permitted, and largely free of statutory interference. However, in some circumstances, employee representatives may have to be consulted where this is provided for under a collective agreement. Temporary agency employees remain employees of the agency, which is responsible for payments and deductions.

There is a trade association for agencies, which operate under a code of conduct. This includes guidelines on the form of contract, which must be in writing, pay, sick pay, holidays and termination arrangements.

Temporary agency employees do not count as part of the user employer's workforce for the purpose of calculating whether the establishment crosses various statutory thresholds.

Sex discrimination

The Equal Opportunities Act (*Ligebehandlingsloven*) prohibits discrimination on the grounds of gender, pregnancy or matrimonial status. This provision applies during both recruitment and employment. Questions concerning intentions to have children or about pregnancy, and any indication of gender preference in job advertisements, are therefore illegal under the Act. The Equal Pay Act (*Ligelønsloven*) requires that men and women receive equal pay for work of equal value.

Finding the applicant

Application documents

The use of application forms for jobs is uncommon. When applying for a job it is usual to enclose a CV and covering letter; both are usually concise – the letter of application being no more than one A4 side and the CV no more than two – and should be typewritten.

CVs usually contain the following items (in this order): personal details; education (in chronological order, latest last), including on-the-job vocational training; previous job experience (chronological order as above) including job descriptions and military service; hobbies and interests.

It is not common for detailed references to be included in CVs, but it is usual to end a CV by stating that references will be supplied on request. References are often requested at the end of a first interview and are taken up at this point, but referees are contacted only with the interviewee's agreement. No more than three references are usually supplied.

Placement services

Prior to 1990 the state job placement service (AF) had a monopoly on placements. Private employment agencies were in general prohibited, although private temporary agencies, mainly in the clerical field, were allowed to operate with the permission of the Ministry of Labour, which was also responsible for supervising the agencies. The 1990 legislation removed all restrictions, and no special permission is now required for any type of job placement activity.

The state placement service – AF

Although the state no longer enjoys a monopoly, Denmark still retains a comprehensive public placement service. The role of the AF has changed since its inception in 1969, from being just a placement service; it now occupies a much more central role in active labour market measures, being involved in monitoring the labour market, co-ordinating various employment measures and advising both the unemployed and employers. Its monitoring activity includes the compilation by its 14 regional offices of employment information and possible employment bottlenecks to be included in a quarterly report published by the Labour Market Board (*Arbejdsmarkedsstyrelsen*). AF has recently been given increased responsibility in the sphere of active labour market policy, because of the recently-introduced requirement for the jobless to formulate, in conjunction with AF, an 'individual action plan' after three months' unemployment.

Placement remains at the core of AF's activity. The organisation has a nation-wide database – AF-MATCH – which contains details of the qualifications and work experience of job applicants, as well as a register of vacancies (including qualification requirements), a register of companies (including product range, staff and training requirements) and a register of training courses.

Placement is effected through about 200 local offices staffed by a variety of consultants and vocational guidance officers. Great emphasis is placed on visiting local companies to discuss needs for both labour and training.

Private agencies

Since the abolition in 1990 of the state monopoly on job placement, private agencies have been permitted to operate freely. The familiar majors are represented, as well as numerous home-grown operations. As well as these, some trade unions are active in job placement activities, among them metalworkers' union, Metal, which operates a service called JOBbank for its members. The various professional associations for university graduates (see below) are also active in job placement.

Executive recruitment

There are no restrictions on executive search companies. Although about a third of vacancies at this level are filled through advertisements in newspapers and specialist journals, search companies account for a quarter of jobs filled, and more than this at the more senior levels.

There are branches of several international executive search companies in Denmark, as well as locally-based operations. The Danish Institute of Personnel Management (IP) also maintains an extensive executive recruitment database.

Selection

Two interviews are the norm. The first may be conducted by one person or a panel, and is designed to draw up a shortlist of two or three candidates for the second interview. Those who reach the second stage are also usually interviewed by their prospective immediate superior.

The use of different types of test – mainly psychological – is fairly common in conjunction with recruitment. It is estimated that there are currently about 100 tests in use on the Danish market. They are used mainly to support overall impressions about an applicant, rather than as a selection method in themselves. Health tests – and particularly genetic tests – are currently under scrutiny with a view to restricting their use.

Education

The education system

Compulsory education lasts for nine years between the ages of 7 and 16. There is also an optional tenth year, which is necessary for some types of upper secondary education, for example the *Højere Forberedelseseksamen* (see below). These years are most often spent in a single school known as the *folkeskole*. After completing *folkeskole*, those who wish to continue at school – as the majority do – may choose between various forms of training and education.

According to OECD figures, public expenditure on education in Denmark accounted for 7.2 per cent of GDP in 1994, the highest proportion in the OECD.

Secondary education

Lower secondary education   Every child attends a *folkeskole* (municipal primary and lower secondary school) or its private equivalent for at least seven years. In 1993/4, there were about 517,000 pupils in the 1,680 *folkeskoler*, and roughly 66,000 pupils in some 400 private schools. Education at this level is therefore principally in municipal schools. These schools, which do not charge fees, are by far the most widespread form of basic education, attended by about 90 per cent of Danish children.

Private schools of various kinds, which take 10 per cent of children at *folkeskole* level, receive government subsidies of 80 to 85 per cent of their operating expenses, the balance being made up through fees charged. These are on average about DKr 600 (£60) a month. Loans can be obtained on favourable terms for the establishment of private schools. Government subsidies to private schools are seen as important in safeguarding the rights of those parents who wish their children to receive an alternative education on ideological, political, religious or educational grounds.

The *folkeskole* aims to provide a broad general education in which the core academic subjects are combined with art, music and more practical skills, together with contemporary and vocational studies. There is an emphasis on taking and sharing responsibility for solving problems, and on developing the ability to form independent judgements. Educational and vocational guidance is also compulsory in years one to nine.

There is no compulsory examination when leaving *folkeskole* at age 16. All students are given a leaving certificate stating the subjects they have taken and the marks for their last year's work. However, students may decide to sit one of two examinations:

- the Leaving Examination (LE) after year nine or ten
- the Advanced Leaving Examination (ALE) after year ten.

The ALE is available in Danish, mathematics, English, physics/chemistry and German; the LE is available in these subjects plus art, woodwork, home economics, Latin and typing. Within this framework pupils may take as many or as few subjects as they wish. The decision on which subjects to study at which level is taken at the end of year seven of *folkeskole*.

An alternative to the last three years of *folkeskole* is provided by the *efterskole* or continuation school. These are residential independent schools whose curricula are based mainly on particular political, religious or educational ideas. They are intended as an alternative form of education for young people who do not feel at ease in the usual system, and they tend to place greater emphasis on social and recreational skills and practical work.

Upper secondary education   On leaving lower secondary education, students may make a number of choices. They can look for a job; go to folk high school or a specialised boarding school; choose general upper secondary education at a *gymnasium*; or opt for vocational training.

Only about 5 per cent of *folkeskole*-leavers choose to quit the education system at this point, although as recently as 1983 the figure was double this. The vast majority continue in some form of upper secondary or vocational education. Roughly 40 per cent go on to complete vocational training and 30 per cent to gain a qualification from a *gymnasium*. But about 25 per cent of any given year-group drop out from vocational or upper secondary education.

General upper secondary education   The most common types of general upper secondary education are three-year courses at a state *gymnasium*, leading to the Upper Secondary School Leaving Examination (*Studentereksamen*) (although this may also be gained by two-year day or evening classes) and two-year courses leading to the Higher Preparatory Examination (*Højere Forberedelseseksamen*, HF) – the latter requiring the completion of the optional tenth year at *folkeskole*. There are about 20 private *gymnasia* which benefit from similar types of public grants. However, unlike *folkeskoler*, the requirement that they prepare pupils for the same final examination as state schools means that they have much less control over their own curricula.

In addition, *gymnasia* also offer the Higher Commercial Examination (*Højere Handelseksamen*, HHX) or the Higher Technical Examination (*Højere Teknisk Eksamen*, HTX), both three-year courses which are comparable to the *Studentereksamen*, but more vocationally oriented.

Admission to *gymnasia* is governed by recommendation from a *folkeskole*, and it may be a requirement that students should have achieved satisfactory results in the LE in certain subjects. Students choose either of two main 'lines' – mathematics (science) or languages (arts). A common core of subjects is taught at intermediate level, with students choosing at least two subjects from their 'line' to study at advanced level.

Students who pass the *Studentereksamen* receive a certificate showing their examination grades and the marks for their last year's work. The certificate gives access to higher education, although admission to some faculties is granted only to students with passes in particular branches of study. Other students may be required to pass supplementary examinations in subjects relevant to their chosen field of study.

While traditional *gymnasium* courses are felt to be the natural preparation for tertiary education for 16-year-olds, older people who have spent time in commerce or industry often opt for the Higher Preparatory Examination (HF). Introduced in 1967, HF can be taken by anyone over the age of 18, and confers the right of admission to further education. Since most people cannot pass an examination of this kind without tuition, two-year courses have been set up at *gymnasia*, teacher training colleges and other institutions. There are also three- and four-year day and evening classes which enable people to sit the HF on a single-subject basis. Work experience is taken into account when deciding on admission to HF courses, although most HF students have passed the LE or its equivalent. A certificate is awarded for passing the examination.

The HF concept has been a great success since its introduction, and the courses have become an important type of continuing adult education.

Technical and commercial education: HHX and HTX   Preparation for these courses normally takes place at commercial schools (HHX) or technical schools (HTX). Admission to courses, which last for three years, is on the same basis as admission to *gymnasium*, that is by recommendation from *folkeskole*.

HHX and HTX are not vocational qualifications as such – rather they are an alternative, more vocationally oriented route into higher education for those interested in, for example, engineering (HTX) or business administration (HHX).

Den frie ungdomsuddanelse (FU)   Established in 1995, FU is an alternative to other secondary education structures for those who cannot find a niche in the system. FU lasts for two to three years. The subjects to be studied are chosen by the student, although the final course design must be approved by the local authority. Both academic and practical topics may be covered. At the moment about 1,200 pupils have chosen FU, and forecasts are that it will become more popular.

Higher education

Entry to higher and further education requires individuals to hold either a *Studentereksamen*, the HF, HHX or HTX. However, applicants may be admitted to some institutions with other recognised qualifications, including foreign ones. About 40,000 people were admitted to higher education in 1995, and 43,500 places were available in 1996.

It has been uncommon for foreign students to enrol at Danish universities – in 1994, there were only about 1,600 of them. However, the number of foreigners studying in Denmark is increasing, especially under the EU ERASMUS programme. It is reckoned that 2,500 EU students were at Danish universities under this programme in 1995/6.

Most further education courses have nominally free admission, with establishments deciding on intake size, but quotas are set. However, some areas of study have admission restricted by the Ministry of Education. This is particularly true of lengthy, expensive and oversubscribed courses such as medicine. When fixing admission quotas, consideration is given to the estimated future need for graduates, the capacity of the various institutions and the geographical distribution of applicants.

A co-ordinated clearing system permits applicants to apply for admission to more than one institution, thus increasing their chances of getting a place. Applications are screened to check whether they meet admission requirements, and admission is granted to the institution or course highest on the prospective student's list, provided sufficient places are available. No applicant is offered a place at more than one institution in the final allocation. This system applies only to full-length degree courses – admission to shorter further education courses is arranged by the individual institutions themselves.

Types of institution   Although there are about 130 higher education institutions offering study programmes of varying lengths and levels, Denmark has only three universities (Copenhagen, Århus and Odense) and two university centres (Roskilde and Ålborg), all administered by the Ministry of Education. The newest of these – Ålborg university centre – was opened in 1974, and brought together a number of previously independent institutions, including two engineering academies, a school of social work and business economics schools.

There are also a large number of specialised institutions administered mainly by the Ministry of Education but also, as in the cases of, for example, architecture and music, by the Ministry of Cultural Affairs. These offer advanced and professional education and training in a wide range of occupations. As well as the *Teknika* (technical colleges), which provide shorter engineering courses than the universities (see *Types of degree* below), there are commercial colleges and single-specialism schools of, for example, dentistry, veterinary science, the graphic arts and pharmacy.

Types of degree   There are three types of degree awarded: a bachelor's degree after three years of study, which as yet is not a common qualification, and a *Kandidat* degree, equivalent to a master's, after five years. Postgraduate degrees include a *Magister Artium* (MA), the traditional postgraduate qualification, and a full doctorate.

The *Kandidat* degrees are commonly known by abbreviated Latin titles. For business purposes perhaps the most relevant are *cand polyt* (civil engineer) and *cand polit/cand oecon* (business studies).

One step below this level there is another set of business and engineering qualifications. The University centre at Ålborg, the Danish Technical College at Lyngby and the engineering colleges have a 3.5-year course awarding the degree of *diplom-ingeniør*, which includes a six-month training period in a company. This replaces the former *teknikum-ingeniør* qualification, which was less theoretically oriented.

In commerce, as well as the degrees mentioned above there is another university-level degree in business studies – *cand merc* – offered by Odense University, the

University Centre at Ålborg and the business schools (*Handelshøjskoler*). The *Handelshøjskoler* also offer courses leading to a lower-level commercial qualification – one full-time (HA) and one part-time (HD).

Administration of the further education system

Funding for higher education is provided by the state and forms part of the national budget. In 1995, government expenditure on higher education amounted to DKr 8.5 billion (£850 million). The administration of universities and other institutions by the Ministry of Education is regulated by an Act adopted in 1992.

Research normally takes place within the institutions themselves, although many non-university vocationally oriented higher education institutions, such as the *handelshøjskoler*, do not carry out their own research but make use of results from other institutes of further education. The distribution of research tasks within each institution is decided by a committee.

Teaching staff, students and technical and administrative staff are represented on all the collegiate boards and committees.

Denmark has had a state financial support scheme for students since the 1950s. The current scheme was introduced in 1988, and consists of two elements: state grants and state study loans. (From the middle of the 1960s there were also bank loans guaranteed by the state – this practice was abandoned in 1988.)

Each element is subject to an upper limit, with different rates for students living away from home, and those either living with their parents or engaged in upper secondary education. In 1993 these rates were DKr 3,310 (£330) and DKr 1,890 (£190) a month respectively. Both categories of students can also obtain state loans of (1993) DKr 1,489 (£150) a month. Before the student's 19th birthday, the level of awards is also dependent upon parental income. In any event, awards are means-tested, and are reduced if an upper income limit is exceeded.

The system for paying grants is fairly flexible. Students are allocated a number of units, each unit representing one month's support, the exact number depending upon the duration of the course. They are also allocated an extra 'pool' of 12 units which may be used in specific circumstances, such as having to retake an examination or upon switching courses during the first year of study. The ordinary units may be used at will throughout the course, and thus the system gives students considerable flexibility in arranging their own individual course of study.

Graduate recruitment

There is no 'season' for the recruitment of graduates in Denmark, and therefore no equivalent to the British 'milkround'. However, some companies do make presentations at some institutions of higher education. There are also a limited number of job fairs.

Most of the universities have some kind of department giving study and vocational advice, but their involvement in actual job-broking is minimal.

The public recruitment service is of limited use to those at graduate level, since many such positions never reach it; indeed, it is estimated that 60 per cent of all jobs are filled by word of mouth.

Speculative applications are therefore fairly common. Information on companies may be gained from many sources, including *Kompass Danmark*. Perhaps the most useful source for graduates is *Karriere Vejviser*, which gives general advice on job seeking and the labour market, as well as giving detailed profiles of many companies, including company culture and recruiting procedures.

There are two other main routes for graduates seeking jobs – advertisements and trade unions.

Press advertisements are still an important source of graduate jobs. For general vacancies, the national daily *Berlingske Tidende* (especially the Wednesday and Sunday editions) carries about 80 per cent of private-sector job advertisements; its closest rival is another national daily – *Politiken* (Wednesday and Sunday) – with about 10 per cent. Other important sources are *Jyllands-Posten*, the local paper for Jutland, and *Børsen*, the business daily.

For more specialised vacancies, the most important places to consider are the journals published by the various trade unions and professional organisations. For private-sector jobs, perhaps the most significant are *Ingeniøren* for graduate engineers – where an estimated 90 per cent of all engineering vacancies are advertised; *DJØF-bladet*, published by DJØF, the association of law and economics graduates; and *Civiløkonomen Jobbørs*, published by the business studies graduates' association FDC.

Apart from producing these publications, the various unions and associations (and their associated unemployment insurance funds) are able to provide other services to their members. Many of them have some kind of job placement service, mainly in the form of a 'job bank', where members may enter their CV, which can then be matched with relevant vacancies; the job banks do not advertise. The associations are also able to help on matters such as determining the 'going rate' for jobs.

Vocational training

Basic vocational training

Denmark's system of basic vocational training is well organised and comprehensive, with a long tradition of involvement by the social partners in policy-making and administration, at central and local level, on both practical and theoretical sides. The system is overseen by the Ministry of Education, although much of the administration and decision-making is done by bodies formed mostly, and sometimes entirely, of employer and employee representatives.

Initiatives for reform during the lifetime of the system have largely come from the trade unions and employers themselves, who in turn attach great value to the qualifications awarded by the system. Vocational training is the most common option for *folkeskole* leavers, being chosen by 50 per cent, compared to 45 per cent who enter a *gymnasium*.

The first Apprenticeship Act was passed in 1889, and made training compulsory for craft trades. This was mainly carried out through evening classes. In the 1920s the first Trade Committee was set up as a representative body where master craftspeople and trade unions could discuss apprentice training measures.

The Apprenticeship Act of 1956 shifted the education and training of apprentices from evening to day classes. The Act provided for the restructuring and modernisation of training curricula, and made them subject to supervision by thirty-four joint trade committees – thirty-one for trade and industry and one each for retailing, commerce and office work. Under this system, successful completion of an apprenticeship was the basis for the award of a Journeyman's Certificate (*svendebrev*). In the clerical and commercial fields it was sometimes necessary for apprentices to pass examinations on the theoretical side of their training – either the Commercial Assistant's Examination (*handelsmedhjælpereksamen*) or the more comprehensive Commercial Examination (*handelseksamen*).

The joint committees also produced recommendations which, after an experimental period, became the Basic Vocational Training Act of 1977 (*erhvervsfaglige grunduddannelser*, EFG). The EFG was designed as a parallel to the apprenticeship system, starting with a one-year period of full-time education providing a broad introduction to a number of related trades. After choosing a particular trade, pupils would continue with a combination of theory and practical work along the lines of a traditional apprenticeship.

The 1956 Apprenticeship Act and the 1977 EFG Act have since been replaced by legislation bringing together vocational training and apprenticeship under a single umbrella. On completion of vocational training, a nationally-recognised training certificate is issued. In the craft trades this is usually called a *svendebrev*; elsewhere, an *uddannelsesbevis*. According to EU comparability standards, these are deemed equivalent, for the engineering industry, to a UK National Vocational Qualification Level 3 or City and Guilds Mechanical Craft Studies 1 and 2. In commerce, it is equivalent to a UK NVQ Level 1–2.

There are about 55 technical schools and the same number of commercial schools responsible for initial vocational training. There are also a number of small specialist schools offering courses in the agriculture and health sectors, for example.

There are generally no restrictions on admission to vocational education and training courses, except for a requirement that nine years' (ten years' in a few cases) basic schooling has been completed. However, it is possible that admission may sometimes be restricted to courses that are reckoned to be oversubscribed in relation to projected employment prospects. There is a free choice of schools.

Course structure   Courses are divided first into technical and commercial/clerical, then into a number of vocational areas, each with several associated courses which in turn contain a number of specialisations. For instance, technical vocational training has a road transport area containing a driver training course – within this there are specialisations in driving; for instance, refrigerated vehicles or tankers. There are about 80 courses in the technical area.

As far as clerical/commercial training is concerned, the structure is broadly the same. There is only one area and five courses, but a similar degree of specialisation – the clerical course has specialisations in, for instance, shipping, accounts, and travel. There is at present – perhaps surprisingly – no basic vocational training aimed at the finance sector. However, a proposal for such a course is currently under consideration.

Courses are all of the 'sandwich' type, ie they alternate between practical work and classroom instruction. However, the size of the sandwich and the relative amounts of 'bread' and 'filling' vary between courses and, to some extent, according to individual preference.

For instance, a student may choose to start technical vocational training with an optional 5- to 40-week (the average is 20 weeks) 'first school period' which gives an introduction to a wide range of specialisations within a course area. This consists of practical and theoretical teaching, as well as information on the possibility of further education and training in the area, and on individual trades within the area. This aids students in choosing a particular course to follow.

But it is also possible, if a training contract (see below) has already been agreed, for a student to start training with a period of practical experience in a company. Both routes converge at the 20-week 'second school period'. It is also possible for students aged over 18 to start straight away on the 'second school period'. Thereafter, training alternates between practical experience in a company and school-based instruction. The average length of courses is four years, ranging from two years (eg general industrial worker) to five and a half years (industrial engineer), and total school-based training takes up no more than 80 weeks. Again, it is possible for those – especially older workers – who already have a good deal of practical experience to skip the two initial school periods and start immediately on the 'sandwich' part of the course. But all routes are of equal value and lead to a full vocational qualification.

In the commercial/clerical field, the first and second school periods are combined, and total 40 weeks. The instruction during these periods is of a less specialised nature than for technical training, and consists mainly of eight basic subjects – Danish, English, a second foreign language, IT, economics, civics, sales and service, and accountancy and finance – but there is some specialised instruction. Students may choose to spend this time by beginning work in a company and alternating with short periods in school (no more than 18 weeks). But one of the courses on offer in the sector – computer assistant – is the only training which is purely school-based, and therefore cannot be entered by this route.

After this initial period, training continues with alternating school and practical periods. The amount of time spent in school is less than in technical training – six to twelve weeks – and the total length of courses is only three years.

There has long been a problem with providing the requisite number of company training places for vocational students. Therefore, since 1990 it has been possible to complete training entirely in school, although the practice is not very common. The provision of training places is voluntary, and responsibility for finding a training place is theoretically up to individual students; but in practice a good deal of assistance is available from college counselling and guidance services. Local education and training committees – a majority of whose members are required by law to be representatives of local employer and trade union organisations – are also set up by colleges for each course area; they are responsible for promoting co-operation between the school and local businesses, and for ensuring that there are adequate training places in local companies for the school's trainees.

Classroom instruction is financed by the state, with periods of practice being financed by the firms involved. Compensation for trainees is financed from a reimbursement fund *Arbejdsgivernes Elevrefusion* (AER), which is financed by compulsory employer contributions.

Training contracts Company training can proceed only on the basis of a legally-binding contract between the student and the company, covering the whole period of the course. Contracts may be concluded only with companies approved by the Trade Committees (see below).

Pay and conditions during periods spent at the company are usually set by collective agreement. For instance, the 1995 Industrial Agreement has a ten-page supplement covering such matters as holidays, sick leave and pay and working time, including overtime and shiftwork. For 1996, minimum pay rates range from DKr 31.25 to DKr 67 an hour (£3.10–£6.70), depending upon the stage of education reached.

Some agreements may cover other matters. For instance, the 1995 agreement for shop and office workers, while covering broadly the same topics and setting a minimum monthly salary of DKr 6,000 to DKr 7,200 (£600–£720) for 1996, also specifies the proportion of trainees who may be taken on in relation to other employees.

Adult vocational education

There are three main strands to adult vocational training in Denmark. Semi-skilled training is designed to offer vocational training to unskilled workers and the unemployed; 'refresher' vocational training updates and refreshes skills acquired during basic vocational training; and training upgrades provide a chance to go beyond the basic training level.

Semi-skilled training

These courses are administered by the Ministry of Labour, and are regulated by a law passed in 1985 (although a systematic, legally regulated system has been in existence since 1960). They apply only to the private sector, and cover metal-working, road transport and construction. There are 25 sectoral committees, composed equally of employer and union representatives, who draw up and monitor the courses available, which currently total about 500.

Course are modular, with a variety of levels enabling participants to enter according to their skills. Modules are short – one to eight weeks – but may be combined into longer courses of up to seven months. Instruction tends to be practically oriented and has traditionally been fairly narrowly based, although general subjects such as the working environment, first aid and labour market conditions have assumed increased importance. A certificate is awarded to those successfully completing courses.

Teaching takes place at 24 centres – 19 of which are independent and five state-owned – as well as in-company. There is free admission provided the prospective trainee either has, or is interested in, a job in the relevant sector. Remuneration is paid to those attending courses; the amount is the same as unemployment benefit (up to 90 per cent of earnings). Expenses for schools and compensation are met by the Labour Market Training Fund (*Arbejdsmarkedets Uddannelsesfond*, AUD), which is financed by employee (20 per cent) and employer (80 per cent) contributions. There are also collectively-agreed sectoral training funds.

'Refresher' vocational training

There are two types of scheme under this heading. The main function of the scheme managed by the Ministry of Education is to provide grants to encourage the development of training schemes, especially in exporting companies. Activities are planned and implemented locally to ensure relevance. Applicants for grants may be educational institutions, other public institutions or private course organisers. Much of the effect of the scheme on vocational training is therefore indirect, although it has led to the development of the IDV and VTP (company oriented) courses run by vocational schools.

The second scheme, under the aegis of the Ministry of Labour, is established under the same legislation as that for semi-skilled workers and is very similar in style and structure. There are 28 sectors with some 900 courses, and entry is open to those over 18 years of age with a relevant basic vocational qualification (or equivalent practical experience). Courses are conducted in a number of places – technical and commercial schools, companies, AMU centres – and participants receive a certificate of completion. Running costs and participants' compensation (at the same level as for semi-skilled course) are again met by the AUD.

Training upgrades

Technical schools run various – usually two-year – courses for those who already have basic vocational training and wish to upgrade their skills. There are about

25 such courses, all of which confer a nationally-recognised qualification. Instruction, although mainly theoretical, is very closely linked to practical, specialised topics.

In commerce there are a number of courses which allow for skills upgrading. For example, there are two-year courses for computer technicians, marketing economists and more general commercial matters run by commercial schools. There is also a four-year 'export technician' course, organised on a sandwich basis, which teaches both technical and commercial skills. However, entry requirements for all of these are one of the four upper secondary leaving qualifications.

Perhaps of more relevance to those with basic vocational training and some practical experience are the one- to three-year part-time courses. These are paid for from public funds, with participants paying a fixed fee (often paid by employers). They lead to the nationally-recognised qualifications of *merkonom*, *datanom* and *teknonom*, and are all commercially oriented courses with specialities in marketing, data processing and technology respectively. They are also highly popular with employers.

'Open' education and training for the unemployed

The Act on Open Education came into force in 1990. Its aim is to give adults the opportunity to take vocationally oriented part-time and single-subject courses – the exact construction of the course is left to individual students – in their own time.

Courses are offered at technical and commercial schools, and at centres of further education (universities, business schools, engineering colleges, etc).

Admission criteria take full account of work experience, and no age limit is specified. By law, teaching must be organised so that it can be followed outside normal working time by those in full-time employment. Supplementary legislation secures the right of unemployed people to pursue such courses during working hours without loss of benefit, subject to proof that it will help their job prospects.

Participation in open education does not entitle students to state financial support, and tuition is not necessarily free. However, the state awards grants to approved courses so as to reduce student payments. These cover about 80 per cent of operational expenditure, with the balance being made up from student fees. Institutions may apportion grants between courses as they wish, so that fees on one course may be set higher to offset free tuition in others. This makes it possible to offer courses to the unemployed free of charge.

Training for the unemployed

There are also schemes targeted specifically at the unemployed, and taking them is a condition of continuing to receive unemployment benefit. These include

one- to two-week 'inspirational' courses after three months' unemployment and
three- to six-month UTB (training offer) courses after four years.

Educational leave

As part of the paid leave (*orlov*) schemes, employees are entitled to one year off
– at 100 per cent of unemployment benefit – to pursue their education. In 1995, a
monthly average of 25,000 people were making use of this arrangement.

Educational attainment of the population

Level	Percentage of 25–64 age-group
Lower secondary	40
Upper secondary	40
Higher education (non-university)	6
University	14

Source: OECD (1994)

Organisations

Landsorganisationen i Danmark (LO)
(Danish Confederation of
Trade Unions)
Rosenørns Allé 12
DK-1634 Copenhagen V
Tel. +45 31 35 35 41
Fax +45 35 37 37 41

Dansk Arbejdsgiverforening (DA)
(Danish Employers' Federation)
Vester Voldgade 113
DK-1790 Copenhagen V
Tel. +45 33 93 40 00
Fax +45 33 12 29 76

Arbejdsministeriet
(Ministry of Labour)
Laksegade 19
DK-1063 Copenhagen K
Tel. +45 33 92 59 00
Fax +45 33 12 13 78

IP
(Danish Institute of Personnel
Management)
Hauser Plads 20
1127 Copenhagen
Tel. +45 33 13 15 70
Fax +45 33 32 51 56

CO–Industri
(Industrial unions'
bargaining cartel)
Vester Søgade 12, 2.
DK-1790 Copenhagen V
Tel. +45 33 15 12 66
Fax +45 33 15 12 66

Dansk Industri
(Industrial employers'
federation)
HC Andersens Boulevard 18
DK-1553 Copenhagen V
Tel. +45 33 77 33 77
Fax +45 33 77 37 00

Media

Berlingske Tidende
Pilestraede 34
1147 Copenhagen
Tel. +45 33 75 75 75
Fax +45 33 75 20 72

Børsen
Montergade 19
1116 Copenhagen
Tel. + 45 33 32 01 02
Fax + 45 33 91 10 50

Politiken
Raadhuspladsen 37
1785 Copenhagen
Tel. +45 33 11 85 11
Fax +45 33 15 41 17

Ingeniøren
Skelbaekgade 4
1780 Copenhagen
Tel. +45 31 21 68 01
Fax +45 31 21 23 96

Main sources

CEDEFOP. *Vocational education and training in Denmark.* CEDEFOP, Berlin, 1995
UNDERVISNINGSMINISTERIET. *Factsheets: The folkeskole, General upper secondary education, Vocational upper secondary education, Higher education, Vocational education and training.* Undervisningsministeriet, Copenhagen, 1996
UNDERVISNINGSMINISTERIET. *Education in Denmark: The education system.* Undervisningsministeriet, Copenhagen, 1991
ARBEJDSMINISTERIET. *Adult vocational training.* Arbejdsministeriet, Copenhagen, 1994
BERLINGSKE TIDENDE. *Hva' ska' du være.* Berlingske Tidende, Copenhagen, 1996

4

France

Although the French labour market is comparatively highly regulated in many spheres, employers are largely free to hire whom they choose, and are under no obligation, for example, to use the state placement system. However, formal notification of vacancies is required. And, in contrast to the UK, areas such as temporary working are subject both to national bipartite agreement and to legislative regulation.

The labour market

The labour force in 1995 stood at 25,659,000, a labour force participation rate of 56 per cent – 64 per cent for men and 48 per cent for women, both on the low side internationally. Women now make up 41 per cent of the labour force.

France's potential work force grew by about 0.5 per cent a year during the 1980s, slightly slower than the OECD European average but faster than the UK. Although growth in the 15 to 24 age population flattened markedly during the 1980s, and will fall back during the 1990s, rapid population growth during the 1960s means that the overall population of working age will continue to grow during the 1990s at well above the rates expected elsewhere in the EU.

The structure of youth unemployment has changed. Whereas those without qualifications used to represent half of the young unemployed, they now account for only a quarter, while young graduates now make up half of young job seekers. Unemployment has risen for the 20 to 24 age-group over the last 20 years, increasing from 6 per cent to 28 per cent.

Part-time work is becoming increasingly important: it grew by some 20 per cent between 1991 and 1994, to cover 15 per cent of the employed labour force. The rise has been attributed to various bargaining objectives as well as to state subsidies for part-time recruitment. (see below)

Recruitment

Official notification and work permits

Work permits and papers   A distinction is drawn between nationals of the European Union and other foreign workers. Citizens of member states of the EU and the European Economic Area (Iceland and Norway) who wish to work in

France can do so without having to obtain a work permit. However, they must have a residence permit (*carte de séjour de ressortissant d'un état membre de la UE*), which has to be obtained within three months of arrival in France. The application can be refused only on medical grounds or for reasons of public order. The permit is valid for five years, and then for a further ten if renewed.

Citizens of other countries must obtain a visa before entering France. Access to employment in France is determined by the authorities in the light of the employment situation in the country. Certain categories of foreign nationals have a privileged right of entry and employment: these include former members of the Foreign Legion, stateless persons and refugees who hold an OFPRA card, conference interpreters, and citizens of Cambodia, Vietnam, Laos and Lebanon.

Foreign nationals who are not European Union citizens must obtain a residence permit (*titre de séjour*) and a work permit (*titre de travail*) before taking up employment. If the nature of the employment is permanent, both permits can be incorporated into one card. Temporary residence permits are valid for one year (*carte de séjour temporaire*). Longer-term residence permits are valid for 10 years (*carte de résident*) and can be obtained only by foreigners who are married to a French national, who have immediate members of family who are French nationals or who have been living in France for at least three years continuously.

A work permit will not be granted unless the prospective employee has a confirmed offer of employment. The work permit may be refused by the authorities, but certain categories of employee are more favourably regarded. These include academics, researchers, senior managers, students on work placements, and seasonal workers. The employer must initiate application proceedings in France by taking the relevant documentation to the local labour authorities in their area.

French companies who want to recruit foreign workers must use the state agency OMI (*Office des Migrations Internationales*). OMI charges employers fees which vary by category of employee. Employers are responsible for checking that an employee has a valid residence and work permit and are liable to a fine and imprisonment for contraventions.

Employment notification All companies with at least 50 employees must make a monthly declaration of all new contracts (hirings) lasting one month or more, and all terminations which took place in the preceding month, to the local office of the Ministry of Labour (*directeur départemental du travail*). Employers who fail to provide this information are liable to a fine of FF 5,000 (£550) or more. All vacancies have to be notified to the state employment service, Agence Nationale pour l'Emploi (ANPE), whose role is outlined below. As part of a drive to curb illegal employment, employers must also notify the relevant social security organisations before hiring an employee.

Until recently companies had to fill in about 10 different forms when recruiting an employee to comply with the above requirements. Since 1 January 1996 this has been simplified and replaced by one single form – the single recruitment procedure. This is aimed at cutting back paperwork from 37 million forms a year to just nine million. Procedures will be simplified in a similar way for apprenticeship contracts (see below).

Workforce consultation

Companies are not required by law to consult works councils or employee representatives on the recruitment of individual employees. However, under the Labour Code, managements must meet the works council in their establishment once a year to discuss the movement of labour within the company over the previous year and to outline proposals and policy for the coming year. Works councils (*comités d'entreprise*) are mandatory in companies with 50 employees or more, although compliance tends to be patchy in smaller companies. The discussion must include part-time and temporary work, and provision for disabled workers.

If works councils request it, companies with fewer than 300 workers must provide information not less than twice a year on the movement of labour within the company, together with staff qualifications, atypical working and training programmes. Companies with more than 300 employees must provide this information, if requested, at least three times a year.

Collective agreements do not contain provisions on personnel planning but often specify procedures to be followed when recruiting: these are binding on those covered by the agreement (these are set out in more detail under *Finding the applicant* below). Typical provisions include: a stipulation that all vacancies should be initially advertised internally; that existing employees should always be given priority for new vacancies; and that advertisements should not contain any age limit. Employers should always check whether they are covered by a collective agreement containing specific provisions.

Using part-timers and temps

Part-time work

Part-time working is defined in statute law as any employment of four-fifths or less of either the statutory working week (thirty-nine hours) or the appropriate collectively agreed working week. Contracts for part-time employees must be in writing, and specify the number of hours to be worked: any changes in working hours must be notified to the employee at least seven days in advance. Overtime may not exceed one-third of the agreed working time and must not increase the part-time employee's hours beyond the statutory or collectively agreed limit. Part-time workers are entitled, on a pro rata basis, to all benefits enjoyed by their full-time colleagues and are given priority of consideration for full-time vacancies if they so wish.

Works councils or employee representatives need not be consulted in the case of individual part-time appointments, but consultation must take place on the general principle of part-time working in a company or if the proportion of part-time workers in the company changes significantly. Full-time employees have the right to refuse to change their working hours to a part-time basis at the request of the employer.

The proportion of women working part-time increased from 21 per cent to almost 30 per cent, and of men from 3 per cent to 5 per cent, between 1985 and 1995. In all, 15 per cent of employees worked part-time in 1995. Much of the growth has been in the area of imposed part-time work as companies have intensified their search for increased flexibility and productivity.

Fixed-term contracts

Recent years have seen a substantial move towards fixed-term and temporary contracts of employment, together with the use of agency employees. In 1995, two-thirds of all new job offers made via the state employment service ANPE were on a fixed-term or temporary basis. A fifth were fixed-term contracts lasting more than seven months; only a third were permanent. In proportional terms, temporary and fixed-term employment has grown from 3.5 per cent to 6.5 per cent of the workforce in the decade to 1995. With the growth in the number of government programmes to (re-)integrate job seekers, the proportion of those on government aided contracts and work placements has also gone up (from 0.3 per cent to 2.3 per cent of total paid employment) over the same period. Mainly aimed at the long-term unemployed, these contracts were initially intended to ease the transition from unemployment to stable employment.

The rapid growth of temporary work in the late 1980s prompted the government to introduce legislation to regulate the use of agency employment and fixed-term and temporary hirings in 1990. This defines the circumstances under which an employer may have justifiable recourse to temporary staff: they embrace replacing an absent employee (or filling in for a permanent employee who has been redeployed); meeting temporary increases in workload; and undertaking work that is seasonal or temporary in nature. Temporary workers may not be used to replace strikers, or work on dangerous tasks, as listed by the authorities.

The law also limits the total length of a fixed-term or temporary contract, which is renewable only once, to 18 months, extendable to 24 months under some limited circumstances.

Importantly, the law prohibits establishments from taking on any temporary staff to meet an increase in the workload in the six months following a dismissal for economic reasons, with two exceptions. In the first, short-term contracts of less than three months can be concluded. And in the second, temporary workers can be taken on to meet an increase in workload provided this is for export. However, temporary workers can continue to be hired to replace an absent employee or to perform tasks customarily regarded as temporary by nature in that business. Works councils must be consulted on these exemptions.

Fixed-term contracts may default to permanent employment if found to be defective on the above grounds. On completion of their period of employment, employees on fixed-term contracts are entitled to a termination payment of 6 per cent of their overall pay.

Temporary work agencies

Compared with the UK, temporary work via agencies is tightly regulated by law in France. Temporary work agencies are freely permitted to operate, provided they inform the local office of the employment authorities. The employee must have a written contract with the agency and there must also be written agreement between the agency and the client employer stating the reasons why temporary workers are needed, the duration of the assignment, a job description, and the agreed pay. Prospective users of temporary workers must justify recourse to them within strictly defined criteria which are the same as for fixed-term contracts and temporary work not through an agency set out above.

A trial period is permitted. Temps may be employed on an assignment for up to 18 months in general, and up to 24 months under special circumstances (for example, if the contract is executed abroad). The contract may be renewed once as long as the renewal and the initial mission together do not exceed 18 or 24 months. However, once the contract has expired, the employer may not place another temporary worker in that post until a period of time equal to one-third of the expired contract has elapsed.

Although temporary employees are not employed by the user company they must be entered into the company's register of personnel movements. Temps are also entitled to all normal company benefits for employees, such as holiday and overtime pay, sick pay and advice from workers' representatives. Pay should be as for a similar employee in the user company, but does not have to include any additional elements payable because of seniority if the temp is replacing a long-service employee. Any pay increases applicable during the assignment must also be paid.

By law, temporary workers are entitled to an 'insecurity allowance' when they complete their assignment, assuming they are not hired by the user company: this is set at 10 per cent of their overall pay for the period.

There are statutory obligations which a temporary employment agency must meet, both when setting up and while in operation. Agencies must inform the labour inspectorate and obtain a guarantee from a financial institution to ensure continuing payment of salaries and benefits in the event of insolvency. The temporary employment agency also has to inform the body responsible for managing local unemployment insurance funds, ASSEDIC (*Association pour l'emploi dans l'industrie et le commerce*), once a month about working contracts concluded in the previous month. There are penalties for not concluding a written contract with both the user company and the employee setting out the full terms and conditions of employment.

User companies can be penalised for unauthorised recourse to temporary employment, unlawful renewal of contracts, not having a written contract with the agency or preventing the access of temporary workers to staff facilities.

There are two trade organisations, which collaborate via a co-operation agreement, representing temporary employment agencies: PROMATT (Syndicat des professionels du travail temporaire) and UNETT (Union Nationale des Entreprises du Travail Temporaire). Their combined membership totals 500 firms, accounting for more than 80 per cent of the sector.

Anti-discrimination provisions

Sex equality The principle of 'equal pay for equal work' is laid down in the constitution of 1946 as well as in the ILO convention ratified by France in 1953. However, it is only relatively recently that the principle of non-discrimination between men and women was legally formulated via the 'Roudy law' of 13 July 1983, which brought French legislation into line with the 1976 EC Directive on equal treatment.

Employers must refrain from issuing job descriptions or job advertisements which specify a particular gender, unless a particular gender is an indispensable prerequisite. A person cannot be refused employment, offered an amended contract, or be discriminated against on the issues of remuneration, training, grading and promotion on the grounds of gender or marital status.

Any contravention of these provisions by the employer is punishable by a fine of up to FF 25,000 (£2,800) or one year's imprisonment. The court may also allow a partial or full report of the case to appear in the press. A judge may also stay the penalty to allow an employer to rectify the situation. In the event that a dismissal is found to be unwarranted because it is on grounds of sex, the tribunal may propose re-engagement. Should either party refuse, the employee is entitled to a compensatory award of not less than six months' pay.

A multi-industry agreement on equality at work, signed in November 1989 by the CNPF national employers' organisation and main union confederations, reaffirms the 'equal work, equal pay' principle. It required collective agreements to be brought into line with the EC Directive (76/207) on equal treatment of men and women, which has largely been achieved. The agreement also contains commitments to:

- encourage initial and continuous professional training as a means of ensuring equal opportunities, especially after a period of parental leave
- collect better information on the situation of women in the labour market, possibly by means of government-financed research
- find ways in which to make it easier for employees of both sexes to combine professional and family life, and in particular, provisions to ensure the care of a sick child.

In order to encourage companies to employ more women and to comply with the 1976 EC directive on professional equality, the government has created two incentive schemes, the *Plan pour l'égalité professionelle dans l'entreprise* (occupational equality plan) and *Contrats pour la mixité des emplois* (equal opportunity contracts). The occupational equality plan may be drawn up on a company basis and would typically include such things as reserving a recruitment and promotion quota for women and having training schemes for women only. The equal opportunity contracts are aimed specifically at small and middle-sized companies with fewer than 200 employees, and aim to promote the interests of individual female employees through training and improving working conditions and the working environment: this includes reducing the amount of physically demanding work or fitting extra showers and cloakrooms. If the government approves the plan, employers are entitled to reimbursement of up to 50 per cent of the training costs incurred, up to 50 per cent of other costs incurred and up to 30 per cent of salaries paid during the training period.

Disabled workers and veterans (*travailleurs handicappés et mutilés de guerre*)   Under the law of 30 June 1986, all companies employing 20 or more staff must employ, on a full-time or part-time basis, a proportion of disabled workers, equal to a sixth of the workforce as from 1 January 1991. These employees must be registered as either physically or mentally disabled but capable of working. Disabled persons are not classed as specially protected employees but are entitled to a longer notice period.

Alternatively, employers may make payments into a special fund established to facilitate the training of the disabled, with the amount related to the statutory minimum wage (SMIC) and size of firm. A firm that fails to fulfil its annual reporting requirement on disabled employees is obliged to pay this sum, plus 25 per cent, into the fund.

In practice, companies tend to pay into the fund rather than employ disabled workers. Less than one in three companies employs the prescribed 6 per cent disabled workers: two-fifths choose to pay into the fund. (The rest mix the various options, contributions to the fund, sectoral agreements and subcontracting.) This has resulted in large sums of money accumulating in the fund and an ongoing debate on how to use the money.

Companies may apply for various state subsidies available for employing the disabled. They include: financial aid to meet the cost of modifying equipment or the working environment in order to improve disabled access, and any additional costs incurred. Those offering an apprenticeship to a disabled person can obtain a bonus of 520 times the hourly rate of SMIC per apprentice. A company is eligible for aid of FF 30,000 to 40,000 (£3,300–£4,400) per disabled employee recruited. Works councils must be notified of all plans. A number of agreements concerning the recruitment of disabled workers have been concluded at sectoral level.

Finding the applicant

Press advertisements and personal connections remain the dominant form for recruiting managers, with placement services accounting for only a small minority of posts filled. In 1995, according to a survey conducted by APEC, the state executive recruitment service, 33 per cent of managers were recruited on the basis of recommendation or connections, 26 per cent through press advertisements, 15 per cent from speculative applications, 17 per cent through recruitment consultants and 9 per cent through state placement agencies.

Agreed provisions

Before embarking on recruitment, employers need to know whether or not they are covered by any collective agreements – either national or at industry level – which require them to follow some set procedures or limit what they can and cannot do during the recruitment process. Some examples are set out below.

In distribution and retailing, vacancies must be advertised internally to give existing staff priority and the terms, conditions and proposed pay rate must be set down in writing. In chemicals, employers must inform interested parties, such as other employees, of general staff needs across all grades and inform the works council of any appointments apart from temporary and seasonal workers. Where employment levels fluctuate markedly, priority in hiring should be given to any employees terminated in the previous twelve months because of lack of work. Age must not be a discriminatory factor in making appointments. All appointments have to be confirmed by letter or other written notification, and new employees have to be given a copy of the company agreement and the relevant collective agreement.

In hotels and catering, existing employees have preference for newly arisen vacancies. Any employee terminated for economic reasons during the previous twelve months also has priority, but this is forfeited if the first offer is rejected, or if no reply is made within eight working days. All employees must receive written confirmation of employment. A 'technical test' may be required for certain jobs, but it may not last for more than one day. Any test lasting longer than two hours is paid for by the employer at the minimum rate for the grade.

Application documents

Companies typically issue application forms requesting details of candidates' education, employment history and other observations. Employers are not allowed to include on application forms questions about union membership, political opinions, religious convictions, family situation or pregnancy. Indeed, applicants may either refuse to answer or give false answers to personal questions. Alternatively firms often prefer to invite submission of a CV together with a handwritten letter. There are no statutory restrictions requiring employers to seek the permission of candidates before submitting their applications to graphology tests. This practice is widespread in France and is often contracted out to graphology experts by companies, and sometimes even by recruitment agencies.

Placement services

The state placement system

The state job placement system ANPE (*Agence Nationale pour l'Emploi*) provides recruitment services for blue- and white-collar workers and managerial staff.

Employers wishing to recruit externally may use ANPE or registered private employment agencies, provided they have an agreement with ANPE. These organisations include public bodies such as chambers of commerce and bodies which are jointly controlled by employer and employee organisations such as the executive placement organisation APEC (see below).

Irrespective of the placement route chosen by the employer, all vacancies must still be notified to one of ANPE's local regional offices, with fines for failure to comply. Similarly, until recently all workers seeking employment and who wanted to receive unemployment benefit needed to register with ANPE and renew their registration regularly, although this was not legally enforceable. Registration and management of unemployment benefits were transferred to the managers' unemployment insurance fund ASSEDIC in March 1996 to lighten ANPE's administrative load, free some of its resources and hence help it to exercise its active placement and advisory role more efficiently. In areas where there is no regional office, the town hall (*mairie*) must be notified of vacant posts. On employing an ANPE-registered worker an employer must notify ANPE within 48 hours. Employers are not bound to employ workers recommended by ANPE, and, similarly, workers are not obliged to accept job offers made by companies through ANPE. ANPE collects up to 20 per cent of job offers and wants to double this figure.

ANPE provides services to people looking for a job as well as to companies looking for staff. The agency will also carry out some pre-selection and testing of candidates.

A total of two million job offers were made via ANPE in 1995 (an increase of 26 per cent on 1994) with 1.7 million people being placed. Recent years have seen a significant increase in the placement of qualified employees, including executives, with an especially large rise in the supervisor and technician categories. Services for executives are often managed jointly with the specialist official executive placement service APEC.

In 1995 ANPE filled 85 per cent of the vacancies notified to it. Sixty per cent of vacancies for unskilled jobs were filled in less than 15 days, 70 per cent of skilled jobs in less than a month, and 83 per cent of executive job offers in under three months. This marks an increase in its success rate, partly as as result of new developments within the agency, such as a commitment to build closer relationships with businesses, especially small and medium-sized companies. For example, ANPE officials made 700,000 company visits in 1995, a 40 per cent increase. Companies can sign partnership contracts with ANPE giving it the monopoly to recruit for them.

ANPE's efficiency and ability to cope with the volume of placements required have been the subject of a good deal of criticism in recent years. Many blame the agency for the bad functioning of the employment market, while some employers are dissatisfied with the standard of service provided. However, 90 per cent of those companies actually using the ANPE feel that they have built an effective partnership with the agency.

In the face of high unemployment and a changing labour market, ANPE itself had to embark on change. Recent changes to improve efficiency have included a move towards greater decentralisation, the opening of more local agencies and the modernisation of existing ones. Since 1990 ANPE has concluded two 'accords for progress' with the state, which commit the agency to develop its internal organisation and achieve targets on placement rates, and increase speed and quality of the service for employers and job seekers. The government for its part committed itself to supporting the agency in these tasks. In order to reach its objectives the ANPE has been increasing the competence of its staff, and reorganised and updated sites and equipment. In its second accord ANPE has set out to embrace 40 per cent of the placement market by 1998. Elements include continuing modernisation and decentralisation, improved candidate selection methods, and incentives for companies contracting out all recruitment to ANPE.

Some unions, and the CGT in particular, have been critical of ANPE's 'commercial attitude' and what is seen as a 'cheap sell-off of a public service'.

The state executive placement service

The state executive placement organisation APEC (*Association pour l'Emploi des Cadres*) provides its services free to users in the private sector. It is financed by charges levied on employees registered in the state executive pension scheme AGIRC and their employers, amounting to 0.036 per cent for the employer and 0.024 per cent of gross salary for the employee. This is supplemented by a lump sum payable by employees and employers once a year, which varies according to the ceiling on social security contributions. The amount in 1996 was FF 58.08 (£6.50) for employers and FF 38.72 (£4.30) for employees. According to a study carried out by APEC itself, and based on the recruitment practices of some eighty companies, in 1989 37 per cent of companies used APEC for finding middle managers, 21 per cent for senior managers and 23 per cent for new executives.

APEC has a homepage on the World Wide Web, which includes vacancy details: as it has a mind-numbingly long Web reference, it is probably more convenient to find it via a Web search engine.

Recruitment agencies

Recruitment agencies for permanent employment are widespread in France, although predominantly small in scale. The state placement monopoly was formally abolished in 1986, and independent agencies were allowed to operate provided they had an agreement with the state agency ANPE. Private agencies may not charge users of their service a placement fee unless special official authorisation has been obtained. Moreover, all vacancies must be notified to ANPE.

Recruitment agencies suffered during the recession and are only slowly recovering. At present it seems unlikely that they will reach the activity levels seen in the late 1980s. Companies also tend to make use of their own resources before calling on an external recruiter.

Executive recruitment consultants

Search and selection is permitted for executive-level employees. Agencies must register any computerised databases with the authorities. Search activities are on a smaller scale than in the UK. In the past, senior managers in the public sector – embracing a much bigger range of activities than in the UK – were not appointed through executive search, and the prevalence of tight networks between large organisations and the top-flight business, technical and administrative universities – the *grandes écoles* – often meant that outside search organisations were not needed or, perhaps more pertinently, were viewed with scepticism.

This pattern has been changing over the last 10 years, with executive search largely introduced by multinational companies needing to recruit in the local market. Search companies have gained in credibility and are now more widely used. The market for consultants is expanding with growing internationalisation. While internal recruitment is still a common means of filling the top jobs, this is not always possible or desirable. International management experience as an added value is in demand, with services such as job-finding for spouses in dual-career couples also on the increase. Other associated services, such as management appraisal, audit and human resources consulting, and non-executive board director search are also growing. The largest search consultants (by turnover) are: Heidrick & Struggles, Egon Zehnder, GKR Neumann, Progress and Russell Reynolds.

For posts in the range FF 120,000–300,000 (£13,000–£33,000) p.a. advertisement only is typically used. Selection backed up by search is customary between FF 300,000 and 600,000 (£33,000–£67,000). Above this figure, search only would be used. The usual fee charged by consultants is in the region of 20 per cent of annual salary for a placement using advertisements and pre-selection, 25 per cent for a mixture of advertisements and direct search, and 30–35 per cent for search only.

According to APEC, consultants place about 17 per cent of all executives recruited. The average processing time for recruitment requests is put at five to seven weeks for recruitment by advertisement and eight to twelve weeks for a search.

If a selected candidate leaves the job within a year of recruitment, consultants will generally look for a replacement free of charge.

The central organisation for executive search consultancies is APROCERD (Association Professionelle des Conseils d'Entreprise pour la Recherche des Cadres). APROCERD members are expected to work to a code of ethics which includes:

- Consultants may accept business only from companies or organisations looking for managers, not from individuals looking for work. Individual advice must be provided free of charge and only occasionally.
- The professional obligation of search consultants is that of providing an efficient service to the best of their ability, and is therefore an obligation of effort, not of result.
- Fees must be established by written contract at the beginning of the assignment on the basis of scale, difficulty and duration.
- Assignments should be carried out solely by direct approach.
- Consultants are bound to secrecy unless instructed otherwise.
- Consultants should not recontact candidates already placed by themselves as long as that person remains with the company in which placement took place, and should not contact employees of former clients for a period of two years.
- Consultants should refuse all non-exclusive assignments and should refuse all unofficial methods of payment.

A copy of the full code of conduct and a list of member companies can be obtained from APROCERD. APROCERD also recommends a recruitment approach to its members, which should consist of: identification of potential candidates and contacts; confidential interview with candidates; presentation of selected candidates to clients; assessment of candidates' employment history, with candidates' permission; assistance in final negotiations; and follow-up assistance in integrating the chosen candidate into the new employment.

Membership of APROCERD is not compulsory and many of the larger search consultancies are not members.

Recruitment media

The press

Advertising is subject to a number of statutory regulations. ANPE and the local labour department – or the Paris department if the advertisement appears in a national newspaper – must be notified of advertised vacancies. Advertisements must not contain:

- an upper age limit
- knowingly false or misleading statements about the nature of the employment, the salary or the place of work
- discriminating statements on the grounds of race, religion or sex
- any foreign expressions or words if a French equivalent exists. If no French equivalent exists, then an explanation of the term in French must also be given. Exceptions are granted when the place of work will not be on French soil, when the advertiser is particularly seeking applicants from another country, or if the advertisement appears in a foreign-language journal.

There are financial penalties for contravention of these restrictions, with up to a year's imprisonment if misleading information is given.

Although in the past salaries were never indicated, this may be beginning to change, and salary ranges are sometimes – though still rarely – illustrated.

Main publications

L'Express, *Le Point*, *Le Monde* and *Le Figaro Economie* carry advertisements for senior managerial positions. The main newspapers for advertising for technicians, supervisory staff and specialist staff are *Le Figaro* and *France-Soir*. The daily *Liberation* also runs a small jobs column. *Les Echos* and *Le Monde* share the market for financial, managerial and administrative positions. Computing posts are advertised in the specialist journal *01 Informatique* and engineering jobs in *L'Usine Nouvelle* and *Le Moniteur*. Personnel positions are advertised in *Liaisons Sociales*.

Courrier Cadres, published by APEC (and available from it), carries about 800 management vacancies each week.

Adverts can trigger a flood of responses, leading many smaller firms – that lack large personnel departments – to concentrate on internal recruitment as their preferred strategy.

Radio and television

There are a number of radio programmes on which companies can advertise vacancies and invite listeners to apply. ANPE for example, regularly broadcasts some of its job offers on television.

Poster advertising

This is not a widespread method of recruitment but it was used successfully by

Spie-Batignolle in 1988 when it advertised for staff on 1,800 posters and received 3,000 telephone calls and 1,200 letters.

Using Minitel

The computerised information service Minitel, which can be accessed from the home through a television screen, is now used regularly by many French households, and can also give help to both job seekers and employers. If a Minitel number is given when a post is advertised in the press, potential candidates can obtain further information via the system about the company and the advertised post. The candidate may then do a short 'pre-selection' test devised by the company that placed the advertisement, which, if they pass, gives access to more details, such as the name and telephone number of who to contact about the post. This is an inexpensive method of pre-selection and can save time and money for both employers and candidates by weeding out the utterly unsuitable at an early stage without the direct involvement of the company. Minitel is accessed within France through the telephone and television network by means of a special installation. Research carried out by Minitel shows that out of 100 candidates accessing information about an advertised post, 60 do the pre-selection test, 25 are pre-selected and ten actually apply for the job. Some consultants and job placement agencies such as APEC can also be accessed via Minitel.

Internet advertising

The state executive recruitment agency APEC has a home page with a selection of vacancies for young technicians and engineers: the APEC page also has extensive links to other employment-related Web sites (see above).

In 1990 a group of leading recruitment consultants collaborated to establish *cadremploi*, a system to publish vacancies via the electronic media, including Minitel and now the World Wide Web. The Web page (http://www.cadremploi.tm.fr) currently carries about 1,000 vacancies. The system, which is managed by the electronic media firm SETEC, can be contacted via the address listed under *Organisations*.

Jobs On Line is a Web recruitment service, managed by CEGOS (http://www.cegos.fr).

Selection methods

Employers are free to choose their means and methods of selection. None of the conventional methods of employee selection are proscribed by law, although there are statutory provisions on employee privacy and equal opportunities (see below).

Selection procedures vary widely between companies. Psychological tests may be used, but the employer is not legally bound to make the selection according to the results. According to APEC, the recruitment process for a manager in France typically involves: sorting of CVs and first weeding out of applicants; further sorting, often using graphology, leading to the second round of elimination; candidates may then be tested, followed by the third round of elimination; interviews precede the fourth round, and may be followed by a second graphological analysis, the checking of references, contact with the previous employer and then a final interview.

A survey carried out by the journal *L'Etudiant* in 1995 asked 124 participating companies to list their main methods of selection for graduates: the companies were tracked from October 1994 to January 1995. The methods, and the proportion of companies using them, were as follows: interviews (100 per cent); personality tests (50 per cent); aptitude tests (36 per cent); graphology (34 per cent); intelligence tests (23 per cent). On average, companies carried out three interviews. Recruitment procedures hardly vary whether a *Bac+2* or a *Bac+5* is hired (for explanation of qualifications, see below).

Graphology, although still going strong, may be gradually losing some of its importance. Other estimates have suggested that some 57 per cent of companies and consultants use it, with other figures as high as 80–90 per cent. Graphology is used both to pre-select candidates and, more widely, to 'verify' the impression derived from an interview. There is a professional association (*Groupement des Graphologues Conseil de France*, GGCF) which requires its members to have undertaken a formal course of training. However, the organisation embraces only some 230 of the estimated 2,000 practising graphologists in France.

By contrast, professional tests are on the increase, with the proportion of companies using them rising from 12 per cent in 1993 to 35 per cent in 1995. Time taken to recruit varies between a fortnight and three months.

Psychometric testing seems to have lost credibility among personnel managers and has declined in popularity. Personality tests, intelligence tests and job simulation tests are also used, especially by consultants. There is a statutory obligation to inform candidates of the results of the tests.

There have also been reports of firms and consultants using palmistry, astrology, phrenology and haematology to assess the character of candidates and their compatibility with existing employees. Although these appear to have peaked in the early 1990s, the whole issue of esoteric methods has become an increasing source of concern among many practitioners and organisations representing more conventional assessment techniques. Quite why these techniques appear to be more prevalent in France – only the Swiss show a comparable interest in graphology, with reports of astrology in Italy – remains unclear.

Privacy

Care needs to be exercised in obtaining information from and about candidates, both from the point of view of French practice and the provisions of the law on privacy. For example, the employment certificate (*le certificat de travail*), which an employer gives to an employee on termination, is a purely factual record and may not contain information about the employee's performance, irrespective of whether this is true or false. Whilst references may be taken up in the case of managerial appointments, this would not necessarily apply at other levels. Previous employers may be approached for a reference only if they have been cited by the applicant.

Under the Labour Code, reference to the sex or family situation of a candidate is prohibited when making an offer of employment or in any publicity relating to recruitment. It is also illegal to refuse employment on the grounds of sex or family situation. These restrictions apply not only to the employer but also to any organisation involved directly or indirectly in the recruitment process, such as employment agencies or newspapers.

Employers may ask candidates about their civil status, military obligations, qualifications and professional history, and may request certain documents, such as examination certificates, employment certificates and, if applicable, letters of dismissal, but only if they are deemed directly relevant to the proposed employment. For example, it is permissible to ask a candidate about school performance and examination results, as they may give an indication of competence for the job, but not to request a school report, as it might contain private information concerning the social and personal circumstances of the candidate.

References are taken up in 70 per cent of managerial recruitments carried out via consultants. However, this rarely applies to academic references for fresh graduates. The type and amount of information that can be legally gained about a prospective employee is limited under Article 9 of the Civil Code, under which all persons have the right to respect for their privacy – an employer has no right to enquire into an employee's private life except when it is deemed relevant to the proper operation of the employer's business. Under law 78–17, the collection, storage and distribution of personal information by computer are subject to data protection, and companies wishing to start up a database must notify the National Commission on Freedom of Computerised Information (Commission Nationale de l'Informatique et des Libertés). No persons, excepting next of kin and legal representatives, are allowed access to the personal identification numbers issued to all French citizens. Certain types of financial information, such as bankruptcies, are available in public registers, but the disclosure of information which would be obtainable only from a bank is a violation of article 378 of the Criminal Code. Public records, tax and property archives may be consulted by the public only 70 years after the date of the relevant entries.

Candidates have the right to withhold information, or give incorrect answers, if they feel that an employer is asking inappropriate questions, without prejudice to their subsequent employment rights. Employers are allowed to ask candidates about a possible criminal record only if it is directly related to the position applied for, such as where the post involves the handling of large amounts of money or the security of premises or persons.

Medical examinations

All employees are required to have a medical examination before an appointment and, if applicable, before the end of the probationary period of employment. The purpose of the examination is to ensure that a prospective employee is fit enough to do the job in question. If an employee does not prove to be fit enough, the employer may offer a different post, although this is not obligatory. Medical examinations are not necessary if the employee has already been examined when being appointed to a similar job during the preceding six months, and another examination is not required for twelve months if the job is with the same employer. Employees are required to have a further medical examination once a year, or whenever requested by the employer. A refusal by the employee to undergo medical examination could constitute grounds for dismissal.

Employment incentives

There are a number of government incentives designed to increase general employment or to encourage employers to take on certain categories of worker. The main incentives are listed below.

The Five-year Jobs Plan

In the face of high and rising unemployment, during the summer of 1993 the government decided to boost job creation by cutting employer social security charges and providing incentives to hire new employees and implement working time reductions and job-sharing initiatives. In August 1993 plans were unveiled for a Five-year Jobs Plan. This was adopted by parliament in late 1993 and became law during 1994 via a series of decrees. It contains provisions on reducing employer social costs, promoting flexible working and job sharing, integrating the unemployed into the workforce, and a commitment to promote training. The main provisions, together with other incentives currently in force, are set out below.

Reductions in social charges   Employers' social charges, at about 42.5 per cent of pay, are among the highest in the EU. The programme contains a number of reductions and exemptions, such as total exemption from all social charges for a first employee until 1998. Employer family allowance contributions (5.4 per cent of gross pay) are waived for employees earning less than 120 per cent of the national minimum wage (SMIC), with the threshold rising to 150 per cent of SMIC by 1 January 1998; contributions are halved for those earning 140 per cent of SMIC, rising to 160 per cent of SMIC by 1998.

The cuts in employers' social charges for the recruitment of a first employee led to more than 100,000 hirings in 1994, an increase of 17 per cent on the previous year.

Incentives to encourage part-time working Employees will be encouraged to transfer to part-time work under a company's social plan (which must be drawn up if a company wishes to make redundancies) by a guarantee of a maximum of 90 per cent of former earnings (previously 80 per cent). Similarly, employees considering early retirement will be encouraged to decrease their working hours gradually. The scope of the 50 per cent reduction in social charges for changing full-time jobs to part-time jobs is enlarged, allowing weekly hours to be calculated over a month or a year. Pensions contributions are reduced until 1999 for newly created part-time contracts.

Part-time work has become a means of integrating young people into the labour market, with the development of apprenticeships and special help contracts for the under-25s – many of which are part-time – and exemption from employers' social charges. In two years 210,000 such contracts have been signed, mainly in small catering, services and retail firms.

Flexible working provisions The programme extends the powers of the 1987 Flexible Working Law, under which weekly working time can be varied to deal with temporary increases or reductions in demand without recourse to overtime payments or short-time working. Hours may be averaged over a year or part of a year within weekly and daily limits specified by an industry collective agreement. Under legislation which was passed in 1996 (*loi Robien*), companies that reduced their working hours by at least 10 per cent, and increase their workforce by the same percentage, may benefit from a 40 per cent reduction in a variety of employer charges in the first year and from a 30 per cent reduction in the following two years.

Training and employment for the young unemployed Companies that employ young people aged between 16 and 25 on apprenticeship contracts of one to three years are exempt from employer social security contributions for those employees, and benefit from a lump sum of up to FF 7,000 (£800). Companies employing young people aged 16–22 on six-month 'orientation contracts' pay no employer social charges for these employees and receive FF 50 (£6) per training hour supplied.

Companies employing young people with no formal qualifications for between six months and two years on a 'qualification contract' pay no social charges and receive FF 60 (£6.50) per training hour and a lump sum of FF 5,000 (£550) for contracts up to 18 months and a lump sum of FF 7,000 (£800) for contracts over 18 months.

Vocational training The programme introduces the principle of a 'bank' of training hours for individual employees to carry with them throughout their careers (*capital temps formation*). Details are to be agreed in the form of a national multi-industry agreement or by industry agreement. The law also tightens up controls on apprentice training. There will be an annual obligation to negotiate on apprenticeships at industry level.

The government also aims to decentralise the administration of training for those under 26 to the regions by 1998.

'Solidarity contracts'   A further government job creation measure is the so-called solidarity contract (*'contrat emploi-solidarité'*), which has been in place since 1982. The purpose of a solidarity contract is to extend financial assistance to employers who conclude an agreement with the National Employment Fund to take on those people who are finding it difficult to enter the labour market. It is available to young people aged 18–26 with little or no professional qualifications; the unemployed aged 50 years or over; those who have been unemployed for at least 12 months in the preceding 18 months; and those on RMI minimum state assistance. In order to set up a solidarity contract, a company needs to conclude an agreement with the authorities (applications to the departmental labour office) and inform the company works council or staff representatives. A report must be given to them each year on the progress of these contracts.

Solidarity contracts are fixed-term renewable contracts for a working week of 20 hours for three to twelve months. The maximum duration may be extended up to 36 months in some cases. There is a trial period of one month, unless a collective or house agreement stipulates a shorter term. Each person on a solidarity contract is allotted a tutor to oversee the running of the contract. It cannot be broken by the employer but the employee can terminate it if he or she has found a job or some other form of training to pursue.

Remuneration for these employees is the national minimum wage, SMIC. The state will reimburse companies for 65 per cent of this sum, or 85 per cent in the case of longer contracts in special cases. The state will also pay all or part of training costs incurred, at a rate of FF 22 (£2.50) per hour, up to a ceiling of 400 hours, if there is a formal agreement for training between the company and a training organisation. Companies are exempt from employer social security contributions for pay up to SMIC, but these are levied on pay above the rate of SMIC.

Those who cannot find work after the expiry of a solidarity contract may conclude further contracts with the company, provided that at the time of entering into a solidarity contract they are over 50 years of age or eligible for state RMI income assistance and have been unemployed for at least 12 months or are handicapped. Subsequent contracts of 12 months, renewable up to five times, may then be signed, with progressively diminishing state subsidies. The state will also pay all or part of training costs and companies are exempt from certain social security contributions.

'Employment initiative contract'   In July 1996 a law introducing the 'Employment initiative contract' (*Contrat initiative-emploi*, CIE) was passed, targeting the long-term unemployed, the young jobless, the unemployed over 50 and those on RMI minimum state assistance. Employers recruiting from these categories are entitled to a monthly grant of FF 2,000 (£220) for up to 24 months, as well as a two-year total exemption from social charges on pay up to the level of SMIC. Further conditions stipulate that any job offered must be permanent, or last for at least a year, and that no redundancies have occurred in the firm over the previous six months. Although this measure has been heralded as a success by the ANPE it was viewed as a failure by a commentator from the central employers' confederation, CNPF.

Early retirement to aid recruitment In September 1996, the major trade union and employers' federations agreed on the implementation of a joint employment fund which is to pay for the early retirement of employees aged 58 who have made social security contributions for 40 years (160 quarters). The scheme guarantees eligible voluntary retirees 65 per cent of their last gross salary until state retirement age (60). A company is obliged to replace any such early retirees with new staff on permanent contracts, preferably full-time, within three months. It is also possible to recruit several employees on a part-time basis. Preference should be given to unemployed people under 26. Details of all these schemes can be obtained from the Ministry of Labour or ANPE.

Critics of the employment measures have pointed out that it is often difficult for companies to pick the right ones as there is such a multitude of them, with many closely resembling each other. Even Jean Gandois, the president of the employers' federation CNPF, has recently gone on record criticising the excessive number of schemes available, most of which were useless in his view, and pleaded for a smaller number of targeted initiatives: 740 different measures to promote employment have been taken over the past 20 years. A commission has recently been set up by the government to rationalise existing provisions (about 50 at present) for the sake of transparency and efficiency.

Another point of criticism is that some of the outlined measures are abused by companies to benefit from cheap labour.

One survey found that 60 per cent of the small and medium-sized companies which benefited from state aid for recruiting claimed that the latter did not constitute an incentive for recruiting. Only 4 per cent of employers admitted recruiting because of the subsidies available.

Military service

If requested by the employee, a company must make every effort to reinstate an employee who has been engaged in military service and who used to work for the company. If it is not possible, the employee is entitled to priority of reinstatement for the period of one year. Military service lasts for one year – students usually choose to undertake it after graduation. Military service may be replaced by a slightly longer period of voluntary civilian service. As part of the government's move to restrain public spending, substantial defence spending cuts have been included in the 1997 budget, with plans to move to a wholly professional army by 2002.

In 1995, while the government was considering reform of the army and national service, 3,000 young people were given the opportunity to do their military service in a French company based abroad under a scheme created in the 1980s (*coopérants du service national en entreprise*, CSNE). Candidates typically come from an engineering school but increasingly frequently also from business schools. While this measure is at present reserved mainly for big firms, it is becoming more and more accessible for small and medium-sized companies.

Making the offer

Appointment formalities Employers must notify the relevant social security organisations before hiring an employee. This measure was introduced by the government as part of a drive to curb illegal employment. Employers are also obliged to provide new employees with a written contract of employment within two months of hiring.

Employees are usually required to present employers with their identity card, examination certificates and, if they have already been in employment, their social security registration card and a certificate of employment from their previous employer.

There is no set procedure that employers are required to follow when making an offer of employment. However, most companies would prefer to have a written record of a job offer. A letter offering a job may constitute a contract of employment (*lettre d'engagement*), in which case it should clearly set out the employee's grade, pay, hours, other main terms and conditions of employment, and the place of work.

Handling rejection There is no statutory formula for handling the rejection of unsuccessful applicants. However, as with offers of employment, rejections tend to be in writing. The average time taken by companies to process job applications varies, according to the *L'Etudiant* survey, from two weeks to three months.

Education, training and development

Initial vocational training takes place primarily through the state education system, with apprenticeships accounting for a small proportion of trainees, frequently outside mainstream industrial and technical sectors. However, the apprenticeship system was subject to reform in 1992. Continuing training is carried out via the employer, although drawing on external providers.

Tertiary education is structured in two tiers, with state universities providing a general and more arts-oriented education and the élite *grandes écoles* providing more directly professional education – principally in engineering and business studies – for the country's potential top managers and administrators. In addition, there are some specialised technical universities and prestigious business schools with an international reputation and intake, notably INSEAD, located at Fontainebleau.

Training is subject to a number of statutory requirements, including compulsory employer funding, the requirement to establish a company training plan, and time-off rights for employees. The persistence of high unemployment has spurred national training efforts, evidenced in new laws and national collective agreements on training and apprenticeships. High unemployment is also the rationale for the plethora of work experience and insertion courses. Education ranks high on the national political agenda, and has been emphasised in recent budgets.

Secondary and tertiary education

Secondary education   School attendance is compulsory until the age of 16. Curricula and staff appointments are highly centralised. The period from the age of 11 to 16, termed the 'first cycle', takes place in general schools (*collèges*), which are not formally selective, and involves a broad education. In all stages of the system, including much of tertiary education, there is marked emphasis on mathematics. Some secondary schools students with academic difficulties may leave the general schools earlier, at 14 or 15, to pursue a preliminary vocational education certificate (CEP) at a technical school (*lycée d'enseignement professionel*, LEP), or take a pre-apprenticeship course.

The 'second cycle' of secondary education entails either further general education, as a preparation for higher education, or a move into initial vocational or technical training. (For initial vocational and technical education in the state system see *Vocational training* below.)

Education post-16 takes place either in general secondary schools (*lycées*) or in technical secondary schools (*lycées techniques*). In the general secondary schools this cycle culminates after three years in the leaving certificate (*baccalauréat*), with a technical *baccalauréat* option in the technical schools. Technical secondary schools may also train students for a technical certificate (BT), although this is being increasingly supplanted by the technical *baccalauréat*.

In common with much of the rest of Europe, the number of school leavers taking an advanced school leaving certificate has increased rapidly. In 1995 65 per cent of young people took the *baccalauréat* compared to 36 per cent in 1985. However, about 65,000 school leavers (8 per cent of the cohort) in 1995 emerged from the school system without any qualifications, compared to 220,000 in 1973. Five to 10 per cent of each age cohort are held not to have command of basic reading and mathematics requirements.

The *baccalauréat*, which is considerably broader than the UK A-level and regarded as more difficult, entails some specialisation, with science options, arts, technology and management variants. It is a prerequisite of access to tertiary education and gives the right of entry into state universities. The crucial *baccalauréat* from the point of view of further advance into a managerial position is '*Bac C*', the mathematics and physical sciences option.

Subsequent advance through the education system, and the status of qualifications, are often expressed in terms of years of study after the *baccalauréat* (and written as '*Bac+x*' – see below).

Tertiary education

About 2.2 million students were in higher education in 1995/6. Higher education is notable for the division between the universities and the *grandes écoles*, although the rigidity of the separation has diminished somewhat and there is now scope for interchange, especially at postgraduate level (see below). Managerial recruits from tertiary education come predominantly from the technical specialisations of the universities or from the *grandes écoles*. Great emphasis is placed on the acquisition of quantitative and technical skills, which are regarded as offering the best foundation for the analytical capacity demanded of managers (see also *managerial and supervisory training* below). The main institutions and courses are as follows.

Technical studies

Technical universities (*instituts universitaires de technologie*, IUTs), established in 1969 in response to the need for less protracted technical education, offer two- and three-year courses located mid-way between the *baccalauréat* and longer university courses. There are about 70 of these technical universities, with a total of some 110,000 students. Entrance to IUTs is selective, based on school reports.

The qualifications offered by the technical universities, rated as '*Bac+2*', include the university diploma of technology (*Diplôme universitaire de technologie*, DUT). The acquisition of a DUT diploma may lead on to further studies at one of the state universities. Technical sections of *lycées* also offer technical training, leading to the higher technical certificate (*Brevet de technicien supérieur*, BTS). (According to the UK National Institute of Economic Research, this is a 'higher intermediate qualification' and rated as equivalent to HND or HNC in the UK.)

Universities

Universities, of which there are over 70, are state run and have a non-selective admission policy as long as students have obtained the school-leaving certificate, the *baccalauréat*. This has led to a high drop-out rate after the first-year exams, with only about 50 per cent of new admissions actually graduating. One exception to the rule is the University of Paris Dauphine, which concentrates on management courses and operates an effective selection policy.

There are currently about 1.6 million students enrolled in the state universities. University courses are divided into three 'cycles', each cycle lasting about two years. The first two-year cycle is a general preparatory study course in a variety of subjects, leading to a general university studies diploma, the DEUG (*Diplôme d'études universitaires générales*) or the more vocationally relevant DEUST (*Diplôme d'études universitaires scientifiques et techniques*). Both would be classified as *Bac+2*.

The second cycle is more specialised and can lead to a variety of qualifications, depending on the subjects studied. A qualification taken after one year of this cycle confers the *licence*, or bachelor's degree (*Bac+3*). Two years of study culminate in the *maîtrise*, or master's degree (*Bac+4*), the most common university qualification. Vocationally relevant examples include the MST (*Maîtrise des sciences et techniques*), the management science degree, MSG (*Maîtrise de sciences de gestion*) or the information sciences degree, MIAGE (*Maîtrise de méthodes informatiques appliquées à la gestion*). There is also a three-year second-cycle qualification in engineering, the *magistère*, which requires both academic work and a practical spell in industry (*stage*).

The third cycle is for postgraduate work, leading either to a diploma in higher specialist studies (the DESS, *Diplôme d'études supérieures specialisées*) or the DEA (*Diplôme d'études approfondies*). Both are conferred after one year's third-cycle study. The DEA also typically leads on to research and study for a doctorate.

Grandes écoles   The *grandes écoles* are a unique feature of the French system of higher education and management training, and represent the apotheosis of its technical and quantitative bias. Founded in the nineteenth century, originally for the education of the country's military élite, *grandes écoles* now train the country's top administrators and politicians. Most of the top managers in French industry have also been educated at a *grande école*. Whilst some *grandes écoles* are run directly by the national Ministry of Education, and in the case of the Ecole Polytechnique by the Defence Ministry, others are operated by local chambers of commerce or are private. There are thought to be about 160 *grandes écoles* in all.

Among the best known and most-widely respected *grandes écoles* are the Ecole Polytechnique, known as 'X', and the Ecole Nationale d'Administration, ENA, both of which confer engineering diplomas. In the area of business administration the three Paris-based *grandes écoles* are the Ecole des Hautes Etudes Commerciales (HEC), the Ecole Supérieure des Sciences Economiques et Commerciales (ESSEC) and the Ecole Supérieure de Commerce de Paris (ESCP). The Ecole Supérieure de Commerce in Lyon is the leading provincial business school. However, there are also many smaller local *écoles*, and applicants may apply for several, and accept the offer of the most highly regarded.

The *grandes écoles* are highly selective, and entrance to them is gained only through a stiff entrance exam. Students prepare for it by undertaking two years of preparatory studies in *classes préparatoires*, organised by the lycées, following acquisition of the *baccalauréat*.

Courses are for three years and lead to a diploma (usually rated as *Bac+5* because of the period of preparation prior to entry). *Grandes écoles* specialising in business administration may also offer supplementary MBA courses. Most *grandes écoles* courses include at least one placement (*stage*), and in some business schools students are encouraged to offer consultancy expertise to companies. As a rule the *grandes écoles* do not offer postgraduate education, as the diploma (or equivalent qualification) is regarded as a sufficient and easily understood high-level qualification for prospective employers.

In order to improve the efficiency of their teaching many of the *grandes écoles* have recently been introducing a greater information technology element into their courses. Following ESSEC, some have also opened apprenticeship training centres (*centres de formation d'apprentis*) encouraging interactive learning and work simulation problem-solving.

Among the criticisms of the system are that it is too élitist, emphasises analytical at the expense of social competences and does not meet the needs of students. Jacques Chirac promised reform of the education system during his 1995 election campaign. Since then a wide-ranging consultation on the subject has been launched. Reforms are likely to touch on the funding system, the structure of school teaching, integration of students into the workforce and the university curriculum, and are likely to become the subject of a referendum. Reform of the education system is traditionally an extremely sensitive issue in France. Early in 1995 the Balladur administration had to withdraw education reforms in the face of mass protests.

Graduate recruitment   Managerial recruits from tertiary education come predominantly from the technical specialisations of the universities or from the *grandes écoles* (see above). There was until fairly recently no tradition of recruiting liberal arts graduates into management.

The labour market for graduates has changed considerably since the years of rapid growth in the mid- to late 1980s when graduates in some disciplines could expect two or three job offers on completion of their course. 1994 marked the worst crisis for the graduate labour market since the war. This crisis imposed new rules. The gap between those students who can offer real 'competence' – that is, work experience in their field – and those who 'just' hold a degree, even a prestigious one, is increasing. A degree alone is less and less the determinant of pay and the gap between different higher education establishments is diminishing. This trend was confirmed by salaries awarded in 1995. Although the starting salary of a graduate has increased little in 1995 compared to 1992, pay after three years of service in the company will on average be 10 per cent higher. In other words, once in employment graduate salaries grow more rapidly (almost twice as fast in the first two or three years of employment) as three years ago. Depending on which institution they come from, some graduates may have lower starting salaries than others but in compensation may increase their pay more rapidly once in employment. A further change is that university graduates are becoming more popular as companies challenge the special status of the *grandes écoles*.

The average salary that graduates can expect in their first job depends both on sector and on educational background. In the past, graduates tended to be assessed very much by the educational institution attended rather than by details of academic performance: this is in a process of change. Graduates from *grandes écoles* can never the less generally command higher salaries than graduates from technical colleges or universities.

Recruitment practice varies for graduates, depending on the type of higher education establishment. The *grandes écoles* usually have both developed counselling and placement offices as well as active societies of former students. Although most universities – whose degrees are not as accepted by French employers as directly relevant to business – have careers information offices, their placement activities are not as highly developed.

Recruitment fairs are organised each year, usually in March, by a number of technical colleges and higher education establishments, where companies set up shop to provide graduates with details of themselves and their vacancies. Details are published in a guide issued each November by the journal *L'Usine Nouvelle*. Fairs can be expensive and need to be booked in advance. A stall space can cost anything between FF 5,000 and FF 30,000 (£550–£3,300) plus the cost for the stall itself. Other recruitment activity on campus tends to take place somewhat later, usually after Easter.

As far as recruitment methods are concerned, unsolicited applications and work experience *(stages* – see below), even though slightly down on 1994, remained the most widespread means of recruitment in 1995. The following methods were the most frequently cited in a survey by the publication *Le Guide des Entreprises qui Recrutent*: 83 per cent of companies recruited from speculative letters received, 72 per cent recruited among people doing a work-experience placement at their company (see below), 70 per cent of companies advertised in the press, 60 per cent used contacts with schools and universities, and recruitment fairs, and 52 per cent took on those who had been on fixed-term contracts. Some 40 per cent used the state executive placement service APEC (see above), 39 per cent recruited on the recommendation of relations, 30 per cent used recruitment consultants and 15 per cent used the state employment service ANPE.

In fact, speculative applications have become so popular – some large employers receive up to 30,000 a year – that some firms have contracted out part of the management of these CVs to outside companies such as Média PA, for example.

Le Guide des Entreprises qui Recrutent also lists the main graduate recruiters and starting pay for graduates by sector and educational background. The top ten companies in terms of the number of graduates taken on each year in 1995 were as follows: Crédit agricole 1,400; Société Générale 880; Elf 750; Bouygues 650; Auchan 600; Crédit mutuel 600; Valeo 600; Altran 500; Carrefour France 500; Décathlon 500.

Average starting salaries in 1995 in order of type of degree, were FF 191,000 –210,000 (£21,000–£23,000) for graduates of the top business schools (the Ecole des Hautes Etudes Commerciales, the Ecole Supérieure des Sciences Economiques et Commerciales and the Ecole Supérieure de Commerce de Paris); FF 150,000–190,000 (£16,500–£21,000) for graduates of other business schools; FF 196,000–215,000 (£21,800–£24,000) plus for graduates of the leading engineering schools (Polytechnique, Ecole Centrale de Paris, Mines, Ponts et Chaussées, Télécommunications de Paris, Supélec, Sup Aéro); and FF 170,000–195,000 (£19,000–£27,800) for graduates of other engineering schools. Salaries for those completing a four-year university course were running at FF 150,000–160,000, (£16,700–£17,800) and for those completing a five-year university course FF 161,000–186,000 (£17,900–£20,700).

According to a survey by Hewitt Associates conducted in 1995 among 81 companies, the majority of employers questioned stated that they kept graduate starting salaries for 1995 at the same level as those for 1994. An increasingly common means to reward competence is the introduction of variable pay as part of the remuneration package from the outset of the graduate's career. One in two of the companies surveyed complement the fixed salary with premiums or a performance-related bonus. These are given selectively rather than across the board. This flexible element is worth about 11 per cent of fixed salary and is expected to rise over the next years. Remuneration remains the prerogative of the recruiting companies, who prefer people who can offer more than just a diploma.

Work placements (Stages)   The practice of allowing a young person to work in a company for a particular length of time or to carry out a certain assignment, either in or out of term-time, is very common in France and is often deemed one of the best ways in which to assess potential recruits, as practical work-experience is involved. The likelihood of a *stage* leading to a permanent position has increased and is now the second most widespread method of recruitment. At Citroën for example, 30 per cent of *stages* lead to recruitment. A *stage* may be offered either during or after completion of a degree course and gives both sides an opportunity to work together before a commitment is made. Many companies take on graduates for a longer placement or a fixed-term contract prior to offering a permanent post. Usually, there is no official employment contract for those working on a *stage*. However, they are covered by all health and safety conditions, disciplinary measures and working-time provisions relevant to the permanent workforce of the company.

Recent trends   Over the last ten years an explosion in the number of young graduates has been taking place, with 65 per cent of young people now reaching the *baccalauréat* compared to 36 per cent in 1985. A notable increase is also evident in higher education. In return, the number of graduates who will obtain *cadre* status straight away has fallen dramatically.

For the first time since 1991 managerial recruitment is improving. An increase in management positions advertised in the press (up by 37 per cent in 1995 compared to 1993 – a particularly bleak year in employment terms) is an indication of the recovery of the graduate labour market. However, while companies are foreseeing an increase in executive recruitment, the axing of jobs is continuing. Also, the increasingly frequent use of fixed-term and short-term contracts, notably for young graduates, shows that *cadres* on the whole are not yet safe from job uncertainty.

During economically difficult years companies prefer promoting staff internally rather than hiring externally. This trend seems to have been reversed in 1995, with companies recruiting again. Paradoxically in a country where youth unemployment is among the highest in Europe, 44 per cent of new recruits in 1995 were young *cadres* who had just graduated. Judging by jobs advertised in the press, almost half of them are in the commercial and information technology sectors.

Besides the new forms of integration into the labour market, particularly sandwich courses and apprenticeships for young graduates, temporary and fixed-term contracts have become new tools of human resource management. However, such practices are often met with hostility. In fact about three in four *cadres* judge solutions such as part-time work, working-time reduction with a reduction in salary or shared posts, as not very realistic.

Companies have taken advantage of their stronger market position by taking their time in making recruitment decisions. While at the beginning of the 1990s it hardly ever took more than two months to recruit, it now often takes up to three months. At the same time probationary periods are getting longer. Fixed-term contracts are becoming more common, with 41 per cent of graduates being recruited on that basis. Even more striking is that, according to APEC, 43 per cent of young graduates have started their careers as non-*cadres* (not as executives). Even the prestigious *grandes écoles* are not immune to this development.

Consequently, young graduates adapt – becoming more professional, more flexible and more mobile than, for example, even four years ago. Moreover, they now venture into territory they might not be expert in or go for less prestigious jobs. They are also more willing to take up employment in small and medium-sized companies. According to APEC, 70 per cent of *grandes écoles* graduates are now finding their first employment in companies with less than 1,000 employees. Graduates are also increasingly geographically mobile, considering less popular areas where employment is often easier to obtain.

Vocational training

A distinction is drawn between initial training, the bulk of which takes place in state educational institutions, and continuing or supplementary training, which is organised via employers. Apprenticeships are still of less importance than the state system in providing initial training, although recent reforms are intended to bolster this form of training (see below).

While the education system classifies qualifications in terms of years after the *baccalauréat*, the vocational training system has its own hierarchy, beginning with Level V (for skilled workers with an initial vocational training qualification) and rising to Levels I and II (for managers and engineers with at least *Bac+4*).

Initial vocational training: the state system

Most initial vocational training follows the end of compulsory education at 16. However, as noted above, some school students may leave secondary school at 14 or 15, go on to a vocational training school (*lycée d'enseignement profes-sionel*) and begin working towards one of the recognised initial vocational quali-fications, the CAP or BEP (see below). Others in the age-group move on to these schools at the age of 16 and pursue the same qualifications.

The principal initial vocational qualification is the vocational training certifi-cate (*Certificat d'aptitude professionelle*, CAP) which takes three years to acquire, and entails practical and theoretical training. (Young people who leave school without any qualification are often those who have had difficulty with the theoretical parts of the CAP.) The less specialised vocational studies certificate (*Brevet d'études professionelles*, BEP) takes two years, with qualifications pri-marily for occupations in the service sector. Both would be regarded as initial qualifications for a skilled or semi-skilled worker. In all, 93 per cent of students pass their CAP or BEP exams the first time, and 75 per cent at the second attempt. Forty per cent of those then qualified go into employment while the rest opt for further training. (In a comparative study carried out by the UK NIESR, the CAP/BEP qualifications were rated as equivalent to a City and Guilds Part II pass.)

A higher degree of technical education is provided initially in specialised *lycées*. As noted above, it may be for either a technical or a vocational *baccalau-réat* or for the technician certificate (*Brevet de technicien*, BT). According the NIESR study referred to above, this level of qualification was deemed 'lower intermediate', and rated as equivalent to a BTEC National Certificate and National Diploma.

Apprenticeship   There is a recognised system of apprenticeship, accounting for training primarily in craft occupations in small enterprises. The system was over-hauled in 1992, through a national collective agreement and corresponding legis-lation. Part of the reason lay in the continuing high level of unemployment, some criticism of the usefulness of the state-provided CAP qualification, and the stag-nating number of apprenticeships (at about 230,000 in all, compared with approximately 1.3 million in vocational and technical secondary schools).

Apprenticeships had also acquired the image of providing a source of cheap temporary labour, with many firms failing to offer a job to apprentices on qualifying. In public discussion it was emphasised that the best direction in which to move would be towards the comprehensive German 'dual system', built on the apprenticeship relationship and based on experience of employment as well as theoretical training. The national collective agreement of 8 January 1992 increased pay for apprentices, expressed as a percentage of the statutory national minimum wage, the SMIC. The agreement also increased flexibility regarding the length of apprenticeship contracts and the content of courses, which is determined at branch level, and increased the amount of information available to prospective apprentices. The main provisions of the agreement were incorporated into a law on apprenticeship passed on 17 July 1992. Since then the number of apprentices has increased by 25 per cent, and in 1996 stood at 290,000.

Apprenticeship is defined in the Labour Code as 'a means of affording to young people . . . general theoretical and practical training leading to a vocational qualification'. The training may be carried out partly on company premises and partly at an apprentice training centre (*centre de formation d'apprentis*, CFA). All apprenticeships must be registered at a CFA.

A law reforming the financing of apprenticeships was adopted by Parliament in April 1996. The new law foresees a unified and simplified system of grants linked to the recruitment and training of apprentices to replace the different schemes and exemptions from apprenticeship tax and social charges in force previously. Tax credits for training (*crédits d'impôt formation*) which had been introduced in the 1988 budget for companies whose expenditure on training is over and above basic legal requirements were also abolished.

Under the new law companies will receive FF 6,000 (£670) on recruiting an apprentice and a further FF 10,000 (£1,100) at the end of each of the two training years. The total amount payable for each apprentice over the period of two years would hence be at least FF 26,000 (£2,900). This amount can vary up to FF 50,000 (£5,500) over two years depending on the age of the apprentice and the kind of training received.

Apprenticeship training is financed by the apprenticeship training tax, which totals 0.5 per cent of the wage bill and is payable by all employers. The above-mentioned reform of the apprenticeship financing foresees that 0.2 per cent (0.1 per cent previously) of the 0.5 per cent directly finances apprenticeships. (The rest of the revenue raised from the tax goes to finance other training and educational institutions, including higher education.)

Apprentices must be aged 16–25 at the beginning of the contract, which must be in writing and registered with the relevant labour authorities. The length of the contract must be at least equal to the length of the course to be undertaken, and is customarily one to three years. The majority of contracts are for two years. Contracts may be extended in the case of failed examinations, if the apprentice is handicapped, or by special derogation (for example, in the case of military service).

Apprenticeship training contracts generally lead to recognised vocational qualifications such as the basic CAP, the BT and the BEP, or in some cases to more advanced qualifications such as the BTS and DUT technical qualifications (see above). The number of people embarking on apprenticeships has soared over the last two years and is expected to reach the number of 340,000 apprentices in 2004/5.

Duties of the employer   An employer who takes on trainees under an apprenticeship contract must register them with an apprentice training centre (CFA). The employer must ensure that the apprentice receives the appropriate practical experience within the company and that the experience progresses in line with the theoretical training. Training may be carried out jointly at the workplace and at the training centre. The employer must also oversee the apprentice's entry for a vocational training diploma, and consult the works committee on apprentice training. Time spent by the apprentice on theoretical training is counted as working time. Apprentices enjoy the same employment protection as that offered to permanent employees.

Payment of apprentices   Apprentices are paid a percentage of the national minimum wage, the SMIC, which varies from 25 per cent (for a 16–17-year-old in the first year of training) to 78 per cent (for a 21+-year-old in the third year). In May 1996 the SMIC stood at FF 6,374.68 (£700) per month. This is the legal minimum rate and may be improved upon by collective agreement.

Apprenticeship contracts terminate at the agreed date, although the contract may be ended by either party within two months of commencement without the need for any reason to be given; the CFA, however, must be informed. Should the apprentice fail the exams, the contract is usually extended by one year. When the contract has expired the apprentice may be taken on by the company in question. If not, the apprentice may continue in training by means of a further apprenticeship contract or may claim unemployment benefit.

Initial vocational training for the unemployed: sandwich courses   A number of schemes exist to encourage firms to take on and train the unemployed, many of whom obtained no vocational qualifications at school, or lack work experience. For those people not in employment a range of training courses is provided under the heading *formation en alternance* or sandwich courses. Such courses are usually governed by a fixed-term contract and are designed to combine theoretical instruction with practical training, on the job. Originally devised for young people under 26, this type of training contract has since been extended to the long-term unemployed. Employers are offered a range of incentives, such as exemption from social security contributions, state financial aid and exemption from the obligation to count such employees as part of the company's registered workforce. The main types of sandwich training contracts and work-experience contracts are as follows.

- Solidarity contract (*contrat emploi-solidarité*). (see *Employment incentives* above).
- 'Orientation' contracts (*contrats d'orientation*), established by legislation passed in December 1991, are fixed-term, lasting between six months, non-renewable and available to young people aged between 16 and 22 who are experiencing difficulty in finding work. They are paid, at a rate varying between 30 per cent and 65 per cent of the national minimum wage, by the employer, who is exempt from social charges for such employees during the period of the contract and will receive FF 50 (£5.50) per training hour.
- Adaptation contracts (*contrat d'adaptation à un emploi*) may be on either a permanent or fixed-term basis of six to 12 months and are aimed at the young between 16 and 26 already holding a qualification, offering them complementary training and practical experience. Remuneration during the adaptation period may not be lower than 80 per cent of the minimum rate fixed by collective agreement. The employer can demand reimbursement of FF 50 (£5.50) per training hour.

Training in the public sector   Like private-sector employees, people employed in the public sector have access to training in two main ways – through training plans devised by the employing organisation, or by taking training leave, which is nationally administered and financed by special funds (see above). A framework agreement on training in the civil service was signed by the social partners concerned in June 1989. The agreement provided for a minimum of 2 per cent of the wage bill to be spent on training measures. This target has been attained, although it is generally accepted that the average amount spent on training in the private sector is 3 per cent of the wage bill. A total of 1.85 million civil servants received some form of training in each year of the three-year agreement, although the spread between Ministries was reported to be uneven.

A new agreement was signed on 7 July 1992 with the aim of ensuring the continuation of training provision over the next three years and raising the minimum amount spent on it to 3.2 per cent of the wage bill. Employees continue to be entitled to a minimum of three or four days' training per year, depending on their status. The agreement increases remuneration for employees on training leave, and provides 100 per cent of pay for those on training leave necessitated by departmental restructuring (*congé de restructuration*).

A new three-year framework agreement was concluded in February 1996. Following social unrest in the public sector at the end of 1995, this agreement represents the revival of social dialogue between government and trade unions. The main elements of the agreement are an increase in the percentage of the pay-bill dedicated to training, and an extension of the minimum training entitlement, varying depending on employee category.

Training initiatives at industry level

Training arrangements have recently been incorporated into a wide range of industry collective agreements, reflecting the higher profile which training has acquired.

The incorporation of a clause in an industry agreement obliging companies to spend 2 or 3 per cent of the wage bill on training is quite common. This commitment is considerably higher than the statutory minimum of 1.5 per cent (for companies with 10 or more employees), although the average amount spent by companies on training is thought to be about 3 per cent.

Recent collective agreements also contain clauses on training provisions and their financing in the face of working-time reductions and flexibilisation. Also integrated are provisions for sandwich courses based on recent national multi-industry agreements, notably those of 23 June and 26 July 1995 dealing with the integration of young people into the labour market.

Managerial and supervisory training

The ranks of supervisor (*agent de maîtrise*) and manager (*cadre*) enjoy legal recognition in France, and their status is defined in collective agreements. There is a recognised qualification for supervisors which is validated by the relevant trade associations in collaboration with ANFOPPE (*Association nationale pour la formation et le perfectionnement du personnel d'entreprise*). Whereas first-line managers and lower-level *cadres* will typically be included in industry job classification schemes, with their grade often defined in terms of the formal qualifications they possess, senior managers will be outside such classification schemes but often be dealt with in industry agreements. Access to the status of *cadre* may be by internal promotion, with the acquisition of appropriate formal technical qualifications and several years' experience, or following recruitment as a graduate and some experience, depending on the employee's higher education qualification. A *grande école* graduate would usually be classified as a *cadre* from the outset: an employee with a basic technical education would need to acquire several years' experience. Entry to the ranks of the most senior management is overwhelmingly via higher education and the possession of a university, or *grande école*, diploma. In general, managers are more highly educated than their British counterparts, and about 60 per cent have qualifications rated as *Bac+4–5* (that is, either a university *maîtrise* or a *grande école* diploma).

However, practice is likely to differ between small and large companies, the former tending to train managers with technical qualifications on the job rather than attempting to recruit *grande école* graduates, whose ultimate destination is likely to be a large organisation.

According to a 1996 survey carried out by the magazine *l'Expansion*, 63 per cent of graduates recruited had been educated at *grandes écoles*; 22 per cent followed a longer state university course of *Bac+3* and over, and 15 per cent had completed shorter university courses such as DUT, BTS and DEUG.

Even though the bias towards recruiting *grande école* graduates still exists, the prestigious schools have been suffering substantial losses in enrolments over the last few years, mainly due to the fact that entrance requirements are deemed too difficult and their courses too long and expensive.

MBAs

MBAs are offered by some private business schools, but are not generally considered by recruiting companies to be essential as a management training qualification. MBAs tend to be favoured by consultancies and the staff of business schools. Two-thirds of staff time at INSEAD, originally established to provide MBA courses, is now spent on short courses for existing managers.

Most higher education qualifications involve a period of practical experience in industry or commerce, and male graduates will also have undergone a period of compulsory military service.

Although the 1980s saw a broadening of managerial training style and content, with greater emphasis on interpersonal and overall management skills to supplement the analytical capacity fostered in the *grandes écoles*, there is still concern about the narrow social base and heavily theoretical training of French managers.

Consultation on training

There are obligations on employers both at sectoral level, through collective agreements, and at enterprise level, where they must prepare a training plan (*plan de formation*) and consult their works councils.

Industry level   It is obligatory for negotiations to take place at industry level every five years between the relevant unions and employer organisations. The topics covered by the negotiations were widened under the training law of 31 December 1991 (No. 91–1405). Negotiations must cover the following main areas:

- the type of training schemes in operation or preparation
- recognition of the qualifications obtained by this training
- the position of young people in the company with regard to vocational training
- the training needs of those with few or no qualifications or skills
- equality for men and women with regard to training
- the particular training problems encountered by companies with fewer than ten employees
- how companies can give practical effect to provisions agreed at branch level.

A date for the next consultation meeting must be arranged at the end of the meeting.

Company level　Companies bound by a sectoral collective agreement should have a programme of several discussions a year (*programme pluriannuel*) to outline the kind of training made available by the company and the way in which it is being used. Meetings should take into account:

- economic factors
- investment levels
- technology
- work organisation
- working time within the company.

The Social Partners' Agreement on Training of 3 July 1991 recommends that such meetings should be held twice a year.

The training plan　Under the Labour Code, the employer must draw up a training plan (*plan de formation*) each year in consultation with the works committee or, in establishments with under 50 employees, with staff representatives. The plan should contain details of existing training schemes within the company and schemes proposed for the coming year. The plan is to be drawn up in conjunction with the obligations upon employers to consult employee representatives annually on training (see below). According to a report on management training in France, published by the UK National Economic Development Office, training plans were seen as a useful means of dialogue by companies, but regarded by training organisations as rarely matching the expectations raised and often 'very basic'.

Informing and consulting works councils　There is an obligation to consult works councils (or staff representatives in smaller firms) on the implementation of the training plan, and on proposals for the coming year. Works councils or staff representatives must be informed two or three times a year, depending on the size of the company, of the number of employees on sandwich course training contracts (see above). They must also be kept up to date on the facilities available for young people on training contracts and for tutors and trainers. Works councils must be consulted on the facilities available to people on work experience programmes which form a compulsory part of training for professional diplomas.

Continuing vocational training

Vocational training is regarded as highly important in France and approximately one major collective agreement is signed on the subject each year. Continuing vocational training (*formation professionelle continue*) is available to all employees by law, with the aim of adapting skills to technological change and maintaining or improving existing skills. Company training programmes must be set out in a formal training plan, and there are statutory requirements on the minimum level of expenditure. The employers' federation CNPF has been pushing for change in the established system, which it considers is outdated and inadequate. A major focus of the discussion has been whether to centralise or decentralise the system.

The 1993 five-year law on employment made some initial moves in this area, and in July 1994 the social partners agreed to reorganise the system totally. The debate over whether to collect funds at regional or sectoral level is ongoing and until a compromise has been reached two funding organisations, OPCAREG and OPCA, are working in parallel.

The Five-year Jobs Plan   The Five-year Law on Employment, passed in December 1993, enshrined a commitment that all young people should be offered some sort of professional training before leaving the education system, irrespective of their qualifications. The law also instituted regional plans for the development of vocational training for the young covering all forms of education: initial training (school and apprenticeship), sandwich course training and continuing vocational training. As well as extensive decentralisation of training responsibilities and some funding to the regions for training young people, the law also introduced various incentive schemes – including cuts in social charges and grants for companies recruiting and training the young and the long-term unemployed.

Legislative framework   Continuing training is regulated by legislation passed in December 1991 which incorporated the provisions of a national collective agreement concluded in July 1991. The main aim was to increase the funding of training and to raise awareness of training opportunities at sectoral level. All firms are required to meet the minimum levels of training expenditure, or pay a levy to training funds: the levy was increased from 1.2 per cent of the wage bill to 1.4 per cent in 1992 and again to 1.5 per cent on 1 January 1993.

When the system was reorganised in 1994 the company contribution rate of 1.5 per cent of the wage bill for training was not raised. However, actual average expenditure is about 3 per cent, with banking and insurance leading the field with about 8 per cent of the wage bill dedicated to training. This does not cover introductory on-the-job training.

Training can be carried out within the company or at a variety of public and private training institutions. The main public institutions are:

• those under the supervision of the Ministry of National Education, such as the 5,000 *lycées* and public colleges offering courses
• technical universities

- engineering schools and universities
- the national centre for correspondence course education, CNED.

The tripartite national adult training association (*Association nationale pour la formation professionelle des adultes*) is overseen by the Ministry of Labour and Vocational Training. Training is also provided by private organisations, including chambers of commerce, which must be registered with the state. They organise work placements, particularly in small and medium-sized companies. Similarly, work placements may be organised by a variety of non-profit-making organisations, such as trade unions. In addition, a number of profit-making organisations, such as language training companies or management training organisations, run a variety of courses.

The Vocational Training Federation (*Fédération de la formation professionelle*, FFP) was created in June 1991, and encompasses three large private national organisations offering vocational training and advice: *Union nationale des organismes privés de formation continue, Syntec formation* and *Chambre syndicale nationale des organismes de formation*. Together these bodies represent over 300 private training organisations that have agreed to be bound by a code of conduct and to maintain minimum quality standards. Overall there are about 600 apprentice training centres (CFA) in France, of which 450 offer diplomas recognised by the Ministry of Education, and 150 award diplomas recognised in the agricultural sector. Just under half of them are managed by private organisations, with the balance run by professional chambers (*chambres de métiers*) and public educational establishments.

Employee time-off rights

Continuing vocational training is governed by the Labour Code, the provisions of which may be improved upon by collective or company agreement. By law, all employees are entitled to continuing vocational training. This may take a variety of forms. One of the most common is individual training leave (*congé individuel de formation*), which is paid absence of up to one year for full-time training or 1,200 hours for part-time training outside the company. In order to qualify for such leave, employees must have at least 24 months' non-consecutive general work experience and 12 months' employment with their current employer.

Employers may refuse to grant, or may decide to defer, leave if the number of employees absent would exceed 2 per cent of the workforce. Employees who have already been on individual training leave may not request a further period of training leave within certain time limits, depending on the length of leave already taken. Employees must notify their employer of a request to take training leave at least 60 days in advance for leave of up to six months or for part-time training, and 120 days for leave of more than six months. The employer has

30 days in which to accept or refuse the employee's request. Reasons must be given for a refusal.

The remuneration of an employee on vocational training leave is fixed at 80 per cent (90 per cent in special cases) of the previous salary as long as the training leave does not exceed one year or 1,200 hours on a part-time basis. After that period, 60 per cent of previous salary is paid. However long the training, payment may not be lower than twice SMIC, or lower than the previous salary if the latter was below twice SMIC. To be paid during leave the employee has to apply to one of the jointly-run OPACIFs (*organismes paritaires collecteurs agréés*) which administer pay and which in turn are financed by statutory annual company payments (see below). Salary is paid by the employer, who is then reimbursed by the official OPACIF body. In 1995 about 30,000 employees benefited from training leave administered by OPACIFs – equivalent to 62 per cent of all requests submitted.

Financing

Vocational training is financed principally by companies, with the state and regional authorities also providing some funding. A proportion of finance is raised by levies on firms, some of which are paid in any event (the apprentice training tax – 0.5 per cent of the paybill) while others are payable only if the firm spends less than the legally prescribed total. Companies contribute 0.2 per cent of their wage bill to financing training leave (see below).

Legal requirements   Since 1971 there has been a statutory obligation for all companies to devote a certain sum to staff training. In companies with under 10 employees a sum equivalent to 0.15 per cent of the total wage bill must be made available; in companies of 10 or more employees this sum is 1.5 per cent of the wage bill. Of this, 0.4 per cent must be devoted to the training of young workers and 0.2 per cent must be dedicated to the financing of individual training leave (*congé individuel de formation*). The rest of the money may be used in a variety of ways, such as financing the training activities of the company's own staff, financing training activities for the unemployed, or operating a central training fund (*fonds d'assurance formation*). Whichever option the employer chooses, the works committee has to be consulted first.

The company must submit an estimate of its prospective paybill for the coming financial year, with pay growth accounted for by an estimate, together with allowable training expenses. The return goes to the tax authorities, who are responsible for the monitoring and enforcement of levies and training expenditure.

Investment in training   Companies spent an average of 3 per cent of the wage bill on training in 1995. This average figure naturally varies according to company size and sector, with larger companies investing more in training than smaller, owner-managed companies. Those with high-profile jobs are more likely to receive training. Vocational training appears to be most often used as a means of enhancing employee skills for those who are comparatively highly qualified, rather than offering a means for less qualified employees to gain new skills and embark upon a change of career direction.

The state contributes about FF 60 billion (£6.7 billion) annually to training. It finances schemes for the unemployed and the young unemployed, the disadvantaged and minority groups, and general information on the types of schemes available. Local authorities spend an annual FF 7.8 billion (£0.9 billion) on training, mainly on the formulation of training and apprenticeship policy in their local area.

Educational attainment of the population

Level	Percentage of 25–64 age-group
Lower secondary	33
Upper secondary	50
Higher education (non-university)	8
University	9

Source: OECD (1994)

Organisations

Ministry of Labour and Vocational Training
127 Rue de Grenelle
75700 Paris
Tel. +33 1 44 38 38 38

Association pour l'Emploi des Cadres (APEC):
51 Boulevard Brune
75689 Paris Cedex 14
Tel. +33 1 40 52 20 00
Fax +33 1 45 39 10 22

APEC also has regional offices, including Marseilles:

APEC Marseilles
220 Avenue du Pocado
BP 352
13271 Marseille Cedex 08
Tel. +33 91 91 79 32 52

and in Lyons

APEC Lyons
204 Avenue Bethelot
69361 Lyon Cedex 07
Tel. +33 7 78 69 04 77

Agence Nationale pour l'Emploi (ANPE):
4 Rue Galilée
93198 Noisy-le-Grand
Tel. +33 1 49 31 74 00

Confédération Générale des Cadres (national executives' union):
30 Rue de Gramont
75002 Paris
Tel. +33 1 42 61 81 76

Conseil National du Patronat Français (CNPF) (national employers' organisation)
31 Rue Pierre 1er de Serbie
75016 Paris
Tel. +33 1 40 69 44 44

Syntec (member of FEACO):
3 Rue Léon Bonnat
75016 Paris
Tel. +33 1 45 24 43 53
Fax +33 1 42 88 26 84

APROCERD (search consultants'
organisation):
120 Avenue des Champs-Elysées
75008 Paris
Tel. +33 1 44 20 54 00

PROMATT (union of temporary workers):
94 Rue Saint-Lazare
75009 Paris
Tel. +33 1 48 78 11 21

UNETT (national organisation for
temporary employment agencies):
9 Rue du Mont-Thabor
75001 Paris
Tel. +33 1 42 97 41 50

British Chamber of Commerce:
8 Rue Cimerosa
75118 Paris
Tel. +33 1 45 05 13 08
Fax +33 1 45 53 02 87

Association nationale pour la formation
professionelle des adultes (National
Adult Vocational Training Association):
13 Place du Général de Gaulle
93108 Montreuil-sur-Bois Cedex
Tel. +33 1 48 70 50 00
Fax +33 1 48 58 34 32

Centre d'études et de recherche sur les
qualifications (CEREQ):
9 Rue Sextius Michel
75015 Paris
Tel. +33 1 45 75 62 63

Union nationale des organismes privés
de formation continue
297 Rue de Vaugirard
75015 Paris
Tel. +33 1 48 56 18 00

Centre pour le développement de
l'information sur la formation
permanente (National Training
Information Centre):
Tour Europe Cedex 07
92049 Paris La Défense
Tel. +33 1 47 78 13 50
Fax +33 1 47 73 74 20

Media

cadremploi
(electronic media recruitment service)
SETEC – 3617 Cadremploi
160 Rue de Paris
92771 Boulogne Cedex
Tel. +33 1 4909 0011
Fax +33 1 4909 9229

Le Monde
1 Place Hubert-Beuve-Méry
94852 Ivry-sur-Seine Cedex
Tel. +33 1 49 60 32 90

Les Echos
46 Rue La Boétie
75381 Paris Cedex 08
Tel. +33 1 49 53 65 65
Fax +33 1 45 61 48 92

Le Figaro
25 Avenue Matignon
75398 Paris Cedex 08
Tel. +33 1 42 36 79 19

Le Point
140 Rue de Rennes
75066 Paris
Tel. +33 1 45 44 39 00

Le Guide des Entreprises qui Recrutent
(annually costs FF 98.00 (£11))
L'Etudiant (regular journal)
27 Rue du Chemin-Vert
75543 Paris Cedex 11
Tel. +33 1 48 07 41 41
Fax +33 1 47 00 79 80

<table>
<tr><td>*L'Usine Nouvelle*</td><td>*Liaisons Sociales*</td></tr>
<tr><td>59 Rue du Rocher</td><td>1 Avenue Edouard-Belin</td></tr>
<tr><td>75008 Paris</td><td>92856 Rueil-Malmaison Cedex</td></tr>
<tr><td>Tel. +33 1 43 87 37 88</td><td>Tel. +33 1 41 29 96 96</td></tr>
</table>

Main sources

ANPE, Annual reports for 1994 and 1995, Paris

ANPE, *L'ANPE et les mesures pour l'emploi*, Paris, Nov 1995

APEC, *Cadroscope*, Paris 1995

GROUP ETUDIANT *Le Guide des Entreprises qui Recrutent*, 1996

BARSOUX, JEAN-LOUIS and LAWRENCE, PETER. *Management in France*, Cassell, London, 1991

ÉDITIONS FRANCIS LEFEBVRE, *Mémento Pratique*, Levallois France, 1995

LIAISONS SOCIALES, *Entreprises & Carrières*, various issues

– *Le Mensuel* various issues

– *Legislation Sociale* various issues

– *Bref Social* various issues

MINISTRY OF LABOUR, 'Contrat de progrès entre l'état et l'ANPE 1994–1998', Paris, 1994

MINISTRY OF LABOUR and the EUROPEAN COMMISSION, *La Formation Professionelle en France*, 1995

WILLEMS, JEAN-PIERRE. 'Vocational education and training in France', CEDEFOP, Berlin, 1994

National collective agreements for the chemical industry, banking, metalworking, textiles, catering and retailing. *Journal Officiel*, Paris.

5

Germany

The outstanding feature of education and training in Germany remains the 'dual system' of initial vocational training, with its implied commitment to broad-based skills for all and investment in people across the range of academic ability. The dual system is seen as the foundation of a high skills economy, and an important element in social integration. Although the German system has its internal and external critics, it continues to demonstrate great strengths when assessed in terms of the overall volume of skilled people that emerge. However, the dual system is deeply rooted in a strong tradition of guilds and local self-regulation as well as a dense network of tripartite institutions not easily transplanted elsewhere. Some observers have noted that the German employment culture is also marked by the distinct category of the 'occupation' (*Beruf*), a concept midway between 'jobs' and 'professions' and characterised by a specific combination of formal knowledge, skills and experience which is not tied to a particular workplace and becomes part of the broader social orientation of the individual employee.

High levels of training for skilled workers are reinforced by recognised further training in intermediate skills, tied into the dual system and creating a substantial reservoir of technically and practically trained employees with managerial potential.

Vocational training in Germany is underpinned by financial and institutional support from the public employment system, with grants and loans to help both employers and employees.

Although the early 1990s saw some contraction in the number of training places available, a sustained campaign by politicians, employers' associations, trade unions, and Chambers of Trade and Commerce ensured that roughly enough places were created to match demand in 1996/7. Nevertheless, there are continuing problems in East Germany and some mismatch nationally between vacancies and demand. Supply continues to lag behind demand, and there has been criticism that the corporate sector has failed to keep to its agreed commitments to increase training places, with an increase of just 1.6 per cent in 1995. Moreover, although the training system temporarily absorbs a large proportion of young people, up to 70 per cent in East Germany emerge into unemployment.

Problems in the future are likely to be dominated by the need to remedy training shortcomings in East Germany, overcome the potential shortage of vocational school teachers, solve financing problems, which have seen calls for training levies, and – on some analyses – systematise aspects of continuing training into a more formal model resembling the 'dual system' for initial vocational training. The lack of relevance of the dual system to the service sector also needs to be addressed.

Recruitment

German labour law, and in some instances collective agreements, impose a number of constraints on employers during recruitment. The main areas are: work permit procedures; mandatory workforce consultation on recruitment; anti-discrimination provisions; and limitations on the rights of employers to information about prospective employees.

Official notification

There is no obligation to notify the authorities of hirings. Employers must establish whether the nationality or residence status of the prospective employee allows them to be employed in Germany. A contract of employment concluded without a work permit is void. Citizens of member states of the European Union do not need a work permit (*Arbeitserlaubnis*) but must have a residence permit (*Aufenthaltserlaubnis*), normally granted as a formality. A health certificate, obtained from the local health department, may be required for some occupations.

Citizens of non-EU countries need both a work and a residence permit, which must be applied for in advance. Since large-scale recruitment of foreign workers stopped in 1973, there have been considerable restrictions on the availability of work permits. There are some exceptions where no work permit is needed, such as some categories of manager, technicians working on assignments for a period not exceeding two months, and academics. Under legislation covering the construction industry passed in 1996, all employees should be paid a new national minimum rate and are entitled to other minimum conditions, irrespective of their nationality or that of the employing company.

Workforce consultation

The 1972 Works Constitution Act provides for the establishment of works councils for employees in establishments with at least five permanent employees. These have rights both to co-determination and information in the field of recruitment. The main areas are set out below.

Personnel planning Employers must inform works councils about current or future demand for labour and any proposed personnel measures. The works council can make suggestions on personnel planning and its execution. Personnel planning is held to embrace not simply long-term assessment of future staff needs but also short-term responses to immediate situations.

Internal appointments   Works councils can request that job vacancies be notified internally before external applications are invited – although there is scope for local agreements to exclude specified positions from this requirement.

Application forms or staff questionnaires   The agreement of the works council is required where an employer wishes to use a form to collect information about an applicant or prospective employee. If no agreement is reached, then a conciliation committee, established under works council legislation, can issue a binding ruling.

Guidelines for selection   Guidelines for employee selection require the agreement of works councils. In establishments with fewer than 1,000 employees the employer is free to decide on whether to set out such guidelines. In establishments with more than 1,000 employees the works council can request that such guidelines be drawn up, and apply to a conciliation committee for a binding ruling if no agreement is reached.

Co-determination on appointments and transfers   In establishments with more than 20 employees, employers must inform works councils before any appointment, regrading or transfer. This includes instances where the selection of the employee has been carried out by a recruitment consultant. The works council can refuse its agreement to the appointment or transfer if the appointment would breach the law, a collective or works agreement, or guideline agreed with the works council. (For example, an agreed redundancy scheme may provide for priority re-hiring of former employees). The works council can also object if it considers that existing employees might be disadvantaged.

Should the works council withhold agreement the employer may apply to a labour court for a ruling unless the employer is already bound by an agreed provision. Works councils' rights in this area extend to any person being employed on the employer's premises and subject to the supervision, direction and control of the employer, even if this includes workers formally employed by a third party, such as a contractor or agency employees (*Leiharbeitnehmer*).

Consultation with executive representatives   Legislation also provides for statutory representation for executives on separate executive representation committees (*'Sprecherausschüsse'*). These have a number of rights on appointment issues, including the right to draw up non-binding guidelines on executive contracts and a requirement for the employer to inform the committee about appointments or changes in the employment of an executive.

Using temps and part-timers

Fixed-term contracts   Fixed-term contracts may, in general, be concluded only if there is a 'material reason', such as probationary employment, a specific task or project limited in time (or subject to finite funding), as a stand-in for an absent employee on sick or maternity leave, or at the employee's request. The duration of a fixed-term contract is governed by case law. In the case of a probationary contract, this is set at six months. In the case of scientific or technical staff workers on long-term projects, up to four years might be agreed. Fixed-term contracts may be repeatedly renewed only if there are telling 'material reasons'.

However, under legislation most recently amended in September 1996 a fixed-term agreement can be concluded *once* for up to two years without a 'material reason'. A fixed-term contract can also be renewed three times provided the aggregate duration does not exceed two years. However, the conclusion of a fixed-term contract under this provision will be unlawful if fewer than four months elapse between the end of a previous fixed-term or open-ended contract and the beginning of the new contract and there is a 'close material relation' between the successive periods of employment.

Registered managers' (*Geschäftsführer*) contracts are commonly on a fixed-term basis. A fixed-term contract may also be agreed with a manager covered by the Protection Against Dismissals Act, provided the contract includes a sum in compensation on termination.

In 1993, 5.7 per cent of all employees were on fixed-term contracts in West Germany, but 11 per cent in the East. Younger workers were disproportionately affected, with nearly 16 per cent of under-25s in West Germany and 19 per cent in the East.

Part-time contracts   Part-time employment, which accounts for some 16 per cent of the German labour force, is defined as working time which is less than that worked by full-time employees in the same establishment. Collective agreements may specify minimum periods for part-time work as well as other terms, such as preferential treatment when applying for full-time posts. Part-timers who work less than 15 hours per week and earn a monthly income of less than DM 610 (£245) (in East Germany DM 520 (£210)) are not subject to sickness and pensions insurance contributions and benefits. Part-timers who work less than 19 hours are excluded from unemployment insurance and benefits. When calculating the minimum number of employees required to bring an establishment under the provisions of the Protection Against Dismissals Act, which prohibits unfair dismissal and was amended in September 1996, part-time workers are counted in fractions of an employee, depending on how much they work. For example, employees who work less than 10 hours per week count as 0.25; not more than 20, 0.5; and not more than 30, 0.75. Only workplaces with 10 eligible employees (or their equivalent) are covered by the law. The rights of employees already in post on 30 September 1996 are protected until 30 September 1999.

'Zero hours contracts' ('Work-on-call')   This type of contract, known as 'capacity-oriented variable working time' (KAPOVAZ) or 'work on call', requires employees to work when requested to do so by the employer. (Such arrangements have been termed 'zero hours contracts' in the UK.) Contracts must specify the length of the working week: if not, a minimum period of 10 hours applies, for which the employer is liable to pay the employee. Weekly working time may be averaged over a year, although there is still some uncertainty on how the law should be interpreted. Employers must give at least four days' notice of a call-in and, unless there is a specific agreement on the number of daily hours, the minimum period for which an employee can be employed per day is three successive hours. The introduction of such arrangements must be agreed with works councils (with right of appeal to conciliation machinery).

Job-sharing   Under a job-sharing contract each of the partners is required to specify the period of work for which they are responsible. Contracts may not require that the post be constantly occupied – that is, that one partner should deputise for the other in the case of absence.

Agency employment   Authorised agencies are allowed to supply workers for temporary employment (*Leiharbeitnehmer*), subject to the provisions of the 1972 Law on Commercial Employment Agencies (*Arbeitnehmerüberlassungsgesetz*). Temporary employment via agencies is absolutely forbidden for manual workers in the construction industry. The law currently limits to a maximum of nine months the period for which an agency (known as the lessor) may hire an employee to an employer (known as the lessee). Agency employees are employed by the agency, which is responsible for payment of wages, deduction of tax and social security charges, holidays and sick pay, and for employment documents.

Fixed-term contracts between the agency and the employee are null and void, unless there are material grounds 'connected with the person of the employee'. If the agency terminates the employment relation with the employee, the termination will be null and void if it re-employs the worker within three months. If an unauthorised agency leases workers to an employer, an employment relation will be presumed to exist between the employee and the lessee.

Agency workers do not count as part of an establishment's workforce for the purpose of calculating the number of works council representatives. Works councils must be informed, however, if a company plans to use agency workers. Although there is no obligation to pay agency employees the same as core staff, this may be provided for by local agreement.

In all, there were some 160,000 agency employees at work in December 1995, an increase of 11 per cent on the previous year, with an especially marked rise of 35 per cent in East Germany. The sector employs about 300,000 people in any one year, compared with about 175,000 in the mid-1980s.

The duration of the average assignment is three months, and about one-third of employees are hired permanently on completion of their assignment. Some 80 per cent of agency employees are men working in skilled manual trades in the engineering industries.

There are two – closely co-operating – trade associations: the Bundesverband Zeitarbeit, which tends to lobby for the whole sector; and the Schutzgemeinschaft Zeitarbeit which requires member firms to pay into a fund to cover any failure to pay employees' social insurance contributions. All members of the Schutzgemeinschaft are also in the Bundesverband.

In the past, German trade unions were highly sceptical about the practice and worth of agency employment, which was regarded as a threat to established employees and not far short of the slave trade for those involved. However, under the pressure of high unemployment and a concerted and effective campaign by the agencies themselves, this negative view has been changing in recent years.

Anti-discrimination provisions

Sex equality

The Federal German Basic Law (1949) – the country's constitution – requires that no one be disadvantaged because of their sex, origin, race, language, home, creed, or religious and political beliefs. As noted above, similar provisions apply through the Works Constitution Act, under which a works council's agreement is required for appointments.

Article 3 (2) of the Basic Law states that: 'Men and women shall have equal rights'. This was amended in 1994 to incorporate a clause under which the state pledges itself to promote the implementation of equality between men and women and remove existing disadvantages. Federal Germany has also ratified ILO Conventions 100 and 111 which provide for equal pay and equal treatment at work. Under the 1980 European Community Adjustment Act, the Federal German Civil Code was amended to incorporate EC Directives on equal treatment. Article 611a of the Civil Code forbids discrimination against an employee in the sphere of appointments, promotion or dismissal, except where the gender of the prospective employee is directly relevant to the activity required and where a particular gender is an indispensable precondition for a particular job. Should an employee be able to show that a disadvantage on grounds of sex may be taking place, the burden of proof rests with the employer that any unequal treatment is justified on material grounds not related to the sex of the employee or that a particular gender is an indispensable requirement for the job.

Article 611b of the Civil Code requires employers to refrain from issuing job descriptions or job advertisements which specify a particular gender, unless a particular gender is an indispensable prerequisite. Under the terms of the Civil Code, a violation of the anti-discrimination provisions of Article 611a requires compensation. Following the 1984 rulings of the European Court of Justice in the cases of von Colson and Kamann *v.* North-Rhine Westphalia, and Harz *v.*

Deutsche Tradax GmbH, the German legislature – with some delay – acted to ensure that such compensation had to go beyond reimbursing out-of-pocket expenses, and constitute an effective deterrent to discrimination.

Under a 1994 amendment to article 611a of the Civil Code, discrimination in the course of recruitment will entitle the victim to compensation of up to three months' pay in the prospective job.

The issue of quotas for women has been hotly disputed. Federal legislation applicable in the public sector requires the setting of targets, but these are not binding on organisations. In contrast, at *Land* level there is legislation covering the public services which requires recruiters to appoint women if they have the same qualifications as men, and women are underrepresented in that area of employment. In some cases such legislation contains 'hardship clauses' which allow the provision to be overridden where a male candidate can demonstrate pressing social reasons for his appointment.

In the case of Kalanke *v.* Bremen, in which a man not appointed on these grounds contested the procedure, the ECJ ruled that legislation in Bremen, which provided for the *automatic* appointment of equally qualified women in areas where they were underrepresented, constituted sexual discrimination against male applicants by breaching the Directive on equal treatment.

However, provisions that contribute to strengthening women's position on the labour market to facilitate their promotion would not be in contravention of the Directive.

Quotas have not been employed in equal opportunities programmes in the private sector. However, EOPs have been discussed and agreed both at workplace level and with national industry unions: their status may also have to be re-examined in the light of the judgment if they contain any automatic elements.

People with disabilities

Special provisions apply in the case of disabled persons. Under the 1986 Severely Handicapped Persons Act, all private and public employers with at least 16 posts are required to employ handicapped persons in at least 6 per cent of these posts. 'Handicapped person' for the purposes of the Act is any person suffering at least a 50 per cent disability: persons with a 30 per cent to 50 per cent disability may apply to the local employment office for treatment on the same footing as persons with a 50 per cent disability. Employers who fail to fill their prescribed number of reserved posts are obliged to pay a sum in compensation – currently DM 200 (£80) per month – for each unfilled place. Under Section 14 of the Act employers are required to examine whether any of their vacancies could be filled by a severely handicapped person.

Applications from severely handicapped persons are to be discussed with severely handicapped persons' representatives, elected under the Act. Funds are available under the Act for adapting workplaces to the needs of severely handicapped persons and for covering exceptional expenses in connection with their employment. Fines up to DM 5,000 (£2,000) may be imposed for non-compliance with the Act.

The Federal Labour Authority produces a magazine, *Gut Drauf*, on employment for people with disabilities.

Finding the applicant

This section sets out the main routes by which employers can find staff. Although the shortages of skills seen in the late 1980s, which led many firms to intensify their recruitment efforts and make themselves attractive for career starters through active 'Personnel marketing', has become less acute, the search for high-quality candidates, especially graduates, has meant that this approach remains an important element in personnel strategies.

The total cost of recruiting a qualified employee was DM 28,000 (£10,700) in 1993, of which just under half were induction costs after appointment.

Poaching

The issue of poaching (*Abwerbung*) is regulated by the Law on Unfair Competition (*Gesetz gegen den unlauteren Wettbewerb*) and by Paragraph 826 of the Civil Code. Poaching, as such, is not unlawful. It becomes so if it violates 'good morals'. This would, for example, automatically include inducement to breach the contract of employment – either by breaching notice or offering inducements to make off with confidential documentation. However, there may be a situation in which civil damages might be payable even if notice periods and other contractual terms were adhered to. These might include exerting undue or 'reprehensible' influence, for example by intruding into the employee's private life, making promises which the prospective employer does not intend to keep, or referring to impending redundancies in the current employer's business. Intent to destroy a competitor's business by raiding an entire layer of management or acquire confidential material could also constitute a violation of 'good morals'.

Poaching could also collide with any prospective employees' restrictive covenants on competition with the former employer, and the German courts have been prepared to enforce these. An employer may have to buy out a restrictive covenant or accept a transition period of less than full effectiveness. Exiting employees have also reportedly struck deals not to raid their old departments, in return for being freed from working out notice.

Application documents

Application documents typically include:

- a handwritten letter of application

- a curriculum vitae (*Lebenslauf*), and often a photograph
- school, work or educational and training records, including any placements whilst studying, and leaving certificates (*Arbeitszeugnis*). Employees are entitled to a leaving certificate from their employer, which must include the basic facts about their employment but may, if the employee wishes, include an assessment of their conduct and performance. The leaving certificate must be true but must not unnecessarily impede the career progress of the employee
- other references.

If the company wishes to use an application form, works council consent must be obtained. Some specialists recommend using agreed application forms to avoid subsequent complications with works councils, to simplify and streamline the subsequent pre-selection and interview, and to allow personal questions to be raised – such as illnesses or previous convictions – which might cause embarrassment in a face-to-face meeting.

Data protection

Data protection is provided for by statute law (*Bundesdatenschutzgesetz*), most recently amended in 1990, and the protection of personnel data is also covered by the 1972 Works Constitution Act. There may also be legislation at *Land* level on data protection and privacy in the public sector: in some case these impose additional limitations on the use of certain types of testing for recruitment purposes, and are generally more stringent. 'Data' covers all information on employees, whether manually or electronically stored. Employees have rights of access, and a right to have incorrect entries rectified or deleted. They may also attach their own comments.

Employers may store data on applicants. In general, however, personal data must be returned and/or deleted from computer systems following rejection, unless the employer has a legitimate interest in holding it: however, according to the courts, this covers situations such as a delay in the procedure or impending legal proceedings. Simply hanging on to data as a means of creating a pool of potential future applicants is not allowed without the candidate's express permission.

Placement services

Until 1994 the Federal Employment Service enjoyed a placement monopoly for full-time posts, with the exception of executive recruitment where the activities of search companies were tolerated by the authorities on the basis of an accord which delimited their operations. The position changed fundamentally in August 1994, when the official monopoly was removed, theoretically allowing agencies to engage in permanent placement and charge employers, but not employees, a fee. However, permanent placement via private agencies has yet to take off, with recession and personnel managers' concern about maintaining their own departments intact weakening the need and desire to involve outside agencies: the state system remains by far the dominant force in placement. Private agencies did not expect to make more than 15,000 placements in 1996. This compares with the 1.7 million placements made for more than one week's employment via the state system in 1994 in West Germany, and 750,000 in the East. The new agencies, most of which have been in business as temporary agencies, are keen to overcome some residual suspicion of private businesses operating as 'middlemen' on the labour market, some of which was fuelled by the poor reputation that temporary employment had in the past.

The official employment service

The official employment service is run by the Federal Employment Office (Bundesanstalt für Arbeit, BfA), with its headquarters in Nuremberg. Its management board consists of union, employer and official representatives. The BfA offers a wide range of services both to employers and work seekers, the vast majority of which are provided entirely free of charge. Services include:

- placement, including full placement service through its network of 184 local employment exchanges. As well as conventional placement services, each exchange has an on-line self-service facility for employers and job seekers, *Stellen-Informations-Service*, known as SIS; information about candidates can also be accessed by employers via the service provider T-Online under **Arbeitsamt#*.
- training, career counselling, including a service for school and college leavers
- occupational health care, including a capacity rating service for the disabled
- psychological testing
- a vacancies and job seekers' weekly publication *Markt + Chance*.

The BfA, which is funded jointly from employer and employee levies together with a subsidy from the Federal government, is also responsible for paying and administering unemployment benefits. It also embraces a well-regarded research institute, the Institute für Arbeitsmarkt- und Berufsforschung (IAB).

There is no obligation on employers to accept candidates suggested by the BfA. Specialist services offered by the BfA include the provision of temporary staff (see also *Employment agencies* below), supply of staff for trade fairs, and an executive and specialist service (see below).

The state service is fairly well regarded by employers, although the recent rise in unemployment and cuts in the BfA's budget have stretched its resources and are likely to do so even more in the future.

State placement service for managers and specialists The service for managerial employees, ZAV, operates from Frankfurt. There is also a service for specialists, FVD, with local offices in a number of large cities with universities. Many of these are being closed down and replaced with '*Hochschulzentren*', concentrating on graduates from harder-to-place disciplines.

The ZAV's services include:

- information on executive labour markets, by sector and function
- preparation of job descriptions and contact with managers on the ZAV's books. (According to the ZAV, some two-thirds of managers registered with them are not unemployed or working out notice.)
- formulation and placing of advertisements (with advertising charged to the client by the advertising medium)
- pre-selection and presentation of candidates.

There are specific departments dealing with individual sectors, as well as a service for international placements which makes use of the EURES service. Specialist departments deal with entertainers, film crew, hotel staff, and sailors.

The national management placement service employs 50 consultants and handles about 600 placements a year.

Employment agencies

Under legislation in force since 1994, private employment agencies may operate for both permanent and temporary employment, subject to various regulations. Most agencies have a background in temporary employment, and have yet to build up their permanent placement businesses – something made difficult by the slack labour market and downsizing during the past few years.

The most common placement method is to offer candidates who are already on the agency's books, most of whom are usually not unemployed but are looking for a change. The agency will carry out some pre-selection, and test candidates if the employer asks for this. In practice, according to one agency manager, tests are rare, apart from on-the-job assessments conducted by the employer.

Agencies normally charge employers one-and-a-half to two months' gross salary in the position for a successful placement, and offer guarantees. (The law limits the fee to 12 per cent of annual gross salary for the post.)

The trade organisation for employment agencies is the Bundesverband Personalvermittlung e.V. (Federal Association of Personnel Recruitment Agencies), whose address is given at the end of the chapter.

Executive recruitment consultants

The use of consultants in the recruitment process has grown substantially over the past 15 years or so. On one estimate, about 35 per cent of all job advertisements in the media were under the name of a consultant rather than the prospective employer. And about half of all executive recruitment – and even higher for the top two levels of management, where search is predominant – is now carried out with the participation of consultants.

Recruitment consultants – termed 'personnel consultants' (*Personalberater*) – working in the area of executive recruitment have been allowed to operate for many years, despite the placement monopoly previously exercised by the state system, subject to a number of guidelines agreed between the BfA and the main recruitment consultants' organisations.

The situation changed in 1991, however, when the BfA's formal monopoly in the area of executive recruitment was ruled by the European Court of Justice to be in contravention of EC law, followed in 1994 by the abolition of the ban on employment agencies for permanent placement. However, consultants who wish to practise placement may do so if they obtain a licence from the authorities. The need for licensing under the new legislation has deterred some recruitment agencies from registering as such: they prefer to continue as 'consultants' in order to minimise administrative formalities. Some consultants also lay great weight on being client-driven, not candidate-driven – that is, working on an employer consultancy assignment rather than offloading people from pre-existing databases.

Many recruitment consultants – but not all, and especially excluding some of the larger search organisations – are members of the Federation of German Management Consultants (Bund Deutscher Unternehmensberater, BDU), which has a specialist group for personnel consultants. The BDU operates a code of ethics for the conduct of its members, and publishes a guide to all affiliated firms. There is also a smaller organisation specifically of personnel consultants, the Arbeitskreis der Personalberater in Deutschland (see the end of the chapter for addresses of both organisations).

Executive search and selection is well developed in Germany, with about 1,000 recruitment consultants in operation – although about one-third are small operations, often with a single consultant.

In general, positions advertised above DM 175,000 a year (£70,000) would be handled via executive search only. Positions in the range DM 90,000–200,000 (£36,000–£80,000) would be filled by a mixture of search and selection by a consultant.

In theory, fees for consultancy should be fixed and not contingency-based – although the legal basis for this was weakened by the 1991 ECJ ruling. In practice, they usually run at 25–30 per cent of the annual salary: one-third is paid as a retainer, one-third on presenting a short-list, and the final instalment on payment. However, many firms are pushing for end-loading, with half in advance and a half on successful appointment.

A number of search consultancies have sought and obtained certification under DIN EN ISO 9001.

Recruitment media

The press

Press advertising is widely used for all categories of employee. German papers are highly regionalised, with local supplements in those regional papers which have built a national readership. Purely local and regional papers (or the local supplements of national papers) are used for blue-collar and clerical jobs. However, German regionalism and the large circulation of the regional press means that these are often also used for managers and specialists. The main newspapers used for job advertisements are as follows:

- The daily *Frankfurter Allgemeine Zeitung* (*FAZ*), which has national coverage, remains the predominant vehicle.
- The daily *Süddeutsche Zeitung* (*SZ*), based in Munich but with national circulation, is important for jobs at specialist and manager level in South Germany – especially for jobs in electronics, which is concentrated in the Munich-Augsburg area.
- *Karriere* is the Friday supplement to the main business daily *Handelsblatt*; abbreviated versions of the same advertisements appear in its mid-week editions. *Handelsblatt* has a Web page with access both to *Karriere* advertisements and *Junge Karriere* which is aimed at graduates (http://www.handelsblatt.de).
- The national daily *Die Welt*.
- The daily *Frankfurter Rundschau*, which has national coverage, but regional sections for the Frankfurt (Rhine-Main) area.

There are many other important regional papers which cover their local labour markets, with positions at all levels.

Specialist journals include *VDI-Nachrichten* (for engineers), *Computerwoche* (which carries job advertisements in computing), and *Markt und Technik* (for electronics specialists). Personnel positions are advertised in *Personalführung*, the monthly journal of the personnel management association DGFP. (Selected addresses of publications are included at the end of the chapter.)

Employers may not advertise vacancies for men or women only, unless a specific gender is an indispensable prerequisite. Age limits may be specified, although most employers will accept ±10 per cent of the limit if a good candidate comes forward or is proposed by a consultant. Salaries are almost never indicated. Vacancies are usually advertised under the company name, except where a consultant is being used, although anonymous advertisements with a code number may be found for some executive positions. However, anonymous advertising using a code number only – that is, without the option of getting more information from a consultant – is regarded as bad practice, as it does not allow a potential applicant to make an informed choice about whether to proceed with an application.

Trade fairs

Trade fairs have become an important forum at which employers and prospective managerial and specialist employees can get together, and these events are also sometimes used by recruitment consultants – especially those who are also active more widely in business consultancy.

Details of the main trade fairs, including costs, can be obtained from the Confederation of Trade Fair and Exhibition Industries (AUMA – see the end of the chapter).

The main fairs are: CeBIT (information technology and telecommunications, Hanover), the International Motor Show IAA (Frankfurt), the Hanover Industry Fair, Drupa (printing and paper) and IGEDO (fashion) in Düsseldorf, Systems and electronics (computers and components) and Bau (building materials) both in Munich. However, there are many specialist fairs which graduates in search of employment will use as opportunities. Some further details can be obtained from the publications for engineers and for general management produced under the overall rubric *START* by the Institut für Berufs- und Ausbildungsplanung, Cologne (see the end of the chapter).

The Internet

Internet advertising, mostly using either job exchanges on the World Wide Web or company own home-pages is growing rapidly, especially where companies are looking for technical employees or employees who otherwise match the profile of typical Internet users. Banks, media concerns, and computer companies have been among the most active. Some on-line exchanges report up to 200,000 visits a month.

The service provider T-Online carries job information, including vacancies and details of job seekers, for the state employment service under the title *Arbeitsamt#*.

There are a number of electronic job exchanges (*Stellenbörse*) on which vacancies can be listed, although the quality of information and the frequency of updating have been subject to criticism. Some reproduce vacancy columns published elsewhere. Among those that are well regarded, with addresses, are Adia (adia#), Arbeitsmarkt total (*2206601#), the official employment service, BfA, in the regions of Hamburg, Bochum and Leipzig (*69100#), E-span (http://www.espan.com/), Jobstar (*24088 05#), Jobs & Adverts (http://www.jobs.adverts.de) and Karriere direkt (*karriere direkt and http://www.karrieredirekt.de), which contains jobs advertised in the previous month in *Handelsblatt*, *VDI-Nachrichten*, and *Der Betrieb*. The Institute for Data Processing (*Fachverband für Datenverarbeitung*) maintains a web site with vacancies in IT and data processing under http://www.dv-job.de/. A typical advertisement with an electronic jobs exchange costs DM 300-900 (£120–£360) a month. Some larger employers, especially in the electronics field, also put vacancies on their company's home-page on the Internet.

Special employment grants and employment incentives

Local pockets of structural unemployment in West Germany, combined with the economic consequences of unification, have generated a range of schemes intended to promote job creation, assist in finding employment for hard-to-place social groups, and cushion the employment shock of the entry of the ex-GDR into the market system.

For example, wage subsidies are payable to employers for hiring hard-to-place employees on work associated with improving the environment, providing social services or help to young people. 'Hard-to-place' is defined as people with disabilities, those over 50 or under 25 years of age who have been out of work for at least three months, and those experiencing or facing long-term unemployment. The subsidy will be paid only if the agreed wage does not exceed 90 per cent of the usual agreed wage for that type of work.

In areas affected by higher than average unemployment, wage subsidies of up to 50 per cent to 70 per cent of agreed minimum rates are payable; this can rise to 90 per cent in areas with an unemployment average more than 30 per cent higher than the national average if the employer hires difficult-to-place workers. Subsidies are payable only for employees placed by the official labour exchanges: potential employees have to be unemployed, or have been unemployed for at least six months in the last twelve months, and the employment authorities can recall any employee if they have found them a permanent job or a training place.

Grants for hiring older employees are payable where:

- the person concerned is at least 55 years old
- the person is unemployed or has been unemployed for at least twelve of the previous 18 months.

The grants, which initially may range from 50 per cent to 70 per cent of pay, are progressively reduced each year by at least 10 per cent of pay down to a minimum of 30 per cent; the subsidy ends at the end of the year in which the grant reaches the 30 per cent minimum.

Grants are also available for covering the costs of formerly or potentially unemployed people's induction periods, if additional training is needed to enable them to take up a particular post.

Loans or grants can also be made to the unemployed, or those threatened by imminent redundancy, to enable them to travel to find work, for removals, for buying working clothes or equipment, and to cover other expenses should the family be temporarily separated.

Details of schemes can be obtained from the Bundesanstalt für Arbeit.

Selection procedures

According to a survey of selection methods carried out in 1990, the most common procedures used were as follows:

Procedure	Frequency of use
Analysis of application documents	98%
Additional references	71%
Structured interview with personnel department	70%
Unstructured interview with personnel department	57%
Structured interview with prospective department	49%
Unstructured interview with prospective department	69%
Group discussion	51%
Personality test	21%
Aptitude test	47%
Intelligence test	34%
Ability test	44%
Biographical questionnaire	21%
Assessment centre	39%
Graphology	9%
Medical examination	64%

Source: Schuler *et al, Personalauswahl im europäischen Vergleich*, p. 34.

Other sources confirm that the interview remains the central element in the selection process. Most consultants are sceptical about tests, but will organise them if clients want them. In larger organisations the personnel department still plays a major role in the assessment of application documents and in guiding line managers in the process of selection. Surveys suggest that staff from the personnel department typically attend interviews together with managers to whom the employee will report. According to some practitioners, demand for psychological testing by employers is less now than in the recent past.

Selection guidelines

Any guidelines for selection must be approved by works councils, where elected. If no agreement is reached, either side can apply for a binding ruling from a conciliation committee (see also above, p. 113). Guidelines may include such factors as education, work experience, family size and competence as established by test in the selection process. (Works councils also have a right of co-determination over employee appraisal systems.)

The main legal framework for selection is provided by constitutional principles which guarantee the inviolability of the person, individual dignity and the development of the personality. These have been developed by the courts in particular in the area of the right to privacy – which may have an impact on checking references and background.

There is an obligation on employers to provide accurate and relevant information on the nature of the job, in particular any associated health risks, and any aspects, such as frequent travel, which might prove especially exacting.

Employer's right to ask

Recruitment specialists often recommend the use of an application form, both as a time-saving device and to ensure that certain questions have been put to candidates: this may be of importance, should the employer later wish to contest that the contract of employment was based on false or incomplete statements by the applicant.

The courts have also shaped the law on the conduct of interviews. The general principles outlined below may not always be precisely applicable to an individual situation, where a different combination of factors and respective interests might apply.

In general, interviews may include only questions which are relevant to the job (training, qualification etc), and may not impinge on politics or the political views of an applicant's university teachers, for example. Employers are not entitled to enquire about matters which could lead to discrimination under Article 75 of the Works Constitution Act. This would rule out, for example, questions of political affiliation, trade union membership, or religious belief, except where these are of direct relevance to the proposed employment (such as employment with a trade union). Membership or non-membership of a trade union may not be a condition of employment.

The courts have upheld an applicant's right not to divulge their previous salary where this is held to be of no relevance to the current application, for example where pay rates are largely set by collective agreement. This principle is unlikely to apply to more senior appointments, and especially where salary is an important indicator of performance and achievement (as in sales), or where the candidate has implied that the reason for changing job is to increase the salary.

On the issue of pregnancy, the German courts are bound by the principles set out in the Dekker case heard by the European Court of Justice. Under this ruling, any less favourable treatment of a woman on grounds of pregnancy is automatically sex discrimination, irrespective of whether or not there is a male comparator. Asking whether a woman is pregnant during an application is intended solely to exclude her from employment and, as such, the question is impermissible. The only exception is where there is a statutory ban against employing pregnant women in the advertised post.

On the question of illness, the general test would be the relevance of the illness to the proposed employment and the reasonableness of any possible burden on an employer. There is no requirement to provide information on illnesses from which the employee has long since recovered and which have no after-effects. Opinion holds that candidates are not obliged to disclose their HIV status, and must give an answer only if this might be relevant to their employment. An 'AIDS test', to establish whether an applicant is HIV positive, is permissible for those applying for the status of established civil servant with life-long tenure. In other cases a test for, or question as to, HIV status is generally impermissible. However, an applicant may be asked whether they are suffering from an acute form of the AIDS syndrome. An applicant suffering from AIDS would be expected to inform a prospective employer. Simply agreeing to a blood test as part of a medical examination does not imply consent for a test for HIV status, and such a test would be impermissible without the candidate's consent. As with all medical examinations, a physician is entitled to state only whether an applicant is fit for the position, not their HIV status. (Being ill with AIDS would not qualify an applicant as suitable for employment.)

Applicants with a disability must inform the employer where this is of relevance for the proposed tasks, but not otherwise. Employers have a generalised right to ask about any disability. Questions about an applicant's genetic predisposition to illness are impermissible.

The prospective employer should not ask about the marital status of the applicant at an early state of application (although this interpretation is disputed by some legal authorities). This information would, however, later be needed for tax purposes.

On matters such as previous criminal convictions or personal financial situation, the employer's right to ask will depend on the nature of the prospective employment, and is fairly narrowly restricted. For example, a potential truck driver can be asked about previous traffic offences, or a cashier about previous convictions for embezzlement. A prospective employee can claim to be free of previous convictions if the period after which they lapse has been completed. An employer may not generally request a police certificate of conduct (*Führungszeugnis*) as this might contain more information about the employee than is directly relevant to the prospective employment; however, these are important in a wide range of positions. Imposed sentences are removed from the certificate of conduct after five years. In general, the more senior the post, the more an employer may ask.

Medical examinations and candidate testing

Medical examinations, graphological or psychological tests, and genetic testing are covered by the same principles as the employer's right to information. In the case of graphological and personality tests, the applicant must be informed of, and consent to, the test; the test must seek only to ascertain characteristics relevant to the proposed employment. It is therefore impermissible to use a handwritten application for a graphological test – the employer is liable to civil proceedings for damages if he impinges on the individual's right to privacy through such a test. Aptitude tests for the proposed employment are permissible, but prevailing opinion holds that pure IQ tests are not permissible as they do not have direct relevance to an employment.

There is great scepticism about the ethics of personality testing, not to mention their efficacy. The possibility of recourse to the law in the face of an unfairly administered test, or a deliberately stressful test, is of little use in most circumstances. However, some control over such tests can be exercised in companies with works councils, which have a number of consultation and co-determination rights in this area (see above).

There is some evidence that candidates educated in the former GDR may not perform as well in aptitude tests as their Western counterparts, although differential performance is being eroded as the culture and practices of the West are absorbed. Testing was regarded as 'bourgeois psychology' in the GDR, and work practices in GDR organisations also favoured working with precision, even if this took longer.

In principle, only the candidate's fitness for the particular employment may be communicated to the employer; however, broader information about the candidate's general state of health can be reported with the express permission of the applicant, and this may be simply accepted as part of the preconditions for participating in the selection process. A certificate of medical fitness is mandatory for people under 18 entering employment.

References, in the form of a leaving certificate, are a standard part of all applications and must be provided by the previous employer on request. As noted above, they must be true but must not serve to impede the career of the employee. As a result, they are regarded very sceptically by employers, who have turned unearthing the true meaning of references behind the veil of words into a high art. Guides to recruitment often offer 'translations' to enable personnel specialists – and candidates – to gauge the real feelings of the previous employer. There are codes for conveying confidential information about an employees' personal behaviour and sexuality, extending, allegedly, even to deliberately placed – but innocent-looking – blotches on the certificate to indicate whether the employee was an active trade unionist. It is regarded as bad practice to obtain additional references without the express permission of the candidate.

Whether information can be obtained from a third party depends on the nature of the job, and any rules governing information disclosure by other organisations and agencies. There is no general prohibition on obtaining additional information about a candidate from a former employer, but this must not infringe data protection legislation or the basic right of privacy.

Assessment centres

Assessment centres were originally an invention of the Prussian military, exported to the USA in the 1920s, and re-imported by US multinationals during the 1950s. A number of large German companies now run them, as well as large consultancies that offer them to employers. They are a common approach where fairly large numbers of applicants, such as graduates, need to be exposed to systematically comparable selection exercises.

Rejection of candidates

There are differing opinions on how a rejection should be formulated, and whether those not appointed should be offered detailed grounds or advice. Prevailing legal opinion is that no reason should be given as this opens the way to possible complaint – legal or other – from the rejected applicants.

Appointment of employees

Works council consent

In workplaces with more than 20 employees and where the workforce has elected a works council, the employer must obtain approval: i) for any standard forms used for contracts of employment, ii) of any proposed appointment at least a week in advance, including fixed-term contracts, trainees, and temporary workers. The employer must provide details of the individual, proposed task and grade, and application documents.

This requirement does not apply to board members, managing directors or executives (*leitende Angestellten*). Nevertheless, the employer must still inform the works council executive representation committee.

Works councils may object to the appointment, and the employer may not initially proceed if the objection is lodged because the appointment:

- breaches a law, regulation, court ruling, or agreed guideline
- may prejudice the interests of existing employees, or involves an employee who could disrupt 'industrial peace' at the workplace
- was made without prior internal notification.

The employer may obtain a labour court ruling to overturn the objection. If the court backs the works council, but the employer nevertheless proceeds, the court may impose fines of up DM 500 (£200) per day of the violation. There are procedures which allow appointments to be made urgently, with subsequent consultation with the works council.

The area of appointments (along with transfer and regrading) is an important sphere in which works councils possess considerable latent and actual power, and effectively oblige the employer to share traditional prerogatives on the firm's 'internal labour market'. This power can also be used to slow up other areas of managerial decision-making, should the works council feel that its interests are being neglected or overridden.

Formalities

Before beginning employment, the employee must present to the employer: their tax card for PAYE (*Lohnsteuerkarte*); their social security pass (*Sozialversicherungsausweis*); proof of holiday already taken (*Urlaubsbescheinigung*); for some occupations, for example in the food industry, a medical certificate (*Gesundheitsattest*).

Contesting the appointment

Any party to a contract can bring an action to have the contract nullified if it was brought about through 'malicious deception': the party wishing to void the contract must do so within a year of discovering any misrepresentation, but can have the contract nullified up to 30 years after the deception. As noted above, prospective employees do not have to remain silent if asked an 'impermissible' question. They may, on some legal opinion, give an incorrect answer without legal prejudice to their employee rights if appointed (sometimes dubbed the 'right to lie'). That is, if the employer discovered that the answer was incorrect, the employee could not be summarily dismissed for 'malicious deception'.

Education system

The system of education and many aspects of vocational training are the responsibility of the constituent *Länder* of the Federal Republic. At primary or secondary level there may be differences between the *Länder*, with a more traditional curriculum in Bavaria and more 'progressive' approach in Central and Northern Germany. The vast majority of children, about 98 per cent at primary level and 91 per cent at secondary, go to state schools. This has been attributed both to the overall quality of schooling and the fact that the system contains a large measure of selection, with little pressure to go to the private sector to find traditional academically-oriented education. None the less, of the 3.7 million school students in Germany between the ages of 11 and 17, some 800,000 are estimated to receive supplementary private teaching after school hours, which is sometimes no more than supervised homework – reflecting the early finishing time of schools. The number of pupils in full-time private education grew by 10 per cent between 1990 and 1995.

Compulsory education begins in the year in which children complete their sixth year, and continues for nine or 10 years, depending on the *Land*. Transition from primary to secondary school may take place either from the fifth or sixth year, again depending on *Land*. However, young people who leave school at 15 are required by law to continue some form of education, which may be as part of initial vocational training, until aged 18.

Secondary education

There is selection at the transition to secondary education, based on examination results and teacher assessments. In most *Länder* there are three types of secondary school: the *Gymnasium*, which takes the more academically-gifted; the *Realschule* which offers intermediate-level secondary education, with most of its pupils going directly into vocational training after obtaining a school-leaving certificate (the *Mittlere Reife*); and the *Hauptschule*, which takes lower-ability pupils, most of whom leave at 15 and who can undertake a one-year preparatory vocational course, the *Berufsgrundbildungsjahr*, prior to entering initial vocational training. In some *Länder*, most notably in Berlin, comprehensive schools (*Gesamtschulen*) have been established, although these tend to exist alongside other types of school rather than displacing them. Approximately 30 per cent of pupils are in *Gymnasien*, 30 per cent in a *Realschule*, 35 per cent in a *Hauptschule* and 6 per cent in a comprehensive school.

Initially, only an education at a *Gymnasium* confers a qualification which gives a right to enter a university. This is the *Abitur* exam, which is taken by about a quarter of all school students, typically at age 19. The syllabus is both rigorous and broad. Most pupils take two core subjects but must, in addition, study a foreign language and either maths or a physical science, as well as other subjects. The final mark, which may influence university entrance, is based on examination results and course progress.

However, there are other routes, via vocational training plus supplementary study, which offer access to tertiary education either at a university or a polytechnic. It is possible to study for the *Abitur* at nightschool (*Abendgymnasium*) as an adult. A group of *Länder* have also established *Telekolleg*, a form of distance learning via TV to enable individuals to obtain entry to a polytechnic.

Determining what qualifications and study may be regarded as equivalent to the *Abitur* is a matter for the individual *Länder*.

Higher education

There are two basic types of higher education institution in Germany. Full universities (which may be called *Universität*, *Technische Universität* or *Technische Hochschule*) and polytechnics (*Fachhochschule*). The latter offer shorter and more vocationally-oriented courses, and can be entered directly with a leaving qualification from some forms of vocational training (notably the *Fachoberschulreife*), as well as with the *Abitur*.

There is continuing discussion around widening the entrance requirements for entry into university to include a broader range of vocational training qualifications. At present, individuals with a vocational training qualification can attend a range of courses, including evening classes at a *Gymnasium*, to acquire the equivalent of the *Abitur* and gain entrance to university (the so-called 'second route' to higher education). The individual *Länder* determine how this is implemented, and can set entrance exams or other selection criteria for university entrance.

Students attend university for much longer than in the UK, with an average of five to six years to first degree at a university, although four years are more the norm at a polytechnic.

Students are generally financed by parents, or they work during studies (and in vacations). There is a system of student loans for students from lower-income families, and about 400,000 students are in receipt of loans.

Universities   In theory, possession of the *Abitur* confers the right not only to enter higher education but also to have freedom to study – irrespective of earlier specialisation. In practice, the large numbers of young people passing the *Abitur* compared with the limited places available for some popular specialisms have led universities to introduce a form of selection, the *numerus clausus*, in which certain *Abitur* grades are required. Whether courses need to be regulated by selection, and how this is organised, is decided by a central inter-*Land* body, the ZVS (*Zentralstelle für Vergabe von Studienplätzen*). The *numerus clausus* operates especially in vocationally-oriented university courses such as architecture, medicine, veterinary science, dentistry, and since 1990 also in management science (*Betriebswirtschaftlehre*). At about 30 per cent, drop-out rates tend to be higher in the arts subjects where there is no *numerus clausus*. Overall, according to OECD figures, 87 per cent of students are still attending higher education three years after matriculation.

As well as the state-run universities, there are also a large number of private higher education institutions, some of which provide technical or business education (a guide is available from the Federal Ministry of Education and Science). These include a branch of the European Business School at Oestrich-Winkel, the Koblenz School of Management, a banking college (*Hochschule für Bankwirtschaft*) in Frankfurt, the Private University of Witten/Herdecke, and numerous specialist institutions in technical areas and design.

There is no established hierarchy of universities in Germany. Meagre state support for students means that many continue to live at or near their homes, and the relative dispersion of the population into a number of conurbations has therefore encouraged strong, well-regarded universities throughout the country. However, individual departments or professors may acquire a strong reputation and these may be sought out both by prospective students and employers.

A number of magazines, such as *Stern*, *Der Spiegel* and *Manager-magazin*, have commissioned opinion surveys to rank universities, both in general and for particular specialisms: the results have not always coincided. According to the *Spiegel* survey, carried out in 1993, the top five West German universities were: Düsseldorf, Duisburg GH, Konstanz, Siegen GH and Bielefeld. In East Germany, high ratings were given to Ilmenau Technical University, Bergakademie Freiberg, Dresden Technical University, Berlin (Humboldt) and Jena. For engineering faculties in both Germany and Switzerland, the highest rankings, according to *Manager-magazin*, were given to the Technical University Aachen, the Federal

Technical University Zurich, Karlsruhe Technical University, Darmstadt Technical University, and Stuttgart University.

Polytechnics The polytechnics (*Fachhochschulen*, FH) were established in the late 1960s, and account for some 12 per cent of students in West Germany. Although established only after unification in the East, by the mid-1990s they accounted for 15 per cent there. There are plans to expand this sector, and the university authorities have indicated a target of 40 per cent of all students to be in *Fachhochschulen* by 2010.

FH graduates generally attract slightly lower starting salaries than university graduates; however, the more practical and directed nature of their education, the effective use of work placements, and the fact that many polytechnic students have completed initial vocational training makes them attractive to many employers, especially in small and medium-sized companies. Recruitment from them is forecast to grow more rapidly in the engineering field than from universities over the coming decade. Drop-out rates are lower, and the overall period of study is shorter – at six to eight semesters compared with the 10 to 12 semesters of university education.

On completion of their course (see below), polytechnic students can move to university with credits for courses.

Distance learning universities

It is possible to obtain an academic qualification either at university or polytechnic level through distance learning at a Distance Learning ('Open') University (*Fernuniversität*). The Fernuniversität Hagen is the only public university-level provider. It was founded in 1975 and in 1993 had some 52,000 registered students on part-time courses. There is also a private university offering similar courses, the Akademikergesellschaft für Erwachsenenbildung. Many students already have a first degree or professional qualification and use distance learning to add a dimension, such as business studies or economics for engineers.

Higher education qualifications

Degree subjects are divided into two phases: a foundation period (*Grundstudium*) of four to five semesters leading to an intermediate qualification, the *Vordiplom*; this is followed by the main degree course, lasting usually a minimum of four semesters, but typically longer. The first degree-level qualification awarded in universities in most specialisms is the *Diplom* (written Dipl.Ing., Dipl. Kaufmann., etc.) In certain areas of study where the main employer is the state, such as teaching, students take a qualification termed the *Staatsexamen* instead. In some arts subjects, universities may offer an MA (*Magister Artium*) as an alternative to the *Staatsexamen* for students who do not wish to enter public employment.

The polytechnics award a *Diplom* for all courses, which is usually written as Dipl. (FH) to distinguish it from a university diploma.

Both universities and polytechnics offer courses in management science, with the qualification of either *Diplom-Kaufmann* or *Diplom-Betriebswirtschaft*. Business studies combined with engineering, leading to the qualification as *Wirtschaftsingenieur*, are also a common starting point for careers in management. (See also *Management training* below.)

The *Diplom* usually entails preparation of a dissertation, some examinations and an oral exam. Choice of the dissertation subject (with research in some areas carried out during a company placement – with subsequent useful contacts) may be important in later recruitment into management positions.

Post-graduate work leading to a doctorate is confined to universities, and German output of doctoral graduates is considerably higher than in the UK. Doctoral qualifications are widely found among senior public figures and managers of very large enterprises, especially in technical fields, and PhDs in some fields can command a substantial salary premium on initial appointment.

MBAs may be taught and examined in Germany, but can be conferred by a German educational institution only if they match the standards of a German university education. Representatives of foreign business schools operating in Germany may confer the title: this is the most common way of obtaining MBAs, and there are numerous German 'campuses' of foreign universities or business schools.

The only fully accredited MBA courses taught in German tertiary educational institutions are at the University of Saarland, and at the Armed Services University in Munich, in association with Henley Management College. Most German students or managers wanting an MBA would normally be advised to look outside Germany, both for range of study options and to add an international dimension to their careers.

Criticisms and reform proposals

German universities have been described as 'the weak link in German education . . . mostly overcrowded, inefficient and dispiriting for students' (*Financial Times*, 6 September 1991). The basic difficulty stems from a combination of a tradition of liberal education, with extensive freedom for students to choose and switch subjects, long study periods of up to seven years to first degree level (often necessitated by the need to finance study through periodic paid work), and increasing numbers of school students passing the *Abitur*.

Drop-out rates are quite high – although not as high as in France or Italy. In 1992, the most recent year for which figures were available, 136,000 students left without completing a degree – at an estimated cost of some DM 4.9 billion (£2 billion) to the university system.

There is also concern that the conditions at many universities have meant that foreign students have not been sufficiently attracted to German higher education.

Proposals for reform from various quarters include:

- opportunities for shortening or speeding up the period of study, in particular for more vocationally-oriented courses, including slimming down the curricula in some areas
- greater opportunities for subsequent development to complement shorter study periods
- rationalisation of administrative and political frameworks, and generally tighter management of physical and human resources (ie professors)
- more rigorous selection at university entrance to cut down overall numbers and reduce the drop-out rate.

Legislation was scheduled to be brought forward during 1997 to shorten study periods to a maximum of four years at polytechnics and four-and-a-half years at universities. A finance package was also agreed in 1996 to create better post-graduate research facilities, promote multi-media and distance learning projects, promote equal opportunities for women staff members, and prepare for the fact that 50 per cent of all professors will have had to retire by the year 2005.

Graduate recruitment

Graduates and career starters in Germany tend to be older than in the UK – a factor also expressed in higher German graduate starting salaries. A German graduate with a first degree is, on average, nearly 28 years old, against 22 in Britain. The main reasons are: later school starting and leaving ages; military service – now 10 months, or the alternative of 13 months' community service; longer period of higher education, with an average of seven years of study.

Emerging graduate shortages in the late 1980s, and the prospects of a demographic squeeze in the 1990s, induced many companies to develop high-profile strategies, known as 'personnel marketing', to find and recruit graduates. The recession of the early 1990s, and the tentative recovery since then, initially led to marked cutbacks in, and greater targeting of, recruitment activity – with the emphasis varying by sector and how well it is flourishing. Student course selection also tends to show a lagged reaction to previous downturns: enrolment in engineering fell markedly after the 1993 recession, with an increase in law, economics and the liberal arts. 'Personnel marketing' has now been redefined to policies to narrow down selection from a smaller pool of high-quality graduates, using industrial placements (*Praktika*) to make initial assessments.

The current main methods of graduate recruitment are:

- newspaper advertising, including specialist journals or supplements aimed at graduates and published by some of the main quality or business dailies. Publications worth noting are: *Junge Karriere*, a supplement published each semester in *Handelsblatt*, and available on the World Wide Web; *Forum*, published by DSV Studenten Verlag GmbH based in St. Gallen, Switzerland; and *Allgemeiner Hochschul-Anzeiger* produced by the *Frankfurter Allgemeine Zeitung*.

- company visits to campuses, including presentations, exchanges and 'contact exchanges' organised on campus by student organisations
- industrial placements ('internships') during study which provide recruitment opportunities for 80 per cent of German companies. These are a mandatory part of courses at *Fachhochschulen* but many university students also pursue them to gain experience and make contacts. Degree dissertations also often provide an occasion for students to contact firms, especially in technical subjects
- recruitment fairs (*Hochschulmesse*) and trade fairs (see also above). There are specific graduate recruitment fairs organised by the German Society for Personnel Management (DGFP), the *Forum* organisation, and AIESEC-affiliated student unions. However, there have been criticisms that recruitment fairs are too thronged with potential applicants to allow for discussion, and employers feel swamped; workshops are increasingly preferred.
- specialist publications for graduates. Probably the most authoritative is the 'START' series, produced by the Staufenbiel Institut für Berufs- und Ausbildungsplanung, Cologne. These are substantial volumes offering detailed recruitment information for particular types of graduate (technical, business studies and general management, plus an overview of MBAs in Europe), with company information – including starting pay. The publication *Karriereführer*, offering a range of recruitment advice, with details of company graduate vacancies, is published by Wison Verlag, Cologne. There are two issues a year, each dealing with a career theme. In the past, *Karriereführer* specialised in recruitment from *Fachhochschulen* but now covers the entire tertiary sector.

Graduate salaries   In 1995/6 annual starting salaries for a university graduate were in the range DM 62–70,000 (£25–28,000), although there is considerable variation according to company and specific qualifications. Well qualified graduates in business and engineering can reach up to DM 75,000 (£30,000). Salaries for students from *Fachhochschulen* are slightly less in most fields, at DM 58–64,000 (£25–25,500). Publications such as the *START* series set out company starting pay for firms seeking graduates.

Education fair

There is a biannual trade fair for education and continuing education and training. Named *didacta* it is held at a different location each time. Details can be obtained from the trade fair organisation AUMA.

Initial vocational training system

The core of Germany's system of initial vocational training is the 'dual system' in which on-the-job training under the supervision of qualified employees, paid for by the employer, is combined with off-the-job training in special vocational schools (*Berufsschule*), financed out of the public purse. Young people may enter the system from any of the three basic types of school described above. For example, in 1993 over a third of young people holding an *Abitur* qualification, giving access to higher education, entered the vocational training system, mostly in white-collar occupations – with a steadily rising proportion over the past two decades. As a result, a sixth of all apprentices in West Germany (and a tenth in the East) are theoretically entitled to enter university. There are special training options for those entering vocational training already armed with an *Abitur*.

Attendance at a *Berufsschule*, which also provides continuing general as well as narrowly vocational education, is obligatory for all young people aged between 16 and 18 not otherwise in full-time education.

The provision of training places is entirely the responsibility of employers: there is no obligation to train and no formal right to vocational training. It is estimated that about 70 per cent of enterprises in the small-trades (*Handwerk*) sector train, compared with 30 per cent in industry and commerce.

Whereas the number of training places offered in the early 1980s often fell short of the number of young people of the 1960s 'baby boom' looking for vocational training, by the early 1990s there was an excess of places offered. However, the position reversed again in the mid-1990s; none the less, although not all applicants were able to find a training place in the year 1996/7, there was a small numerical excess of vacant places.

The shortage of places was regionally highly unequal, with the Eastern *Länder* especially hard hit. As with continuing training (see below), this reflects not only the severe economic problems and enterprise closures which have afflicted the ex-GDR, but also the fact that the apprenticeship system which operated in the East was more dependent on in-house provision than its Western counterpart. The number of unplaced trainees exceeded the number of places available by a considerable margin. This can be offset only partially by efforts to build up full-time vocational education.

There was also a shortage of places in the service sector, and an excess in manufacturing in West Germany.

In 1995/6, 573,000 people entered the 'dual system', reversing several years of declining numbers. The year 1996/7 saw a further increase of 7 per cent in applications for training places to 716,500, putting more pressure on business and the authorities to create more training places.

Why train? Accreditation as a training firm offers a number of advantages to an employer. In a society where job mobility has traditionally been less than in the UK, access to a home-grown pool of skilled workers, not only trained in company-specific skills but also socialised into the company's culture, is a competitive advantage, especially where hiring and skilling-up workers to produce highly specialised products is expensive and time-consuming. Many larger companies often train considerably more workers than they need immediately, guaranteeing themselves the best of the group and also releasing trained employees into the rest of the economy without this implying poaching or wage-competition. In the past this overproduction served to compensate for the fact that many small enterprises did not train, in part because of cost and in part because of administrative complexity. However, there are signs that this balance was disturbed in the mid-1990s by cutbacks in the training budgets of larger employers – highlighted by the decline in the number of places referred to above.

Firms may not employ young people in any of the accredited occupations unless they offer training on the terms specified under the Vocational Training Act. Employers who need and want to recruit good-quality young people must offer training opportunities, and a well developed training programme is seen as part of developing a positive corporate image.

As well as providing a supply of skilled workers across a broad range of occupations, with benefits for product quality and service explored in the UK by research carried out by the National Institute of Economic and Social Research, the generally high standard of training also imparts foundation skills which favour the later training of foremen and supervisors.

Training establishments

Companies must meet certain minimum criteria to get approval as a training company. Apart from providing the appropriate facilities, a company wishing to take on trainees must demonstrate that it employs suitably qualified instructors who meet the requirements specified by the Economics Ministry for the occupations offered for training. These typically include people, aged at least 24, with a Master Craftsman's examination (*Meisterprüfung*), completed vocational training in a relevant occupation, a higher education qualification or professional qualification in a relevant occupation and evidence of practical experience. Instructors must pass an aptitude examination, which is part of the *Meister* examination in most craft trades. The Vocational Training Act also regulates training requirements in such professions as the law, accountancy, and medicine.

Training takes place, and must take place, in one of the 380 recognised occupations. Although many English-language publications refer to 'apprenticeships', in fact the German term for apprentice (*Lehrling*) was replaced by the term 'trainee' (*Auszubildende* – abbreviated to *Azubi*) some years ago. About 125 of the classified occupations are in craft trades which would be seen as apprenticeships in the traditional sense.

Competent bodies

Each component of the dual system is the responsibility of a different political authority. On-the-job training is the responsibility of central government, acting on the advice of the tripartite Federal Institute for Vocational Training. Off-the-job training in vocational schools falls under the authority of the constituent *Länder*. Co-ordination between the *Länder* is achieved through a standing conference of *Land* Ministers of Education.

Chambers of Industry and Commerce

At regional level within each *Land* a major role in the supervision and organisation of training is played by the Chamber of Industry and Commerce (*Industrie-und Handelskammer*). The Chambers embrace industry and commerce, including the liberal professions, crafts (*Handwerk*), and agriculture. Membership of an appropriate chamber is mandatory for any undertaking trading in Germany, despite calls for the introduction of voluntary membership, and companies engaged in specific recognised occupations must employ appropriately qualified staff.

The role of the Chambers is to oversee training at company level, register training agreements, advise on the operation of the system, organise examinations and validate the vocational training qualifications; in this way the costs of establishing programmes are much reduced for individual firms.

The training relationship

The basis of the training relationship is the training agreement between the employer and the trainee. The training contract must be in writing and must specify the main terms and conditions of employment during the period of training: the law lists such elements as the division of the working week between on-the-job activity and attendance at a vocational training school, and other off-the-job training measures, length of probationary period, pay, holidays, and terms for terminating the trainee contract.

Trainees' pay is customarily set by collective agreement, although companies may pay more if they wish. It is substantially below entry-level pay once employment begins, and in 1996 was just over 40 per cent of starter rates for trainees in their third year. Pay increases over the three- or four-year period of training, but is still substantially below full-time adult rates. First-year monthly trainee rates in manufacturing industry for 1996 in West Germany ranged between DM 900 and 1,100 (£360–440) rising to DM 1,200–1,500 (£480–600) in the fourth year of training. In the East, rates varied between DM 550 and 900 (£220–360) in the first year of training, rising to DM 900–1,100 (£360–440) in the fourth year.

The training agreement also sets out the mutual obligations of the employer and trainee, once training has begun. Specifically, the employer (or an assigned training provider) is required to ensure that the specified skills and knowledge are imparted to the trainee to ensure that the training objective (the qualification) is obtained, and to provide all the tools, equipment and other training resources free of charge to the trainee, both for on-the-job training and to enable examinations to be taken. The employer must guarantee appropriate time off for attending a vocational school, and ensure that the trainee attends. Trainees may be assigned only tasks which serve the aims of training. At the end of training the employer must issue a certificate specifying the type, length and aim of the training, the skills and knowledge acquired, and, at the trainee's request, a report on the conduct, performance and specialist abilities of the trainee.

Vocational training schools and training centres

The vocational training schools (*Berufsschule*), administered by the respective *Land* governments, provide the theoretical element of vocational training within the dual system, as well offering a basic vocational training preparatory course for those leaving school lacking basic attainments. In addition, trainees in the dual system continue to receive an element of general education, which accounts for about 40 per cent of the time spent in the vocational schools. Instruction in vocational schools is on a daily basis (with one or two days' tuition) combined with full-time block release; this may be in one 12-week block or two periods of six or seven weeks in a year.

The craft training schools, *Berufsfachschulen*, can supplement or replace company training for people in the dual system, and train young people for the qualifications awarded by the Chambers of Commerce. About 12 per cent of those in the 16–19 age-group are in full-time vocational training in one of these schools, especially in specialisms where on-the-job training might be inappropriate. In contrast to entry into the basic dual system, entry to a craft school requires a secondary school-leaving certificate.

Where companies are small, or cannot offer a full range of experience to meet training requirements (on practical or safety grounds, or in sectors where technical change is especially fast), resort is often made to inter-company training centres (*überbetriebliche Ausbildungsstätte*) which complement the theoretical activity of the vocational school with on-the-job experience. These are usually financed by employer associations, with supplementary funding from public authorities, and may serve a broader spectrum of training objectives, including management training.

Length of training and costs

Training lasts for between two and three-and-a-half years, depending on the industry and occupation. Costs of training in-plant are borne solely by companies, which may also bear a portion of the cost of any inter-company training facilities. Vocational schools are paid for by the *Länder*.

Some state aid is available to finance the training of young people who need preparatory training on leaving school before entering the dual system, or to meet other special needs (see below, on the services of *Bundesanstalt für Arbeit*).

Type of qualification

Basic vocational training takes place in one of the approximately 380 occupations recognised by the authorities. Over the past twenty years the number of recognised occupations has fallen from about 600 in 1971, with training now being more comprehensive within each broader occupational category. Training must confer transferable skills, and may not be related solely to a company's narrow skill requirements.

Occupations become recognised as such by the Economics Ministry in collaboration with the Ministry of Education and Science, which sets detailed training regulations. The organisation of examinations and validation of qualifications is the responsibility of the Chambers of Commerce (see above). Examination is by boards of part-time examiners, and entails a written, an oral, and a practical test.

There is a degree of flexibility in the system, and the content and form of training may be revised in consultation with employers' organisations, trade unions, the training and education authorities, with the impetus usually coming from the two sides of industry. For example, the training syllabus for the metalworking industry (including electrical engineering and electronics) was comprehensively overhauled in the late 1980s and the commercial syllabus is currently subject to major reform.

On passing the final examination, trainees receive certificates setting out the grades, the proper title of the qualification, and the company where the training took place.

In 1995, 37 per cent of training places were in manufacturing and 54 per cent in services: this represented a mismatch compared with the overall share of employment in these sectors, with manufacturing employing 31 per cent of workforce and services 60 per cent.

After initial training

On completion of initial training, just under 50 per cent of trainees take on a permanent job in the occupation for which they were trained, of which about 85 per cent initially remain with the company that trained them; 10 per cent then do their military service (or alternative civic service). Some 10 per cent become unemployed, and 13 per cent move on to further training or education. The remainder either work outside their trained field or take up a fixed-term contract, which has become increasingly common since legislation passed in 1985 eased the requirements.

Criticisms and problems

The dual system has been criticised for some of its rigidities, the long period needed to acquire basic skills, too much theoretical training and general inflexibility, and lack of co-ordination between examining bodies, which could lead to inconsistent standards. There are also concerns that growing sectors, such as the media and many areas of business services, do not have any recognised occupations and that employers in these industries either poach skilled staff or rely on a mix of university graduates and individuals with skills acquired unsystematically through continuing training.

Against this have to be set the comprehensiveness and transparency of the system, culminating in a uniform and universally-recognised qualification. Importantly too, the system gives to those who do not take an academic path an opportunity for development and the acquisition of prestige through recognised training – so much so that vocational qualifications are sought by those who are in principle entitled to enter university. The creation of a deep pool of skills and work attitudes also allows the delivery of more complex and efficient goods and services at all levels. The comparative sectoral studies carried out by the UK National Institute for Economic and Social Research (see references in the UK chapter) attest to the contribution that effective initial training makes to both productivity and quality across a range of occupations. The broad character of these skills also facilitates the adoption of technologies and forms of 'Post-Fordist' work organisation which, certainly in manufacturing, have been associated with a high degree of internal flexibility and demand for technically capable generalists.

Steps have been taken towards greater flexibility, for example by reducing the number of training occupations in each sector and broadening the range of skills. However, there is concern that a body of potentially obsolete technical knowledge, rather than learning and social skills, is given too much weight.

In industry, the high level of training of skilled workers in Germany, combined with a large pool of qualified foreman (see below), has been identified as enabling highly qualified technicians or graduate engineers to avoid the need to become involved in day-to-day trouble-shooting on the shop floor, compared with experience reported in the UK.

The system is under pressure from a variety of forces. Its relevance to many sectors is diminishing, and recognised occupations are still weighted towards traditional industry and commerce. Employers in service industries looking for flexible and capable people with a high general education often prefer either those with higher vocational qualification or graduates, who are in ample supply, to whom they can offer short introductory programmes.

Technical and further training

Technical and further vocational training – which overlaps with continuing training (dealt with separately below) – is also available for people with a basic vocational qualification in a variety of vocational training schools. These include trade schools (*Fachschule*), vocational further education colleges (*Berufsaufbauschule*) and vocational colleges (*Fachoberschule*).

While some of these institutions provide training as a foreman or technician, others offer enhanced basic vocational skills and issue their own qualifications which can be used to gain entry to a polytechnic (*Fachhochschule* – see above), ultimately offering an alternative route into tertiary education.

Training of technicians and supervisors *(Meister)*

Individuals with an initial vocational qualification and an appropriate period of experience prescribed by the Vocational Training Act (usually three years) can proceed to acquire more advanced qualifications across the range of industrial, craft and commercial occupations. The best-known title, *Meister*, is found in both craft occupations and in industry (with the qualification *Industrie-Meister*). Those undertaking further training in commerce, which includes areas such as data processing, will bear a title such as *Fachkaufmann/frau*, *Fachwirt* or *Betriebswirt*.

Training at a *Berufsfachschule* for the status of technician (*Techniker*) holding a formal technical qualification (*staatlich geprüfter Techniker*) is open to individuals who have completed their initial vocational training and who have two years' experience. Training, which may be full- or part-time, is undertaken at a special trade school (*Fachschule*). The period of training is one or two years full-time, or three years part-time. Trainees bear their own costs, though some state help is now available. From 1996 a dedicated grant – the *Meister-BAfög* – is available to cover living costs, with support for families, during full-time courses.

Training services of the official employment service

As well as running the official job placement service and providing careers advice and job counselling, the Federal employment service also offers a number of training opportunities both to employers and employees. As well as its more conventional training activities in West Germany, the BfA is also centrally involved in running job creation schemes and training in the former GDR.

The promotion of vocational training is a statutory obligation on the BfA under the 1969 Work Promotion Act (*Arbeitsförderungsgesetz*). It may carry out training itself, make use of training facilities of other public institutions, or resort to other training providers.

The main areas covered are set out below.

Vocational training for individuals   Grants or advances are available to enable individuals to participate in vocational training if either the individual situation of the prospective trainee or the location of the training create financial and practical difficulties. As well as initial or further vocational training, BfA grants may also be used to enable individuals to obtain a secondary school leaving certificate (*Hauptschulabschluß*), which is a prerequisite for entering the dual system, or to remedy any other general educational shortcomings.

Further vocational training   The BfA can support further vocational training for individuals who have completed a course of initial vocational training followed by three years' work, or six years' work experience. Support can be granted where the course offers scope for individual advancement, adapts existing skills to labour market or job requirements, or enables an unemployed or older person to get a job. Support takes the form of grants to meet costs, together with a subsistence allowance for full-time trainees. This amounts to 65 per cent of former income (less statutory deductions), or 73 per cent with dependants. Loans are also available.

Retraining   Grants and subsistence allowances are also available to support individuals undergoing retraining to enable an employee to move to alternative employment and further occupational mobility and flexibility. Grants are available to employers to enable them to finance a period of introductory training for the unemployed, or those threatened with unemployment, if this will facilitate their occupational mobility. Subsidies paid by the BfA to the employer can cover up to 50 per cent of the usual agreed or local rate for the job, and may be paid for up to one year.

Promotion of vocational training institutions   The BfA can provide grants and loans for the construction, expansion and equipping of vocational training institutions. These include the inter-company training centres referred to in the context of the dual system above, as well as other facilities provided by bodies such as Chambers of Trade and Commerce, employers' associations and employees' organisations, and welfare societies. Organisations entitled to seek financial support may not, however, be engaged in training on a commercial basis, or be predominantly intended to serve the needs of a single organisation.

Managerial training and development

Compared with the UK, top managers in German business, and particularly in large companies, are more likely to be graduates of universities or polytechnics. And based on the length of education, together with military service with men, graduates recruited into business are likely to be at least 26 years old and probably nearer 28 (30 for those with a doctorate). Board members of large companies, especially those in fields such as chemicals, are frequently educated to doctoral level, and a doctorate in engineering is a common route to senior management throughout manufacturing industry. Nearly two-thirds of top managers are educated to degree level (including polytechnic graduates).

Whereas larger companies are more inclined to recruit from universities, small and medium-sized companies often opt for graduates from the polytechnics (*Fachhochschulen*). In the first place, they may well have entered higher education through the route of a completed apprenticeship rather than the *Abitur*, and second, their studies will have been more directly vocationally relevant.

Subjects studied have a much greater relevance in recruitment than in the UK, and liberal arts graduates tend to move into teaching rather than enter management. In the past, most German managers did not change company to obtain promotion and the vast majority of senior appointments were filled internally. Managers were therefore recruited after a solid academic performance or from capable skilled workers with *Meister* qualification, and developed internally. Combined with the well established business and management studies options at universities and polytechnics, there was little demand for a transferable managerial qualification, such as an MBA. The weakening of this culture somewhat during the 1980s may well have increased the attraction of an MBA qualification at an American or leading European business school. MBAs are seen as attractive qualifications for individuals looking for a career in consultancy or for a strategic role in a large company. Foreign, especially US, companies seeking to establish a presence in Germany have been active recruiters of German MBA holders.

Post-entry practice varies considerably, depending on company size and the management area into which the graduate is recruited. Specific trainee programmes tend to be reserved for graduates entering general management and identified as strong performers, and are confined to large companies. However, the competition for good-quality graduates in the late 1980s and early 1990s – principally caused by demographic shifts combined with a phase of strong economic growth – has led firms to improve their public presentation and to highlight their development opportunities for graduates.

Management development

Managerial development, especially for those just above first-line supervisor level, is widespread, in particular for developing technical knowledge and skills, as well as managerial capacities.

In the absence of business schools and university departments offering development courses, firms are obliged either to provide their own programmes or to turn to the multitude of external training providers. Chambers of Commerce also offer management development courses and seminars.

A number of not-for-profit organisations, including business universities such as Universitätsseminar der Wirtschaft, involved in the provision of management training are grouped together in the so-called 'Wuppertal Circle' (Wuppertaler Kreis). This sets out to maintain standards in management training, and participating organisations must abide by commitments on the organisation of courses and the maintenance and updating of course contents. Its members organise some 14,000 events with 300,000 participants annually.

The two main annually-published guides are cited under *Continuing training* below.

Compared with other employees, managers enjoy a much greater intensity of post-entry training and development.

Continuing training

Continuing training covers an enormously wide spectrum of activities, including those already referred to above as promoted by the BfA, the training of *Meister*, and management training. It takes place in a multitude of institutions, is often provided in-house by established training departments in large firms, and via distance learning. After rapid expansion in the 1980s, the provision of continuing training by companies was subjected to more rigorous scrutiny on grounds of cost and effectiveness, following the changed economic climate of the early 1990s. Downsizing has also made it more difficult for employees to release staff, especially indispensable skilled employees, for further training.

Some evidence of greater efficiency can be seen in the fact that the increase in costs per employee slowed down considerably between 1987 and 1992, compared with earlier periods, despite higher wage costs and more hours of training provided: on average, the number of hours per participant rose from 13 in 1987 to 20 in 1992.

At the same time, the need to integrate skill acquisition with strategic objectives and sustain the process of learning led to the emergence, at least as an aspiration, of the concept of the 'learning organisation'. In large companies with, traditionally, extensive central training departments offering standardised seminars, this has gone hand-in-hand with a greater decentralisation of the organisation of training, especially for managers, with training managers offering guidance and a framework. The spread of the *Personalreferent*, a personnel manager with responsibility for a group of individuals' careers, has also fostered this trend. However, most large companies continue to run in-house training departments, rather than outsource, although on the basis that they operate as profit centres.

Continuing training in Germany has been referred to as lacking transparency because of the diversity of institutional arrangements, aims, and implementation regulations. Chambers of Trade and Commerce (and in particular their central organisations) and the BfA hold databases of training opportunities, and can provide advice. The BfA, for example, has two databases: KURS and an on-line system KURS-DIREKT, which is organised jointly with the Insitut der deutschen Wirtschaft, the employers' economics research body; a CD-ROM is also available. Access is through local training information centres – BIZ – at labour offices. There are also regional databanks. The Chambers of Trade and Commerce operate a databank on continuing training called WIS (*Weiterbildungs–Informations System*). A biannual fair on further and continuing training is held in Hamburg (*Info-Börse für Aus- und Weiterbildung*). At *Land* level, continuing training may also be regulated by legislation.

The BfA has also developed a set of criteria for quality assurance known as '*FuU*' standards. Institutions offering distance learning are regulated by statute, the Distance Learning Protection Act, 1980, and must register with a central authority which monitors standards. (See also *Distance learning universities* above.)

Continuing training may be carried out in-house, through a public training facility, or through a commercial training provider. Qualifications obtainable range from diplomas issued by the institutions themselves to those set and examined by the authorities or Chambers of Trade.

In 1992, according a survey embracing companies with a total of about 2,000,000 employees carried out by the Institut der deutschen Wirtschaft (IdW) (see R. Weiss, 1994), some 97 per cent of firms regularly or frequently offered some form of continuing training. The most common was on-the-job training related to immediate workplace needs, including in-house workshops, trainee programmes, foreign visits, and instruction programmes from supervisors. Sixty per cent of the firms surveyed regularly sent employees to external training events and 55 per cent held seminars on their own premises (such training also included courses for works council members). The frequency of resort to seminars, whether internal or external, varied considerably by company size: whereas over 90 per cent of companies with 1,000+ employees provided internal or external seminars, less than half of companies with fewer than 50 employees did so.

On a sectoral basis, the highest participation was in retailing, financial services, transport and communications, and the capital goods industries. Participation was lowest in construction, where initial vocational training was held to be the most important source of skill-acquisition, and technical change is possibly slower than in manufacturing.

Scaling up the results of the 1992 IdW survey yields an overall figure of 14.7 million participants in West Germany (compared to 9.5 million in 1987) and 2.8 million in East Germany. In general, participation increases with educational level: 40 per cent of those with tertiary education, for example, undertook some continuing training, compared to 20 per cent with an initial training qualification.

This is confirmed by other survey material from the German personnel management association, DGFP, which carries out an annual personnel benchmarking survey. In 1995, this found that nearly a fifth of all training budgets went on management-related courses, two-thirds on specialist training, and just under a fifth on general continuing education. However, anecdotal evidence points to a recent upsurge in budgets for training in teamwork and in multi-media skills – probably directed more at intermediate grades than management.

Further training in East Germany has been hit hard by the collapse of many of its former leading enterprises and the break-up of their training departments. Efforts to rebuild training capacities have mostly been concentrated on external providers, combined with intensified on-the-job training. The IdW survey noted much lower levels of provision in the area of formal training events or seminars, either in-house or using external providers, in the East; only one-third of companies offer such training compared to two-thirds in the West.

Information on training providers and seminars appears in most of the main business magazines, such as *Wirtschaftswoche* and *Manager-magazin*. There are also two annual publications with a wealth of information: *Jahrbuch Weiterbildung*, published by Handelsblatt, and *Jahrbuch der Management-Weiterbildung*, which focuses on management training.

Workforce consultation on training

Under the 1972 Works Constitution Act, works councils and the employer are required to co-operate on and promote training. Works councils have a right of co-determination in some areas. For example:

- Both parties are required to ensure full access to training opportunities, within and outside of the firm, and in particular to attend to the training needs of older employees.
- Employers must consult on training facilities and schemes, and works councils have a right of co-determination on the implementation of workplace training.
- Works councils have a right to make proposals as to which employees should participate in training opportunities.

Under dismissals-protection legislation, employers are also required to consider whether an employee to be dismissed could work elsewhere in the establishment after a reasonable period of training or retraining.

Agreed training provisions

Continuing training has gained in importance in recent years and has been a focus of trade union as well as employer and governmental activity and consideration. Continuing training, for example, has been at the heart of the reforms outlined by the metalworkers' union IG Metall in its proposal *Tarifreform 2000* which, among other things, has proposed movement towards skill-based pay structures and continuing training and development.

Although there are trade union hopes for a greater training content to collective bargaining in the future, to complement existing union influence in the organisation of initial training in the dual system, as yet detailed sectoral provisions are rare and raise problems of implementation at workplace level. Moreover, although employers appear willing to commit substantial funds to in-company training of their specialists and managers, there is less enthusiasm for broadening the training of less-skilled workers, as called for by the trade unions.

A recent trade union study has highlighted a number of current provisions and approaches, including the important provisions for the employment of trainees after completion of their initial training, in the context of industry agreements to create and conserve employment. The study 'Agreed Measures to Promote Training' (*Förderung der Ausbildung durch Tarifvertrag* – see Bispinck (1996) in *Main sources* below) identified a number of bargaining units in which binding commitments were made in recent negotiating rounds to raise the number of trainee places. Agreed increases were between five and 10 per cent in areas of the chemical industry, wholesaling and banking. In a few instances, agreements to increase the number of trainees were tied to a standstill in trainees' pay. More widespread and enforceable have been agreed commitments to take on trainees into either permanent or, more commonly, temporary employment on completion of initial training. The most common arrangement is employment for a minimum period of six months.

Some collective agreements require employers to examine the possibilities of continued employment for employees after retraining where rationalisation is taking place. These can be accompanied by maintenance of earnings agreements for downgraded employees. As noted above, the law on redundancies requires dismissals to be 'socially warranted'. Employers do not have a free hand in selecting for redundancy and such clauses therefore may take on a particular relevance.

In a very small number of agreements, this approach is complemented by provisions to develop employee skills. One pioneer agreement, made in 1988, covers the 145,000 employees in the metalworking industry in North Württemberg/North Baden. As well as providing a framework for grading and job evaluation, the agreement emphasises the need to develop and extend occupational skills. The agreement requires the employer to assess the need for training, and discuss training needs with works councils. Firms must assess their training requirements each year, and examine the broader training needs of the workforce. Employees who receive training are entitled to be regraded if appropriate, provided the newly-acquired skill is put into practice. Measures aimed at general further training which are not directly related to the employer's training needs, and management seminars, are excluded. However, the agreement has not yet been extended to other regions in the metalworking industry, and take-up of its provisions at company level has been reported as being low.

Time-off rights for education

Paid educational leave has been legislated for in the majority of *Länder*. This usually entails five days' leave a year for participation in vocational and civic education at recognized institutions.

Interpretation of the law has caused problems, and there have been some high-profile court cases where employers have refused to pay for courses which they regarded as nothing more than disguised holidays. In North-Rhine Westphalia, agreement was reached in 1990 between local trade unions and employers to avoid such problems. It provided that courses had to be open to all comers, recognised by the *Land* authorities and take place in recognised institutions; vocational training need not be confined to the employees' immediate workplace, and may include the acquisition of key skills such as computing or a foreign language, and civic education. However, courses may not be intended solely to provide trade union education and training.

Works council members who are released from work are entitled to paid time off to attend courses which may be offered by trade unions as well as employers. All works council members are entitled to three weeks' paid time off during their four-year period of office.

Financing

There are no levies or mandatory requirements on levels of training expenditure. However, there are mandatory requirements on employing only time-served apprentices and *Meister* in certain trades.

On average, companies spend 0.8 per cent of their overall personnel costs on continuing training, with the pharmaceutical sector the biggest spender at about 2 per cent – equivalent to some DM 1,150 (£460) per year per employee.

Concern about cuts in the supply of training places in the mid-1990s has prompted arguments about whether a system of levies on employers (*Bildungsabgabe*) should be introduced. The German Trades Union Confederation (DGB) is strongly in favour, and the opposition SPD is also backing this approach if adequate funds are not available through Chambers of Trade and other organisations.

In theory, an employer can require an employee to agree to repay the cost of any further or continuing training if he or she leaves within a predetermined period following training, and a number of companies take this approach – most notably the airlines on pilot training. A recent survey (see Küpper, 1996) found that 23 out of 49 firms surveyed, employing a total of 813,000 employees, employed this practice. Interestingly, 15 of these firms said they would be prepared to cover any costs incurred by an employee they recruited if they were subject to such an agreement. However, the practice is fraught with legal complications, with the burden on the employer to establish the legitimacy in each case. Some specialists also feel that such clauses can be self-defeating. According to case law, the amount of time for which such a clause could operate depends on the length of the period of training: for example, six months to two years of training could bind the employee for a maximum of three years.

The Federal Employment Service provides funds for training and retraining the employed and unemployed, and provides grants and subsidies to employers and other organisations to extend training facilities and opportunities (see above). Although the public authorities devote large sums to financing continuing training, the vast bulk of finance comes from industry. In 1992, for example, the private sector spent some DM 36.5 billion (£14.6 billion) on continuing training, and individuals contributed DM 9.8 billion (£3.9 billion) (either directly or through forfeited pay and holidays). This compared with public spending by the BfA of DM 19 billion (£7.6 billion) for all training, including retraining and support for employees, of which DM 11 billion (£4.4 billion) was spent in the new *Länder*. Other public bodies spent a further DM 4 billion (£1.6 billion). In 1992, companies in the IdW spent an average of DM 1,924 (£770) per employee – 2.8 per cent of the paybill – on continuing training, of which the lion's share was accounted for by the costs of formal training seminars and events, either external or in-house. The highest expenditure was in financial services, where DM 5,200 (£2,080) was spent per employee.

The average amount spent since German unification has massively increased public spending on training and employment measures in the new *Länder*: as noted above, it accounted for nearly 60 per cent of all training expenditure by the BfA in 1992.

Educational attainment of the population

Level	Percentage of 25–64 age-group
Lower secondary	16
Upper secondary	62
Higher education (non-university)	10
University	13

Source: OECD (1994)

According to forecasts prepared by Prognos and the Federal Institute for Labour Market Research, the proportion of the workforce completing vocational training is expected to rise from the current 59 per cent to 63 per cent by 2010. The proportion of employees without any formal vocational training will fall from 20 per cent to 10 per cent. Demand for graduates is expected to rise, with 17 per cent of the workforce having a university degree, compared to 12 per cent at present.

According to a survey carried out by the personnel managers' association, DGFP, graduates accounted for 15 per cent of respondents' workforces, rising as high as 40 to 50 per cent for businesses such as publishing and consultancy.

Organisations

Federal Ministry of Labour
(Bundesministerium für Arbeit und
Sozialordnung)
5300 Bonn 1
Rochustraße 1
Tel. +49 228 5271

Federal Ministry for Education and
Science
(Bundesministerium für Bildung und
Wissenschaft)
Postfach 20 01 08
5300 Bonn 2
Tel. +49 228 571

Federal Employment Institute
(Bundesanstalt für Arbeit, BfA)
Regensburgerstraße 104
8500 Nuremberg 30
Tel. +49 911 170
Fax +49 911 17 21 23

Federal Institute for Vocational Training
(Bundesinstitut für Berufsbildung)
Fehrbelliner Platz 3
1000 Berlin 31
Tel. +49 30 868 31

German Association for Personnel
Management
(Deutsche Gesellschaft für
Personalführung, DGFP)
4000 Düsseldorf 1
Niederkasseler Lohweg 16
Tel. +49 211 59 78 0
Fax +49 211 59 78 505

German Chamber of Industry and
Commerce
(Deutsche Industrie- und Handelstag)
Postfach 1446
Adenauerallee 148
5300 Bonn 1
Tel. +49 228 1040

AUMA
(German trade fairs umbrella organisation)
Lindenstraße 8
50674 Cologne
Tel. +49 221 209 070
Fax +49 221 209 0712

Bundesverband Zeitarbeit e.V.
Vorgebirgsstraße 39
53119 Bonn
Tel. +49 228 63 24 50
Fax +49 228 65 95 82

Schutzgemeinschaft Zeitarbeit e.V.
Vorgebirggstraße 39
53119 Bonn
Tel. +49 228 69 87 96
Fax +49 228 65 95 82

Bundesverband Personalvermittlung
Vorgebirgsstraße 39
53119 Bonn
Tel. +49 228 63 00 78
Fax +49 228 65 95 82

Media

Berufsplanung für Ingenieure
Berufsplanung für den Management-
 Nachwuchs
Euro-Challenge (in English)
Staufenbiel Institut für Berufs- und
Ausbildungsplanung
Postfach 10 35 43
50475 Cologne
Tel. + 49 221 12 40 38
Fax + 49 221 12 40 30

Handelsblatt
for 'Jahrbuch Weiterbildung'
(annual survey of management training)
and *Karriere*
Kasernenstraße 67
Postfach 10 11 02
4000 Düsseldorf 1
Tel. + 49 211 8 87 0
Fax + 49 211 32 67 59

Karriereführer
Wison Verlag
Weyertal 59
50937 Cologne
Tel. +49 221 41 10 45
Fax +49 221 41 60 43

Frankfurter Allgemeine Zeitung
Hellerhofstraße 2-4
60327 Frankfurt/Main
Tel. +49 69 75 91 0
Fax +49 69 75 91 17 43

Süddeutsche Zeitung
Sendlingerstraße 80
80331 Munich
Tel. + 49 89 218 30
Fax + 49 89 218 37 95

VDI-Nachrichten
Heinrichtstraße 24
Postfach 10 10 54
40001 Düsseldorf
Tel. + 49 211 6188 0
Fax + 49 211 6188 300

Main sources

BISPINCK, R. *Förderung der Ausbildung durch Tarifvertrag.* WSI 'Elemente qualitativer Tarifpolitik' No. 26, September 1996

BÖHM W. and JUSTEN, R. *Bewerberauswahl und Einstellungsgespräch.* Berlin, 1996

KOCH, R. and REULING, J. (eds). *Modernisation, Regulation and the Responsiveness of the Vocational Training System of the Federal Republic of Germany.* Paris, 1994

KÜPPER, W. and PAWLIK, T. 'Rückzahlungsklauseln bei Personalentwicklungsmaßnahmen', *Personalführung,* 6/1996

PILLAT, R. *Neue Mitarbeiter – erfolgreich anwerben, auswählen und einsetzen.* Munich, 1996

SCHULER H. *et.al. Personalauswahl im europäischen Vergleich.* Göttingen, 1993

STEWART, R. *et.al. Managing in Britain and Germany.* Anglo–German Foundation. London, 1994

WEISS, R. *Betriebliche Weiterbildung.* Cologne, 1994

6

Greece

The Greek labour market is characterised by an ample supply of job seekers at all levels, and managers rarely have to struggle to fill vacancies. In fact, recruitment strategies are often designed to minimise the flow of applications. Turnover tends to be low, except in areas such as IT and sales, and recruitment is still characterised by extensive informality, including word-of-mouth recommendation.

Greece is likely to become a key centre for organising business in the Balkan region, and local internationalised firms are eager to develop young managers, many of whom already have good language skills, to fill these roles.

Although employers – especially in Greek-owned companies – are aware of the need to develop management expertise among their staffs, they are confronted by major problems. Small companies, of necessity, are often obliged to concentrate on technical training, and external providers of management training often do not tailor their programmes to the needs of smaller companies.

The provision of EU funds to subsidise training has made an enormous difference to the supply, although larger and foreign-owned companies tend to be better equipped and more willing to make use of the opportunities. The proliferation of training providers has led to problems of quality, or simply lack of fit between a supplier's programme and the employer's needs.

The labour market

Following a long period of low growth and stagnation, the Greek economy began to show definite signs of recovery in 1994, when inflation fell to single figures for the first time since the mid-1970s. The economic upturn has had a positive impact on employment. According to the official employment service, the Organisation for Manpower and Employment (OAED), registered employment has been increasing steadily since 1993: from 2.267 million people at the beginning of 1993 to 2.401 million at the beginning of 1995. This increase has primarily been attributed to women's entry into the labour market. Employment has increased in all but the primary sector, where a steady decline of about 2 per cent per year on average has been observed since 1973.

The two most distinctive features of the Greek labour market are the relatively high proportion of employers and self-employed people, and of people declaring more than one job – in both cases Greece has the highest rates in the EU. About half of the people in employment are employers, self-employed or family workers. In 1994, 35.4 per cent of the working population were employers and

155

self-employed people (compared to an average of 15.9 per cent in the EU) and about 4 per cent of the active population has more than one job (compared to an average of 2.7 per cent in the EU).

Older workers (aged 60 and over) are a significant part of the labour force, standing at more than 7 per cent of the working population, the second highest in the EU, reflecting the low levels of pensions for certain occupations, and the highest life expectancy in the EU.

Unemployment has increasingly been of a long-term character. In 1994 half the unemployed had been without a job for more than 12 months. The unemployment rate of about 10 per cent remains below the EU average. However, unemployment among certain categories, such as the under-25s, is worse than the EU average. Unemployment benefits tend to be very low, with support for the unemployed critically dependent on strong family links.

Recruitment

Official notification

New hirings have to be notified to the employment authorities (OAED) within eight days of the appointment. Failure to do so does not invalidate the contract of employment but can incur a fine. This procedure is a relaxation of the requirement for all appointments to be made via the official employment service. Notification also has to be made to the statutory social insurance agency, IKA, and failure to do so may incur additional social insurance contributions.

Employers are required to make three-monthly returns of employee numbers to the employment authorities, with six-monthly returns on hours and pay to the Labour Inspectorate.

Work permits

EU nationals are free to enter Greece, subject to limitations imposed by the authorities on grounds of public policy, public security or public health, in order to:

- take up or search for employment (no work permit is needed)
- exercise the right to establishment
- as a spouse or dependant of a worker or established resident.

No formalities are necessary for a visit of up to three months, provided the individual holds a full passport or a valid ID card. After that, a residence permit is required, issued by the Aliens Department of the Ministry of Public Order for would-be residents in Athens, or by a local police station elsewhere. Applicants need a medical certificate, obtainable from a hospital in Greece, and notification of their employment intentions. An initial six months' residence permit will be issued, and following that a five-year permit.

Non-EU nationals who wish to work in Greece must have a work permit and a residence permit, both of which must be applied for by the prospective employer to the relevant prefecture. During the period of application, the prospective employee should not be in Greece. If granted, permission to enter will be recorded on the employee's passport at the Greek Consulate in their country of residence. On entering Greece the employee must report to the Aliens Department to obtain the residence permit, and to the competent prefecture to obtain the work permit. The work permit is made out in the name of the holder and specifies occupation or profession, employer and place and duration of employment. It is issued for a specific length of time and may be renewed. In order for a non-EU national to work in Greece, in theory the prospective employer must normally demonstrate that no Greek employee with comparable skills or experience is available to perform the task. There are, however, a few exemptions from this procedure in the fields of tourism, language teaching and sport. Spouses of Greek nationals are also exempt after two years of marriage.

Since the late 1980s there has been an influx of migrants from Eastern and Central Europe and from the Third World. This prompted the enactment of law 1975/91 which made entry and residence criteria stricter. For instance, there is an obligation to pay a deposit which is held by the Reserves and Loans Fund; the maximum length of stay is fixed at five years for migrants living in Greece; and there is an obligation to join a major insurance organisation. Also, penal and administrative sanctions have been made stricter, with fines of between Dr 20,000 (£50) and Dr 300,000 (£750) for employers who hire foreign workers illegally.

At the time this book was written, deliberations were in progress for the introduction of legislation in 1997 to control the employment activities of illegal migrants: these would be required to register for a work card which would allow them to be employed for six months. Failure to register could lead to their expulsion from Greece.

Legal foreign workers enjoy the same civil rights as nationals, and from the point of view of labour legislation there is no discrimination with regard to remuneration, conditions of employment and social benefits.

Other formalities

Information on social security and health entitlement and procedures can be obtained from OAED or the local office of the social security agency, IKA.

Workforce notification

There are no general mandatory rules on workforce notification. Where employees have elected a works council, this should be informed of changes in staff organisation or numbers of employees. Part-timers have a right to priority application for full-time positions. Larger companies tend to have policies on career and manpower planning, but this is certainly not typical of Greek companies.

Employment incentives

Wage subsidies are available to private enterprises, with certain exemptions, that recruit unemployed people. Emphasis is placed on firms recruiting vocational school-leavers from the OAED apprenticeship, Technical Vocational Schools (TES), Technical and Vocational Secondary Schools (TEL), Institutes for Vocational Training (IEK) or other institutions. A daily rate of between Dr 3,200 and 5,000 (£8–£12.50) is paid for a nine-month employment period. A special programme for women entering the labour market for the first time, or re-entering it after at least a three-year break, offers a daily grant of between Dr 3,000 and 4,000 (£7.50–£10) for a nine-month employment period. Special provisions apply for unemployed people in areas of high unemployment. In order to be entitled to the grants, firms may not have reduced the size of their workforce during the three months prior to application, and 50 per cent of the unemployed must be taken via the OAED. Funds come from the European Social Fund and OAED.

A programme for young entrepreneurs provides a grant of Dr 800,000 (£2,000) for setting up a new enterprise by unemployed people aged 18–25. Special provisions apply for older unemployed workers, the long-term unemployed, women entering the labour market for the first time or re-entering after three years. Extra financial assistance is given to women to participate in management skills training programmes; 8,500 women participated in 1994.

Additional programmes apply to people with disabilities, returning immigrants, single parents, prisoners, ex-convicts, juvenile delinquents, drug addicts, those with atypical cultural and religious characteristics, and the population of remote mountain and island regions.

Industrial and commercial enterprises in border regions receive a 10 per cent wage-cost subsidy for skilled graduates, up to a maximum monthly salary of Dr 80,000 (£200). In order to be entitled to support, enterprises must employ at least 10 employees for each graduate employee supported.

Private firms providing work experience for students of TEI (see below) or the College for Vocational School Teachers (SELETE), during their six-month work experience, receive grants of 50 per cent of the remuneration paid.

Enterprises in industrial, craft and mining sectors, agro-industrial animal production, and hotels and shipping companies receive wage-cost subsidies of between 20 per cent (only in Thrace) and 1 per cent, depending on the type of enterprise and region. Firms must be economically sound, have favourable growth prospects and employ staff on regular terms.

Unemployed persons who leave their place of residence to take up seasonal employment harvesting agricultural products receive a subsidy of two-thirds of the prevailing daily wage of an unskilled worker.

Using part-timers and temps

The main forms of non-standard contracts are fixed-term and part-time. Job sharing and work-on-call contracts are non-existent.

Part-time work

The official labour force survey recorded 162,000 part-time workers in 1993, some 4.5 per cent of the labour force. It is believed, however, that the actual number of part-time employees is significantly higher, standing currently at an estimated 15 per cent of the workforce. According to a survey carried out by the General Confederation of the Workers of Greece (GSEE) in 1993, 32 per cent of the part-timers are blue-collar workers in manufacturing, 24 per cent are professionals and self-employed and 17 per cent are office workers. Part-time work is mainly concentrated in services, and 70 to 90 per cent of part-time employees are female. Multinational employers use part-time staff only for manual and production jobs.

While part-time employment has existed in practice for many years, it received legal cover only in 1990. Part-time contracts of employment are subject to the provisions of the Development Law 1892/90 and Presidential Decree 410/88, and have to be in writing. Before the 1990 legislation, the trade unions maintained a mild opposition towards part-time work. However, it no longer features as a major item on the trade union agenda, and home-working and other forms of sub-contracting have become a growing source of concern.

The legal normal working week is 40 hours, as set by the nationally-binding National General Collective Bargaining Agreement (EGSSE). Law 1892/90 provided a legal basis for part-time work (defined as less than 40 hours a week, or the industry norm), and provided for social security cover for such employees. The law requires that part-timers be paid on pro rata basis, with pro rata entitlement to annual leave and other benefits (Christmas and Easter bonuses and holiday benefits). The employer cannot terminate the contract of an employee who has refused to work part time. Part-timers may not be called on to work beyond the agreed number of hours per week if this would clash with other responsibilities. They also have a right to priority application for any full-time vacancies.

Under the 1993 National General Collective Bargaining Agreement, the social partners made a number of provisions for part-time employees. These included: opportunities for participation in company vocational training facilities under equivalent conditions to those for full-time permanent employees; equal access to company social benefits; and equal (proportional) treatment with full-time and open-ended contract employees for annual leave, indemnity and redundancy pay, benefits, and supplementary social security services.

The 1993 National Agreement also called on the official employment service, OAED, to maintain and circulate a list of part-time vacancies; the employers agreed to ensure that member companies informed employee representatives about the proportion of part-timers in their workforces and the prospects for recruiting part-time employees.

Hourly rates for part-time work are calculated by dividing the monthly salary by 25 (the working days in a month), multiplying the quotient by 6 (the working days in a week), and dividing by 40 (working hours per week); that is, monthly salary multiplied by 0.006. Similarly, the monthly salary is calculated as: monthly salary = hourly rate × hours of employment per week × 4.1666.

Law 1892/90 also provided a special category of social security cover for part-timers, based on a presumed daily wage of Dr 900 (£2.25) for calculating later pension benefits. For social insurance purposes, a day of part-time work, irrespective of the number of hours worked, is recognised as one day, and cover is provided as if for full-time employees. However, since the salary class is the lowest, pensions are also the lowest. In practice that means that while part-timers would need the same numbers of days worked to qualify for a basic pension, that pension would be a fraction of the basic pension of the lowest paid full-time employees.

The 1990 Development Law (Law 1892/90) allows employees to be hired to work at weekends for only two alternate shifts of 12 hours a day. The total remuneration for 24 hours' work, including overtime, Sunday and night work, is equal to the remuneration for 40 hours (unless a shorter number of hours is worked per week).

Fixed-term contracts

Fixed-term contracts may be agreed, either for a short term or for defined tasks – such as seasonal work or sales campaigns – provided that they are justified by the nature of the business. Otherwise contracts could be deemed by the courts to be open ended. Seasonal work is very common in a number of industries. If they are in writing, such contracts must specify the proposed period and task. There is no statutory provision on the renewal of fixed-term contracts. However, the courts could deem that the employment contract has become open-ended if the employee can establish that it covers regular, non-temporary needs of the firm. A fixed-term contract will be held to have been renewed for an indefinite period of time if after the expiration date the employee continues to be employed without the employer's objection.

Conversion of an open-ended contract to a fixed-term one is possible under certain circumstances. Changing the terms of employment, however, can be problematic where the change involves not necessarily or solely pay or material benefits, but also any diminution of the employee's status within an enterprise. Such a change, without the employee's agreement or without a development in the business environment that could justify it, can be successfully contested in the courts. The duration of a fixed-term contract can also be set by the employee reaching an agreed age limit.

A probationary period is often agreed for managerial positions, but this is not a common practice for most ordinary blue-collar employees. The two parties may agree a probationary period of a few months, even up to a year, after which a permanent post will be offered subject to satisfactory performance. If the employer does not indicate in writing the intention to dismiss the employee, the contract is deemed to be open-ended. The length of the probationary period, however, may not exceed the time needed by the employer, acting in good faith, to determine the knowledge and capability of the employee.

Temporary employment

Although Greece has not ratified ILO Convention 96, it nevertheless bans private employment agencies for both temporary work and permanent placement. There is pressure for change within Greece, and the employers' organisation, SEB, and the official employment service, OAED, are in favour – the latter on condition that adequate safeguards are provided. The union federation, GSEE, has reservations about allowing agencies to operate, but is not absolutely opposed. The Greek position might shift if the ILO proceeds with its planned review of the Convention.

Temporary employment, including seasonal work, is covered by exactly the same provisions as regular employment. Some employers prefer to take on people on the basis of a fixed-term contract rather than seek any form of temporary or casual help.

Anti-discrimination provisions

Sex equality in employment is provided for under the 1975 Constitution, and by law (46/75 and 1414/84). Law 1414/84 forbids any discrimination on grounds of sex or marital status in relation to access to, content and implementation of programmes and systems of careers guidance, vocational training, apprenticeships, further training, retraining, training for a change of occupation, open retraining courses, refresher courses and information for workers. It guarantees access to all branches and levels of employment, irrespective of sex and marital status, as well as equal pay for work of equal value. It also forbids termination of employment for reasons relating to sex, and specifies fines for employers.

Trade unions have the right to inform employees of their rights under the act, and employers must facilitate this, if requested, by allowing use of company notice boards and distribution of pamphlets (provided this is done outside of working hours). Employees also have recourse to the civil courts in the event of unfair dismissal on grounds of sex, and under Law 1264/82 trade unions may act on behalf of members in such procedures.

Under the 1984 Act, a department of the Ministry of Labour was established to monitor equality issues and compile statistics. The General Secretariat for Equality, established by law in 1982, and with enhanced responsibilities under 1985 legislation, is an autonomous department within the Ministry to the Presidency and is entrusted with the task of 'promoting and achieving the legal and substantive equality of men and women in Greece'. The Secretariat also compiles statistics on pay and can provide information on equality initiatives, and company positive-action programmes under the auspices of the European Union.

Despite the lack of equal opportunities practices, women occupy a large segment of personnel management positions at senior and middle level, and certain professions (such as law, lower judicial ranks and computing) are female-dominated. Public-sector life-long employment, favourable working conditions and benefits for women, early retirement rights at full pension, and promotions based only on seniority, attract considerable numbers of female workers. In professions where entrance is regulated by examinations and carry a high social recognition, such as law and the judiciary, a large proportion of women is not uncommon.

In the private sector, local practitioners, while acknowledging some bias in employing women in senior and technical positions, exhibit low awareness of equal-opportunity policies. Some women in senior managerial positions might resent any 'different' treatment for women. Equal opportunities and pay are generally not a live issue. No advertisement in the Greek press will identify a company as 'an equal opportunities employer' (including multinational employers). Sex is often stipulated in advertisements for blue-collar employees, or (low-pay) single-sex-dominated occupations. Age is also routinely specified in media advertisements.

Separate lists of examination results for men and women, widely used in the past in the public sector and banks, have been deemed to be illegal.

Finding the applicant

Personal reference and word-of-mouth remain a key element in the search for employees at all levels, and predominate in numerical terms. Companies only rarely advertise blue-collar and routine white-collar vacancies or use the state system. There may be strong pressures to fill vacancies which might involve promotion internally. More senior white-collar positions and managerial vacancies are filled using direct advertising or agencies, with executive search growing in importance for top management.

For many employers, the steady flow of unsolicited applications is often sufficient to meet any vacancies that occur, or fill seasonal gaps. This certainly applies for operatives, clerical staff and new graduates.

The prevalence of word-of-mouth recruitment, the use of existing employees' family members and the mobilisation of informal influence to get jobs can appear problematic to outsiders – and would certainly raise concerns about race discrimination in the UK. However, Greek practitioners regard it as almost an 'unwritten law' of recruitment, and note that it also enables quite large enterprises to retain a 'family feel'. Managing post-recruitment family clashes or the emergence of alternative networks of power in companies is achieved either formally or informally by avoiding placing relatives in the same department, and not putting family members in subordinate/superior positions.

The official employment service, OAED

The official employment service, the Manpower Employment Organisation (OAED), enjoys a placement monopoly, although firms may recruit directly. However, employment agencies are, strictly speaking, illegal, although their activities are accepted in some areas, such as executive recruitment (see below).

A new system of unemployment registration – vacancy notification – has been developed in order to alleviate the problem of low levels of registration of the unemployed, and to create a national database of potential recruits. This is intended to assist OAED in its task of matching supply and demand in the labour market. The organisation also contacts employers to assess the state of the labour market. Legislation passed in August 1996 also sets out to establish unified data on the labour market, to be collected by a new institute (PIEKA), to modernise the operation of OAED and involve the social partners in its administration, and transform labour exchanges into centres for employment promotion.

The state placement system is little used for the recruitment of skilled employees, although it may be used for recruiting less skilled blue-collar workers. Moreover, it may be used as part of broader recruitment campaigns, especially in the provinces. Some official placement services are organised under the aegis of OAED at municipality level, and these have been reported as being locally useful for finding less skilled employees.

However, overall OAED accounts for only a small proportion of total vacancies filled each year -- some 8 per cent compared to the 20 per cent customary in most other EU countries. This reflects both its own organisational status – although great efforts are being made to reform the service – and the persistence of informal methods of recruitment.

Advertising media

Advertising in the media may be undertaken either directly or through a selection firm: according to a 1990 survey, about 30 per cent of foreign-owned firms used consultants for placing advertisements. Company policies on whether to publish the company name or quote a box number (or possibly use an agency citing a reference number) in job advertisements vary. Some personnel managers feel that publication of vacancies with their company name can lead to a flood of personal approaches from candidates, which is time-consuming and may be unwelcome. However, employers eager to establish a corporate image argue that citing the firm's name is vital.

The main vehicle for job advertisements for manual, administrative, specialist and some managerial positions is the daily national newspaper *Ta Nea*. Other media of relevance are: the business and financial daily *Express* (white-collar jobs), and the weeklies *Kathimerini* and *To Vima*. The professional engineers' association TEE (Technical Chamber of Greece) has its own fortnightly publication *Enimerotiko Deltio* which also carries extensive job vacancies as well as notices from job-seeking engineers. *Ta Nea* and *To Vima*, as well as the English-language *Athens News* all have home pages on the Web.

One recent innovation in newspaper advertising is the bi-weekly classified advertisement-based *Chrise Eukairia* ('Golden Opportunity') which allows employers to put in small ads free of charge, with box numbers.

Positions may be advertised in Greek or English or German (and sometimes in French if appropriate to the employer), an approach often used for pre-selection by inviting replies in the language of the advertisement. Age limits may be specified, but salaries are rarely indicated.

Recruitment consultants and executive search

Executive search and selection are widely practised for senior appointments, especially by foreign-owned companies. Although there are some pure search companies, this may be backed up by selection if possible candidates are likely to be thin on the ground. There are a number of local consultancies, some of which operate in association with major international networks, as well as UK-based accountancy/consultancy firms. The market is essentially self-regulating, with customary off-limits provisions. But some employers expressed reservations about the regulation of the market, and felt that standards still had to mature for some participants in the business. However, good consultancies were very well regarded. Demand for them is also increasing, reflecting the need for specialist advice as local family-owned businesses grow and need to attract experienced managers. As a result, search consultants often get drawn into providing broader advice on succession planning and business organisation.

Local consultancies charge about 20–25 per cent of the first year's base salary and expected bonuses plus expenses. For selection, the cost is nearer 15 per cent of salary plus the cost of advertising, or an all-in fee of about 18 per cent.

One third is usually paid in advance, a third on presentation of a short-list, and a third on selection. Six-month guarantees or a free replacement if the person leaves are also customary.

Although technically in contravention of national regulations on placement, executive search is permitted within the context of a broader provision of consultancy services.

Employment agencies

Law 1346/83 forbids the establishment of private employment agencies. Anyone who violates the law is liable to a fine and imprisonment of up to three months. Some agencies exist for the supply of staff for temporary contract work, such as cleaning and security.

There are also a number of agencies or organisations involved in placement which operate illegally, and several have been prosecuted by OAED and have stopped operating.

Selection

There is little statutory regulation in the field of selection. There is a general requirement to maintain confidentiality, enforceable in civil law, and consultants may include confidentiality clauses in contracts and candidate submission reports.

By law, a woman may not be asked if she is pregnant (and is protected against dismissal if she is). However, in general the culture of recruitment does seem to allow greater questioning of personal circumstances than might be accepted (or be legal) elsewhere in Europe.

Selection procedures will depend primarily on employee level. Interviewing is the prime technique, with two or three interviews for a graduate appointment, and up to five for a senior manager. Psychometric tests are rarely used in normal recruitment, but may be used by consultants for some senior appointments. Aptitude tests might be required for some clerical or technical occupations. While younger employees by and large accept tests, it was felt that people above their mid-30s might baulk at the requirement.

Employers normally ask for proof of educational qualifications, a medical certificate, and details of criminal offences. (Appointed candidates can obtain this from the authorities: offences become 'spent' after a predetermined period.) It is customary to take up references.

Some larger internationalised companies that formerly used headhunters for executive recruitment have begun to move towards assessment centres – which are still in their infancy in Greece – especially where companies want to integrate recruitment and subsequent career planning.

Education, training and employee development

Initial vocational training in Greece takes place primarily in public institutions, either in the form of technical and vocational education within schools or through apprenticeships organised via the state employment service, OAED. Although on-the-job and continuing training have been at a low level in the bulk of the small and medium-sized enterprises which make up the Greek economy, EU funds have stimulated greater interest among larger, foreign-owned and more export-oriented firms. The Greek trade unions have also identified training as a national priority, and training issues have begun to appear on the bargaining agenda for the the first time in recent years.

Educational system

The nine-year compulsory education system consists of six years of primary (*Demotico*) and three years of lower-cycle secondary (*Gymnasio*) education. On completion of compulsory education, school-leavers are awarded a diploma (*Apolyterio*). Apart from then joining the labour market, they can either choose to continue their general education or engage in vocational education/training. Four options are available:

- general secondary education (*Lykeio*)
- Technical–Vocational *Lykeio* (TEL)
- Integrated Comprehensive *Lykeio* (EPL)
- Technical–Vocational School (TES) and an apprenticeship under the auspices of the official employment and training agency, OAED.

Over the past two decades there has been a substantial decrease in the number of pupils in primary education as a result of a declining birth rate. The ratio of the 0–14 age-group to the whole of the population has dropped from 22 per cent in 1982 to 17 per cent in 1993. In contrast, the pupil population in the other age-groups has remained constant or even increased, reflecting a burgeoning interest in education.

The profession of teacher has remained relatively attractive for young people and ranks have swollen during the last twenty years. Teachers of all levels of primary and secondary education are appointed to the civil service (usually after a few years on a waiting list) and as such enjoy constitutionally-guaranteed life-long employment and attractive pension benefits. The average number of pupils per teacher in primary education dropped from 31 in 1970 to 22 in 1990.

The number of pupils in private primary schools is relatively low – with 4 per cent in private kindergartens and 6 per cent in private elementary schools.

Between 1983 and 1989, the proportion of young people aged 14 to 18 years staying on at school increased by 9 per cent, reaching 80 per cent of the population of that age, the sixth highest in the EU.

The three-year General *Lykeio* provides general education for those *Gymnasio* graduates – up to 18 years old – who wish to continue their studies at tertiary level. Young people who are older or who work during the day can attend an evening General *Lykeio*, where the period of study, with a shorter teaching timetable, is four years. This level includes an initial common curriculum followed by a core curriculum with special options in the physical and biological sciences, classics and literature, and mathematics/history/sociology, which leads to economics and business studies. At the end of the third year all students sit the examinations for the school-leaving certificate (*Apolyterio* – comparable to GCSE standard, grades A, B and C). A pass in the *Apolyterio* allows students of the four streams to sit the general entrance examinations, held in late June each year, for a place in higher education.

Candidates can apply to up to 60 different departments in various institutions throughout Greece (including the Military Academies of all branches, as well as Police and Fire Brigade Schools). Each year a quota is announced for every department in higher education. Selection is based on performance in the general entrance examinations as well as on the order of preference of each department that the student wishes to attend.

Candidates who fail to gain entry to higher education can resit at least one subject the following year. After two unsuccessful attempts they have to resit all subjects. Alternatively, they can enter the labour market or join the second year of a Technical–Vocational *Lykeio* or the first year of a Technical–Vocational School, or study at an institution of tertiary education, outside the general examinations system.

The Technical–Vocational *Lykeio* (TEL) provides general and vocational education. The duration of studies is three years for *Gymnasio* graduates and two years for graduates of any other type of *Lykeio*. Evening courses are also available for four or three years respectively. In the first year, students are taught general subjects for 21 teaching hours a week and special subjects, common to all, for 13 hours. In the second year, they attend common general subjects for 19 hours per week and 15 hours of vocational specialisms, which they choose from a range of options.

In the third year, TEL students attend general subjects for 13 hours a week and can either specialise further in an area of their vocational sector for 21 hours a week or choose one of the three streams available to them in order to sit the general examinations.

TEL graduates receive either a specialisation 'degree' (*Ptychio*) or a diploma (*Apolyterio*) for those who chose a stream. *Ptychio* holders have the following options:

- to join the labour market, equipped with the vocational training they had at school
- to continue in higher education at the Technical Education Institutions (TEI), after examinations in a specialism subject for 25 per cent of the seats available. Selection is based on the total points each graduate has gathered from the examination results, final degree grade and achievement during the last year in the subjects of essay writing and mathematics, as well as a specialism subject.
- to change specialisation area, within the same sector, by enrolling in the third year, or change sector by attending the second and third years again.

Apolyterio holders can:

- sit the general examinations
- continue at the Technical Education Institutions (TEI), without examinations on the basis of their scholastic performance, as described above for the *Ptychio* holders
- enrol again at the third year to obtain a specialisation degree in the sector they chose in their second year.

Technical–Vocational Schools (TES) train their students in specific occupations. They are integrated with the TEL (as described above), forming the Vocational and Technical Training Centres (KETEK). Courses last for two years (three at the evening schools). In the first year, students choose to specialise in one of fourteen vocational options (depending on the availability of the sector in a TES). The options include industrial skills (together with electronics), craft skills (gold and silver-smithing, watchmaking), commerce and agriculture.

In the second year TES students pursue their specialisation further. Out of a total of 30 teaching hours per week, six are devoted to general education subjects and 24 to vocational specialisms. Complementary in-company training is also available to TES students on a non-compulsory basis, for a limited period of three months. However, since it is practically impossible for such a large number of work places to be secured, few students are able to take advantage of such a scheme.

TES graduates can join the labour market, or the second year of a TEL if they want to continue their studies at tertiary level.

The Integrated–Comprehensive *Lykeio* (EPL), also called 'Unified Multidisciplinary Lykeio', is the most recently established form of *Lykeio*. In 1984, the first fourteen EPLs were opened with 4,458 students. In 1986, enrolment reached 15,565 students in 22 EPLs.

EPL provides both general education and vocational training. There is a core curriculum, including options in health, the natural sciences and social welfare, economics and management, together with technical subjects. EPL graduates can attend any institution of tertiary education, outside the general examination system. Alternatively, they may move straight to the labour market or acquire additional vocational training.

The OAED Apprenticeship is provided by the Organisation for Manpower and Employment (OAED). It is the only programme that combines vocational education with practical on-the-job training. Young people aged 15–18 years who have finished compulsory education may enrol.

In 1995, about 12,700 students were attending courses in 45 Technical and Vocational Training Centres (KETEK) throughout Greece and every year about 3,200 students graduate from them, with qualifications in 20 to 30 professions, according to local needs. When applications exceed available places (and this is usually the case in most centres), candidates are selected by interview. The duration of apprenticeship courses varies between four and six semesters depending on the particular course of study, and is based on the 'dual system'. In the first year, students attend lectures and workshops in the apprenticeship centres on a full-time basis (37 hours a week, five days a week). In the second and third years students attend lectures in the centres and also undergo practical in-company training, which grows in importance throughout the course, reaching 100 per cent of attendance time in the final term. Each year the OAED places 8,000 apprentices in companies.

Apprentices are paid by their employer, in accordance with the youth pay rates (50 per cent of the national minimum wage in the first term, on a sliding scale up to 100 per cent in the sixth) as laid down in the National Collective Agreement. They also have full medical and hospital insurance, the cost of which is at first covered wholly by the OAED (in the first year) and subsequently by the employer. Moreover, for those away from home, the OAED provides free board and lodging or free meal vouchers where no facilities are available.

Apprenticeship graduates join the labour market. The apprenticeship is not linked directly with the rest of the secondary education and qualified apprentices cannot join the educational system at a level higher than that at which they left it.

Other institutions of secondary education

Beside the above institutions, a number of others operate, which are of lesser importance – at least in quantitative terms:

- the Classical *Lykeio*, with an emphasis in classics and humanities
- the Greek Merchant Navy *Lykeio* for Navy Cadets, offering programmes in captaincy, marine engineering and radiotelegraphic operation
- the School for Tourist Professions (STE), including the Hotel and Restaurant Department, the Catering Department and the Hotel Client Account Management Department
- the Ecclesiastical *Lykeio*, which prepares boys for the priesthood
- various privately-owned Technical and Vocational *Lykeia*, which offer a wide range of programmes (from aircraft mechanics to paramedics).

Higher education

Higher education in Greece is under state control, in accordance with the Greek Constitution. It is provided by the university-level Institutions of Higher Education (*Anotata Ekpedevtika Idrymata*, AEI) and by the Technical Education Institutions (*Technologika Ekpedevtika Idrymata*, TF¹). There has been considerable growth in the proportion of young people attending higher education courses, from 9 per cent of the relevant age-group in 1970/1 to about 17 per cent in 1986/7, and by 1992 47 per cent of the 18–21 age group were attending tertiary-level education. The level of participation is higher than in the Netherlands or Italy, and about double that in the UK. Additionally, a large number of students – about a quarter to a third – attend universities abroad. It is not uncommon to find, for example, in maritime studies departments of universities in the UK that the vast majority of students – and in some cases lecturers – are of Greek origin. In 1992 28,380 students were attending university studies abroad, rising to 29,213 in 1994, of whom 5,738 in 1992 and 6,500 in 1994 were postgraduate students. Every year about 25,000 students are admitted to university-level institutions and about 21,000 to TEIs. Female participation in higher education is extensive but is also concentrated in some disciplines. In 1989/90 university departments with more than 60 per cent of female students included Preschool Education (95 per cent), French (93 per cent), English (90 per cent), Humanities and Psychology (84 per cent), Education (82 per cent), Law School (64 per cent), and Social Sciences (64 per cent). The lowest female student participation is in engineering (25 per cent). In TEIs the numbers of men and women are about equal on average.

AEIs include 18 universities (*Panepistimia*) and technical universities (*Polytechnia*) as well as two Highest Schools of Fine Arts (ASKT). At universities courses last a minimum of four years (eight semesters). In engineering, agriculture, veterinary medicine and dentistry the duration of studies is five years (ten semesters); six years (twelve semesters) in medicine. University graduates receive a *Ptychio* (the equivalent of a BA or BSc) and Technical University graduates a Diploma (BSc). In all technical universities, and in several other colleges, a graduation project is required.

University studies are mainly of an academic nature. However, there is student demand for industrial placements during the summer vacations, depending on the discipline, and an increasing number of companies provide opportunities. Placements also afford students a chance to work on their theses in an industrial context.

University graduates with a vocationally relevant degree can exercise their profession after registering with the appropriate professional body (such as holders of engineering diplomas with the Technical Chamber of Greece (TEE); and law degree holders with the local section of the Bar Association, etc).

TEIs train 'technologists' at the level of advanced vocational training. Courses last three or four years (six to eight semesters, including eight months' obligatory practical training and a graduation project). Graduates are awarded a *Ptychio* (rated above the BTEC Higher National Diploma). However, TEI graduates enjoy no professional recognition in law, and often their qualifications overlap those of university graduates.

This situation is a result, among other things, of the policies of various conservative and socialist governments which have viewed the creation of institutions of higher education as a way of meeting public demand for a university-level education (or at least something close to it) as well as a means of promoting regional development. Hence, universities, faculties and departments have been established all over Greece, accepting thousands of students each year, often with little relevance to local or national labour market requirements.

Postgraduate studies Postgraduate studies in Greece are developing rapidly. The increasing number of master's programmes that exist are organised at a university-specific level. They last from one to three years and lead to a 'Diploma in Postgraduate Specialisation'. More often, however, individual departments offer examinations for 'Special Postgraduate Scholars' (EMY). Selection is through competitive tests on a few relevant subjects and on a major foreign language. Successful students assist their academic advisers in teaching while studying for their PhD. EMYs receive a monthly stipend.

The Mediterranean Agronomic Institute of Chania (MAICH) is an independent centre for postgraduate studies and is one of the four institutions of the International Centre of Higher Mediterranean Agronomic Studies (CIHEAM). Subjects are taught in English. Studies lead to a one-year postgraduate diploma and – upon continuation for a second year – to an MSc.

Nevertheless, postgraduate studies share the general weaknesses of undergraduate-level education. Libraries and laboratories are often poorly equipped and staffed; the inadequacy of resources is reflected in the fact that the EMY grant is less than the national minimum wage for unskilled manual workers.

Other institutions of tertiary education

The Higher Public Schools of the Merchant Navy (ADSEN) accept *Lykeio* graduates of not more than 24 years of age, without examinations, on the basis of their grades, prior service in the sea, family membership in the armed forces, the coast guard or the merchant navy, or membership of a large family. Studies follow the 'dual system' with training places in the Greek merchant navy ships. Graduates can subsequently begin work as 'C' class captains or marine engineers, in merchant navy ships, maritime companies, shipyards, or offshore oil-drilling platforms, and advance to higher captaincy grades after further experience and examinations.

Several other public and private institutions – including some foreign ones – offer courses at tertiary level, mostly related to specific professions. Some claim to offer university-level education. Their qualifications, however, are not recognised officially, since, according to the Greek Constitution, universities are under state control. Officially, all kinds of private institutions at the tertiary level can operate only as 'workshops of freelance/liberal studies' (EES) and award their students with certificates of attendance.

Many foreign universities operate campuses in Greece: however, there are some complications with their status – although some enjoy high prestige (see below).

Adult education

The large demand for higher education, and lack of opportunities for adults out-side the national examinations system, facilitated the establishment of the Hellenic Open University. It will admit, without examinations, students of 25 years of age or older who have completed secondary education (any type of *Lykeio* or equivalent). Its status is equal to that of other universities (AEI) and is based in Patras. It will offer undergraduate and postgraduate courses in four departments: Social Sciences and Humanities, Economics and Management, Sciences and Technology, and Applied Arts. Degree courses were scheduled to start in January 1997.

Overall assessment

All types of diplomas from a *Lykeio* (that is an *Apolyterio* from any institution, public or private, that operates as a *Lykeio*) carry the same legal value. Nevertheless, each type – apart from its perceived status – offers its holder different opportunities and qualifications. TEL graduates, in theory, enjoy most scope. They can continue their studies at tertiary education or join the labour market after vocational training. In contrast, General *Lykeio* graduates are only prepared for a place in tertiary education, while apprentices and TES graduates are trained for a job.

In practice the situation is far less promising. The vocational training of all secondary education graduates is mainly academic, with no on-the-job experience. Moreover, TEL graduates lack any official recognition of their specialisation. As far as General *Lykeio* graduates are concerned, they lack any form of vocational education. On the other hand, an OAED apprenticeship is the only reliable alternative for a young person not aiming at higher education, offering its students training, job experience and income. In practice, however, the OAED training scheme is fraught with problems. Demand for training positions is high, and availability limited. Most placements are in small companies or workshops, where training is unsystematic and unsupervised. The shortage of places leads apprentices to accept anything on offer, even when the type of training is unsuited to their theoretical background or interests. Their instructors are experienced workers with no special training or qualifications for the role of mentor to young people. Nevertheless, the specialised training that the apprenticeship provides, coupled with some job experience, makes it highly attractive to youngsters seeking entry to an occupation, even though – in most cases – it leads to no formal recognition or accreditation. The lack of other, better trained, personnel makes demand for apprenticeship graduates high among employers.

There is currently no list of officially recognised professions and the level of qualifications required for each. As a result, graduation from an institution of secondary technical and vocational education may not constitute (for professions where the entry requirements are laid down by statute) adequate qualification for the practice of a profession. In some cases, for example, a pass in an examination administered by the Ministry of Industry may be required.

In general, technical and vocational education in Greece has never been viewed positively by parents or students. For decades the education system (with a predominantly classical and humanistic curriculum), has concentrated on preparing students for highly regarded university degrees rather than for vocationally-oriented qualifications. Under the circumstances, manual labour and vocational education have traditionally been viewed as inferior to intellectual work and academic studies. This prejudice is reflected in the number of registered students in each type of *Lykeio*: about 74 per cent of students in post-*Gymnasium* secondary education attend General *Lykeio*, 20 per cent TEL and only 4 per cent TES.

Various governments since 1974 have tried to alter the situation, creating new and more attractive types of institutions of vocational education and training. In one such attempt, in 1984, the socialist PASOK Government established the EPLs, with the aim of creating the main type of post-compulsory education. In 1992, the conservative New Democracy government introduced a new legal framework for a National System of Vocational Education and Training (see below).

The question of private universities became highly political and polarised after the electoral victory of the conservative New Democracy Party in 1990. A commitment to the establishment of private universities was included in its manifesto. Soon after it came to power, institutions calling themselves 'colleges' and claiming to offer university-level education were established. Many advertised exclusive partnerships with foreign universities where their graduates could continue their undergraduate or postgraduate studies. The situation led to a public prosecutor's investigation and charges of fraud were brought against some institutions. In an attempt to clarify the situation the government introduced a new legal framework for a National System of Vocational Education and Training. Officially, university degrees from foreign institutions of higher education which include a part or the whole of the study in Greece are not recognised by the state organisation (the Interuniversity Centre for Recognition of Foreign Education Titles, DIKATSA) as equivalent to university degrees. EES which are franchisees of foreign-based universities have maintained that according to EC Directive 48/89, their degrees should be recognised as university titles, a provision which clashes with the Constitutional demand for state-controlled universities. The situation became even more complex when the Higher Administrative Court deemed that DIKATSA should recognise, after further examinations, a foreign university degree obtained with partial study in Greece.

In 1995 a study conducted by the National Technical University of Athens found that 80 such institutions were operating, offering various degree schemes to between 27,000 and 29,000 young people. Their total annual turnover was 26 to 28 billion drachmas (£65 to £70 million). The oldest and largest, with 7,000 students (24.4 per cent of EES students), is Deere College, an American institution, established in Athens in 1945. The University of LaVerne is also well regarded. However, some foreign campuses – including one or two based in the UK – have fallen into disrepute and in some cases were purporting to offer their own degrees when lacking the accreditation to do so in the UK.

The magnitude of Greek young people's desire for a higher level education is displayed by the fact that if the number of Greeks studying abroad (27,000 to 28,000) is added to that of those in EES, the overall number of Greeks attending higher level education (outside of the formal system of national examinations and corresponding university placements) at foreign universities (whether or not officially recognised as such) rises to between 54,000 and 57,000, compared to a mere 21,000 in Greek universities.

Overall, as the OECD reported in its 1995 review, the Greek educational system prepares young people for a 'craft economy' with an overexpanded public sector. It is highly bureaucratic and centralised. Individuals' successes are in spite of the educational system rather than because of it, and can be attributed mainly to the nation's high regard and motivation for education. A major issue is the low expenditure on education: a mere 4.2 per cent of the GDP or 6.8 per cent of public expenditure. Schools are often ill-equipped and most pupils attend classes in rotating morning and evening shifts. Vast amounts are spent on preparatory classes in private schools or for tuition at home. Such 'help' is considered essential for the preparation for university examinations.

Graduate recruitment

The limited supply of places in higher education, compared with the number of qualified school-leavers, has meant that an estimated quarter to a third of university students study abroad, primarily in Europe and the USA. This applies in particular to postgraduate study. The majority of students ultimately return, creating a pool of qualified graduates with two degrees and high levels of proficiency in English or other foreign languages.

Greek employers looking for potential managers will tend to favour graduates with two degrees, preferably with the first degree at a Greek university. There are a number of institutional links, albeit limited, between foreign universities and Greek higher education establishments, with arrangements for courses to be held in Greece with credits counted against final degree qualifications taken at an EU university. Foreign postgraduate qualifications are particularly sought after in the natural sciences, for those entering sales and marketing, and (for foreign-owned companies in Greece) in business administration. Within Greece there are well-regarded business faculties in the Universities of Athens, Piraeus and Thessalonika.

Graduates in accountancy and finance need to hold a Greek qualification and to be a member of the relevant professional association.

Degree subjects tend to be directly relevant to career choice. In the past it was felt that many arts graduates who did not pursue further studies abroad were primarily interested in a career in the public sector. Cuts and privatisation have meant that this is no longer a realistic option, and such graduates now consider working in private industry – including small firms.

Recruitment arrangements at Greek universities are rarely formalised, but careers services are developing rapidly. The American Deere College – whose degrees, however, are not formally recognised by the state authorities (see above) – holds an annual graduate recruitment fair, as does the Athens Laboratory of Business Administration (ALBA – see below). Some student bodies that are members of the Association Internationale des Etudiants Anciens Economiques et Commercials (AIESEC), such as the business faculty at Piraeus, also hold recruitment events. A good deal of recruitment results from contacts between companies (and recruitment consultants) and teaching faculty or university career offices, or professional associations. However, some employers are sceptical about the quality of Greek academic teaching and its relevance to business needs, and they look for graduates of foreign universities almost as a matter of course. Newspaper and campus advertising is used in graduate recruitment. Unsolicited applications also play an important – and for some companies – the major role. There is no particular hiring season for graduates, principally because the flow is evened out by the obligation to perform military service after graduation or on completion of postgraduate studies (12–24 months, depending on which branch of the military and the family situation). Women do not perform obligatory military service.

Male graduates entering the labour market with a first degree will be aged at least 23–26, and with a second degree 27–28 years.

Vocational training

The new legal framework

Law 2009/1992 on the National System of Vocational Education and Training is the most recent attempt to provide a national system of vocational education and training as well as a unified national system of officially recognised professional and vocational qualifications.

The law established a supervisory body, the Organisation of Vocational Education and Training (OEEK). In addition to senior civil servants, its executive board also includes representatives of employer and employee organisations. Education and training are provided by the Institutes for Vocational Training (IEK), which can be public or private institutions. IEK are outside the educational system (qualifications from IEKs cannot be used for access to higher education) and are accountable to the OEEK. In 1995 there were in operation 59 public and 73 private IEKs offering qualifications in 61 occupations.

The OEEK itself is financed by state and EU funds, student fees to IEKs, examination fees, fees for establishing IEKs or recognising vocational qualifications, and revenue from its own programmes.

The law also provides for a national system of professional and vocational qualifications:

- certificate of vocational education at level 1 for adult *Gymnasio* graduates after training of at least two semesters in an IEK
- degree of vocational education and training at level 2 for Technical–Vocational School (TES) graduates
- degree of vocational education at level 3 for graduates of a Technical–Vocational *Lykeio* (TEL) and graduates of a specialisation department of an Integrated–Comprehensive *Lykeio* (EPL)
- diploma of vocational training at a level of post-secondary vocational training for: (a) graduates of a specialisation department of an Integrated–Comprehensive *Lykeio* (EPL) after training of one semester in an IEK; (b) *Ptychio* holders of a Technical–Vocational *Lykeio* (TEL) [TEL graduates with a specialisation degree] after training of one year in an IEK; (c) graduates of an EPL or of a TEL who in their third year attended stream subjects (EPL or TEL graduates with no specialisation), after training of up to a year-and-a-half in an IEK; (d) graduates of a General *Lykeio* or of an EPL who in their third year attended stream subjects, after training of up to two-and-a-half years in an IEK; (e) holders of a level 2 degree of vocational education and training after suitable training.

Nevertheless, many decisive matters (such as a list of officially recognised professions with the level of qualifications required for each) have to be regulated through presidential or ministerial decrees and decisions of the executive board of the newly established OEEK.

A further development is scheduled to establish a national baccalaureate and a new system for entering higher education, starting in the academic year 1996/7. Pupils at the first grade of the *Lykeio* will sit common national examinations at the end of the year in all the subjects they have been taught. This aims to familiarise them with the selection process to be followed in the subsequent two years of study. From the academic year 1997/8, pupils will sit exams in five core subjects (Greek language and literature, mathematics, physics and chemistry, history, and a major foreign language – English, French, German or Italian) and in the rest of the subjects of the curriculum, depending on the type of *Lykeio*. At the third grade of *Lykeio*, from the academic year 1998/9, pupils will sit exams in the same five core subjects as well as in one of three groups of three elective subjects, according to their preferences for higher education. Entrance to universities and TEI will be based on the total number of points that pupils acquire by taking into account 20 per cent of the marks achieved in the second grade and 80 per cent of the marks in the third grade of *Lykeio*, with 2,000 being the top mark.

Institutions for vocational training

While the outcome of this legislation is yet to be seen, in recent years increased financing from EU funds has led to a mosaic of agencies and organisations, ranging from local authorities to private schools and governmental organisations, offering a wide range of training programmes. The most important are set out below.

ELKEPA (Greek Productivity Centre) offers a broad spectrum of specialised short (20 to 50 hours) and long-term (100 to 800 hours) training programmes and seminars covering subjects from management and personal development to finance and accounting. Participants range from senior executives to unemployed university graduates. Training programmes are available through the centre's Institute of Management and Institute of Information Science. It also runs in-house seminars customised to company requirements. The cost is borne by the individuals attending the programmes, by their companies or from the EU Social Fund. Attendance is certified with an unofficial diploma. ELKEPA is considered to be one of the best centres for postgraduate, and especially managerial, training in Greece.

The EEDE (Greek Association of Business Management) provides various long- and short-term programmes and seminars as well as intra-company seminars mainly for higher-level management.

OAED operates an Intensive Vocational Training programme, Intra-Business Schools and Mobile Training Units as well as its initial apprenticeship programme (see above).

The Intensive Vocational Training programme is designed for adults – mainly unskilled unemployed, but also employed people. Courses may last up to 200 days (for boiler fitters, for example) but are usually six to nine months. As with the apprenticeship programme, the Intensive Vocational Training programme is provided in the Centres of Accelerated Vocational Training (KETEK), with similar courses. Trainees are paid, with full medical and health insurance, and the training time is considered as work experience. Selection is through interviews, or tests where applicable. However, completion of a programme does not automatically qualify a trainee to engage in an occupation.

The Intra-Business Schools operate within large firms, with programmes approved and managed by OAED. They aim at the intensive training of unemployed unskilled workers in skills which are of interest to the company as well as to the local community. The OAED also prepares the instructors – who may be employees of the companies themselves – with teaching seminars and provides payment and insurance for the participants. A substantial number of programmes have been subsidised in recent years under the development law 1262/82 or through the EU Social Fund.

The three Mobile Training Units are provided for the training of adults in non-industrial areas where there are no facilities, and where a demand for skilled personnel arises.

EOMMEX (the Hellenic Organisation of Small to Medium-Size-Enterprises and Handicrafts) aims to meet the need for skilled labour in small to medium-sized businesses. Among other services, it offers management and innovation seminars to small manufacturers, and general handicraft, carpet-making, wood-work, weaving and ceramic art seminars to craftsmen. The length of the seminars varies from short (24 to 75 hours) to long (three years in the case of carpet-mak-ing and woodwork). Programmes are carried out in the organisation's workshops and the instructors are organisation personnel or invited specialists.

Skilled labour and vocational training

Improvements since the early 1960s have raised the educational level of the labour force, especially the number of higher education graduates. According to the 1991 census, in the 25 to 64 age-group 12.5 per cent had tertiary-level quali-fications (15 per cent of men and 10 per cent of women), 24.2 per cent had fin-ished secondary education (25.4 per cent men and 23.1 per cent women), 6.9 per cent had finished lower secondary education (7.7 per cent men and 6.1 per cent women), and 43.4 per cent had finished primary education. Nevertheless, 13 per cent had not completed their elementary level of education (9.6 per cent of men and a remarkable 16.3 per cent of women, of whom 56 per cent were older than 50), although in the same year only 1 per cent of the under-45 age-group consid-ered themselves illiterate. The figures indicate a steady and continuous improve-ment. However, when the quality of education received is considered, research in 1988 argued that – in accordance with UNESCO's definition – 20 per cent of the labour force were illiterate and about 80 per cent 'technically illiterate' (having no familiarity with technology or 'no technical culture').

This situation can be explained partially by the fact that the vast majority of the trained workforce acquired its skills through work experience, without any anchoring in theoretical knowledge. An EU study in western Greece found that small and medium-sized firms in the high technology sector experienced severe shortages of clerical, marketing and skilled manual personnel.

Employers and vocational training

On-the-job training is practically non-existent for young people other than those on an OAED apprenticeship and TES, TEI and Technical University students (as described earlier). Employers have to rely almost entirely on in-house training to meet their requirements. Moreover, there seems to be general mistrust by employers of the qualifications offered by graduates of vocational education institutions. This stems from the belief that graduates have no real familiarity with industry and no practical experience, and that their theoretical knowledge is out of date and largely irrelevant to the actual production process. The roots of this mistrust lie in the weaknesses of the educational system itself. After decades of emphasis on the classical–humanistic tradition the present system still suffers isolation from the real economic and social environment.

On the other hand, firms themselves have often appeared to display little interest in fostering vocational training. While they may express strong interest in the training their staff have received, their own involvement is minimal. Rather than making use of the skills of trained staff, it has been argued that their prime concern frequently appears to be merely adapting graduates to existing tasks and routines. The problem is especially acute in small, family businesses – the vast majority of enterprises in Greece.

Nevertheless, some signs of improvement can be discerned. Employers, mainly in large export-oriented companies, have shown a marked interest in establishing and running their own programmes for training and retraining, supported where appropriate by EU funds. The textile and clothing industries and parts of the metalworking sector, in particular, have been involved in these programmes. In 1994, a six-year enterprise-level continuous training and employment promotion programme was established with funds from the EU Social Fund (ESF) and the European Regional Development Fund (ERDF). The aims of this programme include the establishment of a link between training and the labour market, the development of a permanent system of continuous training beyond the duration of the current programme, and the improvement of the vocational skills of workers in public and private sector enterprises. The programme consists of three parts.

Part 1 – creating continuous training structures by building the infrastructure required for continuous training (area 1) and activities to promote the realisation of the enterprise-level programme. Part 2 – continuous employee training in small, medium-sized and large firms, and firms undergoing a restructuring process. Part 3 – training and employment promotion for the unemployed and workers threatened with redundancy, aimed at: young people under 25 seeking to enter the labour market or who have so far been only temporarily integrated into the labour market; women, especially those under 25; the unemployed aged over 25, including the long-term unemployed, but excluding marginalised social groups; the unemployed from high-unemployment areas and threatened by long-term unemployment; and workers under threat of unemployment due to planned lay-offs.

Management training

The educational path for future senior managers, especially in international companies, typically entails a first degree in a technical subject at a Greek university followed by a second, business or technical, qualification at a foreign university. The tendency for Greek graduates to study or work for part of their early life abroad, often in North America, the UK or Germany, has created a pool of qualified managers with excellent foreign language skills and international experience. Graduates in accountancy and finance must have a Greek qualification and be registered with the local professional association. There are well regarded business faculties in the Universities of Athens, Piraeus and Thessalonika.

A significant number of employers provide training for their middle and senior managers, and medium-sized to large companies generally favour a strategy of internal development before external recruitment. A popular form of training is an MBA in a private institution in Greece, of which more than 20 function in association with foreign universities.

One especially sought-after programme in management education is the MBA offered by the Athens Laboratory of Business Administration (ALBA), founded in 1992 by the Greek Association of Business Management (EEDE) in collaboration with the Association of Greek Industries (SEB) to help remedy the shortfall of local managers with a strong local business education, some of whom may have obtained their first degrees abroad. Thirty-six primarily Greek-owned, but internationally active, companies sponsor the Laboratory. The MBA is not formally recognised as a degree by the Greek authorities, and ALBA is therefore obliged to call its qualification an 'MBA Certificate'.

The courses, taught exclusively in English, and its graduates are in considerable demand by local employers, despite the fairly high cost compared with other locally-obtained foreign MBAs. As well as its two MBA programmes, ALBA also offers a general managerial education programme.

Trade unions and vocational training

Until recently, trade unions have been almost wholly concerned with wage bargaining and have not shown great interest in, nor developed any strategy for, training issues. The situation has improved considerably since the establishment of the Institute of Labour (INE) by the GSEE trade union federation (General Confederation of the Workers of Greece). The INE provides support and supervision for all EU programmes in which unions are involved. GSEE itself participates in several Community programmes for intra-company training, retraining unemployed workers, training in new technologies, training trainers, and retraining unemployed women. Costs are covered by EU funds (up to 70 per cent of the total cost of each programme) and from the GSEE's own resources. A similar increasing interest in vocational training is currently expressed by local labour centres and federations. In 1992, 60 per cent of these second-tier unions applied for places in retraining programmes. Again, costs are met jointly from EU funds (up to 60 per cent) and from the unions. The 1991 national collective agreement, in a landmark development, established a scheme under which the employers' organisations agreed to administer jointly with GSEE the 0.45 per cent of the employers' social security contributions earmarked for vocational training and development. GSEE is also pressing for the ratification of the ILO Convention 140 on paid leave for training.

Financing

Training is financed by government funding, EU funds and a levy of 0.45 per cent of the wage bill of companies, and is administered by a joint committee of trade unions and employer associations.

Educational attainment of the population

Level	Percentage of 25–64 age-group
Lower secondary	66
Upper secondary	21
Higher education (non-university)	3
University	10

Source: OECD (1994)

Organisations

Official Manpower and Placement Agency
OAED
Thrakis 8
16610 Glyfada
Tel. +30 1 993 2589
Fax +30 1 993 7301

Ministry of Labour
40 Piraeus St
Athens
Tel. +30 1 523 2110

General Secretariat for Equality
2 Mousseou St.
Plaka
Athens
Tel. +30 1 321 2094

Federation of Greek Industries
5 Xenofontos Street
105 57 Athens
Tel. +30 1 323 7325

Greek Personnel Management Association
3 Karitsi Street
105 61 Athens
Tel. +30 1 322 5704

British–Hellenic Chamber of Commerce
25 Vas. Sofias
106 74 Athens
Tel. +30 1 721 0361
Fax +30 1 721 8571

INE – GSEE
(General Confederation of Greek Labour)
Patision and Pipinou 27
112 51 Athens
Tel. +30 1 883 4611
Fax +30 1 822 9802

ALBA
(Athens Laboratory of Business
Administration)
Athinas Ave. & Areos St 2A
16671 Vouliagmeni
Tel. +30 1 896 4531
Fax +30 1 896 4737

Main sources

MINISTRY OF NATIONAL EDUCATION AND RELIGIOUS AFFAIRS. *Review of the Greek Education System. Report to the OECD.* Athens, 1995
EUROPEAN COMMISSION – MISEP (1995). Employment Observatory. *Basic Information Report. Greece.* Berlin, MISEP, 1995

7

Irish Republic

The Irish economy has been one of the most successful in the European Union over the past decade, although it has taken some considerable time for this to begin to have any positive impact on the labour market. Skills shortages have recently begun to appear in technical professions and some local labour markets. The movement of registered unemployment is partly attributable to rates of outward and return migration, which – paradoxically – can serve to cut unemployment levels in phases of economic slackness and exacerbate it when recovery is established. Much of the strength of the economy is attributable to the impact of foreign direct investment in high-tech sectors, calling for and creating a pool of skilled, mostly young, graduates and employees in the fields of computer engineering and software. This group co-exists with an older workforce who are poorly skilled in comparison with the rest of Europe and of which many have become trapped in long-term unemployment.

Much of the legal structure surrounding recruitment parallels that operating in the UK: there are no major constraints on employers, and considerable freedom to shape contracts to suit operating needs.

The voluntarist principle underlying the system of industrial relations in Ireland extends to the area of training, where there is an absence of any strict legislative framework governing initial and continuing training. Apart from the payment of an apprenticeship levy, employers are not obliged by law to spend any money on training schemes for their employees. Although the system of higher education is regarded as producing generally high-quality graduates, but with less industrial experience than their Continental European counterparts, initial and continuing training has recently attracted considerable criticism, and proposals have been made to intensify and standardise the national training effort.

The labour market

In 1995 the Irish labour force amounted to 1,423,000, equivalent to about 40 per cent of the total population of 3,582,000. Of those at work, men accounted for approximately two-thirds (920,000) and women for around one-third (503,000). In recent years female participation in the labour force for the 25–54 age group has risen considerably and this trend is set to continue in the coming years. However, at some 35 per cent overall female participation in the labour force is well below the EU average.

In 1995 unemployment in Ireland stood at 12.9 per cent of the labour force, compared with an EU average of 11 per cent, according to standardised OECD unemployment rates. Recent figures indicate that over 62 per cent of those unemployed have been so for more than 12 months. The rate of long-term unemployment in Ireland, at almost 10 per cent, is higher than the overall rate of unemployment in many other countries. Almost half of the long-term unemployed have no formal educational qualification.

The level of atypical employment in Ireland is below European averages, although there have been dramatic increases in the incidence of various forms of atypical employment over the last decade. The overwhelming majority of atypical workers are women, a trend consistent with the fact that a majority of new jobs are filled by women and because atypical employment now accounts for ever-increasing numbers of new jobs.

Part-time workers now account for about 11 per cent of the workforce, compared to 6.4 per cent in 1985. The steepest rise has occurred in the retail sector, where part-time employment as a percentage of overall employment increased from 28 per cent in 1985 to 38 per cent in 1994. Fixed-term employment now accounts for almost 10 per cent of total employment, up from below 7.5 per cent in 1985, with women making up almost two-thirds of those on fixed-term contracts.

The description of the Irish labour force as being relatively well educated is justified if the focus is on the proportion of young people who participate in formal academic education and the academic quality of that education, according to labour market experts. However, young people account for only a minority of the labour force and the formal educational qualifications of older workers are relatively poor. This is particularly true of those over 40 years of age, a group which comprises 40 per cent of those at work.

The percentage who have completed second-level education is low by international standards, although the proportion of the Irish workforce with post-compulsory education (45 per cent) is close to the EU average, while lower than some northern European countries. The level of continuing vocational training and education for those already in the workforce seems low when compared to more prosperous European countries, although the statistics in this area are said to be not wholly reliable. A relatively high proportion of highly qualified workers are employed in sectors which are not directly involved in exporting. Fewer graduates follow those disciplines of most relevance to manufacturing than is the case in many other countries.

In 1991 approximately one-fifth of those in employment had third-level qualifications, while almost half had no qualification higher than Junior Certificate (the exam taken at the end of the junior cycle in second-level schools, and which occurs at the age at which compulsory school attendance ends). Qualifications varied by age-group, reflecting the expansion of upper secondary and higher education over the last 25 years. In all age-groups, women workers tended to have higher educational qualifications than men.

Education levels also vary by occupation and across sectors of the economy.

Third-level qualifications were most prevalent among professional and technical workers (80 per cent of whom were so qualified).

The latest official assessment of Irish industry and enterprise concludes that there are no persistent shortages of specific skills in the Irish labour force. However, some employers have expressed difficulty in recruiting people with a combination of appropriate qualifications and relevant experience. In the future, the areas where skills shortages are expected to emerge at graduate or diploma level are in software, in design, in combinations of languages with other disciplines, and in combinations of business subjects with other disciplines.

Employment prospects   The composition and size of the Irish labour force in the future will be a major determinant of the rate of economic progress and the achievement of the broad objectives set in any longer-term strategy, according to a recent report from FORFAS, the Irish industrial policy think tank. 'The increasing trend to employment in services, the continuing development of information and communications technologies and the replacement of the old hierarchical approach to the organisation of work by a new flexible entrepreneurial approach will stimulate the growth in more flexible forms of work including self-employment, part-time and temporary employment'. Demography will be a critical factor, but the underlying elements are already changing rapidly, according to FORFAS.

The structure of Ireland's employed labour force differs substantially from other European countries' in terms of its sectoral composition. In 1994 the numbers employed in agriculture, at some 12 per cent, were more than twice the EU–15 average, while the numbers employed in industry and services, at 28 per cent and 60 per cent respectively, were below the EU averages of 31 per cent and 64 per cent. The outflow from agricultural employment will continue to be substantial and add to the need to achieve significant net job creation in services and manufacturing. The services sector will be the main source of new employment opportunities.

The proportion of Ireland's population in the 0–14 year age category is well above the EU–15 average. The proportion in the 'working age' group of 15–64 years is also below the EU–15 average (63 per cent versus 68 per cent in 1993). Ireland has a large dependency ratio and this has been one of the factors explaining why it has been constrained in moving closer to the EU average of per capita living standards.

While Ireland has experienced a rapid increase in educational participation in recent years, it still lags behind many of the more advanced EU countries. In 1994, the participation rate among 15–19 year olds was 74 per cent. This is expected to increase significantly in the years ahead, with consequent reduction in labour force numbers. Overall, the Irish labour market is seen as constituting a single labour force with that of the UK. This lends great uncertainty to any projections in labour force changes. Between 1986 and 1991, it is estimated there was net outward migration of almost 27,000. FORFAS estimates that the Irish labour force will expand significantly in the period to 2010, rising from 1,423,000 in 1995 to 1,640,000 in 2010.

Official requirements

There are few, if any, requirements laid down by law in regard to the recruitment of employees, apart from the provisions of the Employment Equality Act, 1977 which regulate recruitment and advertising, and set out pitfalls to be avoided in the conduct of interviews.

Work permits are not required by EU nationals. All other foreign workers must apply to the Department of Enterprise and Employment for a work permit before commencing employment. Work permits are issued for a maximum period of one year and are renewable.

Personnel planning

Companies are not legally obliged to consult trade unions or employee representatives on personnel planning issues, but larger companies tend to have in-house agreements. Some companies have union agreements which stipulate that all internal vacancies must be posted up, usually with time limits within which employees must apply. Employers usually reserve the right to recruit externally if no suitable applicants have been found within the company.

Employment incentives

A number of subsidised employment and employment incentive schemes operate in Ireland.

Jobstart is a recruitment subsidy which offers employers Ir£80 per week for one year when filling new and existing jobs with people who have been on the live register of unemployed, and in receipt of unemployment payments, for at least three years. Participants can retain secondary welfare benefits, subject to the Ir£250 per week limit which applies to community employment and the back to work allowance.

Workplace provides work experience for up to five weeks with employers who have an identified vacancy or who can offer 'quality work experience' to people who have been unemployed for six months. Five thousand places have been designated for both the Jobstart and Workplace schemes in 1996/7.

Another new scheme has been introduced which is intended to assist people aged over 35 who have been unemployed for at least five years. Voluntary and statutory organisations in a number of urban areas can apply to become managing agents and employ people in categories deemed to be at greatest risk of never working again: middle-aged, poorly qualified people who have not worked for many years. The 1,000 jobs covered by the scheme are expected to cover areas such as caretaking, energy conservation, landscaping, maintenance work and child care. The scheme is funded by the state job placement agency, FAS. Participants will be paid the 'going rate' and will be guaranteed three years' work. They can participate for only one three-year term.

Using part-timers and temps

Part-time contracts There is no statutory definition of part-time work. However, under the Worker Protection (Regular Part-time Employees) Act, 1991, employees working eight or more hours a week, with 13 weeks' service, are entitled, on a pro rata basis, to benefits enjoyed by full-time staff, such as holidays, workplace health and safety, dismissal notice, redundancy payments and redress for unfair dismissal.

Holiday entitlement is six hours' paid leave for each hundred hours worked and part-time employees are also entitled to public holidays. Part-timers must have two years' service (with at least eight hours a week for thirteen weeks in each year) before being entitled to statutory redundancy compensation. They must have one year's service before pursuing an unfair dismissals claim, although part-time employees are covered under the dismissals legislation from day one if they are dismissed for reasons related to pregnancy or trade union activity.

Fixed-term contracts There is no statutory definition of a fixed-term contract, nor do employers have to justify recourse to such contracts. Where employees on fixed-term contracts fulfil service criteria, they enjoy all associated statutory rights. Although the right to bring a claim of unfair dismissal does not apply to employees with less than one year's service, under the Unfair Dismissals (Amendment) Act, 1993, employees who have been employed under two or more successive fixed-term contracts, each of less than a year, may bring such a claim. Any ruling on the issue would be a matter for individual determination by the EAT or a civil court in the light of all the circumstances.

Temporary agency employment As in the United Kingdom, and in contrast to most other EU member states, the employment status of temporary agency workers is not unambiguously resolved. Although some agencies, and in particular the leading ones, provide holiday pay, sick pay and maternity pay for their staff, and take on the responsibility of employers, some case law has ruled that agency employees are neither employees of the agency nor of the user company, with consequent difficulties in enforcing rights against either. However, under recent legislation (Unfair Dismissals (Amendment) Act, 1993), temporary workers may bring a case of unfair dismissal against the user company.

Agencies are regulated by the 1971 Employment Agency Act, which prescribes licensing arrangements, provides for official approval of fees, and allows for official inspection. Most agencies involved in temporary work are also active as placement agencies for permanent employment (see below).

Temporary employment is concentrated in fields such as catering, cleaning services, retailing and financial services, where there are a number of specialised agencies for professionals.

Recruitment paths

According to the 1992 Price Waterhouse survey on Human Resource Management in Ireland, external advertising is favoured for management and professional/technical vacancies, whereas internal advertising is most common for clerical and manual grades. The sample frame used in the survey was the top 1,000 trading companies and the top 500 non-trading bodies in Ireland.

On the whole, it was found that larger organisations made greater use of the internal labour market, while Irish-owned companies made less use of the internal labour market in the recruitment process than foreign-owned companies for all categories of employees. When recruiting managerial staff, 65 per cent of organisations advertised externally, 53 per cent recruited from among current employees, 42 per cent advertised internally, 41 per cent employed recruitment agencies, 35 per cent used search and selection consultants, and in 9 per cent of cases appointments were made by word of mouth.

For professional and technical staff, 69 per cent of organisations advertised externally, 42 per cent employed recruitment agencies, 39 per cent advertised internally, 35 per cent recruited from among current employees, 24 per cent used search and selection consultants and in 12 per cent of cases appointments were made by word of mouth. Job centres were used by only 1 per cent of organisations.

Word-of-mouth advertising was much more important for clerical and manual staff: 22 per cent of appointments for clerical employees and 38 per cent for manual workers were made in this way – the second most frequent method in the latter case. Job centres also figured much more prominently for manual employees than for other categories.

Recruitment and sex equality

The Employment Equality Agency (EEA) has produced guidelines on recruitment and interview procedures to ensure gender equality.

It is unlawful for an employer to discriminate against an employee or prospective employee regarding access to employment on grounds of sex or marital status under the Employment Equality Act, 1977. Both direct and indirect discrimination are prohibited. It is also unlawful to classify a post by reference to sex, although permitted exceptions cover situations where the sex of the person is an occupational qualification for the job. The EEA provides a free, confidential advisory service on the operation of the Employment Equality Act.

The EEA states that indirect discrimination occurs where a practice or policy which is not essential for the job has a disproportionate impact on one sex or marital status. The reason for the disproportionate impact must be related to gender or marital status. For example, the Labour Court has determined that excluding applicants because of child care responsibilities is a form of indirect discrimination.

In its guidelines, the EEA says employers should examine their job requirements and include only those that are essential for the job. This is necessary to guard against indirect discrimination. Specifying age limits may be unlawful. Unnecessary job requirements may prevent suitable candidates from applying.

Discriminatory job advertisements are unlawful. Job advertisements should clearly indicate that the position is open to men and women, regardless of marital status. The EEA says this can be reinforced by including an appropriate phrase in the advertisement such as 'applications are invited from suitably qualified men and women'. Job titles which specify one sex such as 'waitress' or 'foreman' should be avoided, and inclusive terms such as 'waiting staff' and 'supervisor' should be used instead. Care should also be taken to ensure that photographs or illustrations do not indicate a preference for one sex.

Employers who invite applications from the under-represented sex in order to achieve gender balance should ensure that they keep records to show that no discrimination occurred.

Application forms should seek only essential information which is relevant to the job. Personal details should not be disclosed to those involved in the actual selection of employees. Where personal details are sought, to monitor the effectiveness of a job recruitment policy, it should be made clear that they are sought for this purpose only and will not be disclosed to the selectors.

Interviewers should receive training in the requirements of equality legislation and should guard against unconscious bias, says the EEA. Mixed male and female interview boards are recommended. Questions should be related to the requirements of the job. Where it is necessary to assess whether personal circumstances will adversely affect job performance, for example, if extensive travel or unsocial hours are involved, relevant questions should be asked of all candidates and evaluated in the same way for men and women. Employers should be aware that certain questions may constitute evidence of discrimination, such as questions relating to family circumstances. Where tests are used to eliminate applicants, care should be taken to guard against hidden forms of indirect discrimination. Failure to consider adequately an applicant for a job because of pregnancy constitutes direct discrimination.

The Price Waterhouse survey showed that a relatively small number of organisations targeted women specifically in the recruitment process. The likelihood of targeting women was found to be more strongly related to those organisations that recognise trade unions.

Finding the applicant

Staff may be recruited directly, by advertisement or individual approach, through the state job placement agency, FAS, or through private employment agencies for both temporary and permanent placement.

State placement system

The state job placement and training agency (FAS) plays an active role in job placement and mediation between employers and job seekers as well as in the development of training programmes. It is additionally responsible for the operation of training and employment programmes, the provision of an employment/recruitment service, an advisory service for industry, and support for co-operative and community-based enterprise. Priority is given to those facing greatest difficulties in the labour market, including the long-term unemployed and early school-leavers.

There are no costs involved in using the services provided by FAS. It has the reputation of dealing largely with semi-skilled or unskilled jobs, although it also assists in the recruitment of apprentices and has begun taking steps to broaden its recruitment services to encompass certain skilled and professional positions.

In the Price Waterhouse survey, 26 per cent of organisations used job centres – this refers primarily to FAS offices – in recruiting manual employees and 15 per cent used job centres in the recruitment of clerical employees.

Employment agencies

Employment agencies are used primarily in the recruitment of managerial, professional, technical and clerical employees. The Association of Management Consulting Organisations (AMCO) is a professional body which represents management consultancy firms. Its aims include encouraging higher standards of professional service and promoting a wider understanding and use of consultancy services in industry, commerce and government. AMCO has issued a code of practice for its members which covers recruitment practices and which has been voluntarily adopted by member organisations.

Executive search and selection

One-third of organisations used search and selection consultants in the recruitment of managerial staff and one-quarter used them in the recruitment of professional and technical staff, according to the Price Waterhouse survey. These organisations may operate in one of two ways. They may take over the recruitment task: using information on the vacancy, they will advertise and conduct preliminary interviews and provide the company with a short-list of potential applicants. Alternatively, they may keep a register of specialist candidates who have indicated a willingness to be considered for suitable jobs as they arise.

Although there are only two firms involved in search only, a number of international consultants, such as PA, operate a mixture of search and selection, depending on the level of position.

Recruitment methods

The media

The Employment Equality Act, 1977 sets out rules to be observed in recruitment advertising.

Newspapers are widely used to attract white-collar and management staff. Recruitment consultants Executive Market have conducted regular surveys of recruitment advertising for managerial and professional staff in Ireland. In the 12 months to April 1996, it was found that there was a startling 57 per cent increase over the previous 12 months in the numbers of such jobs advertised. In a survey of the most popular newspaper with recruiting employers, they assessed advertisements for managerial and professional vacancies with the exception of the voluntary sector, all posts in the civil service and local government, medical and veterinary positions and positions such as secretaries, office staff, technicians, computer programmers and operators, craftworkers, shop managers and audit assistants.

The electronics, computer and software sectors were particularly busy, with demand in these sectors up by 107 per cent over the previous year. Within four years, demand in these sectors has increased five-fold. The importance of these sectors, in recruitment terms, is such that they have now been separated into two new categories for survey purposes: software now accounts for 18 per cent of all jobs advertised while electronics manufacturing accounts for 14 per cent. Process industries, including food and pharmaceuticals, report healthy growth in recruitment, while the continued increase in demand for professional and scientific services reflects continued expansion and increased investment. Demand in financial services has also been restored to previous high levels.

Analysed by profession, the two groups for whom demand has increased most rapidly are computer professionals and engineers. The demand for computer professionals doubled between 1995 and 1996, and they now account for 21 per cent of the jobs surveyed. Engineers (other than electronics engineers) and sales and marketing staff also each account for 21 per cent of the advertised vacancies in the survey. Demand for engineers doubled in the 12 months to April 1996, while the demand for electronics engineers surprisingly stood still. Sales and marketing has also been buoyant, increasing in numbers of advertisements by 22 per cent over the previous year. The one profession which has benefited least from the recent upsurge in demand is accountancy, whose share of the overall jobs surveyed has halved from 1990 to a current 6 per cent of all recruitment advertisements.

The increased dominance of *The Irish Times* is the main feature of the survey's analysis of the preferred choice of newspaper by recruiters. In the 12 months surveyed, 79 per cent of all jobs advertised were found in *The Irish Times*, up 12 percentage points on the previous year. This increased share was mainly at the expense of the Independent Group of newspapers, whose two main titles, the *Sunday Independent* (17 per cent) and the daily *Irish Independent* (16 per cent), saw their combined share fall by 11 percentage points from the previous year's total of 44 per cent. The *Sunday Business Post* attracted 13 per cent of all jobs advertised and the *Sunday Tribune* attracted 6 per cent, according to the survey, which noted that both of these newspapers relied heavily on heavily discounted duplication from the daily newspapers. In addition to the newspapers covered in this survey, there are two evening newspapers published daily, the *Evening Herald* and the *Evening News*. Neither attract any great levels of recruitment advertising for professional and managerial jobs.

Recruitment procedures

Recruitment Documents and confidentiality   The Association of Management Consulting Organisations (AMCO) has adopted a code of practice which deals with candidate care and confidentiality. Identifiable details about a candidate or potential candidate can be revealed to a client. Enquiries about a candidate's references should be dealt with only with the consent of the candidate.

Candidates must always have the right to know the client's identity before the consultants disclose the candidate's identity to the client. Information given in confidence by the client or by candidates must be kept confidential, and may be used only in connection with the recruitment exercise.

All candidates should be kept informed of the progress of their application. Unsuccessful candidates should be advised when an appointment is made, or a recruitment exercise otherwise completed. If requested, consultants must destroy an unsuccessful candidate's file. Upon written request, consultants must provide candidates with a copy of their personal history form if it is held on file – no charge should be made to a candidate. Candidates should not be charged a fee in any circumstances.

Selection methods

Relatively little use is made of what are considered to be the more sophisticated methods of selection, the Price Waterhouse survey concludes. The application form, the interview panel and references are the most commonly used methods, while methods such as aptitude tests, psychometric testing, group selection, assessment centres, biodata and graphology are used in a minority of cases.

A higher percentage of large organisations appear to use the more sophisticated methods. While only 8 per cent of organisations employing less than 200 people used psychometric testing as a selection tool, 29 per cent of organisations employing more than 200 employees did so. And while only 22 per cent of the smaller organisations use aptitude tests, 41 per cent of the larger organisations use such tests. There are no substantial differences between large and small organisations in their use of the most common selection methods such as application forms, interview panels and reference checks.

Offer and rejection

There is no legal regulation of the form for making a job offer or receiving confirmation of acceptance. In practice, job offers and acceptances tend to be in writing, mainly to ensure that a record is kept of all transactions.

The Terms of Employment Information Act, 1994 obliges employers to give all new employees a written statement of the terms and conditions of their employment. Existing employees who request it must be given the same information. Employees being posted abroad are entitled to information specific to the posting, such as currency for payment, and return arrangements.

Education, training and employee development

The education system

Attendance at school is compulsory by law for pupils aged between 6 and 15. Primary education is free and generally lasts for eight years between the ages of 4 or 5 and 12. A national curriculum developed by the Department of Education applies to all pupils.

Secondary education

The final three years of compulsory education takes junior-cycle pupils up to about the age of 15. This is followed by a senior-cycle of two or three years' duration, bringing children to the age of 18 or 19.

There are three main types of second-level school: secondary, vocational, and community and comprehensive schools. Secondary schools, educating 61 per cent of second-level students, are privately owned and managed, the majority by religious communities. All except 5 per cent participate in the free education scheme, receive the bulk of their funding from the state, are subject to state supervision and prepare students for state examinations.

Vocational schools, educating 26 per cent of second-level students, are funded by the state and are run under the responsibility of statutory vocational education committees which consist of elected public representatives and others with educational and industrial experience. Community and comprehensive schools, educating 13 per cent of second-level students, are allocated individual budgets by the state, run by boards of management, and provide a full range of practical, academic and vocational subjects.

After compulsory education is completed, students can take part in the Vocational Preparation and Training Programme (VPTP) as an alternative to registering for the senior-cycle Leaving Certificate which is the preference of the majority of those attending second-level schools. VPTP is aimed at young people in the 15 to 18 age group who propose to enter the labour market directly after completing compulsory schooling but who require basic vocational training to enhance their prospects of employment. It operates at two levels: level one is designed as a preparation for work or as a basis for entry into a further year of vocational training. Level two is a self-contained one-year programme aimed at those who have successfully completed level one or an equivalent programme or who have formal qualifications (such as the Leaving Certificate), but lack vocational training or experience. The programme consists of three main components: vocational studies (designations include commerce, construction, engineering, secretarial, catering, agriculture, craft and design, and electrics/electronics), preparation for working life (a school programme and work experience) and general skills (such as communications, mathematics and education for living).

A points system, based on results achieved in senior-level state examinations within second-level schools, regulates applications for entry into higher education. The Irish government has recently removed fees charged for undergraduate third-level education.

In 1994 67,500 students left second-level education, of whom 38 per cent entered further education and 34.5 per cent found employment within a year. Twenty per cent were still unemployed twelve months after leaving school and almost 5 per cent had emigrated. This breakdown applied almost equally among the 34,100 males and 33,400 females.

Tertiary education

There are two main types of higher education establishment, both of which are largely state funded: universities and regional technical colleges. A number of private education establishments also operate. Almost 40 per cent of second-level students opt to register for third-level education.

The National College of Ireland has constituent colleges in Dublin, Cork and Galway. Dublin University has one constituent college, Trinity College, Dublin. The two newest universities are Dublin City University and the University of Limerick.

The Dublin Institute of Technology (DIT) together with a number of regional technical colleges (RTCs), offers vocational and technical courses, some leading to degrees, which can be attended on a full-time or part-time basis. They receive substantial funding from the European Social Fund.

Graduate recruitment

All of the main third-level education institutions provide careers services to assist graduates find employment and offer access for employers to new recruits. The complete list of Irish universities is as follows: University College Dublin, Trinity College Dublin, Dublin City University, University College Cork, University of Limerick, University College Galway and Maynooth College. Careers services are also provided in the regional technical colleges, including the Dublin Institute of Technology, which place a heavy emphasis on applied science and technological education. There is no military service in Ireland.

Adult education

According to the recent White Paper on Education, adult education is characterised by the voluntary nature of participation and the variety of opportunities available from a wide range of sources. The main opportunities for participation in systematic adult education is through schemes such as the Vocational Training Opportunities Scheme (VTOS), the adult literacy community education scheme, and various schemes involving area-based partnerships.

VTOS is administered by the Departments of Education and Social Welfare, and offers the long-term unemployed (ie those unemployed for more than 12 months) over the age of 21 an opportunity to return to full-time vocational education and training. Courses focus on the development of employment-related skills, including technological and business skills, and modules are also provided on personal development. Since it was introduced in 1989, enrolment in VTOS has risen from 247 to 5,000 in 1995.

Training and official employment services

The main industrial training authority, FAS, was established under the Labour Services Act, 1987. FAS offers training to those already in employment and those seeking to enter employment. The Industrial Restructuring Training Programme (IRTP) is the principal means by which FAS assists the retraining requirements of Irish companies. The Training Support Scheme, which is the primary financial component of the IRTP, provided assistance to 1,729 firms in the retraining of 22,417 employees in 1994. Special consideration is given to small enterprise owner/manager development where FAS meets 80 per cent of programme costs. In 1994 companies with less than 50 employees received grants totalling Ir£1.76m or 40 per cent of the total available budget.

In terms of training for those seeking or re-entering employment, a total of 15,178 people completed training programmes at 20 FAS training centres during 1994. In addition, 12,746 completed training programmes run by external contractors on behalf of FAS, while 592 people commenced its Job Training Scheme, an employer-based programme providing training in specific skills.

The FAS training courses for those not already in employment operate under a number of broad headings. Specific Skills Training courses aim to provide participants with an employable skill. The Foundation Skills course offers basic skills training for young school-leavers. Re-integration training covers the retraining of older experienced workers and of women returning to the workforce, in up-to-date job skills and practices. Enterprise courses are special courses to assist people set up their own business. Finally, its apprenticeship programmes offer off-the-job training modules in support of on-the-job practice.

In recent years the apprenticeship system has changed from a time-served to a standards-based model. The recent introduction of the new system means that no one has so far completed the new standards-based apprenticeship, but when it is completed successful participants will be awarded a national craft certificate. The total number of registered apprentices within the time-served system was 10,695 at the end of 1994, and those within the new standards-based system was over 1,000.

The new system provides for broad-based training initially, with the apprentice able to develop specialist skills further into the apprenticeship, thereby increasing flexibility and allowing for cross-skilling and updating of skills in line with technological change. The training takes the form of on- and off-the-job modules, with the duration of the apprenticeship determined by the time it takes to pass the modules, and the particular industry concerned. To encourage employers to recruit women into apprenticeships, FAS introduced a bursary in 1990. In 1994 40 firms were participating in the bursary.

The 1996 White Paper on human resource development backs greater direct involvement by employers in the design and provision of training, largely at the expense of services currently being provided by FAS.

CERT is the national organisation for the education, recruitment and training of personnel for the tourism, hotel and catering industries. It is also responsible for training at hotel and catering schools. CERT provides short-term courses, usually of thirteen weeks' duration full-time, for young people wishing to work in the industry. It also provides skills-update courses for those already in employment and wishing to move to supervisory level. Courses are also organised for the long-term unemployed with multi-skilled courses of 26 weeks' duration, or single-discipline courses lasting 20 weeks, in addition to six-week courses for people wishing to return to catering.

The National Rehabilitation Board (NRB) co-ordinates the rehabilitation and training of disabled persons. It trains disabled people with a view to their working either in companies alongside able-bodied employees, or in special organisations, in either a skilled or unskilled capacity.

In 1995 the Irish government approved the establishment of a new national certification authority, TEASTAS, which operates under the aegis of the Department of Education. Though it has a wide-ranging remit, the authority has four main responsibilities:

- the development, implementation, regulation and supervision of the certification of all non-university third-level programmes, and all further and continuation, education and training programmes
- the establishment, direction, supervision and regulation of a national qualifications framework
- ensuring international recognition of all the qualifications under its remit
- the plans, programmes and budgets necessary for the achievement of the functions set out above, including the plans, programmes and budgets for the National Council for Educational Awards and the National Council for Vocational Awards, which will be reconstituted as sub-boards of TEASTAS.

Vocational training

The voluntary approach which informs industrial relations in Ireland also extends to the system of training. There is minimal legislation governing the provision of training, and employers and trade unions work actively with the state in designing and adopting training schemes and institutions.

Since 1993 a new standards-based apprenticeship system has been introduced on a phased basis. All of the main trades are now operating the new system, which replaces the old time-served system. In addition, a number of new trades have been brought into the new system, including service-sector occupations. A new minimum age limit of 16 also applies.

The new standards-based system operates on the basis of four periods on the job alternating with three periods off the job on courses provided by FAS or the regional technical colleges, including the Dublin Institute of Technology. While apprentices are on the job, employers carry out competency tests and apprentices must complete their tasks twice before they can be deemed to have passed.

To encourage greater female participation in the new system, FAS is offering a bursary of almost Ir£2,500 to each employer recruiting a woman apprentice.

Consultation on training

There is no legal requirement for employers to consult with workers or their representatives in regard to any aspect of training. However, at the macro level, trade unions are well represented on various industry advisory committees that decide on training requirements for various sectors together with employers, civil servants and others. Six statutory Industrial Training Committees are responsible for advising and assisting FAS on all matters relating to training for their respective industrial sectors.

Continuing training

There is no statutory obligation on employers to provide training and no statutory right to time off for training. Consequently, continuing training is relatively neglected in comparison with most other EU member states. Employers can send their employees on a wide variety of training courses to enhance their existing skills or train them in new skills, provided by a variety of state or private institutions.

FAS operates an Industrial Restructuring Training Programme which it claims is its principal vehicle for assisting companies to meet their retraining requirements. In 1994, the Training Support Scheme – the main financial element of the Programme – assisted 1,729 firms in the retraining of almost 22,500 workers. Four-fifths of programme costs for small enterprise owner/manager development were met by FAS.

One official study for FAS found that 7 per cent of workers had participated in some education or training in the previous four weeks. In most cases (77 per cent), those involved were receiving further training for their present job, initial vocational training, or training for a different job from that currently held; each accounted for about 10 per cent of those receiving training.

The level of continuing training varied across age-groups. Just over one in six (18 per cent) of workers aged under 25 had received some training in the previous four weeks, but the numbers receiving training in the previous four weeks and aged over 25 stood at less than 5 per cent.

A recent report for the country's industrial policy think tank, FORFAS, stated 'the concept of lifelong learning is still a long way from becoming a reality for most of the Irish population. Full-time education is still aimed almost entirely at those who have not yet started a career, and part-time vocationally-oriented education is aimed at those early in their careers.' Dramatic changes in Ireland's approach to retraining are apparent.

Ireland's level of continuing education and training, while higher than many countries (including Mediterranean European countries) is significantly lower than best practice as represented by Northern European countries, and indeed, by a number of successful enterprises in Ireland, according to the FORFAS report. 'The low level of continuous training at firm-level limits business competitiveness and demonstrates a lack of commitment to staff development on the part of management. The gap to be bridged is, therefore, a dual one, covering both skill development and management/work organisation'. The report says that expenditure on training, now standing at about 1.2 per cent of labour costs, should probably be in excess of 3 per cent, judging by trends in other countries, and by the fact that many of the firms that are seen to have adequate training programmes spend approximately 5 per cent of payroll. It adds that any focus on training expenditure must also look at the quality.

Workforce appraisal/development

The Price Waterhouse survey found that just 63 per cent of respondents indicated that they analyse the training needs of their employees, with larger organisations much more likely to engage in such analysis than their smaller counterparts.

Over two-thirds – 69 per cent – of private-sector organisations surveyed analysed the training needs of their employees while 53 per cent of public-sector organisations did likewise.

About two-thirds – over 67 per cent – of organisations monitored the effectiveness of their training. The greatest emphasis was placed on informal mechanisms of evaluation, with much less use of more structured mechanisms such as formal evaluation after training, or tests.

Supervisors and managers

The level of management training in Ireland has been the subject of continuing criticism. The most comprehensive analysis of management training, the so-called Galvin report, found that in 1989 'expenditure in Ireland on management development is inadequate, whether measured by comparison with international practice or in relation to national needs'. It found that on average 1.4 per cent of companies' pay bills were devoted to management training.

The FORFAS report found that management and operational deficiencies are seriously damaging the competitiveness of Irish-owned industry. These were particularly concentrated in the small and medium-sized enterprises which have the greatest resource constraints on training. There were also some strategically important deficiencies in the multinational sector. While the main expertise of these managers was in operations management, many had an input into strategic decision-making and could benefit from acquiring additional strategic management skills, the report stated.

Financing the system

Industrial employers pay a levy of 0.25 per cent of their wage bill to fund apprenticeship training. Additional funding is provided by the state and the European Social Fund, which together contribute 65 per cent of total costs.

In 1994, levy schemes to fund training were implemented in five of the designated industries: chemical and allied products; food, drink and tobacco; textiles; clothing and footwear; electronics sector of the engineering industry. A total of 1,023 employers (39 per cent), employing a total of 112,789 (92 per cent of the total workforce in these industries) were assessed to pay the levy.

Educational attainment of the population

Level	Percentage of 25–64 age-group
Lower secondary	55
Upper secondary	27
Higher education (non-university)	6
University	12

Source: OECD (1994)

Organisations

Department of Enterprise and
Employment
Kildare Street
Dublin 2
Tel. + 353 1 6767571
Fax + 353 1 6762285

FAS – Training and Employment
Authority
27–33 Upper Baggot Street
Dublin 2
Tel. + 353 1 6685777
Fax + 353 1 6682691

Industrial Relations News
121-123 Ranelagh
Dublin 6
Tel. + 353 1 4972711
Fax + 353 1 4972779

Irish Business and Employers'
Confederation (IBEC)
84–86 Lower Baggot Street
Dublin 2
Tel. + 353 1 6601011
Fax + 353 1 6601717

Irish Congress of Trade Unions (ICTU)
19 Raglan Road
Dublin 4
Tel. + 353 1 6680641
Fax + 353 1 6609027

Institute of Personnel and Development
35–39 Shelbourne Road, Ballsbridge
Dublin 4
Tel. + 353 1 6686244
Fax + 353 1 6608030

Labour Court
Tom Johnson House, Haddington Road
Dublin 4
Tel. + 353 1 6608444
Fax + 353 1 6685069

Labour Relations Commission
Tom Johnson House, Haddington Road
Dublin 4
Tel. + 353 1 6609662
Fax + 353 1 6685069

Media

The Irish Times
10–16 D'Olier Street
Dublin 2
Tel. + 353 1 6792022
Fax + 353 1 6793029

Sunday Business Post
27–30 Merchants Quay
Dublin 8
Tel. + 353 1 6799777
Fax + 353 1 6796496

Sunday Independent
Irish Independent
90 Middle Abbey Street
Dublin 1
Tel. + 353 1 8731233
Fax + 353 1 8731787

Main sources

Industrial Relations News, IRN Publishing, Dublin, various issues

DEPARTMENT OF EDUCATION. *Charting our Education Future, White Paper on Education*. Dublin, 1995

ECONOMIC AND SOCIAL RESEARCH INSTITUTE. *The Economic Status of School Leavers 1992–1994*. Dublin, 1995

FORFAS. *Shaping our Future: A Strategy for Enterprise in Ireland in the 21st Century*. Dublin, 1996

GUNNIGLE P. and FLOOD, P. *Personnel Management in Ireland: Practice, trends, developments*. Dublin, 1990

GUNNIGLE, P. *et al. Continuity and Change in Irish Employee Relations*. Oak Tree Press, Dublin, 1994

MCGRATH, J. 'The Qualifications of the Irish Workforce', *Labour Market Review*, Winter 1995, FAS, Dublin

8

Italy

Recruitment in Italy remains one of the most complex and legally constrained procedures in the European Union. Although some of the more Byzantine requirements have been relaxed in the recent past, legally prescribed recruitment routes and quotas can appear formidable at first glance. However, these frequently apply only to narrow categories of potential employees, are less arduous on a second reading than on initial impression, and can often be softened through discussion and negotiation with the labour authorities if the employer can show reasonable cause.

None the less, the state still holds a placement monopoly, and all forms of employment agencies – whether for temporary or permanent work – are illegal.

Operating successfully in the Italian labour market calls for both an intimate understanding of how officialdom works and an ability to deal with it effectively, together with a range of personal contacts for encountering potential recruits and a willingness to cultivate them – all criteria which are best met by employing a local national in sensitive personnel positions. Employee mobility is fairly low, and local ties remain important. Labour turnover is low, reflecting this culture and the difficulties in external recruitment.

The labour market

In 1995 the labour force totalled 22,914,000 workers, of which some 2,673,000 were seeking work: while the participation rate, at just over 50 per cent, is fairly low in European terms, the unemployment rate of 11.7 per cent is among the highest in the EU. Major regional and demographic imbalances lurk behind the bald figures, however. Historically there has always been an imbalance between unemployment in the North and that in the South. During the 1990s this divergence widened still further. By July 1995, with economic expansion in its second year, the unemployment rate in the South stood at 20 per cent compared with 6 per cent in the North.

There has also been a substantial rise in structural unemployment among women and young people. At nearly 16 per cent in 1994, the female unemployment rate is nearly 7 percentage points higher that the male rate, and is rising. The rate of youth unemployment in 1994 was also one of the highest in Europe at 32 per cent. Added to this is the high rate of long-term unemployment at 61 per cent of total unemployment, in part a function of low labour turnover. In 1992 52 per cent of all employed people reported that they had never had any other employment.

In 1993 the OECD calculated that some 36 per cent of women of working age were in the labour force – one of the lowest rates of female participation in the EU, and approximately half the Swedish rate of female participation – although a rise from the early 1970s when the figure was just under 30 per cent. This low participation rate could be connected to the fact that non-standard forms of employment, such as fixed-term and part-time work, still only make up about 6 per cent of total employment. Although this percentage is rising, it is still among the lowest in Europe.

The OECD found that in contrast to circumstances in other countries, Italians with low education levels do not experience particularly high unemployment, and their participation rate seems to be close to the OECD average.

Compared with other EU countries, Italy has a high proportion both of self-employed persons (24 per cent of the total) and of small to medium-sized companies (with an estimated 4 million employees in 1994). This has been held out as one important factor behind the dynamism of the Italian private sector, despite poor performance on unemployment, and is a vital buttress for the formal sector.

Recruitment

Official requirements on recruitment

Although recruitment restrictions have been relaxed significantly since 1991, the official procedures involved in recruitment remain often lengthy and bureaucratic by contrast with other EU states. Many employers, therefore, delegate the task of recruitment to consultants. Although the law prevents consultants from actually placing personnel, they often do all the preparatory work necessary, such as procuring the list of candidates available for work, arranging for the required documentation and setting up medicals, as well as providing the state placement service with the obligatory notification.

Since the period of the Berlusconi government (1994/5) recruitment procedures have been considerably liberalised. However, until late 1996 employers had to operate in a very uncertain regulatory environment as the new provisions were governed by a stream of decree laws which had only a short shelf-life – reflecting the blockages within the Italian legislative system. A decree lasts for only 60 days and must then be re-introduced into parliament if it fails to complete the procedure for coming into force permanently.

An important decree covering recruitment, which came to be known as the *milleproroghe* ('decree of a thousand extensions'), was finally enacted in late 1996. Under its provisions employers no longer require prior approval from the state placement service for all new hirings. Instead they merely have to inform the service of new hirings within five calendar days. They must also specify whether or not the new hiring is compatible with the requirement that 12 per cent of an employer's new hirings in each calendar year (from May 1996) must be drawn from the ranks of special categories of unemployed people with priority rights to be re-hired (the so-called *riserva*) and 15 per cent from the people with disabilities.

These proportions are not usually calculated on the basis of the total work-force, but on the workforce less certain categories of employee, such as apprentices, people employed on training and work-experience contracts, and any workers recruited through the most common recuitment procedures, the *passaggio diretto* (see below).

Employers who contravene the quota requirement can be fined between L. 500,000 (£200) and L. 3,000,000 (£1,200) for each illegal hiring. However, the employer is not required to comply with the requirement if there is a shortage of suitably qualified employees, or where the employer has a specific recruitment plan agreed with the competent authority.

Official notification

All employers must provide the labour inspectorate (*l'ispettorato di lavoro*) and the national social insurance fund, INPS, with the following information:

- the names of all persons recruited
- names and qualifications of all employees terminating their employment – within five days of the contract ending
- the total number employed, analysed according to plant, sex and type of work undertaken, as well as the names of people employed who are disabled or entitled to compulsory placement. The information must be supplied every six months in January and June.

All employers must also provide the labour inspectorate with copies of all part-time work contracts within 30 days of the contract's commencing.

Work registration card

All citizens of a European Union member state require a work registration card (*libretto di lavoro*) which can be obtained from their local Italian authority (*sindaco*). To do this the citizen will need to produce a residence permit or documentation indicating their intention to reside. An EU residence permit, issued in accordance with EC Directive 68/360, is obtainable from the local police authority (*questura*). This is valid for three months and must then be renewed. Renewals can be obtained at the *questura* or from the local authority, and must be made on special official paper, *carta bollata*, available at most tobacconists. Dependants will also be granted a right to reside, even if not EU nationals themselves. The conclusion of formalities to obtain a right to reside in Italy may not prevent persons from carrying out contracts of employment already agreed.

Citizens of member states of the EU who wish to work in Italy must also be in possession of an EU passport valid for at least five years.

Non-EU nationals need a visa from the Italian consulate in their country of origin plus authorisation from the provincial labour authorities in Italy. The employer must apply for this in relation to a specific task. In general, the procedure is not unduly restrictive for incoming executives.

There are some exemptions to these provisions. They include:

- foreign students
- foreign workers employed by organisations operating in Italy who have been admitted at the request of the employer to carry out specific duties for a predetermined period and who must leave the country once these duties have been fulfilled
- foreign workers employed in institutions dealing with international law
- artists and entertainers
- maritime personnel.

Workforce consultation

There are no legal obligations on employers to consult trade unions or employee representatives on manpower-planning issues or on the recruitment of individuals.

Collective agreements

Nearly all employees are covered by national collective agreements laying down minimum terms and conditions. Since collective agreements are effectively legally binding on all employers and employees in the sector concerned, even if they are not signatories to the agreement, recruiters will need to know which agreement operates in their sector. The relevant collective agreement (*contratto collettivo nazionale di lavoro*, CCNL) must be indicated on the form used for obtaining permission to proceed with the engagement of an employee. In contrast to many other EU member states, managers (*dirigenti*) are covered by their own collective agreement with its specific legally binding requirements.

Agreed provisions on job creation

Some recent industry agreements contain concessions on minimum pay rates and the percentage of atypical work contracts permissible in any particular workforce. For example, the tourism industry agreement includes clauses aimed at extending the use of fixed-term contracts without the need to negotiate but merely to inform workplace representatives, as well as the introduction of a new type of contract, the *contratto di inserimento*. This allows employers to recruit young people at lower initial starting rates for a fixed term. The use of part-time contracts has also been relaxed.

In metalworking the quota of part-time contracts remains low at 2 per cent of the total, but for the first time the recent national industry agreement recognises the value of this type of contract for creating new jobs.

Employment incentives

The government offers a number of incentives designed to boost youth employment and encourage companies to take on unemployed workers. The incentives normally take the form of reductions in employer social security contributions, which are among the highest in Europe. In some cases additional incentive payments are available. In this section we have not taken account of measures contained in decree laws, which by their nature may be only temporary or subject to substantial amendment.

Recruitment of workers from the 'mobility' lists

Permanent contracts   All employers recruiting a worker from the lists of people recently made redundant, termed 'mobility lists' (*liste di mobilità*), pay reduced social security contributions on behalf of the worker for the first 18 months of the contract, and are entitled to monthly payments equal to half the unemployment benefit which the worker would have received.

Short-term contracts   Workers can be recruited on short-term contracts lasting for a maximum of 12 months, during which the employer pays reduced social security contributions. If the short-term contract is converted to a permanent one then the employer is entitled to the reduction in social contributions for a further 12 months as well as 50 per cent of the monthly unemployment benefit to which the employee would have been entitled.

Recruitment of workers in receipt of *'cassa integrazione'* payments or unemployed for at least 24 months   Employers recruiting people in receipt of benefits from the special unemployment fund (*'cassa integrazione'* – see Vol 1 in this series, *Contracts and Terms and Conditions of Employment*, p. 251) are entitled to a 50 per cent reduction in social security contributions on their behalf for the first 36 months of the contract. The contract must be full-time and permanent and must not replace employees either suspended or laid off by the same employer.

Re-employment contracts (*contratti di reinserimento*)   Employers recruiting workers who have been in receipt of the special unemployment benefit (*trattamento di disoccupazione speciale*) for at least 12 months are entitled to a 75 per cent reduction in social security contributions on behalf of such workers, lasting for 12 months if the worker has been unemployed for less than two years; 24

months if the worker has been unemployed for two to three years; and 36 months if the worker has been unemployed for more than three years.

Training and work-experience contracts   This type of contract is aimed at the employment of young people under the age of 29. The employer benefits from a 25 per cent reduction in social security contributions – and in some cases, a 40 per cent reduction. There are limitations placed on the use of these contracts to prevent employers abusing the incentives they attract.

Using part-timers and temps

In law any contract of employment which is not permanent and full-time is considered to be 'special'. 'Special' employment contracts are regulated by the appropriate legislation and are permissible either as part of a job creation scheme or because they are inherent in the nature of the work involved – such as sporting activities or the entertainment business. Other 'special' employment contracts apply to domestic work or the work undertaken by building caretakers. The main types of contract, together with their requirements, are as follows.

Part-time contracts   Collective agreements can establish the percentage of the workforce on part-time contracts, and the permitted range of tasks. Overtime working is not permitted, and pay and benefits must be pro rata to full-time employees. Part-time work is not widespread in Italy and accounts for less than 6 per cent of official employment.

There is no statutory definition of part-time work other than that it is work for fewer hours than that defined in law, and by collective agreement, as full-time work. Three types of part-time contracts are currently in use and are permitted, provided they are in writing and a copy is sent to the appropriate provincial labour inspectorate within thirty days of commencement.

They are: 'horizontal' part-time – with a shorter working day than full-time contracts; 'vertical' part-time – where employees work for only part of the week; and 'cyclical part-time' – where employees work for several weeks a month, or several months a year. Failure to notify the inspectorate will entail a fine of L 300,000 (£120).

'Solidarity contracts'   These are intended to assist in maintaining employment during periods of business difficulty. There are two types.

i) Temporary solidarity contracts may be used where economic circumstances require a temporary reduction in working time with a proportionate reduction in pay. The shortfall in pay is then partially made up by the wage-support fund, the *cassa integrazione guadagni* (CIG), which makes payments for up to two years. (The CIG is a form of long-term lay-off fund, jointly financed by employer contributions and state funds, which effectively forms the basis for income support during periods of unemployment.)

ii) Permanent solidarity contracts can be used as part of a job creation scheme where employees work shorter hours for a proportionately lower level of pay, on a permanent basis. Employers benefit from reduced social security contributions, and in some cases, additional subsidies. The procedure is also relatively straightforward compared with implementing redundancies.

Fixed-term-contracts   These are permitted in certain circumstances, such as the inherent nature of the work involved, when cover is required for an individual on leave (eg maternity, or military service), or to accomplish a specific task. Contracts must be in writing. They are renewable only once and for a term no longer than the original. Pay and benefits should be pro rata to full-time employees. In certain circumstances workers on fixed-term contracts are given priority of consideration for full-time vacancies, if desired.

Collective agreements may make more detailed provisions, including the setting of maximum quotas for fixed-term contracts as a proportion of total employees.

Contracts for managers (*dirigenti*)   The special nature of this type of contract embraces enhanced powers and responsibilities within and on behalf of the enterprise; rights of supervision over other employees; exclusion from social legislation such as the duty to register at the placement office and to carry an employment record (*libretto di lavoro*); exclusion from legislation on working time and on fixed-term contracts. However, *dirigenti* are covered by their own collective agreements setting minimum pay levels.

Training and work-experience contracts   Applicants should be between 15 and 29 years of age. The maximum duration of the contract is 24 months, and the employer benefits from reduced social security contributions.

Apprenticeships   Applicants must appear on a special list at state job placement offices. There are a limited number of apprenticeships for each company, and authorization from the labour inspectorate is required. Apprentices may not be younger than 15 nor older than 20, and the maximum duration of the contract is 5 years. Piece-work is not permitted.

Temporary work agencies

Temporary employment agencies remain illegal, although draft legislation to allow them to operate has been proposed. However, employees may be temporarily posted between enterprises belonging to the same group.

Finding the applicant

The recruitment culture in Italy combines a good deal of legal and procedural formality with a major role for personal contacts and informality in job and employee search.

Italy is a signatory to ILO Convention 96 which outlaws the operation of commercial employment agencies and makes placement a monopoly of the official system. The operation of employment agencies for temporary workers, or for the permanent placement of all but managerial employees, is severely circumscribed. Although draft legislation has been presented to Parliament which would allow their introduction in the future, it has not yet been adopted.

Until recently the mainstay of the state system was the statutory-based procedure whereby recruitment was undertaken 'by number' (*chiamata numerica*). That is, employers were obliged to take workers from lists of the registered unemployed ranked according to certain criteria by the labour authorities: when recruiting, the employer was obliged to take the next person on the list as offered by the state placement system. In practice, however, so many new procedures were attached to the basic system over the years that 'recruitment by number' became the exception rather than the rule, and was really relevant only when recruiting unskilled or semi-skilled workers. Law 223/1991, promulgated on 23 July 1991, abolished this requirement, though other procedures which often resulted in circumvention of the *chiamata numerica* remain.

The state placement system

The Italian public employment service has only a very limited role in the practice of placement, especially since the waning of requirements on employers to take a substantial volume of new hiring from official lists of the unemployed. The main role of the public employment service now is to approve hirings made by other means, and ensure that prescribed quotas are met.

All hirings, with few exceptions, have to be communicated to the local employment office (*la sezione circoscrizionale per l'impiego*, SCI) even if the service has played no direct role in finding the new employee. This must be done within five calendar days and notification must specify the employee's name, personal data, date of recruitment, qualifications, grade, applicable national industry agreement and registration number.

Where no national industry agreement applies and the contract is a private one, then the employer must supply the following information: the gross monthly salary, weekly working time, holiday entitlement and notice period.

Below we set out the various procedures available for recruiting different types of employee.

Direct recruitment (*assunzioni dirette*)

Direct recruitment – that is, without the involvement of the state placement service, by advertisement, individual contact or unsolicited application – is possible for some categories of employee, including managers (*dirigenti*) and people recruited in an emergency to prevent harm to property (although the authorities must be informed if they are employed for more than three days).

'Direct passage' (*passaggio diretto*)

This procedure covers instances in which an employee transfers from another employer immediately and without a break in employment. The local placement office must be informed within five days and supplied with the necessary information.

Recruitment requiring registration at the placement office

All persons seeking employment are required to register at the state placement office, and will need a *libretto di lavoro* (which can be obtained from the same office) and a form verifying that they are unemployed.

'Recruitment by name'

Following the passage of law 223/1991 employers are free to select employees 'by name' – that is, individually – from all categories of employee registered at the placement office (and unlike *passaggio diretto*, irrespective of their current employment status).

Reserve lists for priority hiring *(riserva)*

Workers qualifying for the reserve lists are as follows:

* those who have been registered on an official placement list for more than two years and who have kept their registration up to date by stamping their unemployment form (C1) regularly
* those on so-called 'mobility lists' of the recently unemployed, drawn up by the regional employment offices
* those coming from companies which have been using the long-term lay-off fund (*cassa integrazione guadagni straordinaria*) for more than six months, and who have been individually laid-off for at least three months
* those drawing from the long-term lay-off fund for more than 24 months.

Companies hiring workers from these reserve lists pay lower social insurance contributions for them.

Press advertising

The press is essentially regional, although some papers have achieved national status and readership. The main vehicle for job advertisements, _Il Corriere della Sera_, originally based in Milan, now publishes regional editions and is also printed in Rome.

Other important potential vehicles for managerial and specialist recruitment with local roots but a wider readership include _Il Resto del Carlino_ in Bologna, _Il Mattino_ in Naples, _Il Messaggero_ in Rome, _La Repubblica_ also in Rome, and _La Stampa_ in northern Italy. More local newspapers can be used for manual and routine white-collar jobs.

The main business daily, _Il Sole–24 Ore_, carries very few job advertisements, although it does play a role – with other specialist papers – in graduate recruitment.

Equal opportunity legislation forbids the specification of gender in job advertisements. However, there are no restrictions on setting age limits. The wording of advertisements must comply with the Workers' Statute, which forbids discrimination on the grounds of political opinion, race, religion or trade union affiliation. However, employment advertisements never positively assert that an employer is an equal opportunity employer.

Salaries are very rarely mentioned in job advertisements, nor is the company name always stated.

Employment agencies

Employment agencies for the direct recruitment of temporary or permanent employees are illegal in Italy, which has ratified the ILO conventions forbidding private employment agencies. Although some local agencies for temporary work do exist, the major temporary work agencies familiar to UK practitioners do not operate in Italy because of the illegality of this form of activity. Temporary work via agencies is not an available or well-regarded alternative in Italy. Agencies are tolerated in the field of management and executive recruitment (see below).

All this, however, could be set to change since unions, government and employers approved the introduction of such agencies under the terms of the national framework agreement signed in July 1993, and more recently in September 1996. Although draft legislation has been proposed, no new provisions had been passed by Parliament at the time of writing.

Recruitment consultants

The use of recruitment consultants for selecting candidates across all categories is widespread and growing, particularly in northern Italy, reflecting the lack of an effective official or graduate recruitment infrastructure. Consultants may only advise employers on candidates for jobs, as private placement is illegal. Services provided by recruitment consultants range from drafting and placing advertisements in newspapers to shortlisting candidates for final selection by the company concerned. The cost of consultant services would typically be 15 per cent of the candidate's first year's salary plus the cost of the advertisement, or 20 per cent of the candidate's first year's salary without an advertisement. Consultants are allowed to hold files of job seekers.

Executive search

The use of executive search consultants for the recruitment of executives (*dirigenti*) and senior technical staff (*quadri*) has been growing rapidly in recent years, particularly in northern Italy. Most of the major international executive search organisations are represented in the market, and have achieved market dominance in recent years, although a number of smaller local independents also operate.

Executives are one of the few categories of employee who may enter into an employment contract directly with the employer. Like other employees, they are covered by national agreements providing basic minimum terms and conditions, which all employers need to take into account. In a business environment where lack of employee mobility is a concern to employers, many executive posts are filled by internal promotion. However, shortages in key areas such as engineering and finance in the 1980s changed this culture. There are no legal restrictions on how these consultants operate, except for equal opportunity legislation and the Workers' Statute.

Application documents

Job advertisements typically ask for a detailed CV, including a telephone number. Males should indicate whether military service has been completed. (Usually candidates will be expected to have fulfilled this requirement.)

The Workers' Statute and equal opportunity legislation forbid employers putting questions on application forms which seek information about union membership, political opinions, religious beliefs, family situation or pregnancy. There are no other statutory restrictions on what may be asked. Recruitment specialists within large multinational employers will almost always be expected to adhere to company codes of practice. However, there are no recognised broader codes of practice guiding recruitment and selection.

There are no mandatory regulations on how information returned by an applicant may be used. For example, a graphology test could be performed on a handwritten letter without the candidate's express permission. Many consultants, though, would tell candidates if such tests were to be carried out.

Employment quotas

There are numerous items of legislation setting quotas for the employment of people with a disability, war invalids, widows and orphans, as well as employment protection for these groups. Details of such potential employees are held by placement offices. In firms with more than 35 employees, the quota is 15 per cent of hirings.

Selection

Employers are free to choose their methods of selection, with the precise course of the process determined by the level of job involved. A senior appointment via a recruitment consultant would typically involve, after assessment of the CV, three interviews plus tests of various kinds which might involve graphology, and psychometric tests. For routine white-collar positions, CVs would be sorted and those entering the next stage put through an aptitude and/or a job simulation test. There is no obligation to inform applicants about the results of tests, although some employers and consultants will do so.

What can be asked during an interview is governed, as with application forms, by the Workers' Statute and equal opportunity legislation. It is unlawful to discriminate on grounds of sex either directly – by asking about a candidate's marital status, family circumstances or pregnancy – or indirectly by indicating via preselection procedures or the advertisement of vacancies that a particular sex is required. Nevertheless, more searching questions may be put and expected than is normal in the UK, equal opportunity legislation notwithstanding.

Infringements of the Workers' Statute and equal opportunity legislation are punishable by fines or in extreme cases, theoretically, by imprisonment.

Medical examinations may be requested by employers prior to engagement. They can be carried out either by a company doctor or independent physician and the outcome, but not the detailed results, given to the employer. In certain industries, such as food or chemicals and when recruiting young people, employers are legally required to carry out a medical examination, at their own expense.

There is a certain amount of controversy concerning medical examinations, as the Workers' Statute makes them illegal unless undertaken by a doctor in the public service. However, a 1974 ruling of the Constitutional Court stated that this provision applied only to workers already in post, and not to applicants.

Military service currently lasts 12 to 14 months. When recruiting personnel it is unlawful to stipulate that candidates should have completed or be exempt from military service. The law also states that employees who undertake military service have a right to reinstatement provided they report back for work within 30 days of discharge. Some national industry agreements, such as retailing and distribution, state that the period spent on military service counts towards seniority.

The form of the offer

There is no mandatory procedure that employers are constrained to follow when making an offer of employment, although the law does require that it must be in writing if the contract is part-time or fixed-term. Most companies choose to have a written record of the job offer. Some national industry agreements, such as in chemicals, stipulate that the offer must be in writing and must contain the following:

- the date on which employment starts
- the grade
- the starting salary
- the length of any probationary period
- the place of work
- all other agreed conditions.

There is no prescribed formula for rejecting candidates.

Appointment formalities

Documents expected of an employee are set down by law and collective agreement. Law N. 122 (10 January 1935) makes it illegal for an employer to engage anyone – with some exceptions – who does not have a valid official work registration card (*libretto di lavoro*), which effectively functions as a work permit but also as an employee's work record. The *libretto di lavoro* can be obtained from the local placement office.

On engagement, the employer will check the *libretto di lavoro* and retain it during the period of employment. Workers employed by more than one employer must deposit their permit with one employer, who is then required to inform any other employers. On termination of employment the employer must return this document to the employee no later than one day following the end of the employment, in return for a receipt from the employee. Employees who have been on training contracts (*contratti di formazione e lavoro*) will have a record of their work and of the training received.

Newly-appointed employees will also need to provide a social insurance record, which consists of a block of certificates, one of which is completed each year and sent to the national social insurance fund, INPS, giving details of the preceding year's income.

Some collective agreements also require employees to produce other documentation, such as an identity card (which all Italian citizens carry), proof of eligibility for family allowance, and certificates establishing vocational qualifications. Employees in the metalworking, chemical and pharmaceutical industries also need to keep a health record (*libretto sanitario personale*), which contains information on the results of medical examinations, accidents at work, occupational disease, and absence through sickness or accident.

Education and training

Overview of the education system

Compared with other EU countries, Italy still has a relatively short period of compulsory education, with the school-leaving age at 14. However, this is compensated for to some degree by the large proportion of young people who transfer to the various forms of continuing schooling. The bulk of initial vocational training, including intermediate and technical skills, is provided through the state education system, with apprenticeship playing an important but subsidiary role, and primarily concentrated in small firms. Italy, however, lacks a continuous training system.

Secondary and tertiary education

Secondary education is highly centralised and is administered by the Ministry of Public Education. The system has not changed for 70 years. Approximately 5 per cent of lower secondary school students and 11 per cent of upper secondary school students are in non-state-run schools (which include those administered by local authorities as well as purely private institutions). Private schools must, however, conform to national legislation and regulations issued by the Ministry.

Education is compulsory between the ages of 6 and 14. Secondary education is divided into two cycles: lower secondary (*scuola media*), which extends to the age of 14 and is compulsory, and upper secondary. However, a large proportion of pupils continue beyond the age of 14 (91 per cent), principally because initial vocational and technical training is provided through the state education system.

Lower secondary education

Pupils complete compulsory education in lower secondary school. These schools provide three years of free, standard comprehensive schooling for all children from the age of 11 to 14. For some years there has been a proposal to increase the school-leaving age to 16 in order to bring Italy into line with other European countries.

At the end of lower secondary schooling successful students are awarded a leaving certificate, the *Diploma di Licenza Media* and can proceed to upper secondary school. In 1994, 92 per cent of lower secondary pupils obtained the *licenza media* and 69 per cent per cent proceeded to acquire the upper secondary school certificate.

Upper secondary education (including initial vocational and technical training)

There is a variety of upper secondary educational institutions providing courses lasting three, four or five years. Students may also opt for vocational training at one of the regional centres.

Academic courses leading to university entrance are provided by *licei*. These are differentiated further into:

- the classical lyceum (*liceo classico*), where subjects such as Latin and Greek are included in the curriculum
- the scientific lyceum (*liceo scientifico*), where the curriculum places greater emphasis on scientific subjects
- the artistic lyceum (*liceo artistico*), with students specialising in artistic and technical subjects
- the linguistic lyceum (*liceo linguistico*), with students specialising in modern languages.

Courses at these schools last five years, except in the case of the liceo artistico, where they last four years. Successful students are awarded a high school certificate (*diploma di maturità*). Those receiving either a classical, scientific or linguistic diploma can proceed to university, while those with a *diploma artistica* can go either to an academy of fine arts or to a university faculty of architecture. Students with a *diploma artistica* wishing to enrol at other faculties must complete a further year's study.

Teacher training

Teacher training is undertaken by the special institutes – *istituti magistrali* – for primary school-teachers or *scuole magistrali* for nursery school-teachers. The *istituti* provide four-year courses leading to university, while the *scuole* provide three-year courses which do not.

Technical, commercial and intermediate-level skills

Technical and commercial upper secondary education providing intermediate-level skills is well developed and takes place at technical institutes (the *istituti tecnici*). This is the single most important study option at upper secondary level, with 1.3 million students in 1990/1 (see below). Most courses last five years, and just over 50 per cent of all enrolled students follow courses in commerce. The final qualification for students leaving such schools is the *diploma di maturità tecnica*, which is fully recognised by employers in industry, commerce and agriculture and also entitles the holder to enter university. There is some institutional specialisation, with separate *istituti* for agriculture, commerce and accountancy, business management, tourism, surveying, industrial technology, aerospace, maritime skills and home economics. (Accountancy, for example, is not primarily a graduate profession in Italy.)

Tertiary education

Access to university education depends on the possession of either the school-leaving certificate or a technical qualification. Admission is restricted only in a few selected institutions or for high-demand specialisms (such as dentistry and medicine). This very open structure, combined with fairly long courses, has produced notoriously overcrowded institutions and high drop-out rates: in 1992, for example, just over 30 per cent of Italian students completed their degree, compared with 94 per cent in the UK. Some measures to combat this were taken in the early 1990s in the form of an expansion of capacity and some – though very limited – selection for courses.

Tertiary education takes place almost exclusively in universities (although in technical specialisms these may be termed *politecnici*). They are mainly administered by the state, with a small number in the private sector that are also funded largely by the state and are obliged to conform to national regulations. While the private institutions account for only a small minority of student numbers, they include some of the most highly regarded universities, such as the Bocconi in Milan, the LUISS in Rome and the Catholic universities in both those cities. Many of these institutions have developed close links with business and, unlike most state universities, frequently operate a system of selection. The Bocconi has a well-regarded school of business administration (*Scuola di Direzione Aziendale*) offering an MBA. There are also business schools offering MBAs at the universities of Padua, Genoa, Bari and Turin. (However, the master's degree is not a recognised academic qualification in Italian law – see below).

Italian universities produce roughly 75,000 graduates a year. The most popular subjects studied are the arts, law, economics, and engineering, although the numbers studying economics and engineering have declined recently.

University qualifications   There are two main types of academic qualification:

- the university diploma (*diploma universitario*, DU), also known as a 'short degree' (*laurea breve*), was introduced in 1990. It is a first-level degree course lasting two or three years. The change was intended to bring Italy into line with other European university systems such as those of Britain, Germany and France. It also aims to keep up with rapid technological change, particularly in engineering, economics and medicine, and to reduce the high drop-out rate among students, as well as to provide more flexible courses in growing subject areas. Having achieved the *laurea breve*, students can proceed to study for the full *diploma di laurea*, although it is also a preparation for entering the labour market direct. The latest figures show that only 3.3 per cent of university students opted for the *laurea breve*.
- the *diploma di laurea* is the standard degree after a full course of university study of four or five years, depending on specialism, and those holding it will call themselves *Dottore* (or *Dottoressa* for women). The qualification means

passing annual examinations over the entire course, as well as the submission of a thesis. Students can choose between a wide variety of major and minor options, graduation exams taking place three times a year.

Postgraduate studies   Universities are responsible for postgraduate studies and run the *scuole di specializzazione* – specialization schools – offering courses lasting one to five years, depending on the field of study, which lead to the *diploma di specialista*.

Students wishing to further their studies in their own field rather than specialise in a new one, can attend a *corso di perfezionamento* – a specialisation course, lasting a maximum of one year. At the end of it they are awarded an *attestato di frequenza*, an attendance certificate.

Only since the University Reform Act, 1980, have students been able formally to pursue academic research leading to a doctoral qualification (*Dottorato di Ricerca*). Master's degrees, mainly in business studies, are awarded by some universities. Although not formally recognised in law, they are accepted by employers.

Graduate recruitment

There is as yet a relatively undeveloped infrastructure for graduate recruitment in terms of university careers services or recruitment events. Fairs for graduate recruitment do take place but cannot be equated to the 'milk round' operating in the UK. Companies make presentations at the fairs but do not interview there and then. The private universities tend to be more effective in promoting recruitment and fostering contacts between potential employers and their graduates. Universities and schools sell lists of their graduates to employers, and companies that sponsor schools or universities have priority of access to such lists. Students graduate throughout the academic year.

Some newspapers, such as the finance and business daily *Il Sole–24 Ore*, regularly publish lists of graduates from various universities, giving details of the student's name, date of birth, address and telephone number, subject, class of degree, knowledge of languages, whether male or female, whether or not they have done military service or are exempted, and their preferences regarding location of employment, sector, and function. The *Il Sole–24 Ore* list is published as a regular supplement in conjunction with Assolombarda, the industrial employers' organisation in the Lombardy region around Milan in northern Italy. Information is collected from the universities in Milan, including the Bocconi (business school), the Cattolica, the Statale and the Politecnico, and permission is obtained from new graduates to publish their details. There are also some specialised guides for students, notably *Campus* and an annual directory *Azienda Informa*.

Unsolicited applications also account for a large proportion of the initial contact between graduates and employers.

Training and the official employment services

It is a widely held view that the official training and employment service seriously fails to match the training requirements of companies despite the plethora of initiatives. In its annual report the Institute of Professional Training, ISFOL, singles out few examples of excellence. Action was promised by government under the terms of the national framework agreement of July 1993 but this has failed to materialise. Frustrated by years of only halting progress, the main business employers' association, Confindustria, and the main trade union confederations CGIL, CISL and UIL have come up with their own agreement on the way forward. This was signed in February 1996 and aims primarily to identify on a national basis what training needs exist and where, plus likely projections for the future. This will then inform those organisations responsible for providing training courses.

Initial vocational training: *Istituti professionali*

The main bodies providing initial vocational training are the vocational training institutes (*istituti professionali*). These are open to students with a lower secondary school certificate or to any candidate over 14 years of age who passes an entrance examination. Successful students obtain a *diploma di qualifica* in the specialisation taken. Courses are two to three years long and cover a variety of fields, such as industry, agriculture, crafts and trade. On completion, students are awarded a vocational skills diploma (*diploma di qualifica professionale*) attesting to their skill in a particular trade and they can attempt the entrance examination to one of the technical institutes to follow a course to develop their basic skills. (According to the EU's rating of comparable qualifications, the *diploma di qualifica* is counted as equivalent to UK NVQ Level 3 in engineering or metalworking, and Levels 2/3 in commerce and banking.)

Some *istituti professionali* offer more specialised courses which extend the usual three years to five, culminating in the award of a *diploma di maturità professionale*. This entitles the holder to enrol at a university. There are specialised vocational institutes for agriculture, hotels and catering, industry and crafts, tourism, traditional 'female' occupations (shorthand and typing, fashion design, secretarial, graphic design, dressmaking), the food industries, woodworking (including musical instruments), maritime skills, commerce, and education for the blind.

Most vocational training is conducted on a full-time basis, and there are only a small number of pilot schemes offering work experience or placements. Some special employment/training contracts also entail a combination of instruction and work experience.

Despite a number of reforms introduced since the late 1970s, vocational training continues to exhibit a number of problematic features already tackled elsewhere in the EU. For example, there is no centralised system for the certification of training courses, and no corresponding institutional network developing nationally-accepted training standards or materials. Links between vocational training and higher education are also virtually non-existent.

Vocational training is provided in several ways, funded both by the state and privately.

The weakness of guilds or similar associations, combined with attempts to establish a national model via the state, has led to the concentration of training provision within the public education system and under the control of the state.

The state system – dual provision, three institutions

State provision is delivered by three institutions. The state-run technical and vocational training institutes provide initial and intermediate training, are regulated by the Ministry of Public Education, and are part of the general system of education (for details see above). All costs of initial training within this system are borne by the public exchequer. In addition, there are regional training centres (*centri di formazione professionale regionale*) which are co-ordinated by the Ministry of Labour. Training provided by the regions is described below. Apprenticeship is underdeveloped, and serves mainly as a special scheme to encourage the employment of young people, with concessions on social security contributions for employers (see below).

In recent years one of the most important developments in state provision has been a pilot study, 'Project '92', which aims to reform vocational education as first step towards reforming all secondary schooling, including raising the school-leaving age to 16.

Regional centres

The regions have legal responsibility for all vocational training, although in practice it is mainly carried out within the national state system. Relatively few school-leavers were attending regional centres (CFPs) in 1994/5, compared with 1.2 million in technical institutes. The centres train people for all three sectors of the economy – agriculture, industry and services. Courses vary considerably from region to region, and national data on provision are notoriously difficult to collect because of their fragmented nature.

Students undertaking any of the basic (first- and second-level) courses provided by the regional centres do not need a lower secondary school certificate (*licenza di scuola media*) unless they are planning to progress to the second level. Courses at the first level last for two years, while those at the second level generally last one year. None of the courses qualifies a student upon completion to enter university. Nor do those trained at these centres enjoy the same opportunities for employment as those trained in the state vocational training institutions and technical institutes. There is pressure for reform, and it is envisaged that change can be attempted within the framework of the draft legislation to reform secondary schooling and to raise the school-leaving age.

The regional centres also provide some adult vocational training, mainly aimed at the unemployed and those made redundant owing to company restructuring.

Workforce consultation on training

There are no statutory requirements for employers to consult with their workforce on training requirements. However, many company agreements make provision for the joint examination of training needs and how they are to be met.

Time-off rights for education and training

The Workers' Statute of 1970 gave all employees in companies employing more than 15 people certain rights to facilitate study. Article 10 of this law distinguishes between employees attending university (where attendance at lectures is not compulsory) and workers 'enrolled and regularly attending classes at primary, secondary or vocational schools which are public, state-approved or authorised to award legally-recognised qualifications'. The latter – but not the former – are entitled to hours of work arranged to facilitate attendance at classes and preparation for examinations. In addition, they may not be compelled to work overtime or during weekly rest periods.

All employees, including university students, are entitled to paid leave in order to sit examinations.

Collective agreements

Many collective agreements contain additional provisions on study leave. The pace-setting agreement in this field was the national engineering agreement of 1973, which specified that workers wishing to attend certain schools (that is, state schools or others agreed by the employers and unions) were entitled to total paid leave of up to 150 hours over a period of three years. (This leave could be used up in one year by any individual employee.) The allowance was subsequently increased to 250 hours for workers attending primary school courses (that is, completing their basic education under the Italian system). There are certain limitations on the use of study leave under the engineering agreement:

- Student workers must produce a school certificate verifying their attendance for a number of hours which must be two-thirds more than the number paid for by the employer.
- No more than 2 per cent of the workforce may be simultaneously absent from work for study reasons.
- Absence from work for study reasons must not hamper normal production.

In addition, the agreement provides for 120 hours of unpaid leave per annum for all workers, provided that it can be scheduled to take account of the company's organisational and production needs. Similar agreements exist in most sectors, although the number of hours' leave and the limitations may vary slightly from sector to sector.

Sector-level agreements along these lines are aimed at improving the educational standard of workers in general. For individual workers following courses other than the approved ones, other provisions may exist at company level or may be worked out on an informal basis.

Continuing training

There is no real system of continuing training in Italy, although a significant number of initiatives can be observed for training both employed and unemployed adults by companies, universities and training centres. It is only in the 1990s in an EU context that the concept of continuous training has really taken hold.

Officially, the regional training centres are responsible for continuous training and there has been a series of government job creation and training initiatives between 1970 and the present day. The 1993 framework agreement between the social partners signalled the latest phase of training development. A part of the agreement aims to address issues such as reform of the unemployment benefit system, temporary work agencies and both initial and continuous training. Also in 1993, law 236 provided for setting up a single fund for continuous training. Unfortunately, little practical progress has been made to rationalise the funding and the provision of continuous training.

Various types of scheme have been developed to foster training on the job or provide a mixture of training and work experience. Such schemes can be a route into work for those without any skills, or may follow completion of initial vocational training in the public education system. The main schemes, which are administered through the regions, are as follows.

Training/employment contracts (*contratti di formazione e lavoro*, CFL) together with apprenticeship contracts (*apprendistato*) have been developed and given statutory backing to induce employers to take on and train young people. Employers are offered reduced social security contributions and are required by law to commit themselves to providing training, but there are no formal systems to verify that proper training actually takes place. Employers have always tended to rely on older, more experienced workers passing on their knowledge in an informal way. For this reason unions have exerted pressure and have achieved the establishment of a small number of more formalised on-the-job training schemes. The schemes are aimed at young people with a low level of basic education.

Apprenticeships   Apprenticeships are regulated by a specific statute (law 25/1955) and are concentrated overwhelmingly in craft firms. Apprentices may be aged between 14 and 20, and are allowed to work on apprenticeship contracts – at special rates of pay – for up to five years. The primary criticism of apprenticeship training is the failure of the system to guarantee that apprentices attend the prescribed eight hours' school instruction intended to accompany the on-the-job element. The apprenticeship system, which none the less still embraces some 560,000 young people, has been perceived as losing its value as a general vocational qualification because of the lack of a systematic theoretical component.

Job retraining (*riconversione professionale*) is aimed at the unemployed, those in *cassa integrazione* (the wage fund that supplies payment to workers in companies undertaking restructuring exercises) and those seeking to change their occupation.

In-company training

There is no legal obligation on employers to provide training, although employees may enjoy certain statutory or agreed rights to time off for education and training (see below). Substantial differences in practice and organisation are found, primarily depending on company size. Whereas training in smaller concerns is informal, and conducted without the help of an in-company training department, larger firms have training departments which in many cases have become independent organisations offering training to other firms. (Both Fiat and Olivetti have established such agencies, for example.) Because a good deal of basic vocational training is provided by public bodies (see above), much company-based training is concerned with training and developing managers.

Medium-sized firms tend to provide more formalised training, often with the help of a small training department. This will usually have recourse to the outside market to provide the actual training. An exception would be firms that, although small or medium-sized, have a high level of investment in information technology and therefore more stringent training needs. Such organisations are much more likely to have a larger, more structured training department in-house.

Resort to outside providers appears to be growing and, according to a survey of consultants carried out in the mid-1980s, training services accounted for just over 10 per cent of the fee income of management consultancy companies (the largest single source of income after computer consultancy). This trend is attributed both to a growing interest in in-company training (spurred on by technical change) and organisational streamlining in which more functions are subcontracted.

Some industry associations also function as external training providers to member companies, especially for the development of sectoral-specific skills. One example is IFA, the National Association for Vocational Training in the Insurance Sector, which offers a broad range of courses for all skill levels for its

80 member companies. Courses include specialised programmes for brokers, general management in the industry, and foundation and induction courses for employees.

Confindustria, the national employers' organisation (see *Organisations*), also operates its own training agency, ENFAPI, which is run as an independent limited company jointly with a number of major employers (including Fiat, Pirelli, Zanussi, IBM Italia and Montedison).

Hard facts on the incidence and costs of continuing training in Italy are notoriously hard to come by, reflecting the lack of national standards and statistics in the training field beyond the public education service. However, in 1989 it was estimated that some 1,640,000 individuals received some form of in-company training.

Workforce appraisal and development approaches

This is often carried out collectively between management and workforce representatives. Individual appraisal in indigenous companies is unusual, but is more common in multinational companies. However, the recent expansion of the scope for productivity- or quality-related bonuses under industry agreements may be leading to some extension of appraisal to wider groups of employees.

Supervisors and managers

There is no national supervisory qualification although these employees form a separate category of employees, '*quadri*'. *Quadri* are often university graduates and often developed within the organisation. Their training will typically be a mixture of learning on the job and specific and generic training. The training can be undertaken either internally or subcontracted to external private providers.

Management education and development

Most senior managers in large and medium-sized companies will be graduates. Although the large number of small firms, which play an especially important role in the Italian economy, are likely to be led by entrepreneurs (and their families), these are now also increasingly likely to be university-trained. Degrees in economics and business (*economica e commercio*) and law (*giurisprudenza*) are common for entrants into general management as well as into technical specialisms. The Bocconi in Milan, which has its own business school, is the most prestigious university for those looking for careers in top management (see also above, *Tertiary education*). There are also other well-regarded organisations in the Milan area offering managerial education, such as IPSOA's Master in Business Strategy, Master in Company Taxation and Master in Organisational Communication. As with supervisors, managerial training needs will either be met internally or subcontracted to outside providers.

Managerial qualifications

Although MBAs are not formally recognised in Italy, some business schools offer them, and this is bolstered by institutional and many personal links with the USA. Formal management education, as well as the use of external seminars and short courses, has also been fostered by the increased demand for professional managers from medium-sized and small companies, where attitudes to training have become much more positive in the past decade or so. In common with Germany, Italy is experiencing much greater managerial mobility than previously, both in the form of executives changing company to advance their careers and in an increased readiness of businesses to dismiss underperforming managers. Both phenomena are likely to raise demand for a transferable management qualification.

Management development is given a high priority by both large and medium-sized companies. The latter more typically use consultants as providers of training. All large firms, however, have in-house facilities for management training. Recruits into larger organisations will generally join a two-year graduate programme which combines a theoretical element with circulation through the various departments. Furthermore, whereas in the past larger firms kept to established programmes for such issues as succession planning and triennial career reviews, there is now increasing experimentation with more flexible approaches designed to foster internal entrepreneurship and the devolution of decision-making.

Financing the system

Levies   There are no training levies on employers in Italy but these are currently being mooted by the social partners.

State support for workplace training   There is no state support for workplace training other than that which is provided by the public training system.

Educational attainment of the population

Level	Percentage of 25–64 age-group
Lower secondary	67
Upper secondary	26
Higher education (non-university)	–
University	8

Source: OECD (1994)

Organisations

Ministry of Labour and Social Security
(Ministero del Lavoro e
della Previdenza Sociale)
Via Flavia 6
00187 Rome
Tel. +39 6 4683

Ministry of Public Education
(Ministero della Pubblica Istruzione)
Viale Trastevere
00100 Rome
Tel. + 39 6 58491

ISFOL
Institute of Vocational Training
(Istituto per lo Sviluppo della
Formazione Professionale dei
Lavoratori)
Via G.B.Morgagni 33
00161 Rome
Tel. + 39 6 854 1744

AIDP (Italian personnel managers'
association)
Via Cornalia 19
20124 Milan
Tel. + 39 2 67 09 558

Confindustria (central employers'
organisation)
Viale dell'Astronomia 30
00144 Rome EUR
Tel. + 39 6 59031

AIF – Associazione italiana formatori
(Italian association of trainers)
Via Vincenzo Ponti 4
20123 Milan
Tel. + 39 2 480 1320
Fax + 39 2 481 95756

ASSCO
(Association of management consultants)
Via S. Paolo
20121 Milan
Tel. + 39 2 796 157
Fax + 39 2 760 14282

ELEA Olivetti Spa – Formazione
Consulenza – Direzione e amminis-
trazione (Training consultancy)
Via Nuova 21
10010 Burolo
Tel. + 39 125 57578 – 577327

ENFAP – Ente nazionale formazione
addestramento professionale (national
training organisation)
Larga Ascianzi 5
00198 Rome
Tel. +39 6 85281
Fax +39 6 5884326

ENFAPI – Ente nazionale per la
formazione e l'addestramento
professionale nell'industria (national
training organisation for industry)
Viale Pasteur 10
00144 Rome
Tel. +39 6 5903433
Fax +39 6 5903427

FORMEZ – Centro di formazione e
studi per il Mezzogiorno (education and
training centre for the South)
Via Salaria 229
00199 Rome
Tel. +39 6 84891
Fax +39 6 84893242

IPSOA – Scuola d'impresa (management
school)
Milanofiori strade 3, Palazzo B5
20090 Assago (Milan)
Tel. + 39 2 57557554
Fax + 39 2 8253234

Istituto 'Piero Pirelli'
Viale F. Testi 223
20162 Milan
Tel. + 39 2 644 23400
Fax + 39 2 644 29 213

LUISS – Scuola di management
Via Cosimo de Giorgi 8
00158 Rome
Tel. +39 6 451 0337/418 2135
Fax +39 6 451 2863

SDA – Scuola di direzione aziendale
dell'Università L. Bocconi
Via Bocconi 8
00196 Roma
Tel. +39 6 39 62 696

Media

Il Corriere della Sera
Via Solferino 28
20121 Milan
Tel. + 39 2 6339
Fax + 39 2 29009668

La Stampa
Via Marenco 32
10126 Turin
Tel. + 39 11 65681
Fax + 39 11 655 306

Il Messaggero
Via del Tritone 152
00187 Rome
Tel. + 39 6 47201

Il Sole–24 Ore
Via Paolo Lomazzo 52
20154 Milan
Tel. + 39 2 31031
Fax + 39 2 312055

La Repubblica
Piazza Independenza 11/b
00185 Rome
Tel. + 39 6 49821
Fax + 39 6 498 229 23

Main sources

Collective agreements including: *Contratto di Lavoro, Industria Metalmeccanica Privata* (engineering); *Contratto Collettivo Nazionale di Lavoro – Industria Chimica* (chemicals)
CEDEFOP. *I Sistemi di Formazione Professionale in Italia.* Berlin, 1995
DURANTE, B. and FILADORO, C. *Enciclopedia dei Diritti dei Lavoratori.* Nicola Teti Editore, Milan, 1991
ISFOL. *Rapporto Isfol 1995.* Rome, 1995
MAGGIOLI EDITORE, *Codice Civile a Leggi Complementari.* Rimini, 1991
VOLPINI, F. (ed.). *Agenda per l'Amministrazione del Personale delle Aziende Industriali 1994.* Jandi Sapi Editori, Rome, 1993

9

The Netherlands

Despite its small size there are considerable regional variations in the Dutch labour market which influence company recruitment strategies. Recruitment techniques also depend on the size and nature of the company: large well-known firms have less trouble getting responses from general advertisements and can often rely on numerous unsolicited applications. Although a legislative framework covering recruitment was proposed as a concept in the early 1980s, this never materialised, but various guidelines, collectively-agreed provisions, and custom and practice are well established.

The Dutch education system is well regarded, with some 20 per cent of the adult population holding a higher education qualification – the highest rate in the industrialised world except the USA. However, there has also been much debate in business circles about the overly theoretical education often provided. Many industry representatives have called for, and to some extent achieved, a reduction in the length of university courses and a greater bias towards practical experience and application. Hand in hand with this is the demographic problem of an ageing population and a low birth rate which will result in the next century in fewer young people entering the labour market. Generally speaking, the Netherlands has a highly educated and mobile workforce with impressive language skills and a truly international focus.

The labour market

During the recession of the early 1990s the unemployment rate rose to over 10 per cent, and squeezed recruitment and training off most companies' agendas. To some extent this trend was reversed after 1994. Unemployment fell slowly in 1995/6 to 6.5 per cent, largely through strong job creation measures. Some 90,000 people a year have been forecast to join the labour market in 1996 and 1997. However, this trend will level off and eventually start to decrease, as an ageing population and low birth rate take effect.

The Netherlands has the highest percentage of part-time employment in the EU, with about one-third of employees working less than 32 hours a week. This is particularly true of women, two-thirds of whom work fewer than 32 hours per week, often in low-skill, low-pay sectors and jobs. Most work between 15 and 25 hours per week, although 13 per cent work fewer than 15 hours. The overall female participation rate on the other hand is relatively low: it stood at 55 per cent in 1993 – none the less a substantial increase on the 30 per cent at which it stood in 1973 – and only 5 per cent of working mothers have a full-time job, compared to 17 per cent in the UK.

Recruitment

Official requirements

There is no legal framework governing the recruitment and selection of job applicants. Although legislation was proposed in the early 1980s, it never materialised. Instead a set of recruitment guidelines was drawn up within the bipartite Labour Foundation (*Stichting van de Arbeid*), dubbed the STAR recommendations. These cover recruitment, interviewing, taking up references, procedures for testing candidates and a complaints procedure. The Dutch institute for personnel management (*Nederlandse Vereniging voor Personeelsbeleid*, NVP) also has a code of practice (*sollicitatiecode*) offering more detailed guidance. The two codes were combined by a joint NVP and Ministry committee at the beginning of 1994 in order to draw up a national code of practice (*Nederlandse sollicitatiecode*), including the establishment of a complaints authority – something that the unions had been requesting for some time. However, to date the national code has not been finalised due to union and employer differences over the complaints procedure.

There is no statutory obligation to notify the authorities of any vacancies that arise within a company, but collective agreements may detail certain procedures that are to be followed in recruiting for certain positions via the public employment bureaux (see below).

Work permits

No work permits are required for nationals from other EU states, although they do have to obtain a residence permit from the local police department where the individual is resident.

Work permits are required for most non-EU nationals. Employers must obtain a work permit (*tewerkstellingsvergunning*) from the regional employment office. Such a permit will be issued only where the employee has a valid residence permit. In cases where an establishment employs more than 20 foreign nationals requiring work permits, a limit may be imposed. If a work permit is revoked or expires, this is not automatic cause for termination of the employment contract.

Work permits for temporary workers from outside the EU must be obtained by the client employer and not by the temporary work agency.

Personnel planning

Employers are required to consult with their works councils on general issues relating to personnel planning. However, the works council does not have any influence over the appointment of individuals. Collective agreements often require employers to consult and inform works councils regularly on company recruitment policies and may restrict or encourage the use of certain recruitment methods.

Agreed job creation provisions

Trade unions have pushed very hard over the last three years for job creation measures to be included in collective agreements at every level. However, few specific measures have been achieved. A number of industry agreements such as in banking, textiles or transport, cut their working hours (most commonly from 38 per week to 36) but little evidence is available to show that this resulted in increased recruitment. Others have encouraged early retirement, although this has been countered by the efforts made by many companies to cut the cost of early retirement schemes. Most recently the civil service and the textile sector introduced a new funded group pension plan to replace their early retirement schemes, with staff allowed to choose when to retire from age 62 but with payments adjusted accordingly.

Employment incentives

A number of government schemes and subsidies are available to employers recruiting from certain target groups. These tend to be the long-term unemployed, the young or low-skilled, ethnic minorities, and in some cases women and the disabled. The 1996 budget extended some of these measures. Most involve some form of reduction of employer social security charges relating to new recruits from the above-mentioned groups. These are usually up to 20 per cent rebate for a maximum of four years. However, 25 per cent rebates may apply to recruits at the very bottom of the labour market – defined as those earning up to 115 per cent of the national minimum wage. Employers recruiting from the long-term unemployed in areas of high unemployment may have their contributions waived entirely for a limited period.

There may be other criteria attached to the subsidies or rebates. The national scheme for ethnic minorities for example, requires the contract to be open-ended and for at least 15 hours per week. A second national scheme linked to training provisions (see below) entitles employers taking on recruits from the target groups to subsidies of between Fl 3,000 and Fl 6,000 (£1,000–£2,000) to be channelled into training (for apprentices this increases to between Fl 7,500 and Fl 15,000 [£2,500–£5,000]). The amount is based on age, experience and hours to be worked.

Jobs pools

The long-term unemployed (at least three years) may be eligible to join a jobs pool (*banenpool*). These organisations place people in temporary posts, usually in public sector organisations. They remain employees of the jobs pool which pays them a minimum wage. The government provides subsidies to the jobs pool of Fl 3,500 (£1,150) per unemployed person recruited to the organisation.

Long-term disability subsidies have been available since 1993 for employers taking on people classed as disabled and receiving long-term disability benefit (WAO). These amount to some 20 per cent of salary paid to the WAO recipient plus a one-off payment of Fl 4,000 (£1,300). This is intended to allow the employer to make any necessary adaptations to the working environment in order to cater for the particular disability.

Collective agreements may also lay down targets for recruitment from certain disadvantaged groups; the textile industry agreement (1994/6) states that priority should be given to long-term unemployed and young people so that over the period of the agreement 2 per cent of the workforce has been recruited from these groups. The recruits may be taken on with fixed-term contracts at a rate of pay that is between the national minimum wage and the agreed minimum rate for the job. Training opportunities should also be offered to such recruits.

Using part-timers and temps

Part-time work

As stated above, the Netherlands has the highest incidence of part-time working in Europe: some 33 per cent of all employees work fewer than 32 hours per week. Most of these work between 15 and 25 hours, although 13 per cent work fewer than 15 hours. Part-time work is particularly common in low-skill, low-pay jobs and is predominantly female; 66 per cent of women and 15 per cent of men work part-time. The unions have been largely successful in obtaining equal rights and status for part-timers on a par with full-time employees, and in a number of recent collective agreements various terms have been extended to part-time staff: in its 1996 agreement for example, retailer Vroom & Dreesman extended overtime pay to part-timers working outside their normal contractual hours.

Fixed-term contracts

According to the Civil Code, a fixed-term contract can be concluded for a specific length of time or in order to carry out a specific task, including the temporary replacement of a particular employee. There is no statutory maximum or minimum duration, although there are limits on renewals that are implied rather than expressly concluded. Any such implied extension to a fixed-term contract will be presumed to be for the same length of time as the original contract – but with a maximum of one year – with the same terms and conditions unless stipulated otherwise. In practice, successive fixed-term contracts are not common, except for fields such as scientific or academic research dependent on specific funding.

All employment rights granted by virtue of the existence of an employment contract also apply to a fixed-term contract, with the exception of dismissal procedures (notice periods, authorisation, etc). However, once a fixed-term contract has been renewed, or continued without notice that is not to be renewed, then the full dismissal procedures automatically become applicable, unless a period of more than 31 days lies between the two fixed-term contracts. (Note, however, that the law stipulates that if an employer uses the same worker during the period between fixed-term contracts, via an agency, then all dismissal procedures also apply to the second fixed-term contract – see below.) Moreover, where an employee on a permanent contract is put on to a fixed-term contract, the dismissal provisions also apply immediately.

Temporary work

Temporary agencies (*uitzendbureaux*) are well established. They require authorisation from the Ministry of Employment in order to operate. In law, agency workers are deemed to be in an 'employment relationship' (*arbeidsrelatie*) with the temping agency through which they are carrying out work for the client company, for the duration of the work to be carried out. However, they do not have a contract of employment (*arbeidsovereenkomst*) – as defined in law – with the agency and therefore they do not enjoy the same rights and protection that other employees do by virtue of being under a legally-defined contract of employment. They are, however, covered by a collective agreement which lays down a number of binding terms and conditions. The agreement is signed by the trade association, Algemene Bond Uitzendondernemingen (ABU), and all ABU-affiliated agencies must abide by its terms, These include minimum hourly pay rates, which are payable by the agency, and it is the agency that is liable for any breaches of terms laid down in the agreement. A number of conditions are also attached to the use of temporary workers by client companies, although some of these are due to be changed.

Under the present law, agencies may not normally hire out a temporary worker to the same employer for more than three months, but this can usually be extended to six months, and even up to one year in exceptional circumstances. Agencies are also forbidden to collude with employers in so-called 'revolving door' arrangements, under which an employer seeks to alternate its workers between fixed-term contracts and agency employment to avoid the limitations of the laws on dismissals and on fixed-term contracts (see above).

An agreement in the bipartite Labour Foundation (STAR) in March 1996 stated that anyone who had worked for one or more agencies for more than one year would be deemed to be under a full contract of employment with the agency. This would mean that the agency will be required to continue wage payments to a worker for three months even if no work is available. Legislation is in preparation to translate the agreement into statute. Under the STAR provisions the collective agreement will now also cover issues such as pensions and training for workers deemed to have an employment contract. The STAR accord also amended a number of the restrictions on use of temporary agency workers such as allowing one-year contracts to be renewed up to three times before being deemed a permanent contract, and it abolished the maximum of six months for temping with one employer.

Sectoral or company collective agreements may limit the use of agency workers. For example the banking agreement (1995/8) stipulates that agency workers may be used only during unexpected peaks, coverage for sickness or holidays, coverage between a vacancy arising and it being filled, or during temporary restructuring. The agreement for cleaning workers stipulates that a maximum of 7.5 per cent of quarterly hours may be covered by agency workers. Most agreements lay down that only authorised agencies that fall under the ABU collective agreement may be used to hire such staff.

Internal recruitment

This is still common practice. Many collective agreements require there to be internal advertisement of vacancies prior to outside recruitment, for example in banking, insurance, or cleaning. This is usually done by advertising on company notice boards or in-house magazines. Some firms require part-time staff to be given an option on full-time vacancies that have arisen or that employees made redundant for economic reasons must be informed of suitable vacancies prior to, or at the same time as, external advertising taking place. In the context of job creation, a number of agreements state specifically that, in consultation with the works council, the suitability of any vacancies for targeted groups should be considered, for example the long-term unemployed or the disabled (see above).

Recruitment and anti-discrimination provisions

The right to equal pay and equal treatment is laid down in the 1989 Act on the equal treatment of men and women. The Act stipulates that employers must make no distinction between men and women as regards recruitment, terms of employment, job category allocation, training, pay, or termination of contract. Nor may any distinction be made on the basis of marital status or family situation.

Following the Act a new Equal Treatment Commission was set up. The commission has an advisory and investigative role in alleged cases of discrimination. However, it can impose no sanctions. This is also one of the criticisms levelled at the proposed new recruitment complaints authority under the national code of practice: it would have no powers to fine or sanction those who disregard the code. It could, however, advise complainants as to the possible legal bases of their complaints, and it is hoped that the authority would act as a deterrent.

Discrimination on grounds of race is forbidden under the Constitution and the Penal Code. The provisions of the Penal Code have been held to cover both direct and indirect discrimination (such as excessive or irrelevant qualifications for routine work). However, investigative machinery is weak and the penalties for a breach of the Penal Code are minimal. Complainants may also resort to civil law, which allows for damages for the results of unlawful acts. However, awards remain small. In an attempt to boost the recruitment of ethnic minorities, companies were to complete a survey of the ethnic make-up of their workforces by June 1995. However, only 37 per cent of firms did so, and the government debated the imposition of quotas. So far this has not been settled, but an agreement between the social partners was extended into 1996 in order to help up to 60,000 people from ethnic minorities find work. Under its terms, collective agreements are meant to contain specific measures, although few do so other than in the context of general measures targeted at certain groups (see above).

There is no specific legislation prohibiting discrimination in the recruitment process on grounds of disability. Under a 1986 law, employers, their organisations and trade unions are called on to co-operate to promote the employment of disabled people. The law requires employers to employ a quota of people with disabilities – initially set at 5 per cent and later moved to between 3 per cent and 7 per cent of the company workforce, depending on sector and type of business. Employers who do not meet the quota can, in theory, be required to contribute to the General Disability Fund, which finances some disability benefits. Employers may gain exemption if they can show that they have undertaken other measures to facilitate the employment of disabled people. In reality, quotas are rarely met: a study carried out by the Ministry in 1990 found that the average proportion of disabled workers in any company was 2.2 per cent.

Finding the applicant

The official employment service

The official employment service (*Centraal Bestuur voor de Arbeidsvoorziening*, CBA) was created in its current form in 1991. At that date the old system was decentralised and the social partners were co-opted into management of the service. This is now operated on a regional basis with 28 offices geared to the regional labour markets. The central office draws up policy guidelines annually, but there is significant input from, and variation across, the regions. These provide job targets, vacancy numbers and target groups.

The service is funded by the state, but individual offices may make limited charges for additional services, such as consultancy or training. It was hoped in

1991 that the changes would lead to a more effective and streamlined system. However, the CBA as a whole is still regarded as bureaucratic and unwieldy, particularly by employers. Most of the jobs offered through the CBA continue to be at the lower end of the labour market, with few management or graduate positions. In theory, vacancies not filled by internal company recruitment should be notified to the relevant regional office, and many collective agreements specifically restate this requirement. However there is no sanction for failure to notify.

In 1991 the ban on private recruitment agencies (*arbeidsbemiddelingsbureaux*) was lifted and these are now allowed to operate alongside the official service. They do, however, need a licence from the Ministry of Labour.

Employment agencies and consultants

There is an increasing use of employment agencies and search bureaux (*bureaux voor werving en selectie*), especially by medium-sized and large firms, with between 50 and 1,500 employees. Recruitment consultants are finding that not only top executive and managerial posts are being referred to them, but also more middle management and specialist functions. Most selection bureaux and consultants charge hourly fees of up to Fl 300 (£100), or anything between Fl 10,000 and Fl 25,000 (£3,300–£8,300) for a complete recruitment package.

Executive search

Much executive recruitment takes place via executive consultancies. Some specialise in certain sectors or professions and usually deal with positions with minimum salary levels of over Fl 100,000 (£33,000). Some companies may stipulate a higher minimum. Executive consultancies normally charge a percentage of the annual salary for the position. This is usually between 20 and 25 per cent of the first year's salary for senior executives; 15 to 20 per cent for other executives. There is a professional body for search and selection bureaux, the Organisatie van Adviesbureaux voor Werving en Selectie (OAWS). The OAWS has a code of practice to which all member companies must conform. It has almost 100 member companies which are bound by the code of practice. This, for example, forbids agencies from accepting fees from job seekers, makes provisions on confidentiality and data protection, and sets 'off-limits' rules to prevent agencies approaching former successful candidates for up to two years, unless the candidate contacts them. Members may accept an assignment only if the client is able to guarantee that no other consultancy has been approached for the same post; on the other hand more than one consultancy can be engaged to handle separate assignments for the same client. An independent monitoring body ensures compliance, and a full list of members and fees charged is available from the OAWS (see address at the end of the chapter).

Recruitment methods

The media

Almost 40 per cent of recruitment is through media advertising of one sort or another. Large companies use the media more often than smaller ones, and most prefer to draft their own advertisements. The NVP recruitment code also covers advertising, detailing what the advertisement should contain, including:

- job description and title
- workplace location
- hours of work, with indication of shift work or unsocial hours
- closing date for applications and estimated time for selection procedures
- whether a psychological test will be required
- contact name and address.

The code recommends that the salary level should be mentioned where possible; however, this is rarely done. In addition, advertisements should not contain false or misleading information or be discriminatory in any way. At present there are no restrictions on age limits in job adverts, and a survey in 1993 showed that only 9 per cent of adverts stipulating age limits were open to the over-40s. However, under proposals issued in 1996 the government is due to introduce legislation making all age discrimination in job adverts unlawful.

Most national papers carry regular job adverts, often in their weekend supplements. Many have a niche for particular types of jobs or sectors. So the *NRC Handelsblad*'s Saturday supplement carries advertisements for managerial positions, lawyers, economists, consultants and general managers, whereas *De Telegraaf* is more commonly used for commercial posts, and the *Algemene Dagblad* is aimed at middle management across most sectors. The financial daily, *Het Financieele Dagblad*, advertises for accountants, economists and banking or finance staff. Some regional papers are also used – particularly outside the Randstad area, where they may be read in preference to the nationals.

Specialist journals or trade magazines are used for advertising for specialist and technical staff: for example, personnel functions in *Personeelsbeleid* or *Gids*; engineering in *PolyTechnisch tydschrift*. A weekly paper distributed to final year students and graduates, *Intermediair Weekblad*, has jobs in all sectors, with emphasis on management trainee positions. *Intermediair Jaarboek* gives a comprehensive list of employers of graduates, together with a series of practical employment guides. The publishers of *Gids* also produce an annual review, *Jaargids*, including a detailed list of recruitment bureaux, outplacement services, and training institutions.

Recruitment documents

Advertisements in the media will usually specify whether an application form needs to be filled out by the applicant, and by when this should be completed. Initial selection is done on the basis of the letter of application, a CV and, where required, an application form. Some smaller firms may hold an initial telephone discussion as well. Any documentation provided by the candidate should be returned by the employer as soon as possible, and in any case within four weeks of the appointment or rejection being made.

References are taken up by about 70 per cent of employers, particularly for more senior positions. Only 50 per cent of employers take up references for lower-level jobs. References from current employers are taken up only if the candidate has no objections. During the interview and selection procedure there should be no invasion of the candidate's privacy, and only relevant questions should be asked. The results of any medical or psychological tests must be made known to the candidate.

Selection methods

The main method of selecting new employees is through an interview. Most companies make their short-list on the basis of application form, CV and letter, and usually contact only applicants to be invited to interview. The letter of invitation to an interview will usually state the name and titles of those who will be carrying out the interview, the estimated length of the interview and whether any tests will be set before or during the interview.

The NVP and national codes recommend that employers provide adequate company information, details of the job itself, salary level and other conditions of employment during the interview. Any training requirements should also be stated. Only questions relating directly to the job should be posed during the interview, but this is often broadly interpreted.

Graphology and psychological testing are normally used for managerial posts only. The NVP code states that candidates should receive the results of such tests, but a 1992 survey found that only 50 per cent did. Psychological tests should only be carried out under the guidelines of the Netherlands' Institute of Psychologists (NIP). Any costs for carrying out such tests are borne by the company.

Medical examinations are often standard practice at all levels. This mostly involves a routine check-up as required for company pension schemes. According to the NVP code, examinations must be conducted by a qualified physician. In addition, legislation may require that appointment to a certain position is dependent on the outcome of a medical examination. The government has opposed the use of HIV/AIDS testing and genetic testing in the context of recruitment, although there are no specific prohibitions on either practice, and HIV testing does take place.

Offer and rejection

According to the various codes of practice, offers of employment should be made and accepted in writing. However, there are no statutory requirements governing appointment procedures. The NVP code recommends that the letter of appointment should contain details of general terms and conditions of employment, salary, probationary period and notice periods, as well as specific provisions agreed during the interview. The code also recommends that the whole selection and appointment procedure should take no longer than three months.

Unsuccessful candidates should be informed in writing as soon as possible (the NVP code recommends within one week). Reasons for the rejection should be given in the letter, and any psychological test results returned to the centre that carried them out. In the absence of a complaints authority it is most often the personnel manager within the company who handles complaints.

Military service

Men may be called up for military service from age 19, usually for 18 months. Conscientious objectors can complete a slightly longer spell of community service. In the case of employees over 21 the employer must take them back after military service in a job at the same grade as the one they formerly held. Jobs of those under age 21 are similarly protected provided they have at least one year's service with the employer. After 1998 compulsory military service will be abolished, although it will still be possible to undertake voluntary military service.

Education, training and employee development

Overview

The Netherlands has one of the most egalitarian higher education systems in Europe, with a long-standing tradition of decentralisation and freedom of choice. Much of the emphasis is on providing study opportunities for all, geared to preparing the individual for a specific career. Education in the Netherlands has traditionally been established along religious lines, with a constitutionally guaranteed freedom that education may be made available by any provider. The government therefore funds all schools, state (*openbaare school*) and private (*bijzondere school*), provided they meet a certain set of criteria and standards. In practice, approximately 70 per cent of all schools in the Netherlands are publicly funded but privately run. This has led to a bewildering array of education establishments. The system also has a built-in flexibility for moving from one stream to another and for continuing into higher education. However, the emphasis is still strongly on obtaining formal qualifications, with some qualification required for almost every kind of work.

Throughout the 1990s a series of reforms have been implemented to stream-line the system and allow greater movement between institutions as well as encouraging individual flexibility and adaptability in vocational training. The latest of these reforms was the 1995 law on vocational education and training, which comes into force in stages (see below). This has led to an enormous diversity of organisations and structures providing education and training, and the whole system is still in flux.

Responsibility for education is divided between central, regional and local authorities, with an increasing tendency to decentralisation – including local management of schools. There have been moves by the government to allow local authorities to distribute education funding, for example. Central control is exerted to maintain national standards and qualifications, to stipulate minimum numbers of students, set broad curricular requirements, monitor teaching standards and allocate funds. Provision of state schools remains the responsibility of the regional authorities.

In contrast to many other European countries – where pay and career prospects for graduates can be determined by which institution a graduate has attended and the duration of their studies – the emphasis in the Netherlands is more on market conditions and individual performance.

Much vocational training is provided under the state education system, with a vocationally-oriented stream from age 12, and various gradations extending up to vocationally-geared tertiary education. There is also a well developed apprenticeship system (amended by the 1995 law – see below).

Education system

Education starts at the age of 4, although it is compulsory only from age 5, and continues until at least age 16. However, there is a legal obligation for all 16–17-year-olds to attend part-time vocational classes for two days per week for a further year.

Secondary education: general

Secondary education (*voortgezet onderwijs*) begins at age 12 and is structured along two paths: vocational and general. Since amendments to the legislation in 1993, all secondary education now begins with a common curriculum (*basisvorming*), although this may be taught over different lengths of time, depending on the school. Nevertheless, the integration of initial secondary education allows for transfer between the streams. General secondary education is divided into four streams, with the top three often requiring an entrance exam to be taken:

- Junior pre-vocational secondary education (*lager beroepsonderwijs*, LBO) lasts four years to age 16. Although termed vocational, the course has a substantial general content, with more vocational emphasis in the later years. Numbers attending LBO courses have dropped considerably in the last few years. An LBO certificate permits entry to higher vocational training or an apprenticeship (see below).
- Junior general secondary education (*middelbaar algemeen voortgezet onderwijs*, MAVO) lasts four years to age 16. Pupils who obtain an MAVO certificate can either enter the labour market directly, follow intermediate vocational training (see below) or transfer to higher general secondary education in order to gain entry to higher vocational education.
- Higher general secondary education (*hoger algemeen voortgezet onderwijs*, HAVO) lasts five years to age 17 and confers the right to enter higher vocational education or transfer to pre-university education.
- Pre-university education (*voorbereidend wetenschappelijk onderwijs*, VWO) lasts six years to age 18 and is intended to prepare students for university or higher vocational colleges (see below). There are two types of VWO schools: the *atheneum* and the *gymnasium*, where pupils must learn Greek and Latin, although the two types are often combined within a single *lyceum*.

There is a growing number of combined schools (*scholengemeenschappen*) which encompass two or more types of schools under one headteacher. The government has been encouraging the establishment of such schools in particular since the introduction of the unified curriculum in 1993. In the school year 1994/5, some 759,000 pupils were pursuing general secondary education (MAVO, HAVO and VWO), while 150,000 were in secondary vocational education (see below).

Higher education

A major reform of higher education is under way, following legislation passed in 1993 and 1995, which should be completed by 2004. There are two main sectors of higher education: universities, which offer scientific/academic education (*wetenschappelijk onderwijs*, WO) and higher professional schools offering higher vocational education (*hoger beroepsonderwijs*, HBO). In 1994/5 some 179,000 students were at university while a further 246,000 were in higher vocational education. The two streams of higher education are governed by separate legislation but there are moves towards a more unified system (see below).

There are 13 universities offering over 200 courses (three universities of technology, one university for agriculture and nine general universities) plus an open university. Most are public bodies and are government-funded (up to 80 per cent in most cases) but not all offer the same range of courses. Currently university courses run for four years, although students can take up to six years to complete a course. Higher education aims to be open to as wide a spectrum of the population as possible, and entrance to university is open to anyone with a VWO school-leaving certificate, and to HBO institutions to anyone with a VWO or HAVO certificate. VWO is taken after six years' secondary education at age 18 in six subjects (including Dutch and one foreign language). A quota system may be applied to admissions on a national basis if the number of candidates exceeds the number of places or if there is a glut on the labour market of particular qualifications: this has been applied repeatedly in recent years to medicine, dentistry and veterinary science.

University graduates are awarded the title *docterandus* (drs.) – comparable to the UK master's degree – although in engineering and law the titles are *ingenieur* (Ir.) and *meester van de rechten* (Mr.) respectively. A limited number of students go on to obtain a research degree, *doctorate* (Dr.), which takes a further four years to complete.

In contrast to the universities, most HBO (*hogeschool*) institutions, are privately run. There are 85 *hogescholen* and the number of students on HBO courses has steadily increased from 180,000 in 1989 to 246,000 in 1995. HBO courses may be taken up by anyone with a VWO or HAVO school-leaver's certificate. HAVO is taken after five years in six subjects (including Dutch and one foreign language). HBO courses last between two and four years and are available for agriculture, engineering and technology, health care, economics, social and community work, the arts, and teacher training.

Most HBO courses involve some kind of commercial or industrial placement. They lead to a bachelor's degree (*baccalaureus*, bc.). After passing the first-year examinations HBO students may be able to transfer to a university course.

Just over 21 per cent of the workforce aged 25–64 hold a higher education qualification: 15 per cent from an HBO institute, 7 per cent from a university. Drop-out rates are low by international standards: some 87 per cent of those going into higher education graduate. There is expected to be a continuing move towards HBO education, with forecasts for reductions in the number of university entrants to 149,000 by the year 2000, while HBO numbers are expected to remain stable. According to the CBS, 45 per cent of higher education students are women. However, this varies by subject: 50 per cent of graduates in law are female; 28 per cent in business studies; 20 per cent in economics; 12 per cent in IT; 6 per cent in physics; and 2 per cent in engineering. This is also reflected in graduate recruitment: in 1995, 45 per cent of graduate recruits taken on by the finance company ING were female; 40 per cent at ABN Amro; 33 per cent at KPN; 27 per cent at Akzo Nobel; 20 per cent at Unilever; 18 per cent at Philips; and only 13 per cent at Shell. Many graduates are working in jobs below, or even well below, their qualification levels, amounting to nearly half of VBO graduates and 40 per cent of MAVO certificate holders.

New government proposals for higher education are aimed at reducing the length of most courses and encouraging more students to opt for HBO education. HBO courses would be cut from four to three years for students with a VWO qualification, while universities could choose to have 2 × 2-year cycles with a *baccalaureus* awarded at the end of the first cycle and a Drs/Mr/Ir at the end of the second. The government envisages the first degree to be largely for subjects such as economics, social studies and humanities. Only better students would go through to the second cycle. Employers are less convinced of the idea of shorter HBO courses, saying that they will be insufficient as preparation for work, and will only increase the amount of training to be carried out within companies. Universities and *hogescholen* would be allowed to reduce their intake of students for a particular course if there was a glut on the labour market; at the moment only the government can impose such limits. Funding changes are also proposed: university and *hogeschool* funding would no longer be related strictly to student numbers but would be based on a ten-year projection using research and teaching capacity criteria. For *hogescholen* there is already a general council which would take responsibility for allocation of resources across the individual schools, rather than individual allocation direct from government, as is currently the case. The idea of selective entrance for some courses has also been mooted, as well as allowing HBO schools to set up professional master's courses for students with at least four years' work experience. These courses would be funded by the *hogescholen* themselves, with some financial commitment from companies.

Graduate recruitment

Exams can be taken at different times in the year, and therefore there is no one particular period for graduating. This makes the annual graduate 'milk round' as practised in the UK not possible. However, company presentations, recruitment fairs and open-days at universities are becoming more common, with resulting unsolicited applications from students an important means of recruitment. Direct links with universities and other higher education establishments mean that a number of posts are filled by direct referrals from department heads. Work experience and 'stages' are also commonly used to recruit a growing number of graduates; indeed many graduates are finding that without some kind of work experience jobs are hard to come by.

There are two guides for graduates published by the state services: *Vacant* carries details of vacancies, while *Sollicitant* gives details of students seeking work. Many universities have careers offices, but they tend not to be well developed.

A number of other publications aimed at graduates have recently been developed, including an annual directory, *Orientatiegids*, published by Projekt Media. This gives details of companies seeking to recruit as well as types of vacancies and qualifications sought. The introduction to the directory offers advice on CV writing, interview techniques and other hints. The address is given at the end of this chapter.

Vocational education and training

Vocational secondary education underwent a major overhaul in 1995/6 with the *Wet Educatie en Beroepsonderwijs*. This law came into force on 1 January 1996, although institutions have a period of adjustment with some measures staggered over several years. The law also affects apprenticeships and adult education (see below). Vocational secondary education consists of:

- junior secondary vocational training (*voorbereidend beroepsonderwijs*, VBO) which lasts four years to age 16 and allows entry to a higher vocational education or an apprenticeship (see below)
- senior vocational training (*middelbaar beroepsonderwijs*, MBO) which leads on from VBO or MAVO and lasts three or four years
- a short-term MBO course (KMBO) available since 1979 which lasts two to three years.

Pupils who have completed the MAVO or HAVO secondary schooling can also opt to take up an MBO course or an apprenticeship (see below). The MBO course offers a range of subjects in engineering and technology; economics and commerce; social services and health care; and agriculture and environmental studies. All MBO courses include work placement. Under the 1995 law, qualifications gained during an apprenticeship are to be aligned more closely with the MBO. Four levels of qualication will be set from 1997 (see below) with the fourth level roughly equivalent to a full MBO qualification. Schools providing MBO education will have to merge with national boards for apprenticeships under the umbrella of newly-created regional education centres (ROCs). Schools will still educate and train their students – with the curricula little changed – but examinations and standard controls will largely pass to the national apprenticeship boards.

Attendance at KMBO courses rose considerably in the 1980s but stabilised in the 1990s: in 1994/5 334,000 students were on an MBO course, the vast majority (204,000) in technical or economic/business subjects. Although the number of women in MBO courses overall was roughly equal to the number of men, there was a clear split in subjects: 80,000 men did technical subjects (compared to 22,000 women), while 60,000 women were on social or health care courses (compared to 12,000 men). Short MBO courses are also open to those who have failed pre-vocational education (LBO or MAVO) and need a bridging course as an intoduction to specific training. KMBO courses also include a practical placement.

According to some observers there is a polarisation taking place in education and training with, on the one hand, increasing numbers of students opting for general secondary education rather than vocational training, and within this opting for HAVO rather than MAVO. Those who choose MAVO are going on to MBO more often than their predecessors. On the other hand, within the HAVO group more are going for lower-level further training rather than apprenticeships.

Apprenticeships

Young people aged 16 who are no longer in full-time education are required to attend an educational or training establishment for one or two days per week. Apprenticeships therefore provide a mixture of practical on-the-job training and theoretical study. Most people who embark on an apprenticeship have at least an LBO certificate; where this is not the case the apprenticeship takes one year longer.

Apprenticeships are regulated by statute, overhauled by the 1995 *Wet Educatie en Beroepsonderwijs*. The law stipulates the obligations and rights of the employer, the apprentice, and the teaching establishment. It states that the schooling component of the apprenticeship is the responsibility of the teaching establishment, while the employer is responsible for the practical training. An apprenticeship contract is signed between the apprentice, the employer or company providing practical training and the school and/or regional board for apprentices (see below). The contract requires the consent of parents or guardian within four weeks of the contract being drawn up (this is the case for any contract of employment with someone under age 18). Apprentices usually earn at least the national minimum wage, but collective agreements may also stipulate higher rates. In most cases the apprentice will also sign an employment contract with the employer, although this is not a statutory requirement. This is then governed by legislation applicable to contracts of employment.

Until 1996 most apprenticeships consisted of up to three levels of training; from 1997 this rises to four levels and will parallel more closely the MBO courses. A new qualification structure will be introduced which straddles both apprenticeships and MBO courses in order to allow greater transfer between the two. The new structure consists of an introductory cycle of six months to one year (*assistentopleiding*); a basic cycle of two to three years (*basisopleiding*); a third cycle of two to four years (*vakopleiding*); and two alternative end cycles of one or two years (*specialistenopleiding*) or three or four years (*middenkaderopleiding*) which allow greater technical specialism or development to management positions. However, the broad content of current courses will be little changed to accommodate the new qualification levels. The main difference between MBO and apprenticeship courses will remain the practical content: for MBO courses between 20 and 50 per cent of the course will be practically-oriented, while for apprenticeships it will be at least 60 per cent. The final, managerial-level, qualification will roughly equate to the current full MBO qualification.

Currently each sector of industry has a national sectoral board (*landelijk orgaan*) responsible for apprenticeships. Among other things they co-ordinate theoretical and on-the-job training; draw up general programmes for apprentices on a national basis; set and mark examinations; and monitor apprenticeship contracts. Each board appoints advisers to assist employers in setting up and running apprenticeships. The boards also come together under the Central Office of National Industrial Training Organisations (COLO), which acts as a centre for co-ordination and consultation. In addition, there are 15 regional apprentice-ship boards, although their role is more limited. Under the 1995 law, new regional education centres (ROCs) are to be set up to co-ordinate a number of educational and training institutes for MBO, apprenticeship training and some adult vocational education (although not those aimed at target groups etc – see below). This continues the process begun in the late 1980s. It is envisaged that 45 to 50 ROCs will be created in order to offer a full range of educational and training opportunities in at least three of the following areas: technical, eco-nomics, services, health, agriculture and environmental services. All current MBO and apprenticeship training and education providers will be required to 'find a place' within an ROC by 1 January 1998. Failure to do so will mean that the centre or institute concerned will no longer be eligible for government funding (there are a number of exceptions to this). The national sectoral boards will continue to exert control over quality and standards, including over some MBO courses within the ROCs, and also over placement of apprentices with companies.

Apprenticeships are open to adults, with a number of programmes designed for immigrants, long-term unemployed and women returners (see also below).

Currently the sectoral boards are funded by the government – largely by the Ministry of Education, with three funded by the Ministry of Agriculture. Money can be made available to companies to partly pay for some training of employees or apprentices (see below). The government has been worried for some time about the shrinking numbers of apprentices: in 1991/2 there were 127,000 but in 1994/5 there were only 119,000. Particularly badly hit are sec-tors such as publishing and textiles (down 28 per cent from 1993/4). Employers fear that this will lead to a shortage of skilled and experienced workers in the medium term.

For this reason the government introduced an apprenticeship subsidy from January 1996. Employers receive a wage subsidy for full-time apprentices with an employment contract, and who have been in employment for at least one year, and earning no more than 130 per cent of the national minimum wage. The employer may claim rebates of Fl 4,000–Fl 4,500 (£1,300–£1,500) in tax and social charges payable. There has been some dispute over this from employers in sectors with collective agreements that have minimum scales already higher than 130 per cent of the national minimum wage.

Apprenticeships can also be covered by collective agreements: in banking, for example, the agreement stipulates that apprenticeships for given posts can be offered to employees under 23 for (re)training. Many sectoral agreements have a special training and development fund (*opleiding en ontwikkelingsfonds*) which also partly compensates the employer for the costs of training courses, and funds examinations (see below also).

Schemes for late entrants, returners and unemployed

The complex adult education system that existed for a long time in the Netherlands has been – and to an extent continues to be – streamlined. In the early 1990s two important laws were passed: the Adult Education Act (*Kaderwet Volwasseneneducatie*) in 1991, and the law on short-term vocational training (*Wet op het Cursorisch Beroepsonderwijs*) in 1993.

The Central Employment Service (*Centraal Bestuur voor de Arbeidsvoorziening*, CBA) is responsible for the majority of education centres aimed at late entrants, the unemployed and returners. The CBA was hived off from the Ministry of Labour in 1991 to be run jointly by government, employers and unions. The CBA draws up multi-annual policy programmes for implementation by its 28 regional services. These determine the number of unemployed to be trained, and the appropriate educational requirements. A number of training institutions fall under the control of the CBA: the vocational training centres (*Centra voor Vakopleiding*, CV); centres for job orientation and preparation (*Centra voor Beroepsorientatie en Beroepsoefening*, CBB); women's education centres and apprenticeships for the unemployed. The CVs offer short-term (average seven months) technical and administrative courses. There are 21 technical and 11 administrative centres running highly practical courses aimed largely at the unemployed. Some 20,000 participants are involved each year. The CBB courses are targeted at groups most 'at risk' in the labour market: the long-term unemployed, the low-qualified and immigrants.

A number of women's training centres (*Vrouwenvakscholen*) have been set up under the auspices of the FNV trade union women's organisation. These are aimed at women over 25 with minimal or no qualifications who have not yet been in employment, or who wish to return to work after a significant period of absence. Training programmes are often part-time and designed with mothers of school-aged children in mind. The courses last between one and two years and specialise in information technology. There are nine centres with a total of 1,000 places available. Six of the centres are fully subsidised by the regional services of the CBA, and the other three receive some municipal funding. The success rate, measured by the percentage of women obtaining full-time employment upon completion of the course, is relatively high at 70 to 80 per cent. Some 22 per cent of participants are from ethnic minorities.

Some apprenticeships are also open to job seekers, returners and late entrants through government subsidies introduced in 1990, when the upper age limit for apprentices (27) was abolished. The subsidies are paid into the sectoral training boards and distributed according to programmes drawn up by the boards, or into joint training funds for several companies co-operating in practical training programmes (most often smaller companies). This is termed *Gemeenschappelijke Opleidingsactiviteit*, GOA. Subsidies consist of a basic payment, plus a GOA contribution, plus an additional amount for targeted groups (such as to boost the intake of women into traditionally male occupations). By law, at least 15 hours per week must be devoted to practical training, and a specific policy plan should be submitted in cases where the additional subsidy is to be paid. Since 1990 there has been an increase in the average age of apprentices and a growing tendency towards module-based apprenticeships with greater options for transfering to and from other types of adult vocational training – see also the provisions of new law, above.

Further sectoral training programmes for the registered unemployed are available to small and medium-sized companies. Again, these programmes are drawn up and implemented by employer and employee representatives on a regional basis. Subsidies cover all training costs up to a maximum of Fl 10,000 (£3,300) per place. In 1990 some 5,500 people benefited from these courses.

Further training/technical training

Although the Dutch system of vocational education, principally the various MBO options, is broadly based and offers formal training to a large number of young people, it suffers from disadvantages which employers have to offset through in-house provision. People who complete standard vocational education are often aged at least 21 when they are ready to enter employment but they still lack industrial experience. Set against this is the breadth of vocational education which means that often only a short period of company training is needed to allow the employee to become productive. Company training is carried out either in-house or by external providers (see below). Retraining for employees, and further training options, have become increasingly common features in collective agreements. Some form of educational and training measures are included in agreements covering over 85 per cent of the total number of employees covered by collective agreements. The scope of employee training has also increased, with a corresponding rise in the number of external providers offering training courses. Company training budgets were cut during the early 1990s recession but recovered in 1994/5 with increasing demand for versatile, flexible people. None the less, price and quality awareness is more acute, and many companies are keen to ascertain the effectiveness and medium- to long-term benefits of training courses on offer.

External training providers include independent training institutions as well as educational establishments, especially HBO and MBO centres (see above).

Workforce consultation and agreed provisions

Agreement of the company works council is required by law for company training programmes, provided these are not already laid down by collective agreement. For example, at the chemicals company Akzo Nobel, the collective agreement stipulates that a training inventory should be undertaken annually and a programme drawn up in consultation with employee representatives. The banking agreement stipulates that the works council be informed annually of training details, notably which category of workers has undergone training, what type of training, what funding was required and an assessment of the success. Some firms have in-house training departments which are open to all on application. Courses are advertised in in-house magazines and on notice boards.

Time-off rights

Educational leave is not covered by law, other than for young people who have not completed their legal schooling requirement. Employers are obliged to release such employees to attend the relevant training for the required number of hours per week, usually one or two days. The main trade union, FNV, is pushing for the adoption of statutory rights to time off.

Additional educational leave, primarily for young workers but also for retraining for older workers, is provided for by collective agreement. At chemicals firm Akzo Nobel, paid time off is granted to under 21-year-olds wanting to undertake training related to their work, either for a specific post in the company or for furthering an apprenticeship, for up to two half-days per week. Evening courses taking up three or more evenings per week may entitle the employee to a morning off in order to complete homework etc. Akzo Nobel also provide funding towards such training: all costs of training directly related to the job are met, notably exam entry fees, course fees, essential text books and travel expenses up to Fl 0.25 (eight pence) per km. Should the employee not complete the course, the money has to be refunded.

Company training provisions

A study by the Central Bureau of Statistics (CBS), published in 1995 but relating to 1993, gives a breakdown of training provision in the private sector. This shows that on average 50 per cent of all private sector firms undertook some kind of systematic training of their workforce; in almost all large companies (with over 500 employees) training was offered to at least some employees, while only 31 per cent of companies with fewer than 10 employees offered training of any sort. The sector most involved in training was the financial sector, especially banking, and public utilities, with hotel and catering undertaking the least. However, men are more likely to receive training (26 per cent) than women (22 per cent). Economics (including general business studies and management) is the most common subject, followed by administration and commercial courses. One in five training places is in the technical field. The majority of training is done by outside providers (60 per cent) rather than in-house. Of these by far the most common are independent or private training institutions (52 per cent of all external training) and sectoral organisations (23 per cent). The former tend to offer more general, business-oriented courses, while the sectoral provision is more technical in nature. Information technology in any of its many guises is the most sought-after technical training option. Many company training courses require a certain level of education, most often HAVO or MBO. Training courses vary in length from one to seven days, with five days the average. Some 60 per cent of training occurs during working hours (with overall 0.5 per cent of working time devoted to training).

The average costs of training were found to be 1.7 per cent of total labour costs, although this varied depending on the size of the company; large firms with more than 500 staff spent about 3 per cent, while firms with fewer than 100 employees spent 0.7 per cent. This is broken down as follows – (per employee): Fl 380 (£125) in firms of up to 100, Fl 1,750 (£580) in firms over 500; (per course): Fl 2,070 (£690) in firms up to 100, Fl 3,400 (£1,139) in firms over 500 – these figures include wage costs for the employee, costs of the actual training course and other (eg travel) expenses. Collective agreements may detail an amount to be devoted to training; in the textile industry (1994/6), for example, 2 per cent of a company wage bill is to be earmarked for training and skills development needs. The sectoral training organisation offers advice and support for individual companies in setting up training programmes and policies.

The CBS study also noted that between 1986 and 1993 there was growth in the provision of company training, but that since 1990 large firms have stabilised their investment, or even cut back – while small firms have continued to increase (by 13 per cent in the period 1990–1993).

Continuing training: skill- and competency-based pay

There has been much discussion of and some movement towards skill/competency-based pay. Most collectively-agreed pay scales still have a strict hierarchy of increments by age (for the under-23s) and by length of service (for the over-23s). Such automatic progression up the pay scale has been questioned; performance- and/or competency-based criteria are starting to be introduced. Most often this is at managerial level, with company and individual targets set. However, large companies are also increasingly introducing an element of team-based performance pay at lower levels, with salary scales widened to allow for an element of skill/competency-based pay. Nevertheless, 85 per cent of large companies (with over 500 staff) still have job evaluation-based pay scales. Even where an evaluation system of competencies within a department or company has been put in place, the link with pay remains tenuous, according to consultancy Berenschot. A number of job classification systems may also be moving towards incorporating skills or competencies in their structure. One large finance group, for example, recently opted to include in basic pay an element dependent on the achievement of certain skills or targets. However, employers say that high pay at low levels impedes this development.

Appraisal and development

An important means of evaluating core skills and training needs within a company is an effective appraisal system for all employees. These are less likely to be included in collective agreements but may feature in company handbooks etc. For example, at insurance company Delta Lloyd, the appraisal system (*beoordelingssysteem*) is detailed in the handbook. Appraisals take place once a year for every employee and are carried out by the employee's line manager or supervisor. Training needs are discussed as part of any appraisal, with requests for further training most commonly following directly from appraisals. Salary reviews are linked with the outcome of appraisals, but Delta Lloyd deliberately separates the appraisal from the yearly salary review. Nevertheless, salary progression within an allocated salary scale depends partly on achieving a good appraisal. On the other hand, a bad appraisal will not result in reductions in pay. Promotions are also linked to appraisals.

Most appraisals are still carried out individually, but in some firms where team working has been implemented some team appraisals may also be included, with team members evaluating each other.

It should be noted that for a dismissal to be authorised on disciplinary grounds, or for reasons related to performance, a carefully documented history has to be submitted. This means that regular appraisals (particularly where the employee is underperforming) are essential to build a dismissal case. This well-known fact can influence appraisal systems negatively.

Managerial and supervisory training

A large proportion of Dutch managers hold university or HBO degrees. Although the subject pursued at tertiary level is more relevant to subsequent career choice than in the UK, there is some degree of flexibility. Arts graduates, for example, may be drawn into general graduate training programmes or may convert to business studies. There is a difference between large and small companies; the latter tend to have greater difficulty in retaining graduates, and more of their managers are developed from skilled workers and specialists within the company. Both the MBO and apprenticeships have scope for training in aspects of supervision – a feature that will be further strengthened with the new structure of apprenticeship training due to be implemented by 1997 (see above). Large (often multinational) companies spend considerable time and money recruiting high flyers from among graduates, often MBA graduates, for grooming into senior management. Initial training usually involves a programme of assignments in different sectors or units, although all companies stress that management recruits are expected to fill 'real' jobs almost immediately. A number of multinationals are also considering more integrated pan-European recruitment and management training, but few have actually done so. Nevertheless, language skills and international experience are highly rated for development to senior managerial posts.

MBAs have become increasingly popular, and are offered by some universities and private colleges, often with links to the US. Their perceived value varies considerably. The MBA offered at Rotterdam School of Management (Erasmus University) is particularly well regarded.

Financing the system

The Constitution allows any person the freedom to provide education as long as a number of criteria and standards are met. In practice this means that the government funds almost all compulsory education up to age 16. Most of this comes via the Ministry of Education and Science, with the Ministry of Social Affairs responsible for certain educational needs and provision in the context of labour market policies. A number of health courses are funded through the Ministry of Health and some agricultural courses through the Ministry of Agriculture. Higher education and part-time education after age 16 may require some financial contribution from students and/or parents, with loans and limited grants available. (Students at university or *hogeschool*, aged over 18 and living at home, qualify for a monthly basic grant of Fl 225 (£75); those not living at home receive Fl 560 (£185) monthly.) Very often students in the Netherlands have a (part-time) job to supplement their grants, but earnings over Fl 8,000 (£2,650) per year will lead to a reduced grant. Means-tested loans are also available (based on parental or partner's income), with 15 years allowed for repayment.

Total spending on education and training was 5.8 per cent of GDP in 1992, while the Ministry of Education and Culture's budget in 1996 was Fl 37,900 million (£12,600 million).

Estimates from the Ministry of Education put costs per student per year at Fl 14,800 (£4,900) for university and Fl 13,900 (£4,600) for *hogeschool* courses; Fl 10,900 (£3,600) for MBO courses and Fl 4,300 (£1,400) for apprenticeships. Over the past few years cuts in education grants and spending have largely fallen on tertiary education at universities and *hogescholen*. One aim is to reduce the number of students at any one time by cutting the length of courses, and 'forcing' students to complete courses within four years. Also, students who under-achieve will be made to give up their places within three months, rather than within the year as is currently the case. The Ministry of Education estimates that by the year 2004 the number of university students will fall from 180,000 to 142,000, while those on HBO degree courses will remain around the 262,000 mark. 'Funding is to be adjusted accordingly.'

There is no statutory training levy on companies, although many sectoral and company agreements detail some kind of training fund. These are most commonly jointly operated and funded by compulsory contributions. For apprenticeships, companies are required to fund on-the-job training while the theoretical schooling takes place at external institutions funded by government, regional authorities and the companies that use them. In metalworking, for example, the collective agreement on training stipulates a levy of 0.6 per cent (1995/6) of the total wages bill. The agreement also details the amount of funding that will be provided, and the required criteria for entitlement to such funding from the sectoral board for (re)training activities. The amount depends on the type of training followed; where training is primarily carried out (in-house or externally); what course is followed; etc. So, for someone aged less than 27 and in their first apprenticeship, the board will pay Fl 12,000 (£4,000) in the first two years. For those aged less than 27 with no apprenticeship contract but undertaking training the boards pays Fl 12,000 (£4,000) in the first year and Fl 13,250 (£4,400) in the second year of training. For apprentices moving into further levels of training the board will pay between Fl 3,750 (£1,250) and Fl 5,000 (£1,650).

An important development over the last few years is the increased inclusion of broad (re)training schemes in collective agreements. Although they tend to be limited in scope, unions have appeared willing to accept lower pay increases in return for training and jobs investments. In 1996, this tended to diminish as employees became increasingly dissatisfied with the apparent reluctance of employers to translate such principles into hard action, particularly the jobs issue. A number of 1995/6 collective agreements have introduced lower starting rates of pay for low-skilled recruits. In many cases there is an element of training involved in the schemes; most commonly new recruits will be paid at the lower rate while receiving training for up to one year, after which they are assessed and moved up to the normal rate of pay. The success of such schemes – largely intended to encourage recruitment and training at the lower end of the labour market – remains to be evaluated.

The government has moved towards greater decentralisation of training, retaining control over total budgetary expenditure but ceding more and more regional and municipal control over the actual budget allocations. The 1995 law on vocational training stipulates that after the year 2000 funding is to be increasingly linked with numbers attending and completing courses successfully. The newly-created regional centres (ROCs – see above) will have to agree 'contracts' with regional and/or local authorities (*gemeenten*) who will also control a degree of their funding and will have a considerable say in the charges to be levied for different courses or diplomas.

Educational attainment of the population

Level	Percentage of 25–64 age-group
Lower secondary	40
Upper secondary	38
Higher education (non-university)	–
University	21

Source: OECD (1994)

Organisations

Ministry of Education, Culture and
Science
Postbus 25000
2700 LZ Zoetermeer
Tel. +31 79 32 32 323

Ministry of Social Affairs and
Employment
Postbus 90801
2509 LV The Hague
Tel. +31 70 333 4444

Central Employment Service
Postbus 437
Visseringlaan 26
2280 AK Rijswijk
Tel. +31 70 313 09 11
Fax +31 70 313 0260

CIBB – Centre for Innovation in
Vocational Training
Postbus 1585
5200 BP s'Hertogenbosch
Tel. +31 73 6800 800
Fax +31 73 6123 425 (publications
department)

COLO – Central Office for National
Apprenticeship Boards
Bredewater 8
Postbus 7259
2701 A6 Zoetermeer
Tel. +31 79 352 3000
Fax +31 79 351 5478

Organisation of Recruitment Consultants
(OAWS)
Van Stolkweg 34
2585 JR The Hague
Tel. +31 70 350 5995
 Fax +31 70 354 4067

Federation of Temporary Work Agencies
(ABU)
Prins Mauritslaan 29–39
1171 LP Badhoeverdorp
Tel. +31 20 658 0101
Fax +31 20 659 2425

Dutch Association of Personnel
Management (NVP)
Postbus 19124
3501 DC Utrecht
Tel. +31 30 367137
Fax +31 30 343 991

Federation of Dutch Industry (VNO-
NCW)
5 Prinses Beatrixlaan
Postbus 93093
2509 AB The Hague
Tel. +31 70 349 7373
Fax +31 70 381 9508

Media

NRC Handelsblad and
Algemene Dagblad
Marten Meesweg 35
Rotterdam
Tel. +31 10 406 6217
Fax +31 10 406 6950

De Telegraaf
Postbus 376
1000 EB Amsterdam
Tel. +31 20 585 2211
 Fax +31 20 585 2435

Het Financieele Dagblad
Weesperstr. 85–87–101
Postbus 216
1000 AE Amsterdam
Tel. +31 20 557 4511
Fax +31 20 557 4200

PolyTechnisch tydschrift
Postbus 34
2501 AG The Hague
Tel. +31 70 304 5700
Fax +31 70 304 5812

Gids/Jaargids
Intermedia bv
Postbus 4
2400 MA Alphen a/d Rijn
Tel. +31 172 466 855

Orientatiegids 1996
Uitgeverij Projekt Media
Postbus 23413
3001 KK Rotterdam
Tel. +31 10 414 4177
Fax +31 10 414 9306

Main sources

Collective agreements for: banking, insurance, textiles, Akzo Nobel, cleaning and sanitation, metalworking and electrical engineering as well as summaries in *CAOs in Nederland* (published by Sdu Uitgeverij, The Hague), together with relevant legislation on training.
CEDEFOP. *Vocational education and training in the Netherlands*. Berlin, 1994
CENTRAAL BUREAU VOOR DE STATISTIEK. *Bedrijfsopleiding 1993*. The Hague, 1993
CENTRAAL BUREAU VOOR DE STATISTIEK. *Werken en Leren in Nederland*. The Hague
CENTRAAL BUREAU VOOR DE STATISTIEK. *Statistisch Jaarboek 1995*. The Hague

10

Portugal

Introduction

Following its accession to the European Community in 1986, Portugal initially narrowed the income and productivity gap with other EC member states thanks to higher than average growth rates over most of the rest of that decade, and a stream of inward investment. Healthy economic growth generated jobs and saw the unemployment rate drop to about 4 per cent by the beginning of the 1990s. Since 1992, however, the country has been grappling with the combined effects of an economic downturn – from which it was slow to emerge – as well as increased competition in the single European market and globally. This has accelerated the pace of industrial restructuring and modernisation, in turn raising unemployment, now at some 7 per cent, and prompting some changes in recruitment practices. Above all, it has led to a radical reassessment of education and training priorities.

Education and training weaknesses have held back improvements in productivity, stranding industry with goods and services based on low added value and keeping wage levels down. The rise in unemployment evident by 1994, particularly affecting the lower end of the labour market, highlighted existing structural imbalances such as the large number of unskilled employees, combined with shortages at middle management and technical levels, and weak corporate management structures including in the human resources area.

Despite great strides forward, the education gap between Portugal and the rest of the EU is substantial, evidenced by its low rate of staying-on at school. Policies are now being put in place to kick-start the transformation to a better-educated workforce. Owing to a declining birth rate, and to compensate for a historic high drop-out rate from basic education, measures must, of necessity, be targeted on the active working population as well as on those currently in the education system.

The need to strengthen training both within the education system and the labour market, to enhance its status and achieve a closer fit with company requirements are top priorities. The state is dominant in the training domain, as in many other aspects of the economy, and the importance of EU structural funds will assure its key role for some time to come. There is virtually no culture of company training, partly due to the preponderance of small family-owned firms – 70 per cent of the total – although some foreign enterprises, such as Auto Europa, are pointing the way forward. Research has shown that the better educated and those employed in large firms are far more likely to receive training.

Greater social partnership and company involvement will be essential to overcome low participation in training.

The imbalance in allocating resources between regions, perpetuating differences between urban industrial areas and rural areas, is also a source of concern. The objective of regional development programmes and decentralised delivery of education and training is to bridge the gap between advantaged and disadvantaged localities. However, as yet EU funds have proved to be ineffective in reducing regional disparities, resulting in some regions falling even further behind Lisbon, the richest, in terms of per capita income.

The role of EU structural funds

National spending on education exceeds 5 per cent of GDP. Moreover, Portugal is a major beneficiary of EU funds; the whole country is designated as an Objective 1 area qualifying for special help on the basis that per capita income is on average lower than 75 per cent of the EU average. (In addition, to the end of 1999 at least, it is entitled to help for infrastructure and transport projects from EU Cohesion Funds.) European Social Funds finance programmes in the education, vocational training and human resources areas, as well as for industrial modernisation.

It has been estimated that funds channelled through the first European Community Support Framework (CSF) 1989–93 were worth 6.8 per cent of 1989 GDP. With hindsight, this CSF was criticised as being too ambitious, failed to meet training needs in particular, and was difficult to manage, given the necessity of establishing regional structures through which programmes could be administered. Many experts believe the emphasis was on quantity over quality – leading to an ostensible explosion in company training, although firms that were allocated funds often used them inappropriately resulting in outcomes of dubious quality and utility.

The 1994–9 second Community Support Framework (involving Esc 3,250 billion (£13 billion) in grants, and European Investment Bank loans of Esc 1,200 billion (£4.8 billion)) will deliver a level of national and EU investment over the life of the programme equal to 43 per cent of 1993 GDP. European Social Funds can finance up to 75 per cent of the total cost of training and at least 50 per cent of total public expenditure incurred. Programme administration has been streamlined to some extent, with a separation of financial and technical support functions. Procedures on company access to funds have also been tightened up.

The labour market

Portugal's active population in 1995 was 4,550,600, including employees and self-employed; the latter account for just over a quarter of the workforce. The ranks of the self-employed appear to have swelled over recent years, although the authorities fear that self-employment is often simply used as a means of avoiding payment of social security contributions and income tax, and have subsequently instituted a crack-down. Of the total workforce, just over 11 per cent was employed in the primary sector, 32 per cent in industry, construction, and utilities, and 57 per cent in services.

Portuguese activity rates are relatively high at 67 per cent – 75 per cent for men and 59 per cent for women. The workforce has grown slightly, and the rise in the female activity rate has more or less compensated for the decline in activity among older cohorts due to early exit from the labour force, a trend less marked in Portugal than in other EU states. Early retirement options often offer insufficient financial incentives, a subject under discussion by the social partners. Older employees declared redundant sign on for work but commonly need to supplement their income through self-employment or informally.

The age profile of employees is uneven by companies and sector. For example, in large companies (over 100 employees) staff are predominantly within the 30–40 age range, reflecting the effects of restructuring and lay-off of older workers, whereas the over-40s predominate in manufacturing, transport and hotels. Young people must be aged at least 16 years before being allowed to work.

In 1995/6 the unemployment rate hovered around 7 per cent. Some 16 per cent of under-25s were without work, predominantly those with poor education. However, in Portugal it is older unemployed people in their 40s and 50s who cause most concern; often their levels of education and skill are so low that it is difficult to devise suitable retraining programmes to secure re-entry into the labour market.

Of those in employment at the beginning of 1996, 92 per cent were working full-time, and 8 per cent part-time. As a result of restructuring, larger firms are employing fewer people who are performing longer hours. Part-time work has so far not taken off, partly because many households need two full-time incomes, but it might become more prevalent in future.

Some 88 per cent of employees had permanent contracts, 11 per cent had temporary contracts, including contracts for a fixed-term, the remainder being agency temporaries. During the boom years of the late 1980s the percentage of staff on fixed-term contracts rose, but the position now seems to have stabilised. While permanent contracts remain the norm, new entrants are most likely to be on fixed-term contracts, at least initially. Individuals may be employed by the same firm under a succession of contracts – sometimes with very short gaps between – technically in breach of the law (see below) which specifies only two contract renewals and a three-year maximum period with the same employer.

The low level of educational attainment in Portugal has been a preoccupation ever since the 1974 Revolution. Despite improvements over the last two decades, some 40 per cent of men and women in the workforce in December 1994 had completed only four years or less of basic education; just 40 per cent of men (37 per cent of women) had completed the nine years of basic compulsory education; a mere 6 per cent (2.4 per cent of women) had completed a full university education. In practice this means that young people are much more likely than their parents to have a full secondary education (12 years). Nevertheless, the drop-out rate from basic and secondary school is high. Raising educational attainment and increasing its science and technology component are key goals of the CSF 1994–9; a target secondary school enrolment rate of 90 per cent for 15–17-year-olds has been set for the year 2000.

Statistical data show how the skills profile of the working population is skewed towards low-level or no qualifications, with some 80 per cent of employees holding qualifications or skills only at level 2 or below – that is, below basic education level. As yet, training is not regarded as an essential component of an individual's employment portfolio.

Of those in employment in March 1992, only 2.2 per cent were classified as higher management, 4 per cent supervisors, 4.2 per cent highly skilled, 39 per cent skilled, 17 per cent semi-skilled, 11 per cent unskilled, and 11 per cent trainees and apprentices. Large companies employed a higher proportion of the highly qualified: nearly 11 per cent were described as middle or senior management.

A number of employment policies are aimed at rectifying the mismatch of skills sought and offered in labour market; it is still relatively difficult to fill jobs at degree level and above, especially where work experience is required. Employees are rewarded for possessing higher-level qualifications but not necessarily for undertaking training.

Recruitment

Labour laws covering recruitment appear rigid, but are widely flouted. The Portuguese labour market is in the process of evolving from a 'jobs for life' culture, underpinned by stringent dismissal laws, to one with a greater degree of insecurity in which most new posts are offered, at least initially, on a temporary basis. In the past a rigid structure of job classification was rooted in collective agreements, backed up by law – but often freely 'adapted' by firms – which determined an employee's position in the hierarchy, and their subsequent career progression. Employers have long called for flexibility and in 1996 controversial legislation on multi-skilling was passed – which could conflict with provisions in collective agreements – enabling employers to place staff in positions where they could be required to perform a wider range of tasks. The present government has also waged war on illegal employment and spurious 'self-employment' which allows companies and individuals to avoid paying taxes and social charges.

Official notification requirements

Employers have no statutory obligation to consult the authorities on recruitment matters except to ensure that new employees are correctly registered for tax and social security purposes. EU citizens need no work permit but must secure a resident's permit after three months.

Forms of contract

Certain types of employment contract must be in writing – namely, fixed-term contracts, and contracts between a temporary agency and client company, and between the agency and a temporary worker. Where a contract is permanent (open-ended) either party may insist upon its being in writing; if a contract contains an unusual term, such as a restrictive covenant, it must be written. Trainees' contracts, including for an apprenticeship, must also be written (see below). In any event, under decree-law 5/94, which incorporates the EU Directive on proof of employment relationship, an employer is obliged to inform an employee of the main terms and conditions of employment once the contract comes into effect.

Personnel planning

Law 46/79 governing the establishment of enterprise committees, which may be set up in any size of firm, requires the employer to inform and consult on personnel matters including those affecting workforce size. (Further details on enterprise committees can be found in Vol 2 in this series, *Industrial Relations and Collective Bargaining*, pp. 245–7.) This does not impinge on individual recruitment decisions or guidelines for selection. However, collective agreements may specify recruitment and selection requirements, internal advertising of posts, regrading and promotion criteria.

Employment incentives

A national medium-term tripartite agreement on economic development and job creation was agreed in late 1996. The pact aims to stimulate overall job creation via a package of wage moderation combined with government commitments in the area of investment, tax reform and education and training. Despite a rapid rise in unemployment in early 1994, Portugal continues to enjoy a jobless rate below the EU average. Industry and corporate restructuring programmes have highlighted the structural nature of unemployment, which needs to be addressed through a strategy to raise workforce skills rather than boost demand or share out work.

None the less, some specific programmes are aimed at combating unemployment: these tend to target the long-term unemployed in their 40s and young people seeking a first job, groups 'at risk' owing to their age, inexperience and/or lack of qualifications. However, evidence shows that past initiatives were not always backed up by implementing legislation, and budgets earmarked for schemes were often underspent.

A 1995 decree-law (89/95) created a framework of incentives to encourage recruitment among these two 'at risk' groups. For companies making a net increase in their workforces over a set period, two kinds of incentive are available. Those recruiting an employee on a permanent contract are entitled to a lump-sum subsidy of 12 times the national minimum wage for a month, as well as exemptions from employers' social security contributions for 36 months. For employers hiring on fixed-term contracts, a 50 per cent social security contribution reduction is applied for the duration of the contract to the end of 1996. Employers normally pay 23.75 per cent of gross pay in social charges.

A further scheme was introduced by decree-law 34/96 which became operational in June 1996. This is also aimed principally at the young jobless (aged 16 to 30) registered at local employment centres, and the long-term unemployed. Designed to strengthen links between the education system and small companies (with fewer than 50 employees), it envisages recruitment on a permanent contract to perform practical work and training in companies. Again, firms must achieve a net increase in jobs, and stable employment levels over four years, with priority given to companies that increase the number of permanent jobs. Larger firms can take advantage of the scheme if recruitment involves an employee aged 45 or over who has been without work for 18 months. The subsidy involved is equivalent to 12 times the national minimum wage.

Another 1995 programme aims to promote local development initiatives (decree-law 34/95) in order to help maintain levels of activity in the regions to benefit young job seekers and to help narrow regional disparities. Companies with fewer than 10 staff can apply for 75 per cent investment subsidies, and for favourable credit terms and job grants. There is also a scheme to develop the 'social' labour market.

Using part-timers and temps

As mentioned above, part-time employment is not widespread, and no specific employment regulations apply; part-timers are entitled pro rata to the same pay and benefits as other staff. In addition, an employee with a child under 12 is entitled to work part-time for up to three years, with reinstatement to full-time thereafter. Employers wishing to introduce part-time work for the first time need to consult with their enterprise workers' committee, if one exists. Under a 1996 national tripartite short-term pact, the social partners are committed to examine proposals for promoting part-time work.

Fixed-term contracts

Fixed-term contracts are now common for recruits at all levels, although the more senior the position the more likely that the job will become a permanent one. The fixed term is often treated as a probationary period.

The basic law on fixed-term contracts (decree-law 64-A/89) specifies the conditions and time periods over which employers may resort to this type of contract, which are as follows:

- temporary replacement of workers who are absent, or unable to fulfil their obligations
- temporary or exceptional increase in the company's activities
- seasonal work
- performance of an occasional or precisely defined one-off task
- launch of a new activity of uncertain duration, or new activity within an existing enterprise
- performance, management and supervision of operations in construction, public works, industrial building and maintenance
- project development including planning, research, management and supervision which are not a normal part of the employer's activity
- recruiting employees for a first job, and hiring the long-term unemployed.

Some of the same grounds may be used to justify the employment of an agency temporarily (see below).

Fixed-term contracts must be in writing, signed by both parties, and state reasons for the fixed-term status. Because of abuse, in August 1996 the law (38/96) was tightened up and employers are now required to give more details to justify their use of a fixed-term contract.

The contract must set out the position or category of the worker, rate of pay, place of work and working hours. Moreover, it should state the contract term (this can be unspecified for a temporary replacement, seasonal work, construction and project workers where the contract would end when work is completed). By law, a fixed-term renewable contract may not be renewed more than twice, with a total duration of three years – or two years in the case of a new activity launch. Where these limits are exceeded the contract will be regarded as a permanent one. If the employer does not want to renew a contract, he must notify the employee eight days before the contract is due to expire. Failure to do so where a contract has not already been renewed twice will mean that the contract must be renewed for a term at least equal to that of the original contract. The new 1996 law states that where a contract continues beyond, or for a different period from, the original term, the parties must sign a formal addendum – otherwise it will be regarded as open-ended.

Probationary periods range from 15 days (for a six-month contract) to 30 days for longer-term contracts, and 60 days for permanent contracts. This latter probationary period can be reduced or even lengthened to up to six months for complex or highly responsible jobs.

At least three months must elapse between the end of one fixed-term contract exceeding 12 months and hiring a new employee in the same position.

Temporary agencies

The legal framework for temporary employment agencies was established in 1989 by decree–law 358/89, although they had already been operating before this date; the public employment service is not permitted to place temporary staff.

Two separate contracts are signed during the process of hiring agency temporaries: one between the user company and the agency that agrees to supply labour for a fee; the other (the employment contract) is between the agency (the employer) and the temporary worker (the employee) who agrees to perform work in the user company. The contract must be in writing and indicate whether it is fixed-term or open-ended, the names of the parties, reasons for using temporary staff, the nature of the post, its location, hours of work, and pay (which must be at the same rate as the user company pays other staff performing the same tasks). Recent legislation (decree-law 39/96) stipulates that any unlawful contract between a user company and a temporary agency will be regarded as null and void and could mean that a temporary worker is regarded as a permanent employee of the contracting company.

The 1989 law specifies that temporaries can be used:

- to substitute for an absent worker (for as long as the absence lasts) or to fill a job for which recruitment is in train (maximum six months)
- to cope with an exceptional or temporary increase in workload (maximum 12 months)
- to perform clearly-defined but non-permanent tasks, or a seasonal or project-linked nature (between six and 12 months, according to circumstances).

All agencies must be licensed and pay a warranty of 150 per cent of the national minimum monthly wage. As with other private employment agencies, activities are supervised by the Institute of Employment and Vocational Training and the labour inspectorate, although checks are rare. A professional association exists (*Associação Portuguesa das Empresas de Trabalho Temporário*, APETT) but members are not bound by a code of conduct. Unlike private agencies, scale fees are not regulated but fees typically amount to about double basic pay, given that pay, other on-costs and social charges are the responsibility of the agency. Agencies make widespread use of press publicity.

Temporary agencies mostly handle the placement of lower-level industrial and clerical staff; graduates sometimes register in order to gain work experience – often unavailable through university courses. Typically, a temporary employee will work under an agency contract for several months before placement with a firm on a fixed-term contract, possibly leading to permanent recruitment. Before placement, a file is compiled on each applicant and relevant tests are undertaken; references are usually taken up at a later stage. Some agencies place temporaries 'on approval' for a short period at their own expense.

Temporary agencies cover only a small part of the labour market; according to official figures they account for just 0.2 per cent of new hirings. Although some agencies earned the sector a negative reputation during the 1980s when activity mushroomed, their status has since improved owing to the growing trend towards outsourcing by large companies. Nevertheless, in cultural terms Portuguese employees are reluctant to accept very short assignments.

Internal *v.* external recruitment

Many collective agreements lay down requirements for internal promotion; in larger firms jobs have in any case tended to be filled internally. However, the culture is changing and research suggests that as companies' demands for more qualified staff have grown, they often prefer to recruit more employees externally rather than upgrade the skills of their own staff through in-service training – which is another major focus for training policy.

Equality

Under the Portuguese Constitution, discrimination on grounds of gender, race, ideology, political beliefs or country of origin is forbidden. Decree-law 392/79 guarantees equality of opportunity and treatment for men and women in employment. This outlaws advertising jobs in a discriminatory way and specifies that recruitment must be carried out according to objective criteria. Specifying physical attributes which are unrelated to the particular occupation is also unlawful. Age discrimination is not specifically outlawed and its practice is largely linked to the fact that older employees often failed to complete compulsory (basic) schooling, or to acquire qualifications.

Finding the applicant

The main routes for finding applicants are via the state placement service, private agencies and direct advertising. Surveys have also shown that many jobs are still publicised and filled by word of mouth.

The state placement system

The Institute of Employment and Vocational Training (*Instituto do Emprego e Formação Profissional*, IEFP), governed by legislation dating from 1985 and 1986, is responsible for implementing government employment policy, including job placement and vocational training. The Institute is financed by funds raised by employer and employee social security contributions, which contribute about half the overall budget, and EU funds.

One of its principal tasks is the management of a network of 79 local job centres (*centros do emprego*) responsible for job placement. Since the IEFP carries a particular brief for 'at risk' groups, its placement activities tend to focus on the lower end of the market with job seekers who are more difficult to place (school drop-outs, the unqualified, and long-term unemployed). The number of jobs it manages to fill is consequently small (involving 8–10 per cent of the labour market) despite the existence of incentives to employers to take on recruits from among these categories.

There is no official requirement to report vacancies to IEFP and in practice job centres are mostly used by small companies seeking poorly qualified staff or who offer low-level employment. Job centre staff also try to steer job seekers, particularly young school-leavers, into training but often encounter a marked reluctance, since this is still seen as the poor relation to higher education.

The IEFP, like other EU public employment services, is responsible for running the EURES system – the European Union Europe-wide job vacancy information network – which tends to handle posts for the better-qualified. Since there are shortages of such staff in Portugal, the system has been less used than in northern Europe.

The efficiency of the IEFP has become a top priority for the present Socialist government including making its job placement activities more proactive.

Three issues concerning training and information have been identified:

- The service's staffing tends to be older, lacking in certain skills and concentrated at national rather than local level.
- There is an absence of consistent, reliable up-to-date information on local labour markets.
- The system for identifying company needs is still inadequate.

State-supported job start units   The IEFP provides financial and technical support for a network of job start units (*Unidades de Inserção na Vida Activa*), supplementary to job centres, which help and involve the unemployed – mostly those with few skills – in finding a first job, or if appropriate, secure educational or training opportunities. These can be set up in vocational training centres, by the social partners and by other public, private or co-operative bodies.

Private employment agencies and personnel consultants

Portuguese law was amended in 1989 (decree-law 124/89) to allow the functioning of private employment agencies (*agências privadas de colocação*) for all categories of staff in accordance with ILO Convention 96. Agencies may be involved in all stages of the recruitment process: inserting advertisements, preselection, testing, drawing up short-lists, and placing individuals in employment. They may also advise on careers and vocational training. The law prohibits both the recruitment of foreign nationals with no right of residence in Portugal and the placement of Portuguese nationals to work abroad – except when on assignment for Portuguese firms or foreign firms associated with a Portuguese firm (eg members of the same group).

Agency activities are supervised by the Institute of Employment and Vocational Training (IEFP) through its network of local employment offices, and the labour inspectorate. There is no professional association or code of conduct.

The law makes a distinction between agencies that are free of charge and those that levy charges and, in respect of fee-charging agencies, between those trading for profit and those with non-profit objectives. Fee-charging agencies must obtain a licence (with accompanying payment) normally renewable annually. The scale of maximum fees for each placement is regulated, and ranges from 10 per cent of the sectoral monthly minimum wage for work lasting less than three months, to 75 per cent for permanent placements.

Private agencies tend to deal with the recruitment of skilled and specialist staff, as well as executive search and selection, which is not catered for by the state placement service. At a time when outsourcing is gaining ground, agencies may also be required only to deal with advertising and the pre-selection part of the process on behalf of clients. Located in Portugal are branches of some large multinationals such as Cegoc and Egor, as well as local firms.

Executive search and selection

Although the labour market for executives is far less heady than in the late 1980s, good candidates are still hard to find as the proportion of the workforce with high-level qualifications, training and suitable work experience remains low compared to other EU countries. Nevertheless, in line with Portugal's strategy to modernise its industry, qualifications demanded of candidates are becoming more stringent.

This is one reason why age discrimination is quite prevalent; it is widely held that executives aged over forty will not hold the necessary qualifications or qualities to thrive in today's much tougher market place. Therefore younger candidates, better qualified but with less work experience, may be recruited in preference. The most sought-after degrees include engineering and management (and an MBA for a higher management position). Candidates should also be fluent in English or French, possess IT skills and have relevant work experience. In return, recruits will often expect companies to enhance their personal development through the offer of a training plan and assignments abroad, regarded as important elements for career advancement. Often remuneration details are revealed only at the final stage of selection.

Executive search is conducted through press advertising, via direct approach – feasible given the small size of Portugal's executive labour market – and general or specialised agencies. The weekly *Expresso* and dailies *Publico* and *Jornal de Noticias* are used for press advertisements. Some executive search agencies have their own web sites on the Internet, but outside the specialised and small executive labour market this is not widely used.

Since there is no professional association for private agencies, nor code of conduct, off-limit rules vary. Some agencies never resort to seeking candidates in a client company, whereas others may return after a given period has elapsed. Some never ask the present employer for a reference. The fee structure is typically 15–20 per cent of gross annual salary depending on how much of the recruitment process the agency has responsibility for; fees for international consultants tend to be higher.

Jobs, even at executive level, tend to be offered on a fixed-term basis initially – often regarded as a probationary period – with the likelihood of its being converted into an open-ended contract eventually.

Recruitment media

Press advertising is inexpensive in Portugal and is widely used. The Saturday newspaper *Expresso* is the principal national vehicle for specialist and management appointments, which appear in the *Emprego* supplement, while the dailies *Publico*, *Jornal de Noticias*, *Correio da Manhã* carry a wider range of vacancies. *Correio da Manhã* publishes advertisements for skilled and unskilled staff in services, while *Commercio do Porto* deals with vacancies in Oporto and the surrounding district.

Large companies advertise under their own name but smaller firms often use box numbers. While salaries are rarely indicated, age ranges are usually specified. Under sex equality law, advertisements must not contain any restriction, specification or preference based on sex and most now indicate that jobs can be done by males or females.

Recruitment documents

Applicants for specialist and managerial posts are required to submit a curriculum vitae, sometimes with a recent photograph – invariably requested by an agency. Requests for a handwritten introductory letter are rare but a candidate's permission would not be needed if this was subsequently submitted to a graphology test. Copies of educational and professional certificates are usually requested later in the recruitment process. Male applicants may also be required to clarify their status as regards military service, which now lasts four months. A certificate of competence (*carteira profissional*) is needed to fill certain skilled occupations regulated by law, and is issued by the relevant government department. This records that the holder has attained a given level of qualification or has passed the appropriate practical test to qualify them to perform the job.

Privacy, confidentiality, references

At interview, applicants may not be asked about family circumstances, marital status or, in the case of female candidates, possible pregnancy unless the work involved is forbidden to pregnant women under safety regulations. Nevertheless, even in recruiting to specialist and higher-level positions, there is often an assumption that a woman will not wish, or be able, to undertake business trips or foreign travel alone.

Confidentiality can be an important factor, particularly when recruiting to high-level specialist posts where the labour market within the country may be very small. References are taken up well into the recruitment process. Departing employees can ask their employers to supply a statement confirming their period of employment; this does not constitute a reference.

It is not normal practice, even on an application form, to ask about possible criminal convictions, unless the post carries responsibilities for money or security. The individual can obtain a copy of his or her own criminal record from a central office, which lists all offences, including spent ones.

Selection methods

The interview is at the core of the selection process, but aptitude and personality tests are also common, except at the highest levels, and sometimes tests are conducted in a given specialism. Graphology tests are uncommon. Consultancies often perform these services, even if they are not used for the whole recruitment process. Group dynamics involving individual presentations are gradually becoming an accepted part of the scene for specialist and managerial posts. Few assessment centres exist.

Medicals

A medical examination may be carried out prior to engagement. By law, doctors are allowed to disclose only whether the person meets the required standard of fitness for the post. Disclosure of results of an examination to a third party would require the candidate to give his or her authorisation.

Offer and rejection

There are no statutory provisions on making a job offer or notifying candidates of their rejection. Since many forms of contract are required to be written (see above) employers normally confirm offers in writing.

Education, training and employee development

The education system faces enormous challenges in order to overcome the basic weaknesses that permeate all levels. The combination of too many low-skilled, or unskilled, employees with too few highly educated and qualified personnel is seriously impairing the performance of Portuguese companies.

First, the system must curb the high drop-out rate in compulsory (basic) education. In 1991 22 per cent of those in the 15–24 age-group left school before completing compulsory education, which at that time lasted six years (it was extended to nine years in 1996). A majority of these did not subsequently achieve any qualifications. The education system is not entirely responsible for this; drop-out rates are high in the poorer regions such as the islands, indicating the importance of economic factors in prompting young people to join the labour force early. Enrolment rates at other levels in education also need to be improved; and owing to demographic ageing and a falling birth rate, hopes cannot be pinned solely on the next generation. In this context, an important task falls to remedial education. In 1991 the rate of illiteracy was just 6.5 per cent overall, but accounted for 20 per cent of the 50–65 age-group.

The last decade has seen some key reforms including the raising of the school-leaving age to 15 and the expansion of the system, with the private sector meeting some of the increased demand for places in higher education. Now more qualitative issues are gradually being addressed, such as boosting the educational attainment of school-leavers, diversifying the educational choice on offer, particularly for those not wishing to enter higher education, providing courses more relevant to working life, buttressing and raising the status of vocational education (to attract students of a wider ability range), improving teacher training and methods, and redressing regional imbalances. In 1994 over 5 per cent of GDP was devoted to education (of necessity concentrated into primary and secondary sectors), a higher proportion than in most EU states – but from a lower GDP base. But funds are stretched by the sheer scale of structural reforms required. EU support funds have contributed to the strengthening of educational infrastructure in terms of buildings and classroom capacity – although school shifts are still necessary in a few cases – and improving teaching quality and methods.

The 1986 Education Framework Act

The 1986 Education Framework Act (*Lei de bases do sistema educativo,* decree-law 46/86) defines a coherent framework of principles for the education system – including primary, secondary and higher education sectors, as well as education targeted at adults, those with special needs and people seeking vocational education, distance learning, and immigrants to Portugal. It allows private and co-operative establishments to be set up side-by-side with the state sector. The reform was scheduled to be implemented by detailed legislation over a ten-year period, and the pace of change has accelerated with the election of the Socialist government in October 1995. Unlike in many EU states, the Portuguese education and training systems are still in an evolutionary phase. Since many reforms are of recent origin, it is too early to assess their precise impact.

Following the 1986 initiative, laws have been approved on university and school self-government and schools management. Reforms have also been implemented regarding the curriculum, teacher/trainers training, and the establishment of a vocational education system. The latest reform – which, strictly speaking, falls under the training head – was an overhaul of the apprenticeship system, adopted in October 1996 (see below).

Under the 1986 Act, compulsory basic education (*ensino básico*) was extended from six to nine years, ending at age 15 or 16 – a change introduced in 1987 and completed in January 1996. At this age, students may opt to continue on to secondary education (*ensino secundário*) both in order to progress to higher education or follow a more vocational track, undertake vocational training at a separate establishment, or enter the labour market.

Basic education (*ensino básico*)

Pre-school education is optional but expanding, with the objective of offering places to 90 per cent of pre-school children by the year 2000.

Nine years' basic compulsory education is divided into three cycles lasting four, two and three years respectively. The first cycle, which commences when a child reaches the age of 6, imparts basic skills and general education and is taught by one teacher. During the second cycle, the curriculum is taught in integrated subject areas by one teacher per area; a foreign language is introduced and teaching is organised into interdisciplinary areas of basic training – Portuguese, mathematics, history, sciences, arts and physical education. During the third cycle teaching is organised according to a standard curriculum, including some vocational areas. On completion of the nine years, students are awarded a basic education diploma (*diploma do ensino básico*) which is necessary to continue into secondary education, to qualify for entry into vocational schools (integrated into the education system), or to move on to apprenticeships (so-called training in the labour market).

Secondary education (*ensino secundário*)

This comprises a single cycle lasting three years (from age 15 to 17) and caters to the needs both of those destined for higher education, and those who seek to enter working life. In recent years, efforts have been made to avoid steering students prematurely into given streams at too early an age.

Secondary courses are grouped into two integrated streams: general education courses (*cursos gerais*, CSPOPE) geared towards those who seek to go into higher education, and technological education courses (*cursos tecnológicos*, CSOPVA) which are more vocationally-oriented but do not focus on narrowly-based vocational skills. Completion of the latter type of course confers a certificate of vocational qualification Level 3 (*técnico intermedio*), equivalent to qualifications awarded at vocational or technical schools. On completion of secondary education, success in a national examination leads to a *diploma do ensino secundário*.

The slow move towards vocational education

In 1994 only 28 per cent of secondary school students pursued the 'technical/vocational' track at school, with another 7 per cent attending vocational schools; the rest followed general courses, many in order to enter higher education. Curriculum reforms were launched to promote the take-up of science and technology courses at school and higher education levels, supported by improvements in teacher training, infrastructure – for example, more school laboratories – and so on. These endeavours benefit from EU funding channelled through the second Community Support Framework (CSF) 1994–9, specifically by means of 'the education sub-programme', and 'the science and technology programme'. The objective is to achieve a 90 per cent enrolment rate in secondary education, and increase the numbers following science and technology courses.

Initial vocational education

Vocational schools (*escolas profissionais*)   As an alternative to mainstream secondary school, students with nine years' basic education (or exceptionally other young adults seeking to gain vocational skills) may enter a vocational school, first established in 1989 by decree-law 26/89, and governed by 1993 legislation (70/93). These are designed to equip young people for working life, in particular to meet the needs of the local economy, through acquisition of professional skills gained partly in a work environment. Running parallel with the public education network, vocational schools and the courses offered are vetted by the Ministry of Education. Schools may be founded on the initiative of bodies such as local authorities, the social partners or co-operatives, or in conjunction with other educational institutes (eg art schools). Institutions are privately managed on the basis of agreements and programme contracts between the state and the promoting bodies, and provide flexible education via a modular system. Courses can run for up to three years (with half the time devoted to technical/practical subjects and a quarter to general education and sciences) and offer access to qualifications (*certificados de qualificação*) up to EU level III – equivalent to full secondary education (ie years 10 to 12). At the end of 1994 about 165 schools had been founded specialising in 17 areas of training such as computing, accountancy, engineering, hotels, catering and tourism, and management. Some 23,000 students were on their books.

The system, still in its infancy, has been criticised for its concentration in urban areas and the lack of involvement by the social partners. The record on job placement for students qualifying through the system has not been very positive, with unemployment among trainees almost the same as the national youth rate, ie 15 per cent. Firms taking on students as part of these courses are able to set trainee pay rates; study grants are also available.

Higher education

One educational priority pursued immediately after the 1974 Revolution was to open access to higher education beyond its then élitist base, arguably to the detriment of secondary education and with little regard to the specialisms of graduates. By 1991 only 6 per cent of the working population were university graduates, with just 20 per cent having graduated in science and 9 per cent in management specialisms. As a consequence, priorities were reassessed in order to advance the expansion of higher education but at the same time placing greater emphasis on science, technology and managerial disciplines (see also under *Secondary education*). Even today university courses are criticised as being too abstract, theoretical and isolated from the needs of industry, although things are beginning to change.

The Portuguese higher education system encompasses universities, on the one hand, and a non-university sector including polytechnics and specialist institutions, on the other. Some seats of learning date back to medieval times but many were established in the mid-1980s. The considerable expansion in the public sector over recent years has not kept pace with demand, leaving the private sector to fill the vacuum. Currently about 45 per cent of higher education students are in private institutions, due to fixed quotas in the public system.

The Ministry of Education has overall responsibility for the public sector, although institutions are self-governing and award their own degrees, but it assumes a supervisory role and provides some financial support to the private sector. Both universities and polytechnics offer a wide range of courses, with the latter being more oriented towards the professions.

Access to university higher education is now governed by legislation approved in April 1996. The national general entrance examination (*prova geral de acesso*, PGA), heavily criticised for its cultural bias, has been abolished. Under the new rules, candidates for university must have completed 12 years' education and possess a secondary school-leaving diploma (*diploma do ensino secundário*). Examinations can be taken in various groups of subjects and are graded. Individual institutions set their own entry requirements, which may specify the study of certain subjects at secondary level or the achievement of set minimum examination grades; some also set their own entry examinations in subjects studied at secondary level. Special examinations are sometimes held for candidates not holding standard qualifications, for example, those aged over 25, or from other higher education systems. Polytechnics also require applicants to have 12 years' education but they will also consider those with qualifications gained in the training system. National competitions are held for some of the specialist institutions.

Each year the Ministry of Education publishes a comprehensive list of entry requirements for all courses in public institutions, together with the number of places available. A central government department helps to place students on courses according to their preferences, but this is not as systematic as in the UK, nor offered at such an early point in the academic year. Students usually attend a local university and live at home.

University education is provided through a network of public universities, an open university and university institutes, and their equivalents in the private sector. Three main degrees are conferred:

- *Licenciado* – a full degree after four to six years' study; students typically graduate between 22 and 24; attempts to shorten university first degree courses, for example in engineering, have met with some resistance from professional bodies.
- *Mestre* – a master's degree after an additional one or two years' academic study, including the submission of a dissertation.
- *Doutor* – a doctorate following three to six years' research.

Subjects offered are the arts and humanities, fine art, social sciences, management, law, science, mathematics, engineering and technology, architecture, communications, medicine, education and agriculture – mostly taught according to a modular system.

Polytechnics (*ensino politécnico*), which became established from 1979, provide the other arm of higher education. They accept students with 12 years' education but will look at qualifications gained outside the education system proper. There are over 50 establishments in this network, including eight higher schools of management and technology. Fields of study embrace marketing, accountancy, administration and public relations. The first degree, after three years' of study, is the bachelor's (*bacharel*). This may lead on to the diploma of specialist higher studies (*diploma de estudos superiores especializados*, DESE), broadly equivalent to a full degree or *licenciado* in the university system.

Certificates and diplomas may be awarded for shorter courses in both the university and polytechnic sectors. There are close links between both types of institution and transfer between them, as indeed there is between public and private. There are also some higher education institutes under joint ministerial control.

Graduate recruitment

University graduates enter the workforce aged around 24 – or at 21 or 22 for polytechnic students with a bachelor's degree. The 1990s have seen a marked decline in graduate recruitment by large firms, which have been under pressure to streamline their workforces. Furthermore, graduates have been forced to come to terms with the transition in Portuguese society from a 'jobs for life' culture. The graduate unemployment rate remains close to the national average. It should also be noted that graduate employment in Portugal often embraces a wider range of skills, partly to compensate for shortages of skills held by staff at intermediate levels.

The recruitment process is fairly informal. Universities do not run a unified careers service, and therefore it is common practice for students to send companies unsolicited letters seeking work placements or employment. Increasingly, employment consultants and companies are asked to give campus presentations. Firms may also contact universities requesting lists of graduates, or may foster close links with particular departments. Recruitment fairs are gaining a foothold. A frequent complaint is that university courses are too academic and offer few opportunities for work placements. As with other levels of job, most posts are initially offered on fixed-term contracts. Some recent training programmes have been aimed specifically at placing trained graduates in small companies, often on special projects (eg IT and marketing) to help modernise and revitalise the small-firms sector.

Adult education

In the context of a poorly educated workforce, a high priority is attached to adult education with courses often targeted at specific groups and offered in existing education and training centres (law 140/93). Responsibilities are divided between the Education Ministry, as far as remedial and special needs education is concerned, and the IEFP on the vocational training side. The objectives are to boost literacy, help students acquire basic skills and competences, reconvert outdated skills and, where possible, offer 'second chance' education.

Priorities for training

The last decade has seen rapid change in the area of training, with the state taking a decisive role in defining policy, co-ordinating and supporting initiatives and evaluating outcomes. There is a division of responsibilities between different government departments dealing with research and policy formation; policy implementation; and financial and technical support of EU-funded projects. As mentioned earlier, there is virtually no tradition of in-company training; experts have pointed out that this is unlikely to develop fully until company systems for managing human resources become better established.

Community Support Framework funds

While EU membership accelerated the process of change, particularly by creating a more competitive economic environment, it also provided the funds to smooth the process in the area of human resources. An initial downside of this was that while funds were available for all sorts of training, the actors and institutions involved had insufficient time to create the infrastructure for launching new initiatives. Latterly there has been a renewed emphasis on quality as opposed to quantity of training, with more stringent rules applying for access to funds.

As mentioned earlier, the EU Community Support Framework sets the parameters and priorities in the training area. The 1994–9 Framework places particular emphasis on:

- initial training for school-leavers entering the labour market, and 'rescuing' early drop-outs
- upgrading the training of trainers
- targeting training in small firms and companies affected by   technological change
- prioritising the training and management of human resources
- promoting local economic development
- improving labour market information services
- combating social exclusion.

New priorities for the Socialist government

The Socialist government elected in October 1995 has revitalised the training debate. In a speech to Parliament setting out her plans to reform the shortcomings of the present system, the new Minister of Qualification and Training (formerly Employment and Social Security) highlighted the need to stimulate consultation on training at sectoral and regional level with a greater role for the social partners, develop a better system for identifying training needs, streamline financial support, explore new training models appropriate for different types of trainee, and reform the apprenticeship system to avoid overlap with the education system – creating a flexible system of schooling, training and labour market induction. In future, public (IEFP-run) training centres are to respond more directly to the training needs of disadvantaged groups in the labour market, leaving jointly-managed training centres (and other bodies involved in sectoral training) to meet the spectrum of sectoral needs more effectively, including taking account of research and development, international trends, and small and medium-sized firms' needs. Further initiatives were announced in the spring of 1996, including support for developing managerial skills through the creation of a special network of advisers to small and medium-sized firms in areas of personnel management and training, and strengthening training by sector (see also above under *Employment incentives*). Reforms are now in progress in some of these areas.

Tripartite involvement

An agreement of July 1991 was the first tripartite involvement in training to set parameters for the future. Four broad objectives were defined:

- to promote training to meet the country's needs
- to raise the level of educational qualifications
- to boost the efficiency of present system
- to strengthen the role of the social partners.

In addition, the agreement contained draft legislation laying the foundations for initial and continuous vocational training. This legislation was also implemented in 1991, but social partner involvement since then has not been as active as expected (see below).

The 1996 tripartite Short-Term Social Pact, concluded with the help of the new Socialist government, also makes reference to further employment and training measures, underlining the need for more active participation by the social partners in revising the current Community Support Framework, and in ensuring delivery of programmes at regional and local levels.

Framework legislation on initial and continuous training

Decree-law 401/91 created the framework for initial and continuous vocational training offered both through the education system and via the Employment and Training Ministry.

The state is responsible for anticipating training needs, launching programmes for initial training and for developing schemes targeted at specific groups on the labour market (the unemployed, and groups 'with difficulties'), regulating the training of trainers and ensuring that training structures are national in coverage. Companies are expected to focus on continuous and on-the-job training, and to provide training geared towards adaptation to new technology, improving products and raising productivity.

The aim is to set up a comprehensive and flexible training system, favouring a diversity of skills, with courses and programmes structured as modules and linked with the work context. All training is subject to certification (which is linked to systems developed at EU level) issued through officially-sanctioned bodies.

A variety of bodies can be contracted to carrying out this type of training in line with published guidelines, which will be publicly financed:

- education, public (IEFP) training centres, jointly-managed centres, other training centres
- firms and business associations
- unions and professional associations
- local authorities
- private social welfare institutions
- cultural associations.

Framework legislation for labour market vocational training

Decree-law 405/91 deals specifically with vocational training on the labour market – that is, outside the education system – delineating the respective responsibilities of the state, other employment/training bodies and companies.

The state's role is to set policy formation, and to co-ordinate and evaluate implementation. It is directly responsible for training the unemployed and other 'disadvantaged' groups, for accrediting and supporting other training bodies and guaranteeing that training is recognised through certification. Another of its key tasks is the promotion of the training of trainers and appropriate teaching aids. The state training agency, IEFP, implements policies through its directly-managed training centres and jointly-managed centres.

The certification system

The national system for certifying vocational training and skills gained outside the education system was established in 1992 through decree-law 95/92. Its functioning is the responsibility of IEFP, which governs the certificates to be issued within each industry and approves organisations competent to make awards.

The certificate of vocational training (*certificado de formação profissional*) details the level of qualification, the industry for which the trainee has been prepared, and the equivalent educational level. Certificates bear the name of the holder, and details of the course (curriculum, hours of study, final student evaluation).

The certificate of occupational skills (*certificado de aptidão profissional*) testifies to the holder's competence to exercise a given occupation based on training, but also taking into account work experience and qualifications (including those gained from abroad), again specifying the level and equivalent in educational terms. The *carteira profissional* is regarded as equivalent to this award.

The certification system has advanced most in hotels and tourism, car mechanics, graphic design, air transport, and personal services, as well as in the military to help young men secure employment before they are demobilised.

Vocational training in the labour market

IEFP directly managed training centres   The IEFP directly manages a country-wide network of more than 20 vocational training centres, with tripartite involvement (*Centros de Gestão Directa*, CGD) under legislation dating from 1985. These offer practical courses of varying duration (usually less than a year) principally aimed at both initial and continuing training for those aged 18 and over (ie after secondary school) and linked to the needs of the local economy. The major priority is to equip students with a qualification to secure entry into the labour market. Students with more than nine years' schooling have access to more specialised courses comprising technical and practical components, and which offer qualifications at Levels 2 and 3 (at the top end, equivalent to full secondary education). Those who have already acquired work experience can update their skills. Trainees receive an allowance related to the national statutory minimum wage and additional help with transport and accommodation costs, depending on place of residence. In 1993 nearly 20,000 people attended such courses, and over 12,000 in 1994. As mentioned above, the government wishes to see the efforts of these centres concentrated on those at most disadvantage in the labour market, such as the long-term unemployed and the unskilled, and to minimise duplication with courses run by jointly-managed centres.

Jointly-managed centres   There are some 30 jointly-managed vocational training centres (*Centros de Gestão Participada*, CGP) which are principally funded and technically supported by IEFP, but run by agreement between the IEFP, and, for the most part, employers but also trade unions and professional associations. These centres provide more specialised training on a regional basis for a particular sector or sectors. They offer (usually) short continuous training courses for employees working in companies belonging to the respective industrial associations. Such courses may lead to an initial qualification, or round off or convert existing skills. Although the centres are run according to tripartite principles with employers feeding in their training demands, trade union involvement remains low. One criticism levelled at these centres is the excessive bureaucracy involved in setting up training schemes; in 1993 some 33,850 people attended courses, rising to nearly 41,000 in 1994.

Funds are also available to support one-off training activities run through agreements with employers, or unions, and training providers. Initially, unions supported courses set out to meet the needs of the labour market but members have demanded training in IT and languages, rather than in more technical areas. Some sectors provide training programmes through their own schools (as in hotels and tourism) or in existing training centres (industry).

Apprenticeships

As promised in the new government's programme, the apprenticeship system was overhauled by decree-law 205/96, approved in October 1996, which repeals previous legislation on apprenticeships and pre-apprenticeships. The aim is to rationalise the previous schemes, create greater opportunities for transfer between education, training and work, and enlarge the proportion of the workforce with intermediate-level skills. Specifically it aims to equip school-leavers at all levels (including early leavers, and those with basic or full secondary education) with occupational skills acquired through the dual system. Courses which last from six months to three years are held both at training centres of the IEFP (or jointly-managed centres) and on company premises.

Targeted principally at those with at least nine years' basic education up to the age of 24, apprenticeships provide training for particular sectors of the economy. Practical work cannot exceed 50 per cent of training time, with a maximum of 30 per cent of time spent on the job.

The Ministries for Qualification and Employment, and Education, in conjunction with the National Apprenticeship Commission, legally regulate apprenticeships by sector, and specify methods of certification, while the IEFP approves the bodies responsible for co-ordinating and delivering the apprenticeships.

These bodies include local IEFP training centres, jointly-managed centres, state teaching establishments and other bodies; they are responsible for planning courses, admission of trainees, registration of trainees' contracts with the IEFP, recruitment and supervision of trainers, and assessment of outcomes. Requirements of trainers are far more stringent than before, and there is a rigorous student assessment procedure.

As for the types of courses on offer, these are now available at four basic levels:

- induction courses at Level 1
- apprenticeship courses at Level 2 (equivalent to third-cycle basic education)
- apprenticeship courses at Level 3 (equivalent to secondary education)
- post-secondary courses.

These categories are further subdivided to allow access to courses by those with formal education below the stated levels; the content of courses and number of hours' tuition is lengthened accordingly.

For example, students without basic education and deemed unsuitable for immediate acceptance on a course leading to a vocational qualification may be offered a basic induction course lasting about six months, leading to a certificate of occupational skills Level 1. A Level 2 apprenticeship is open to those without basic education provided they are regarded as suitable for a vocational qualification course. Such a course could last from 1,800 to 4,500 hours. Those completing basic education may enter a Level 3 apprenticeship, equivalent to the three years' secondary education, on completion of which the student may transfer into higher education. Other courses are aimed at those with full secondary education but with no vocational qualifications.

Courses cannot exceed 1,500 hours annually, 35 hours weekly, and usually take place between 8 am and 8 pm. Trainees are given 22 days' holiday. Candidates must pass a medical examination and have a right to induction and an assessment of their skills and professional knowledge. On successful completion of courses, candidates are awarded a certificate of occupational skills (*certificado de aptidão profissional*) which must identify the course undertaken, the level of qualification achieved and its educational equivalent.

Training courses for 15-year-old school-leavers

The authorities are employing various strategies to curb the high drop-out rate in basic education. Beside the revamped apprenticeship courses, new vocational education courses were introduced in October 1995 as an alternative for students not seeking higher education, as well as offering a 'second chance' for those without basic education to progress through mainstream education or training. The latter courses which last a year (about 1,200 hours' training), provide access to EU training Levels 1 and 2, and can be provided within a work context, or as alternating training. On completion, trainees are entitled to a vocational training certificate and a certificate of occupational aptitude.

Company in-service training

As mentioned above, company in-service training is as yet barely developed outside the large company sector. Firms often either bring in more qualified staff as their needs change in preference to upgrading the skills of existing staff, or resort to more temporary solutions. Many pilot schemes are in progress, and firms receiving public training subsidies must produce training plans which anticipate the recruitment of additional staff or upgrading of skills levels. However, in a recent survey conducted by the Ministry for Qualification and Employment, about a quarter of the small firms surveyed had no knowledge of government training measures. As yet there is no statutory right for time off for training. Although in practice this does not appear to be a problem, some small firms have indicated that they cannot spare staff to engage in training.

Management training

Better-trained managers is a key objective of government policy and EU-supported programmes. Some of the large industrial associations have their own training organisations which target small firms. Courses aimed at improving human resource development and technical/organisational development are high on the agenda. Some courses are run regularly, others are tailor-made for particular clients. Tuition may take place at a central location (sometimes shared between several firms), at company premises or through distance learning.

Financing the system

Employers and employees make contributions into a general social security fund: currently the employer contribution is 23.75 per cent of gross pay, with employees paying 11 per cent. Five per cent of the total is earmarked to finance the Institute of Vocational Training: this provides about half the IEFP's receipts, with additional funds coming from the national budget and European social funds, which play a central role in supporting training programmes rather than administration. Very little training is financed directly by companies.

Educational attainment of the population

Level	Percentage of 25–64 age-group
Lower secondary	81
Upper secondary	8
Higher education (non-university)	3
University	7

Source: OECD (1994)

Organisations

Ministry for Qualification and
Employment (formerly Employment and
Social Security)
(Ministério para a Qualificação e o
Emprego)
Praça de Londres 2
1000 Lisbon
Tel. +351 1 80 44 60

Institute of Employment and Vocational
Training
(Instituto do Emprego e Formação
Profissional)
11 Avenida José Malhoa 11
1100 Lisbon
Tel. +351 1 726 25 36
Fax +351 1 726 5755

Department of European Social Fund
Affairs
(Departamento para os Assuntos do
Fundo Social Europeu, DAFSE)
Avenida Almirante Reis 72
1100 Lisbon
Tel. +351 1 814 1445
Fax +351 1 820 063

Office of Technological, Artistic and
Vocational Education (Gabinete de
Educação Tecnológica Artistica e
Profissional, GETAP, a section of the
Ministry of Education)
Avenida 24 Julho 140
1300 Lisbon
Tel. +351 1 395 34 07

Association of Portuguese Human
Resource Managers
(Associação Portuguesa de Gestores e
Técnicos de Recursos Humanos, APG)
Avenida do Brasil 194 7o
1700 Lisbon
Tel. +351 1 89 97 66
Fax +351 1 80 93 40

In Oporto:
Rua Formosa, 49 1o
Tel. +351 2 32 32 34
Fax +351 2 200 07 64

Confederation of Portuguese Industry
(Confederação da Indústria Portuguesa,
CIP)
Avenida 5 de Outubro 35 1o
1000 Lisbon
Tel. +351 1 54 74 54
Fax +351 1 54 50 94

Confederation of Portuguese Commerce
(Confederação do Comércio Português,
CCP)
Rua Saraiva de Carvalho 1
1000 Lisbon
Tel. +351 1 66 85 39

Confederação Geral dos Trabalhadores
Portugueses-Intersindical Nacional
(CGTP-IN)
Rua Vitor Cordon 1-3o
1200 Lisbon
Tel. +351 1 34 72 181/8
Fax +351 1 34 22 189

União Geral de Trabalhadores (UGT)
Rua Buenos Aires 11
1200 Lisbon
Tel. +351 1 397 6503
Fax +351 1 397 4612

Portuguese-British Chamber of
Commerce
(Câmara do Comércio Luso-Britânica)
Rua da Estrela 8
1200 Lisbon
Tel. +351 1 396 14 86
Fax +351 1 60 15 13

APETT (Association of Temporary
Employment Agencies)
c/o Marcelina Pena Costa
Rua Quirino da Fonseca 15
1000 Lisbon
Tel. +351 1 57 04 15

Main sources

INSTITUTO DO EMPREGO E FORMAÇÃO PROFISSIONAL. *Vocational Training in Portugal.* Lisbon, 1996

GRILO, M. *O Sistema de Formação Profissional em Portugal.* CEDEFOP, European Community Publications, Luxembourg, 1995

MISEP. *Relatório Sobre Portugal Elaborado no âmbito da Informação sobre Políticas de Emprego.* General Directorate for Employment and Vocational Training. Lisbon 1995.

CPCS (Standing Council for Social Consultation). *Acordo de Política de Formação Profissional.* Lisbon, 1991

KOVACS, I. *Qualificação e Mercados de Emprego.* Estudoes 13, IEFP, Lisbon, 1994

RODRIGUES, M.J. and LOPES, H. *O papel da Empresa no Produção da Qualificação, Dinâmia.* Centro de Estudos sobre a Mudança Socioeconómica, Lisbon, 1995

MINISTRY OF EMPLOYMENT AND SOCIAL SECURITY. *Quadro Comunitário de Apoio 1994–99: Fundo Social Europeu – Guia para o Utilizador Português.* Lisbon, 1994

MINISTRY OF EDUCATION. *Roteiro do Ano Escolar 1996/97.* Lisbon, 1996

11

Spain

One of the major changes in Spanish law on recruitment, and personnel management more generally, during the first half of the 1990s has been the progressive removal of many aspects of legal constraints on employers' decisions, a number of which were vestiges of the Francoist corporate state which had been perpetuated in the legislation which immediately succeeded the dictatorship. Many of these changes were made through the reform of the 1980 Workers' Statute effected in 1994. However, some requirements remain, and some have been added, principally to combat employer abuse of the possibility of concluding more flexible employment contracts. In addition, although no longer subject to detailed statutory provisions, employers may be covered by agreed industry-level provisions, as well as company agreements specifying procedures.

Reflecting the persistence of high levels of unemployment, much of which is concentrated in particular groups in the labour force, there is an extensive structure of state recruitment incentives, involving either a reduction in social security contributions or cash grants on appointment. These tie in with the option of concluding one of a variety of short-term employment contracts, intended to ease the transition from unemployment to work, and to ease employer fears that, once hired permanently, employees would be expensive to dismiss in the event of a downturn.

The 1990s have seen a huge expansion in the university sector, often at the expense of quality. Spain's attempts to catch up with northern Europe in the provision of tertiary education have also been one factor in the creation of a dual employment structure, evident in other southern European countries, in which the older sections of the workforce often lack basic skills but are entrenched in jobs, while a younger, more highly educated and skilled workforce is struggling to gain a foothold in the labour market.

Reforms are in train in the field of vocational training, most of which is provided through state institutions, aimed at integrating it into mainstream education and reconfiguring it into an additional pathway to higher education, rather than an alternative to academic study.

The labour market

In the first quarter of 1996 the Spanish labour force totalled 15,791,000 – up from 13,579,600 in 1985, largely thanks to the rise in young people and women seeking work. 12,173,900 were employed – 60 per cent in the service sector, 21 per cent in industry, 10 per cent in agriculture and 9 per cent in construction. The total participation rate was 49 per cent (63 per cent for men, but only 36 per cent for women, both fairly low by European comparison). About 9 per cent of the labour force was illiterate, 32 per cent had primary schooling, 41 per cent secondary schooling, 12 per cent post-secondary qualifications, and 7 per cent a university degree or equivalent.

Unemployment has remained a persistent and intractable problem, especially for young people. While 58 per cent of 25–54-year-olds were employed, only 12 per cent of the 16–19 and 36 per cent of the 20–24-year-olds were in work.

Recruitment

Work permits

Recruitment procedures are regulated by Article 38 of the Constitution, the 1980 Workers' Statute (*Estatuto de los Trabajadores*) and its subsequent modifications, in particular Act 10/1994 and Article 24 of the Basic Employment Act (*Ley Básica de Empleo*). Until 1994 there were still considerable legal restrictions on employers during the recruiting process; however, the reforms of that year removed the vast bulk of constraints. The official employment service (*Instituto Nacional de Empleo*, INEM) is empowered to vet and reject advertisements which are considered discriminatory, although in practice this is interpreted loosely. The employer is no longer required to notify INEM of vacancies, but is required to notify new contracts to them within 10 days.

The employment of non-European Union citizens in Spain is strictly controlled. They need a work permit for most paid employment and self-employment. There are six categories of permit, depending on the circumstances of the employment and the applicant, although some groups, including media correspondents, performing artists and technicians employed by the Spanish government, do not need permits. Since 1994 a quota system has been in operation to regulate the inflow of foreign employees from non-EU countries: these quotas, totalling some 20,000 permits per annum, also set limits on the number of foreigners allowed to be employed according to sector and country of origin.

EU citizens working for more than three months require a residence permit, which also registers them for income tax status, in order to work. They should request this from their local police station within 15 days of arrival.

Official and workforce notification

An employer must notify the labour authorities within 30 days of opening a workplace, and supply information about the company and its employment plans. Article 64 of the Workers' Statute grants an element of employee participation in the recruitment process, giving works councils the right to receive information quarterly on recruitment plans. In 1991 the government legislated to make participation more formalised, obliging employers to provide a copy of new or renewed employment contracts to the works council within 10 days. Most non-permanent employment contracts are covered by this provision – a step introduced ostensibly to combat social security fraud, but which has greatly irritated employer associations.

Agreed provisions on recruitment

Collective agreements may also include a variety of provisions relating to recruitment, either with the aim of protecting jobs, defining preferred categories of recruits, setting out recruitment procedures, or delineating managerial autonomy on recruitment. Typical provisions include: preference for new jobs to be given to employees already or formerly on non-permanent or atypical contracts, as in the chemical industry-wide agreement; preference to existing employees or their children; internal advertising prior to external recruitment; target recruitment groups in the labour market, such as the young, the over-45s or the disabled; favoured types of contract, such as relief contracts or work-experience contracts. Some agreements may specify the proportion of posts which may be filled by management decision and those requiring consultation with the works council. For example, at Hidroeléctrica de Cataluña, 50 per cent of new recruits may be hired directly by management appointment, with the remaining 50 per cent to be decided by competitive examination. Exceptionally, some agreements offer job security guarantees, as at Iberdrola, where new recruits are offered eight years' job protection in the same workplace.

Employment incentives

There are a variety of state incentives to encourage employment. They include cash grants to employers, usually for concluding permanent full-time contracts, and reductions in social security contributions, usually linked to fixed-term contracts for certain groups and for a variety of permanent contracts. Act 10/1994 modified procedures for assisting employers. The new measures target key groups of potential employees, and give the government the power to decide which groups to target in the annual budget. In 1996, for example, the groups singled out for assistance for temporary job creation contracts were the over-45s, the disabled and the long-term unemployed claimants.

Employers benefited from a 75 per cent reduction in social security contributions (rising to 100 per cent reduction for small firms with fewer than 25 employees) for employing these groups on full-time contracts.

If contracts are subsequently converted from temporary to permanent, employers may receive a cash grant of Pta 400,000 (£2,000) for an employee under 25, Pta 500,000 (£2,500) and a 50 per cent contributions reduction for an employee over 45, and Pta 500,000 (£2,500) and contributions reductions of 70 per cent or

90 per cent for a disabled employee. However, figures for 1995, the most recent year for which they are available, indicate that these incentives are creating only some 10,000 jobs per annum.

Reductions in social security contributions are also available to promote temporary, apprenticeship and part-time contracts. Apprenticeship contracts carry a fixed low contribution rate, and on conversion from temporary to permanent contract the employer may receive a cash grant of Pta 550,000 (£2,750). Since their introduction in 1994, these contracts have proved very popular with employers, with 208,000 registered in the first year. Contributions on 'partial-time' contracts (*contrato a tiempo parcial*) have, since 1994, been pro rata to actual working time, and carry reduced benefits. This form of contract has become the third most common type now issued (after fixed-job contracts and casual contracts), with about 1,000,000 concluded each year (see also below).

There are also incentives to create permanent employment for certain categories of employees. Employers offering a permanent contract to an under-25-year-old may receive a cash grant of Pta 400,000 (£2,000). Currently some 2,000 of these contracts are issued each year. Similarly, a permanent contract for a female employee in an occupation where women are under-represented can attract a grant of Pta 500,000 (£2,500), although only some 500 of these are issued each year. Permanent contracts for disabled employees carry cash grants of Pta 500,000 and contributions reductions of 70 per cent for an under-45-year-old and 90 per cent for an over-45-year-old.

Companies employing an over-45-year-old or a disabled worker on a permanent full-time contract (and maintaining the net payroll increase for at least two years) are entitled to a corporate tax deduction of Pta 1,000,000 (£5,000) for each such new employee.

Since Spain is a major beneficiary of the EU Social Fund and Regional Fund, there are a wide variety of grants, subsidies and other aids available to employers in different regions and sectors. These are managed by INEM, by the Ministry of Labour, or by the governments of the Autonomous Communities. There are also employment promotion schemes run by local authorities and special government incentives for job creation in development areas (*Zonas de Promoción Económica*) and declining industrial areas (*Zonas industrializadas en declive*). There are specific government schemes to support job creation in various sectors affected by industrial restructuring plans, and a scheme known as the Local Employment Initiative (*Promoción de Iniciativas Locales de Empleo*) offers subsidies of Pta 700,000 (£3,500) for each full-time post offered to someone previously unemployed.

Part-timers, fixed-term contracts, and agency workers

Temporary and part-time contracts of various kinds have come to form a large majority of new employment contracts in recent years. More than 90 per cent of all new contracts issued in 1994 were part-time or temporary of some kind.

Part-time and 'partial-time' contracts   Part-time contracts were permitted in Spain for the first time only in 1981, and grew steadily in number until 1993 when 635,000 contracts were issued. In 1994 the contract was redefined, and has now become a major means of imparting flexibility into the labour market. Under Act 10/1994 part-time contracts were redefined as 'partial-time contracts' – defined on the basis of hours per day, per week, per month or per year, where less than normal full-time employment is involved.

An employee working less than 12 hours weekly also now pays pro rata contributions. This effectively makes this contract a 'temporary contract' too, and usable for seasonally fluctuating demand.

Fixed-term contracts   Fixed-term contracts are also a relatively recent development but over the past decade or so these have become overwhelmingly the most common form of new employment contract. In 1995, for example, 5,200,000 fixed-term contracts of various kinds were issued, as against 209,826 permanent contracts.

Legislation does not address the issue of the extent to which employers may use atypical employment contracts, except in the case of apprenticeship contracts, which may apply to no more than a fixed proportion of the workforce.

Collective agreements occasionally include provisions in this area. For example, the agreement for the chemicals industry specifies that fixed-term contracts will be restricted to backlogs or peak orders, or special market circumstances, and may apply only for a maximum of nine months in any 12. Alternatively, an agreement may provide for a preference for fixed-term contracts.

Apprenticeship contract (*Contrato de aprendizaje*)   The phasing out of training contracts, and their replacement by apprenticeship contracts in 1994, provoked bitter trade union protest. Since then, the new type of contract has been taken up very extensively. In 1994 208,975 were issued, and 179,036 in 1995. The contract is available for unqualified people between the ages of 16 and 25. It may last from six months to three years, and must include alternating periods of working time and training time. Training must account for at least 15 per cent of agreed maximum working time. The apprentice must be employed on work formally defined within the company's job evaluation system, and the work must be in line with the training given.

The radical element of the contract is that for the first time in modern Spanish history it permits the employer to pay below the legal minimum wage: apprentices must receive at least 70 per cent of statutory minimum wage (in 1996: Pta 64,920 (£325) monthly for 18-year-olds; Pta 50,220 (£250) for 16–17-year-olds) in their first year, 80 per cent in the second year and 90 per cent in the third year. Rates for 16-17-year-olds must be at least 85 per cent of the statutory minimum. Collective agreements may establish higher rates, and up to half of apprentices are receiving the statutory minimum wage under the requirements of sectoral agreements.

The employer also benefits from a reduced, single-rate social security contribution, which was Pta 4,350 (£22) monthly in 1996. The employer is obliged to assign an apprentice to a mentor for supervision, with no more than three apprentices per mentor.

Work-experience contract (*Contrato en prácticas*) This is available for employing university or vocational training graduates within four years of their qualifying. The contract may be for six months to two years, and pay may either be as collectively agreed, or no less than 60 per cent (in the first year) and 75 per cent (in the second year) of the remuneration set by collective agreement, but in no circumstances less than the statutory minimum wage. If at the end of the contract the employer takes on the trainee as a full-time permanent employee, he may receive a grant of Pta 550,000 (£2,750). There were 50,962 such contracts in 1994, and 69,936 in 1995.

Agency employment Legislation passed in 1993 permitted the operation of temporary employment agencies (*empresas de trabajo temporal*, ETT) for the first time, ending the monopoly on employment services enjoyed up to then by the state employment service INEM. Some 70 per cent of the 342 agencies operating in 1996 were grouped in the largest trade organisation *Asociación Española de Empresas de Trabajo Temporal* (GEESTA). Four companies – Ecco-Adia, Alta Gestión, Laborman and Manpower – accounted for 60 per cent of turnover in the sector.

Agencies employ workers on special service contracts (*contratos de puesta a disposición*), under which the employee is assigned by the employment agency to work in a client company and under that company's authority. Act 14/94 specifies the circumstances in which agencies may supply workers: they may supply employees for a limited term, they may cater for temporary market or seasonal demands, they may replace employees on leave or fill a post temporarily while selection is taking place.

The contract may be for up to six months when catering for special seasonal or market demands, and three months to fill a temporary vacancy during the selection procedure. In other cases the duration of employment is determined by the contract. Should employees continue to work at the client company when their specific assignment is completed, they will be considered to be employed on a permanent contract by the client company.

Agencies are not permitted to supply staff to replace striking employees, to carry out hazardous work, to fill a redundancy created during the previous 12 months, or to assign workers to other temporary employment agencies.

The agency must supply the labour authorities with lists of service contracts issued, which must be in writing. It must dedicate at least 1 per cent of the payroll to training costs, and must not charge the employee any fee. The employee's pay must correspond to collectively-agreed terms, agreed by the agency, or failing that, by the client company. On termination of the fixed-term contract, the employee is entitled to 12 days' pay per year of service. The employee is entitled to be represented by the client company's worker representatives, and also has the right to use company-provided transport to work.

Client companies are responsible for informing agency employees of working conditions and ensuring that health and safety requirements are complied with. They are jointly liable for wages and social security charges incurred under the service contract, although the agency is primarily responsible for paying wages and deducting social security contributions. The employer must also inform employee representatives of details of agency contracts within 10 days.

Temporary agencies placed some 255,000 employees in 1995 – 20 per cent in the public sector and 80 per cent in the private sector, of which about a half were in large companies of 100 employees or more. (This still represented only four out of every 1,000 recruitments, as against 17 per 1,000 in the USA and 16 per 1,000 in France). Between 20 and 30 per cent of the employees contracted on a temporary employment contract via temporary work agencies are subsequently offered permanent contracts. Average annual salaries offered in 1996 by the large Ecco-Adia agency were Pta 2,500,000 (£12,500) for graduates with a higher degree and Pta 1,400,000 (£7,000) for less qualified graduates. The average length of contract was 45 days.

Internal *v.* external recruitment

There are no legislative provisions on this issue, but collective agreements frequently provide for detailed arrangements. Some agree to advertise internally before externally or to fill posts from internal candidates. Preference for permanent appointments is sometimes given to existing employees on fixed-term contracts, as in the chemical industry agreement, and sometimes preference is agreed for employees' families or survivors.

Finding the applicant

Statutory regulations

Article 38 of the 1978 Constitution guarantees the employer freedom to recruit in the labour market. Since the major reform of the Workers' Statute in 1994, employers are no longer required to notify all vacancies to INEM but simply to notify all new employment contracts issued within 10 days. Procedures for recruiting are addressed in Article 1 of Act 10/1994 and Article 24 of the Basic Employment Law.

State placement system

The offical employment service is operated by the government agency INEM

(*Instituto Nacional de Empleo*) which dates back to the Franco period. Before 1994 it had an official monopoly on placement, and employers were formally required to notify all vacancies to it, as well as new contracts issued. Now employers need only notify new contracts. Citizens of Spain and other EU countries may register for employment at INEM offices, and need to produce their national identity card or passport, social security record and vocational or academic qualifications.

Although INEM can be a useful service for finding skilled manual workers, recent surveys reveal persistent dissatisfaction with INEM's effectiveness. Ministry of Labour figures indicate that only a small proportion of new contracts registered by INEM relate to new contacts between employer and employee via INEM – the rest reflect INEM's ratification of a contract already established directly between employer and employee. In 1986, 481,700 out of 3,020,000 total placements resulted from contacts initiated by INEM; in 1995 the equivalent figures were 875,700 out of 7,561,900 – 11.6 per cent.

Permanent employment agencies and personnel consultants

The legislation which enabled temporary employment agencies to operate also permitted non-profit-making placement agencies to operate for permanent placement (*agencias de colocación*), provided this is carried out in co-operation with the official employment service. The first area to pilot this service, Catalonia, established the *Servei Catalá de Collocació*, operated by the Catalan government, which processed 15,000 employee requests from Catalan firms in the first six months of operation; a further 24 agencies began to operate in early 1996. They are operated by a variety of organisations – regional governments, voluntary groups, professional bodies, charitable organisations, and while 60 per cent are free, the rest charge a fee ranging from Pta 5,000 to Pta 40,000 (£25–200). These agencies generally offer counselling to the job seeker as well as placement, and complement the work of INEM offices.

Executive search and selection agencies

Executive search and selection companies do operate, and these have been growing in importance. There are about 25 search and 20 selection companies in Spain, carrying out over 1,000 searches a year. The search market is not legally regulated, and databases, for example, are permitted.

Recruitment media

Job advertisements must comply with anti-discrimination legislation and are vetted by INEM, which may in theory reject them.

The main vehicles for job advertisements are *El País*, which carries a large range of jobs in its Sunday supplement, *ABC* and *La Vanguardia* in Catalonia. The business weekly *Actualidad Económica* carries executive and managerial advertisements.

Recruitment documents

Applicants are usually requested to apply for jobs with a copy of their CV and a photograph. It is fairly usual for them to include copies of certificates of qualifications obtained.

Privacy, confidentiality, references

The procedures for recruiting employees are covered in Article 1 of Act 10/1994, and Article 24 of the Basic Employment Law. Legislation passed in 1982 (the *Ley Orgánica sobre el derecho al honor, a la intimidad y a la propia imagen*) makes general provisions on the protection of privacy of individuals, including job applicants. Revisions to the Penal Code in 1996 radically increase the penalties for injurious exploitation of personal data, which now may carry a prison sentence of up to seven years. The Spanish Data Protection Agency (*Agencia de Protección de datos*) has a monitoring role, and legislation passed in 1992 (the *Ley Orgánica Reguladora del Tratamiento Automatizado de los Datos de Carácter Personal*) prohibits the exploitation of computerised personal information. However, there are no statutory or voluntary codes governing recruitment or the investigation of an applicant's credentials. It is still fairly common in Spain for applicants to include unsolicited testimonials from referees.

Selection methods

It is common in both the public sector and in large private firms in the service sector to select applicants by competitive examination, or by requiring them to pass an induction training course. Aptitude tests, which are the norm for most public-sector positions, consist of general knowledge, technical knowledge and psychological tests. It is not unusual to find employee representatives on the selection panels. Collective agreements may specify the proportion of recruits each year who must be selected by competitive examination, and the proportion that may be recruited solely based on the employer's decision, usually managerial and professional staff.

Collective agreements may also detail selection procedures; the chemicals industry agreement, for example, requires employers to inform employee representatives of selection procedures and to allow them to monitor proceedings. At Ericsson, the company collective agreement provides for a joint management–staff committee to determine recruitment procedures, and at other companies joint committees may determine the details of any psychological, medical, theoretical and practical selection tests to be applied.

A recent survey by the *Centro de Investigaciones Sociológicas* indicated that, after a short interview, psychological or psychometric testing is usually the first step in the selection procedure of most companies, particularly medium-sized or large ones. On passing this preliminary selection phase the candidate will go through a series of interviews, which vary in number but may be as many as six. Group discussions may also be included. Recruitment agencies and selection companies tend to use a battery of tests, ranging from IQ to aptitude and psychometric tests, although rarely in the case of executives.

Handwriting analysis is rarely found in Spain now. Suspicion about unqualified analysis and abuse of the procedure in the past has left a widespread reluctance to use the technique.

Education and training

Overview of the education system

According to the OECD, a quarter of Spain's population have either upper secondary or tertiary-level educational qualifications – one of the highest rates in OECD member states. This reflects the rapid development of the Spanish education system, which the OECD considers to be among the most impressive of its members over the past 25 years. Before 1970 there was little pre-school provision, primary education was far from universal, and secondary schooling was often élitist and concentrated in the private sector. Change began in the 1970s, and improvements have been sustained. Now, 99.7 per cent of 4- and 5-year-olds are in school, compulsory education until 16 is universal, and 65 per cent of pupils take the BUP and COU examinations (approximately equivalent to GCSE and A Level in the UK). The pace of change has also produced a deep split in the population between a poorly educated older age group and a better-educated younger generation: 80 per cent of the over-35 age group do not have higher secondary-level qualifications, while the figure for the younger age group is only 34 per cent.

While completion rates at all levels of education have improved considerably in recent years, there is still concern about the low level of technical and vocational schooling. Only 33 per cent of secondary students currently follow vocational courses, compared with 80 per cent in Germany and 55 per cent in France.

Secondary education

The education system is undergoing considerable upheaval as a result of reforms designed to restructure both primary and secondary schooling. While the Ministry of Education has national responsibility for core provision, standards, legislation and management of the school system, a wide range of powers relating to the curriculum and routine management have been transferred to the regions. However, this process is very patchy, and while by 1996 powers had been transferred to seven regions, the Ministry of Education still controlled education in the other 10. This has made for a very uneven application of the reforms, with regions such as Catalonia, the Basque Country, Andalusia and Valencia making rapid progress (for example, pressing ahead with the incorporation of regional languages into the standard core curriculum), while others find change slow and frustrating.

Public spending on education rose substantially in the first decade of the Socialist PSOE government from Pta 608 billion in 1982 to Pta 2,908 billion in 1993 (£3 bn – £14.5 bn), although it accounted for a fairly constant 8.5 per cent of public spending – considerably below many other EU countries. This rise in spending helped to raise the number of teachers significantly, yielding a teacher–pupil ratio of 18:1 in state primary and 23:1 in private primary, and 14:1 and 17:1 respectively in the corresponding secondary schools. Parents still have to pay for books, meals, transport and extracurricular activities.

The state sector provides 65 per cent of primary and 74 per cent of secondary schooling, although substantial government financing of the private sector (which is largely religious-based) has ensured parity of teacher qualifications, school government and salaries between the sectors.

Education reform

In 1990 legislation was passed aimed at achieving a fundamental restructuring of the education system and curriculum. Among its provisions was the introduction of free pre-school education for the 3–6 age group, the extension of primary schooling from six to 12, secondary schooling from 12 to 16, the reorganisation of education for the 16–18 age group and state vocational training, and the redesign of the curriculum to give greater flexibility, offer a better balance of core and optional subjects, and incorporate technical and humanities subjects into the curriculum for all. Secondary education, now known as *Enseñanza secundario obligatorio* (ESO) culminates at 16 with the BUP (*Bachillerato Unificado Polivalente*) qualification, which may be followed by the BUP 'higher' at 18. Students who want to enter university are required to obtain a university preparation certificate after a one-year course (*Curso de Orientación Universitaria*, COU) and pass an entrance examination.

Vocational training (*Formación profesional reglada*)

State vocational training was given greater priority in the 1990 reforms, although the reforms are not due to affect the 16–18 age group for some years. Until the 1980s, vocational training was largely limited to the state-run *Institutos de Formación Profesional*, essentially technical colleges which offered traditional training programmes largely for traditional occupations. School-leavers not opting for the more 'academic' COU school certificate and university could follow vocational courses lasting two years at level 1 and a further two years at level 2. These institutions retained their popularity during the last decade: there were 726,000 students of levels 1 and 2 in 1984 and 782,000 in 1995 – with the increase largely in level 2 numbers. In 1995, of the 782,000 trainees, 616,000 were accounted for by seven occupations – 291,000 in clerical work, 131,000 in electronics, 58,000 healthcare, 46,000 in motor vehicle trades, 28,000 in design, 32,000 in engineering and 30,000 in hairdressing.

Formación profesional studies have been successful as a preparation for employment: in 1993 83 per cent of those who had completed courses were employed, a higher percentage than for any other educational level, including university graduates, and largely a result of the high success rate of those who had gone on to level 2. However, the mainly traditional nature of the training given, and the generally low prestige of vocational training qualifications, compared with academic qualifications, have prompted the change of direction signalled in the 1990 reforms. In these reforms, due to affect vocational training from 1998, vocational training will be brought more into the mainstream of secondary school activity and turned into another access route to university education instead of an alternative to academic study.

Tertiary education

Spain's universities have undergone a revolution in numbers and in course provision since the 1960s. Most of the growth came after Franco's death in 1975, and expansion continued apace until the mid-1990s. Expansion raised major problems, particularly in the financing of the state system, the governance and administration of universities, course structures and resources. Under Franco, university education was the preserve of a middle-class minority, with traditional courses and methods. Universities were also controlled politically by a highly centralised administration. During that period, when universities were also sources of political protest, student numbers were already starting to rise – from 69,000 in 1960 to 213,000 in 1970. However, it was later, with the bulging baby-boom generation and the exploding demand for information which followed Franco's death and the ending of censorship, that numbers rose rapidly. In 1980 there were 639,000 students. The Socialist government which came to power in 1982 made modernisation of courses and improved access to all levels of education a main priority: by 1990 numbers topped 1,000,000, and in 1996 reached 1,500,000 – a six-fold increase in 25 years.

By 1996 there were 44 state and 10 private universities. While the oldest, Salamanca, dates from 1218, half have been created since 1970. Many of the new universities were created from provincial campuses of existing universities – such as Huelva, Jaén and Vigo – while others were newly created as flagships by regional governments, such as Jaume Primer (Castellón), Castilla la Mancha and

Pompeu Fabra (Barcelona). This left a great imbalance in size, with large traditional universities like the Complutense de Madrid having 126,000 students by 1994, Barcelona 74,000 and Valencia 64,000, but new smaller ones like Pompeu Fabra with only 3,280 and Castellón 6,900.

Within universities, courses may either be taught within faculties (*facultades universitarias*) or 'university schools' (*escuelas universitarias*). Whereas the former teach full degree courses, the latter concentrate on shorter courses leading to a diploma.

The OECD rated Spain second only to the USA for the proportion of 18–21-year-olds in university (at 23 per cent) in 1995. Spanish university provision was then far greater than in other European countries (although non-university higher education was less extensive). Such expansion demanded increased budgets; in this respect the picture was less positive. Funding was very poor when the PSOE took office in 1982; while it increased in the late 1980s and 1990s, the increase was inadequate. Education budgets quintupled in the period 1982–92, but spending is still below the European average. As a proportion of public expenditure, Spain spends only 1.6 per cent on higher education, against the OECD average of 2.8 per cent. In 1994 spending per student in higher education was $4,000 per annum – the lowest figure in Europe. However, its overall public spending on education – as a proportion of GDP – exceeds that of the UK and Italy, for example.

The consequence of expansion on a limited budget was *masificación* – overcrowded lecture rooms, inefficient administrations, neglected students and poor completion rates. In the early 1990s only 6 per cent of the male age group graduated in the target time – one of the lowest rates in Europe. And by 1993 51 per cent of students routinely resat examinations due to failure, and out of a total university population of 1,400,000, only 130,116 graduated. Expansion also made it difficult to realise the academic and administrative targets contained in the 1983 law on university reform, designed to modernise courses and university administration.

Such difficulties explain the rise in private universities in recent years. Although they accounted for only 70,000 students in 1996 (1.7 per cent of the national total), they have been growing in significance. Whereas annual fees in the state sector universities in 1996 averaged Pta 97,000 (£485) for technical courses and Pta 65,000 (£325) for humanities courses, the private sector fees average Pta 1,000,000 (£5,000) and Pta 700,000 (£3,500) respectively. The private universities claim to offer smaller classes, better facilities and more attentive teaching, together with a high employment rate on graduation – some 75 per cent of their graduates find employment immediately. However, they offer a limited range of courses, and only one, San Pablo-CEU in Madrid, offered postgraduate courses in 1996.

One problem of the Spanish graduate profile is that of matching qualifications to demand. Some 55 per cent of recent graduates are in law and social sciences, 13 per cent in technological subjects, 13 per cent in medicine, 10 per cent in humanities and 7 per cent in pure sciences.

Tertiary qualifications   The basic higher education qualification is the *licenciado*, which takes a minimum of five years to complete. There are also courses culminating in a diploma (*diplomado*) which take three years, and which are taught within the university schools. Technical graduates, such as engineers or architects, have their own specific designation. Postgraduate education leading to a doctorate combines research and taught courses.

Graduate recruitment

Spain produces some 100,000 university graduates annually. The *Fundación Universidad Empresa* publishes an annual guide to graduate recruitment patterns in major companies, the *Guía de las Empresas que ofrecen empleo*. The 1996 edition covers the employment policies of 202 companies. It shows a rising trend of graduate recruitment, with graduate representation in the participant company workforces up from 23 per cent to 33 per cent, though 55 per cent of companies recruiting graduates this year are small and medium-size companies.

Graduate employment is primarily concentrated in the areas of consultancy, auditing, human resources, IT, telecommunications and engineering. The lowest demand for graduates is in hotels and catering, the motor industry and electronics.

Much of the employment offered is for temporary contracts, especially work-experience contracts, with permanent contracts accounting for only 25 per cent of the demand; mobility and flexibility are qualities which are, finally, being asked of Spanish graduates – 84 per cent of recruiters now ask for these, with 77 per cent requiring a willingness to travel frequently. Traditional graduate management recruitment sectors, such as chemicals and pharmaceuticals, are increasingly incorporating graduates into commercial, production and organisation functions.

Some 40 per cent of graduates enter direct into the middle levels of companies. Proficiency in a foreign language, especially English, is now required by over 70 per cent of recruiters.

Recruitment methods for graduates   Advertising in the press is the prime recruitment approach, with the main vehicles being the newspapers referred to above: that is, *El País*, *Actualidad Económica*, and *La Vanguardia* in Catalonia. However, unsolicited applications and employer contacts with academics also provide important channels for graduate recruitment.

Campus visits by companies, organised by university placement services or AIESEC, offer opportunities for making contacts, with a particular focus on business and engineering faculties and in the business schools. A number of larger universities have placement services (COIE) run jointly with the official employment service INEM.

Men are liable for military service of one year, normally undertaken after graduation at age 25.

Adult education

Article 4.2.b of the Workers' Statute establishes that employees have a right to vocational training. The FORCEM in-service training schemes (see below) allow for individual employees to apply for financing to take courses such as university degrees or postgraduate qualifications. In 1995, the first time that this type of scheme operated, 162 of the 353 individual training proposals approved were for technical diplomas, 136 were for undergraduate degrees and higher technical diplomas, and 97 were for postgraduate study.

The *Universidad Nacional de Enseñanza a Distancia* (UNED) is structured along similar lines to Britain's Open University, and offers distance-learning higher education to adult learners. However, limitations in resources and financing have inhibited its development.

Training and the official employment services

In recent years Spain has made radical changes to its training arrangements for ali categories – school-leavers, graduates, the unemployed and employees – following considerable dissatisfaction with the previous schemes.

In 1981 the law allowed employers to conclude special training contracts for the unqualified; this was followed in 1982 by the addition of another type of special employment contract, the work-experience contract for qualified job seekers. Throughout the next decade these were widely used by employers, attracted by the fact that they were concluded for a fixed duration and were accompanied by considerable subsidies to employers' social security contributions. Their numbers peaked in 1989, when 335,000 training contracts and 225,000 work-experience contracts were concluded. Concurrently, under the first national vocational training plan, the *Plan de Formación e Inserción Profesional* (FIP) of 1985, a wide range of schemes to support and subsidise the costs of trainees and training centres was also developed. However, the results were disappointing, with poorly motivated trainees, accusations of misuse, and inadequate training. The OECD's 1994 report on Spain spoke of 'serious mismatches between demand and supply of skills'. Of the 173,827 people trained under the FIP in 1992, for example, only 32 per cent were placed in jobs on completion.

Consequently, in anticipation of the measures to partially deregulate the labour market in the 1994 reforms to the Workers' Statute, in 1993 the government concluded a tripartite agreement for a radical overhaul of the FIP and the introduction of new measures for in-service training (*Plan Nacional de Formación Profesional*). These reforms are claimed to have had significant effects.

In January 1997, a new four-year tripartite agreement was concluded to cover both initial and continuing vocational training. Schemes funded by the 0.75 per cent levy on pay, which raises Pta 160 billion (£800 million), will be distributed equally between schemes for the unemployed and for continuing training for those in employment. The agreement also extends access to financial support for continuing training for self-employed workers, casual agricultural labourers and the civil service.

Training for job seekers

Training for job seekers (*Formación Profesional*) under the FIP consists principally of programmes run by INEM or those regional governments that have authority (Catalonia, Galicia,Valencia, Andalusia, Canary Islands) in accordance with the needs identified by INEM's occupational training unit survey. Courses are run either in INEM training centres (14 per cent), in recognised training establishments (57 per cent), or by organisations such as trade unions (14 per cent) and companies (11 per cent). Priority is given to those receiving benefit, the long-term unemployed over 25, disadvantaged groups such as women in certain sectors and the disabled, unemployed under-25s for whom the employer guarantees to employ 60 per cent of the trainees on completion, and unemployed under-25s who have lost a job which they had had for at least six months. Attendance, travel, board and lodging subsidies (Pta 7,600 (£38) daily) are available for some.

Courses involving work experience attract grants to the company, and INEM supports the training of the trainers. Employers are paid Pta 1,500 (£7.50) daily for each trainee being trained in the company.

Some 150 vocational certifications have been established in the 25 occupational categories covered by the FIP, which provide certification on completion. In 1994 38 per cent of trainees were placed in work – but only just over a fifth of these were in jobs related to their training. Some 64 per cent of training courses relate to the service sector, 23 per cent to industry, 7 per cent to construction and 6 per cent to agriculture.

The courses are run at four levels, and range from under 200 hours to more than 800. Although there are more female trainees than males, males have a 10 per cent better employment take-up rate on completion. Those on benefit are required to take a course if a suitable one is offered to them. The financing of the training amounts to 5 per cent of INEM's budget, and the greater part of it comes from the European Social Fund.

Continuing training

Traditionally there has been a very low level of in-service training in Spain, compared with other countries. In 1992, for example, only 3 per cent of the active workforce was involved, compared with 27 per cent in France and Germany, and Spanish companies spent only 0.17 per cent of their total labour costs on it (against the EU average of 1.5 per cent). To address this issue, in 1993 a tripartite agreement between the government, the unions UGT and CC.OO and the employers' organisations CEOE and CEPYME established a three-year plan, the

Acuerdo Nacional de Formación Continua and a training fund dedicated to continuing training, the *Fundación para la Formación Contina* (FORCEM). This radically reshaped the provision and is considered to have been very successful. In 1993 564,000 employees received training, while in 1995 the figure was 1,500,000, representing more than 10 per cent of employees in some regions. FORCEM is financed by part of the employers' 0.7 per cent contribution to social security, and by the European Social Fund. In 1995 the FORCEM budget totalled Pta 62,000 million (£310m), and in 1996 Pta 82,000 million (£410m).

The agreement envisages four types of training: a company training plan, a group training plan devised by several companies, an individual employee plan, and union or employer federation-sponsored plans. Companies with more than 200 employees are encouraged to draw up an annual training plan, in collaboration with unions and employee representatives. Groups of small companies employing at least 200 between them may draw up a group training plan. Individual employees of at least six months' experience with the company and 12 months in the industry may apply for paid training leave of up to 150 hours. These training plan provisions may be incorporated in a collective agreement, or agreed as a separate document in the companies concerned.

Each year the plans are submitted to the national tripartite commission, which then vets them and approves the successful applicants. In 1995 80 per cent of plans were approved, including 828 company plans and 1,192 group plans. A total of 353 individual requests for paid training leave were approved, 78 per cent of them for males. In 1994, of the 61,669 companies involved, all but 823 were participants in a group training plan. Notably, the main beneficiaries of training schemes are employees already holding a qualification: in 1995 they accounted for 46 per cent of the trainees. Of these, 18 per cent were technical staff and 15 per cent middle managers. The largest group in function terms were production staff, accounting for 42 per cent, followed by sales staff (27 per cent). Only 5 per cent of trainees were senior management.

FORCEM also administers EU structural funds for training for the period 1994–9 in Objective 4 regions. Successful applicants may receive between 25 and 100 per cent of their training costs.

As an example of the role of FORCEM in large companies, Michelin stated that 75 per cent of their 6,800 employees participated in some form of FORCEM training in 1994, all of which was conducted in-house in the training centres they have attached to each factory. They estimate that in-house training costs amount to only 33 per cent of external training costs. In 1994 some 25 per cent of all Michelin's training costs were met by FORCEM.

Workshop schools An innovative and successful training scheme are the 'Workshop Schools' (*Escuelas Taller* and *Casas de Oficios*) which have been operating since 1985. These offer a mix of theoretical and practical training for unemployed under-25-year-olds in traditional skills used in building, restoration work, crafts, and environmental skills. There are now 3,283 centres staffed by 25,000 craftspeople who train young people for one or two years. Six hundred of the centres are operated by the local municipality, supported by INEM.

Workforce consultation on training

Article 64 of the Workers' Statute gives statutory rights to works councils to express their opinion before a company puts into practice an occupational training scheme. Under the 1993 tripartite training agreement, the unions have a role in running INEM, which provides post-school occupational training.

Collective agreements often formalise the role to be played in company training plans by employee representatives: for example, Ford submits its training plans twice yearly to the works council for consultation. At industry level, the chemicals national sectoral agreement establishes a joint committee of four trade union representatives and four representatives from the chemical employers' confederation to draw up national industry training plans.

Collectively agreed provisions on training

Collective agreements frequently include provisions on training. They may, for example, openly subscribe to the terms of the national training agreement, the *Acuerdo Nacional sobre la Formación*, as for example in the chemicals national sectoral agreement which endorses the *Acuerdo Nacional* as the 'best way of organising and managing training programmes'. Individual company agreements often adhere to associated sectoral training plans.

Companies may also include training plans in house agreements: these may either provide for consultation, as at Ford, or embrace detailed and substantive training objectives, as at the telecommunications company Sintel.

Some agreements specify sums available for employee training. Ford, for example, provides up to Pta 59,500 (£300) for registration fees and Pta 16,750 (£85) in expenses for employees taking higher education courses, and lower amounts for lower-level courses. Other companies have a global fund to finance individual study grants. Occasionally an agreement may tie pay levels to qualifications achieved; the insurance company Aurora Polar adds 20 per cent to basic pay for those achieving the insurance business's higher diploma, and 10 per cent extra for the lower level. The company also fosters the learning of Catalan, Basque and Galician in the respective regions, and pays 10 per cent extra on basic pay to employees who can demonstrate fluency.

The most recent survey of the effect of collectively agreed measures in 670 of Spain's largest companies showed that in 1994, of the employees receiving training, 93 per cent were effectively receiving some form of retraining, and only 7 per cent were new employees. While 60 per cent of employees in large firms with over 5,000 employees were receiving some training, the proportion fell to 22 per cent in firms of less than 300 employees. On average, training lasted for

38 hours, ranging from 12 hours in agricultural companies to 74 in steel and chemicals. Estimated average annual training costs per employee were Pta 85,000 (£425), ranging from Pta 28,300 (£140) in agriculture to Pta 132,100 (£660) in energy companies.

Time-off rights for education and training

Article 23 of the Workers' Statute establishes that employees have the right to time off for examinations, and also to arrange a suitable shift when shiftworking is operated, to enable them to attend courses. They also have the right to modify their working-time arrangements or to have leave to attend relevant vocational training courses. Details of the implementation of these rights are established by collective agreement. Whereas some companies, such as Ford, grant paid leave to attend examinations for all levels of study, some may restrict this to examinations for vocational qualifications. In the footwear industry, employees must achieve a pass rate of 50 per cent of examinations entered to qualify for fully-paid time off.

Management education and development

A 1996 survey of management training in Spain established that some 30 per cent of companies expressed no concern about the need for management training for their managers. However, the serious shortage of trained executives in the 1980s, which underlay the rapid pay increases for Spanish executives seen in that decade, did prompt a major growth in the provision of such training, largely in the private sector. By the early 1990s there was a total of nearly 1,000 establishments offering management training across the country, and a proliferation of organisations offering MBAs.

Two sources offer basic information on the training available in those centres – the AFIDE (*Asociación Española de las Asociaciones para la Formación y el Desarrollo en la Empresa*) and the DIRFO (*Directorio de la Formación*).

The most established business schools are IESE, EADE and ESADE in Barcelona, ICADE, EOI and ESIC in Madrid, and ESTE and DEUSTO in the Basque Country. In recent years many more have been established. The organisation which represents the private business school sector and monitors standards is the *Asociación Española de Escuelas de Dirección de Empresas* (AEEDE). There is a very wide range of full-time and part-time options on offer, mainly leading to an MBA, available in some 100 establishments, including the Spanish centres of American or British business schools. Some 90 per cent of MBA students pay their own fees, while 80 per cent of executives in post who take an MBA are financed by their employer. A typical MBA programme lasts 800 contact hours. The MBA qualification in Spain may not always be legally recognised, but in practice they are accepted by employers.

Managerial qualifications

A 1995 survey of the qualifications of Spanish management concluded that while 70 per cent of those in all management positions had basic school-leaving quali-fications, and 23 per cent had tertiary vocational training qualificatons, only 7 per cent had a degree or equivalent – although this proportion rose to 44 per cent for senior managers and directors. Just under half held qualifications in economics or management, with 41 per cent in science and engineering. Some 54 per cent spoke English, and 27 per cent French. The survey commented on this duality – a highly professionally qualified senior management and a relatively poorly qual-ified middle and lower management profile.

Financing the system

Vocational training is financed by contributions made by employers and employ-ees. The contribution rates for 1996 were 0.7 per cent (employer 0.6 per cent and employee 0.1 per cent) of pay. Of the funds generated by this levy, FORCEM received 0.20 per cent in 1994, 0.25 per cent in 1995 and 0.30 per cent in 1996. In 1995 FORCEM granted total funds of Pta 48.6 billion (£212 million).

State support for workplace training

When companies agree to admit unemployed trainees for vocational training schemes run by INEM for the purposes of workplace training, they are paid Pta 1,500 (£7.50) per trainee per day (which includes insurance premiums). Trainees who are eligible for financial support (the disabled and under-25s from rural areas who have exhausted special farmworkers' benefit) receive Pta 725 (£3.50) per training day, with travel and meals expenses of Pta 1,100 (£5.50) per day.

Training in the Basque Country

The Basque Country has a long tradition of independent initiatives in the field of employment relations. It has also pioneered some notable training schemes. For example, in 1991 the Basque employers' confederation CONFEBASK, against the wishes of local unions, introduced practical work-experience elements for full-time *Formación Profesional* students. Under this scheme, 100 companies provided practical experience for 600 students, attached to a tutor rather like the apprentice–master relationship, for 30 per cent of their course time. Subsequently in 1993, the Basque regional government created a public agency, EGAILAN, to co-ordinate training policy in the region, and in 1995 the Basque government issued a series of decrees to stimulate all aspects of vocational training. EGAILAN is charged with monitoring the effectiveness of the programmes, which offer incentives ranging up to Pta 1,200,000 (£6,000) to companies pre-pared to employ and train approved unemployed applicants, and which offer sup-port for company training schemes.

Educational attainment of the population

Level	Percentage of 25–64 age-group
Lower secondary	74
Upper secondary	11
Higher education (non-university)	4
University	11

Source: OECD (1994)

Organisations

The Ministry of Labour and Social Security
(*Ministerio de Trabajo y Seguridad Social*)
Agustin de Bethencourt 4
Madrid
Tel. +341 553 6278
Fax +341 533 2996

National Employment Institute
(*Instituto Nacional de Empleo*, INEM)
Condesa de Venadito 9
Madrid
Tel. +341 585 9888
Fax +341 268 3981
INEM is attached to the Ministry of Labour and Social Security, and is charged with the management of the employment offices. It has an office in each provincial capital, entitled *Dirección Provincial del Instituto Nacional de Empleo*, which handles recruitment and registers the unemployed.

The Labour Inspectorate
(*Dieracción General de Inspeccion de Trabajo y Seguridad*)
Agustin de Bethencourt 4
Madrid
Tel. +341 553 6000

Confederation of Spanish Employers
(*Confederación Española de Organizaciones Empresariales*, CEOE)
Diego de Leon 50
28006 Madrid
Tel. +341 563 9641
Fax +341 262 8023

Asociación Española de Directores de Personal (AEDIPE)
Moreto 10
Madrid
Tel. +341 468 2217
AEDIPE is Spain's largest personnel management association and is a member of the European Association of Personnel Management.

Union General de Trabajadores (UGT)
Hortaleza 88
Madrid
Tel. +341 308 3333

Comisiones Obreras (CC.OO)
Fernandez de la Hoz 6
28010 Madrid
Tel. +341 419 5454

Union Sindical Obrera (USO)
Principe de Vergara 13 7o
28001 Madrid
Tel. +341 262 4040

Confederación Sindical Euzko Laguillen Alkatasuna – Solidaridad de Trabajadores Vascos (ELA-STV)
Euskalduna 11 1o
48008 Bilbao
Tel. +344 4442504

Main sources

Consejo Economico y Social. *Economia Trabajo y Sociedad.* Madrid, 1996

Ministerio de Trabajo y Seguridad Social. *Acuerdos Sobre Formación Continua 1993–1996.* Madrid, 1993

Ministerio de Trabajo y Seguridad Social. *Boletín de Estadísticas Laborales.* Various issues

Ministerio de Trabajo y Seguridad Social. *Guía Laboral.* (Annual review of labour legislation). Various issues

Ministerio de Economia y Hacienda. *La Negociación Colectiva en las Grandes Empresas.* (Annual survey of collective bargaining in large companies), various issues

Vidal Soria J. *Codigo de las Leyes Laborales*, B.O.E. Madrid, 1991

Industry collective agreements, published in *Boletín Oficial del Estado* (Official Gazette)

12

Sweden

The remorseless rise in unemployment in the years since 1991, following decades of what would pass for full employment elsewhere in Europe, has not only delivered a shock to confidence in economic management but also posed major challenges to distinctly Swedish approaches to employment and welfare policy, with their emphasis on active measures to return the unemployed to the labour force. Government plans to cut unemployment from its 1996 level of just over 8 per cent to 4 per cent by the end of the decade are centred on ambitious plans to improve workforce skills, with major investment in the education system – including a boost for adult education.

As with many other European countries, the 1990s have seen an end of the state monopoly on placement, and the sanctioning of private agencies. As yet, these have to gain a real foothold in the market and the public service remains at the heart of much of recruitment activity. Recruitment procedures include some reporting requirements to the authorities, both before and after hiring. There is also a statutory requirement to re-hire workers previously dismissed because of a lack of work – this accounts for about a quarter of all new hirings.

The labour market

In the first quarter of 1996 the Swedish labour force consisted of 4,257,000 people, equivalent to 77 per cent of the population between 16 and 64 years of age, and about 50 per cent of the total population – a rate exceeded in Europe only by Denmark. While the male participation rate, at 79 per cent, is broadly in line with the European average and is exceeded by a number of countries, the female rate of 75 per cent is, again, second only to Denmark in Western Europe.

Unemployment, excluding those on state employment schemes, was running at 328,000 or 7.7 per cent of the labour force in 1996, with the female jobless rate at 6.9 per cent, and the male rate at 8.5 per cent – historically unprecedentedly high by Swedish standards. Until the economic recession of the early 1990s unemployment had for a decade been between 1.5 and 3 per cent of the labour force, in part through macro-management but also because of a commitment to high public expenditure on active labour market policies. The unemployment figure rose rapidly to nearly 10 per cent between early 1991 and July 1993. Although the jobless rate eased in the wake of moderate economic recovery, there are no expectations of a quick return to the sustained low figures of the past. The government has set itself the goal of getting unemployment down to 4

303

per cent by 2000, based on a concerted effort to upgrade and update workforce skills.

Public sector employment is high, at 38 per cent of the total, and is dominated by women: the converse is true in the private sector, with more male (63 per cent) than female (37 per cent) workers.

About one-eighth of the workforce is employed on fixed-term contracts, of which the lion's share is accounted for by blue-collar workers. Twenty-eight per cent of employees work part-time (9.4 per cent of men and 45 per cent of women), one of the highest proportions in the EU.

Recruitment

Official notification

Employers have a legal obligation to report most vacant positions to the public job placement system (*arbetsförmedlingen*). This must be done before any steps are taken to fill a vacancy, such as placing an advertisement.

Reporting usually takes place over the telephone, and details must be given of the employer, where the vacancy is located, the duties to be carried out and qualifications required, proposed pay, benefits and hours of work, whether the position is permanent or temporary, the application deadline and the start date.

Exceptions are made for temporary jobs lasting less than 10 days and for vacancies which it is intended should be filled through internal recruitment. In addition, under the Security of Employment Act (LAS), employees dismissed by a company because of a lack of work may have preference if that company subsequently recruits new workers; in cases where it is intended that the vacancy be filled by such a candidate, it need not be reported.

As private job placement is permitted, there is no obligation to employ any candidate provided by the public system; however, there is a legal duty to inform the relevant authorities when a vacancy has been filled.

Workforce consultation

Under the 1976 Co-determination Act (*Medbestämmandelagen*, MBL), employers are obliged to consult union representatives on 'important' alterations to work or employment conditions. The importance of this provision in the recruitment process varies. For example, the appointment of a manager or supervisor would usually constitute such a change. The appointment of other employees may also be considered 'important' if, for instance, it entails a redistribution of work.

The MBL also obliges employers to keep unions informed of developments in personnel policy.

Temporary and part-time work

The Security of Employment Act (*Lagen om anställningsskydd*, LAS) explicitly states that contracts of employment are valid indefinitely unless otherwise agreed.

Part-time work is not defined in legislation, nor usually in collective agreements; it is generally regarded as work for less than full-time contractual hours. The maximum legally-stipulated working week is currently 40 hours.

Collective agreements in sectors where part-time work is common, such as retailing or banking, often contain particular provisions for part-timers. Employers are usually obliged to notify employees that some state and collectively-agreed benefits – the most important being the state supplementary pension – are conditional upon certain minimum numbers of hours being worked, or wages earned. Relevant agreements therefore urge employers, wherever possible, to arrange working hours so that these thresholds are met. Part-timers often have first option to work extra hours when business activity increases.

Overtime for part-time employees is regulated by law, and may be no more than 200 hours annually. Such overtime has a different name from overtime for full-time employees; it is called *mertid* rather than *övertid*. In addition, if the hours of a part-time employee are longer than those of a full-timer, the extra time is called *överskjutande mertid*. It is usually only the latter which attracts overtime supplements.

Other types of 'non-standard' employment are regulated by the Security of Employment Act, which begins from the principle that employment contracts are open ended. Under the Act, fixed-term contracts may be concluded for:

- a certain task, period of time or season, where this is necessitated by the nature of the work
- a specified period as a temporary replacement, a trainee or during a holiday period
- a specified period, up to a maximum of six months in the course of two years, where this is necessitated by an accumulation of work
- the period preceding the commencement by an employee of compulsory military (or other comparable) service lasting more than three months
- probationary employment, provided the period does not exceed six months.

Employers must consult with trade unions over proposals for any fixed-term contracts intended to last longer than one month. In late 1996 proposals were put forward which would eliminate the need to consult with trade unions on some types of fixed-term contract in small and newly established companies.

Equality provisions

There is legislation prohibiting racial and sexual discrimination, both of which include provisions forbidding discrimination in connection with recruitment. There is also a collective agreement between SAF, LO and the white-collar bargaining cartel, PTK, covering sex discrimination. It is inadvisable to ask about marriage prospects and parenthood in a recruitment context.

Finding the applicant

Between 1936 and 1992 the state job placement service had a monopoly on placement activity, with very few exceptions. Private employment agencies were prohibited from operating on a profit-making basis, although non-commercial job placement activity was permitted, but its extent was very limited. In 1992 temporary employment agencies were legalised for contracts of less than four months, and in 1993 this stricture was removed, and employment agencies of all sorts were allowed to operate freely. The most important method of finding employment is, perhaps surprisingly, by prospective employees being contacted by a company. However, this is because of a peculiarity of Swedish law. Under the Security of Employment Act (LAS), employees dismissed for economic reasons have the right of priority if their former employer is undertaking fresh recruitment in their former area of work. This right is contingent upon 12 months' service in the two years preceding dismissal for permanent staff, and lasts for nine months after dismissal for those recruited after 1 January 1997, and for one year for those already in employment at that date. About a quarter of all new hirings originate in this provision, according to research carried out by the National Labour Market Board (AMS). The next most important method of finding a job is through relatives and friends – about a fifth of people obtain employment in this way.

The state placement service (*offentliga arbetsförmedlingen*)

Of all the placement agencies available in Sweden, the public system is by far the most comprehensive, although it no longer enjoys a monopoly.

Overall responsibility for labour market policy lies with the Ministry of Labour (*Arbetsmarknadsdepartementet*), which has jurisdiction over the Labour Market Administration Department (*Arbetsmarknadsverket*). The latter is made up of the National Labour Market Board (*Arbetsmarknadsstyrelsen* or AMS) and the county labour boards (*länsarbetsnämnder*), of which there is one for each of Sweden's 24 counties. The county labour boards are responsible for operating the Public Employment Service (*offentliga arbetsförmedlingen*) and the 'employability institutes' (*arbetsmarknadsinstitut*) which provide vocational training and advice for those with employment difficulties.

AMS is the central administrative body for general labour market policy, and oversees the county boards. It is thus responsible for enacting employment policy decided upon by the Cabinet, and sets policy for the county boards and allocates resources to them. The boards then have responsibility for carrying out policies in their counties.

The public employment service (Af)

The offices of the Employment Service (usually referred to simply as Af) are responsible for providing practical help both to job seekers and employers.

There are almost 400 Af offices spread over the country, including some which specialise in certain particular occupations – there are, for instance, offices for technology, accounting and finance, IT and seafaring. All offices are linked to a central computer system, and are therefore able to provide information on job vacancies over the whole country.

Several larger cities and towns also have a specialised service for those interested in working abroad. Af offices can also supply information on terms and conditions for various occupations, and help in choosing a suitable job.

Most offices have self-service terminals which allow job seekers to look at all reported job vacancies in the whole of Sweden. Current vacancies may also be accessed on Af's home page (http://www.umu.se/af). Af also publishes a number of regionally- and sectorally-based newspapers (*platsjournaler*) detailing current vacancies in relevant areas.

Af's services to employers may take several forms. Af staff make regular visits to local employers in order to gauge current and likely future recruitment needs, and obtain information on the type and level of skills needed. Af is also able to conduct searches for candidates according to employers' criteria, advertise vacancies in the *platsjournaler* and offer other advice.

A survey published by AMS in 1996 shows that about 17 per cent of those obtaining employment do so through contact with the state employment service.

Private employment agencies

Private agencies have been allowed to operate freely since the total abolition of the state monopoly on job placement in 1993. There are, however, a few firms which concentrate on recruiting exclusively for permanent positions, but such services are often also provided by temporary-employment agencies. Research by AMS has shown that, in mid-1996, only about 2 per cent of those obtaining new employment did so through a private employment agency.

Data on the extent of private employment activity – and even the number of companies involved – varies widely. The number of private agencies was estimated by some observers to be about 1,200 in 1995, with about half of these being very small 'one-person' operations; but the commercial employers' organisation, HAO Tjänsteföretagen, estimated that there were about 450 temporary agencies in the country, of which only 100–150 had more than 10 employees, and only 60 belonged to the organisation – mainly the bigger players.

Agencies – both permanent and temporary – are strongly concentrated in

Stockholm, Gothenburg and Malmö, and deal mainly in secretarial jobs, although other types of work (especially those requiring IT skills) are becoming more popular. It is estimated that about 5,000–6,000 people were employed by temporary agencies in 1995, and that this figure will rise to about 20,000 by the end of the century.

Executive recruitment

There are no restrictions on executive search companies. There are branches of several international executive search companies in Sweden, and some local companies, as well as a variety of consultants. The public employment service plays virtually no part in executive recruitment, and there is no legal obligation to report such vacancies to it.

Although some vacancies are advertised in newspapers, most are filled by search companies or by informal networking – as a small country with relatively few executive positions, the personal element is important.

The strong export orientation of the Swedish economy has produced a cadre of internationally-minded executives who are often attractive to non-Swedish companies. On the other hand, there are very few non-Swedes occupying executive positions in Swedish companies.

Recruitment media

The press

Press advertisements are also an important method of recruitment. Of newspapers, the daily *Dagens Nyheter* carries by far the largest number of vacancies. Advertisements appear every day, but most are carried on Sundays; the Thursday edition of the paper has a specialised IT recruitment section. The newspaper also carries a service resulting from a joint initiative with the Stockholm county labour board. Called *Personal Direkt*, it allows job seekers to advertise themselves and their skills. It appears on the first Tuesday of each month.

Two other dailies, *Svenska Dagbladet* and *Dagens Industri*, have fewer advertisements, and concentrate mainly on the business sector. There is also a limited amount of advertisement in technical and professional journals.

The Internet

For those with access to the Internet, there is a growing trend – although at present confined mostly to large companies and those in the IT sector – for firms to carry details of job vacancies on their home pages. Many private recruitment agencies also have such details available, with some enabling job seekers to enter details into a databank free of charge (it is illegal for recruitment agencies in

Sweden to charge job seekers for their services) and apply for advertised vacancies on-line. Companies can either search records of job seekers or advertise vacancies through these services. As a rough guide to costs, one agency charges Skr 3,000 (£273) a year for access to its candidate bank, while another charges Skr 2,900 (£264) for the inclusion of a job advertisement on its home page for two weeks.

Trade unions

Trade unions play a limited part in placement activity, although some whose members are mainly graduates have either established or are testing systems. The main one is *CF-Börsen*, run by civil engineers' union CF, which has about 2,800 job seekers on its database, and which fills about 200–250 vacancies a year.

Recruitment procedures

Recruitment documents

Job applications are usually concise, consisting of a short covering letter and a CV. CVs should include previous employment, education and other activities, eg military service, together with dates. Apart from these, personal details and interests should be included, as should copies of school grades and degrees. Swedish employees are entitled to a certificate of performance (*tjänstgöringsbetyg*) when leaving employment, which includes dates of employment and job description; it may also include details of competence and conduct and reasons for the termination of employment, but these details may be left out at the employee's request. Any such certificates should also be included with the application.

It is usual to include two, or at most three, references, both professional and personal, although prospective employers are entitled to seek other relevant information if they wish, including from previous employers not named as references. Large companies always follow up references, although smaller firms are not always quite so assiduous.

Education

The education system

Basic education (*grundskola*)　Basic, compulsory schooling in elementary schools lasts for nine years between the ages of 7 and 16, and is comprehensive in nature. In 1991 the law was changed to grant parents the option of letting their children start school at age 6 if this option is available in their municipality. Although the aim is to provide this option to all children from

July 1997, the take-up is low as yet, at around 5 per cent.

The system of basic education is currently undergoing structural change, which will be fully introduced by the academic year 1997/8.

School curricula are centrally framed. Earlier curricula were very specific, both in subject criteria and the amount of time per week to be spent on the various subjects at all three levels (*lågstadiet, mellanstadiet, högstadiet*) of basic education. The new curriculum (*Lpo 94*) has abolished this three-level distinction. It specifies a minimum guaranteed teaching time for the whole nine-year period, divided by subject or groups of subjects. Teaching time totals 6,665 hours, with a further 410 hours available for school-elective subjects, from a range which is decided by the local authority. Almost 500 hours of this total are reserved for student-elective options. Most hours are spent on the study of Swedish, English and mathematics.

Schools are free to decide how they distribute these hours over the nine-year period, which is not necessarily all spent in the classroom, but must be teacher-supervised; it may therefore include study visits, field trips and time spent in places of work under the *praktisk arbetslivorientering* (*prao*) scheme. The curriculum is of a more general nature than previously, and is framed in terms of goals to be achieved by the end of the fifth and ninth years. No vocational training is undertaken at this level of education. Schools have a function called *studie- och yrkesorientering* (*syo*) which guides pupils in their choice of further studies or career.

Practically all children – over 99 per cent – attend state-funded primary schools. There are a number of schools for those with various types of disability, where instruction lasts for 10 years. In the north of Sweden about 120 Sami (Lapp) schools exist to provide education with an ethnic emphasis – instruction there corresponds to the first six years of primary education.

Although the number of independent schools has increased in recent years, there are still only about 200. These include schools based on religious denomination, those based on specific teaching methods (such as Montessori schools), those with a special language emphasis (such as Finnish) and those started in sparsely populated rural areas in response to the threatened closure of a state school. There are also international schools, primarily for children of those temporarily resident in the country.

Upper secondary education (*gymnasieskola*)

The pre-reform situation   A transfer to *gymnasieskola*, although not compulsory, has been the choice of the vast majority of those leaving *grundskola*. Take-up increased during the first half of the 1990s, and 97 per cent of pupils now choose this option. This is at least partly because of the large increase in unemployment during the recession in the early years of the decade, although the increase in demand for more knowledge and skills than the *grundskola* can provide has also played a part. There are currently about 310,000 pupils studying at roughly 600 *gymnasieskolor*, just over 10 per cent of which are private schools.

The *gymnasieskola* has been undergoing a process of reform as a result of an Act passed in 1991. The old system consisted of about 25 different 'lines' (*linjer*) and about 500 specialised courses (*specialkurser*). Most of these courses were vocationally-oriented and of two weeks' to two years' duration; there were also a number of three-year lines which prepared students for higher education.

Although certain core subjects – Swedish, English, physical education and 'working-life orientation' – were common to all courses and lines, eligibility requirements, duration, timetables and syllabuses varied widely.

Preparatory lines for higher education were more broadly based and contained more general subjects, with the shorter vocational courses being more sharply focused. There were no examinations; rather, students were awarded marks in each subject every term according to centrally-set achievement targets. After at least two years of study at *gymnasieskola*, it was possible to obtain a leaving certificate which conferred eligibility to further education.

Although the system offered students a good deal of choice, it was often criticised for being inflexible, with little opportunity for transfer between courses. The system was therefore redesigned in 1991, and reforms were gradually introduced.

Post-reform From the autumn of 1995, a new, unified system of upper secondary education came into full effect. The plethora of lines and courses have been replaced by 16 national programmes, although not all schools or local authorities choose to offer the full range of possibilities.

The programmes are:

- an arts programme offering a broadly-based education for those intending to work in arts-related professions
- building and construction
- business administration, embracing private business and public administration
- child care: for work in child care, after-school and recreational activities, sports and libraries
- electrical engineering
- energy, for those interested in working in, for example, electricity and power stations, heating, ventilation and sanitation plants, and on ships
- food processing, sales and distribution
- handicrafts, with a large component of on-the-job training
- health care
- hotels, restaurants and catering
- industry, including manual and technical skills
- media: advertising, design and production of graphic media
- use of natural resources: for work in forestry, agriculture, horticulture and animal husbandry

- vehicle engineering, covering repair and maintenance
- social sciences: for those intending to pursue further studies in social sciences, economics and languages
- natural sciences: for those intending to pursue further studies in mathematics, science subjects and languages.

All programmes last for three years, and all qualify students for further education. About one-third of teaching time is spent on the eight core subjects of English, Swedish, mathematics, civics, religious education, general science, physical education and artistic activities. 10 to 12 per cent of time is spent in three other activities. These are: a project; individually-chosen subjects (such as an extra foreign language or one of a range of locally-decided options) involving extra teaching time or subject-related work experience; in subjects specific to the programme.

The remaining 50 to 60 per cent of teaching time is spent on the subjects special to the particular programme. The first year of the programme covers the chosen area in a general manner; from the second year, students may choose to specialise.

Students who find that their educational needs are not fulfilled by one of the standard programmes may follow one of their own choosing, constructed in conjunction with schools and local authorities. The latter are also mandated to devise their own programmes and offer them to students under their jurisdiction.

Higher education

Until recently, the system of higher education in Sweden had a strong degree of central regulation, with details of study length, financing and curricula laid down by Parliament.

However, the adoption of a new Higher Education Act in 1993 marked a shift away from this approach. Funding is now determined by the number of students at an academic institution, and their performance. Both the organisation of courses and the range of courses on offer are now determined locally. Students have the option of combining courses to 'tailor-make' their own degree within general criteria for the various qualifications.

Entrance requirements

In order to be admitted to higher education in Sweden, students must fulfil a general entrance requirement, and also specific requirements which can be imposed on applicants by individual universities and colleges – which vary according to area of study and type of course.

The general entrance requirement is completion of a three-year programme of study at upper secondary school (see above). This requirement can also be satisfied by an equivalent education at a Swedish or foreign institution, and also by knowledge gained through work experience. Applicants whose mother tongue is not one of the Nordic languages must demonstrate a satisfactory command of Swedish; this may be achieved, for example, by a one-year preparatory course in the language. Another general requirement is a very good command of English.

Within general guidelines, universities and colleges are then free to choose which criteria they wish to use to select students. The allowable criteria are school results; results from the university aptitude test (which is a standard national, but not compulsory, test); previous relevant education; and work experience. Institutions may decide to use as many of these criteria as they wish.

They may also decide whether to carry out the admissions process locally or to use the services of the state National Agency for Higher Education (*Verket för högskoleservice*, VHS) in selecting applicants.

Undergraduate education   Since 1 July 1993 all studies have been conducted in the form of courses whose curricula are set by the individual institution. The goals for courses are set out in the state Degree Ordinance. Students may freely combine courses, for which points are given, into a degree. Individual courses last from about five weeks to one-and-a-half years.

First degree courses generally take between two and five-and-a-half years to complete. There are two types of first degree: professional and general.

Professional degrees (*yrkesexamen*) are awarded upon completion of courses of study leading to specific professions, such as diplomas in teaching and medicine.

General degrees are of three types:

- a diploma (*högskoleexamen*) awarded after two years' full-time study
- a bachelor's degree (*kandidatexamen*) after three years' full-time study, and a thesis
- a master's degree after four years of full-time study, including either one or two dissertations.

Teaching methods are decided by the individual institution, but the most common are large lecture groups (up to 300 students) and smaller seminar groups of about 30. Instruction normally takes place in Swedish, but a great deal of compulsory course literature is often in English.

Assessment and examination procedures are also decided by the institutions themselves. These are commonly a mixture of continuous assessment and examinations, both written and oral, but there are no final examinations on the British model covering a whole three- or five-year syllabus.

Marks are generally given in three grades – Fail, Pass, and Pass with Distinction – although, once again, institutions may decide to use other systems.

As part of a recent government initiative, an extra 30,000 places are to be created in higher education by the autumn of 1997. At least half are in the areas of science and technology, where there is felt to be a lack of graduates.

Institutions   Almost all the institutions of higher education – except for the University of Agricultural Sciences, which is the responsibility of the Ministry of Agriculture – fall under the jurisdiction of the Ministry of Education and Science. The state institutions are:

- the Universities of Uppsala, Gothenburg, Stockholm, Lund, Linköping and Umeå
- specialised institutions for education and research: the Karolinska Institute (medicine), the Royal Institute of Technology, Luleå University College and Institute of Technology and the Stockholm Institute of Education
- seven smaller colleges, covering various areas of the arts, and located in Stockholm
- the University College of Sport in Stockholm
- twenty small and medium-sized university colleges spread over the country.

Until 1994 there was only one major private institution in the higher education system – the Stockholm School of Economics, which is well-known as a source of high-calibre business studies graduates, and is run by a private foundation with central government support. From 1994 both the Chalmers University of Technology in Gothenburg and the University College of Jönköping have also been transferred to non-state ownership, and are now administered by foundations.

Study in all institutions is free of charge.

Financial aid   Financial aid is available to all undergraduate students permanently resident in Sweden, but not generally to those over 45 years of age. While support may be limited for those with high incomes from other sources, no account is taken of the economic situation of the student's parents or spouse.

Study assistance is available for a maximum of twelve semesters and consists of a non-repayable grant plus a larger, repayable loan.

Those eligible to receive study assistance from the Swedish state are not obliged to attend Swedish institutions. In the 1992/3 academic year, about 13,000 Swedes studied abroad, 1,100 of them in Europe under the ERASMUS programme, and 650 in other Nordic countries.

Postgraduate education   All the universities and many of the other further education establishments provide the opportunity to pursue postgraduate studies.
To be admitted to such a course requires the completion of an undergraduate course of at least three years' duration (that is, at least up to *kandidatexamen* standard). In addition, faculty boards in each institution will assess the student's ability to pursue doctoral studies.

Graduate students attend some courses but most importantly must produce a doctoral dissertation, which is defended in public and marked as either Pass or Fail. The process usually takes up to four years to complete. Some institutions have recently introduced a 'licentiate' postgraduate degree; this is based on research training of between two and two-and-a-half years and can be supplemented to earn a doctorate at a later date.

Postgraduate studies are financed out of the research funds – both state and private – of the faculty concerned. The faculty board may decide to spend funds on posts for postgraduate studies or on fellowships, both of which usually run for four years. Fellowships may be divided between two students.

It is common for postgraduate students to finance their studies through teaching or other types of work, such as jobs on research projects funded by one of the national research councils or private industry.

Graduate recruitment

There is no recruitment season for graduates in Sweden, as recruitment takes place all year round. All universities and university colleges have advisory services which give career guidance to students, although they are not involved in placement activity.

There are few recruitment fairs, although one, arranged by the Royal Institute of Technology in Stockholm (which has about a third of all engineering students in Sweden), is popular. Larger companies often arrange presentations targeted at certain institutions; student lawyers, economists and civil engineers are most popular.

Speculative applications are common, and it is common practice to follow up such an application with a telephone call. Research conducted by the Labour Market Board in 1996 found that 20 per cent of all those obtaining employment did so by this means. There is a *Kompass* directory giving comprehensive details of Swedish companies.

Vocational education

Originally, basic vocational training in Sweden took place in the form of apprenticeships in the workplace. But for many years now this function has been mainly the task of the upper secondary school, although apprenticeship training outside the education system still exists in a limited number of occupations.

As noted above, the majority of 'lines' in upper secondary school, both before and after the 1991 reforms, are vocational in nature. The reduction in the number of lines and the increase in the general educational element in the new upper secondary school are an attempt to address perceived weaknesses in the vocational training system, the main one being over-specialisation in the face of an ever-changing labour market.

Matching the rapidly evolving demands of the labour market has led to a shift in emphasis in the basic vocational training system. Since it is increasingly difficult to equip students with all of the professional skills they will need during a lifetime, more weight is being given to 'learning how to learn', with the teaching of specialised skills being left to workplace training.

Thus the actual structure of vocational training varies very little from more academically-oriented study courses. The main difference is that the 13 vocational programmes require 15 per cent of teaching time to be spent at a workplace outside school; this concept is called workplace-based training (*arbetsplatsförlagd utbildning*, APU). Exactly which parts of teaching take place in the workplace is a matter for individual schools. The provision of sufficient places in companies is also the responsibility of individual schools.

There are local bodies, called SSA councils, composed of representatives from employers and unions, that foster co-operation between schools and companies. Although the establishment of such bodies is no longer mandatory, about a third of local councils have one. Over half of local authorities also have other forms of councils which advise schools and companies on, for example, the planning of training and purchase of equipment, and also co-ordinate seminars and informal networks. They often also discuss and plan training for workplace student supervisors.

There is also the opportunity for those taking the non-vocationally-oriented programmes to take part in subject-related work experience. Again, this is decided by and arranged by individual schools during the time allotted for local options.

Company schools A recent development is the establishment of either specially designed programmes or independent upper secondary schools by Swedish companies. There is, for instance, a combination of courses from the car engineering, industry and natural sciences programmes – together with a three-year apprenticeship – offered in the town of Skövde in central Sweden by Volvo in co-operation with a university college and an upper high school. There are similar initiatives by other large companies such as SAAB and SKF; ABB has opened its own *gymnasium* in Västerås, north-west of Stockholm. They are an attempt to encourage students into industry and also to ensure that companies' skill requirements are met.

The number of pupils applying for the industrial vocational study programme has tailed off in recent years – applicants were down from 6,000 in 1987 to 2,000 in 1994. The number of female applicants has dropped even more dramatically – from 900 to 125 over the same period.

Adult education

Folk high schools and study circles About 50 per cent of the adult population of Sweden takes part in some form of adult education, although this is by no means always vocationally-oriented.

The folk high schools (*folkhögskolor*), a mainly residential and specifically Scandinavian form of adult education, were originally founded in the mid-19th century, and offer courses ranging from two days to 80 weeks in length. They are run as non-profit-making organisations, with each school determining its own curriculum. Subjects and levels of study vary widely, although some courses can qualify students for further education. It is reckoned that about 230,000 students enrol annually.

Study circles (*studiecirkler*) attract about 2.8 million people a year. These are organised by 11 voluntary educational organisations, the largest being ABF (*Arbetarnas Bildningsförbund*), the Workers' Educational Association. Classes are 40 per cent state-financed, with the balance coming from fees and local authority grants. Although the subjects studied are mainly in the arts, extra grants have been available for classes in Swedish and mathematics.

Formal adult education

Formal adult education (*kommunal vuxenutbildning* or *komvux*) is offered as a right by local authorities, under legislation introduced in 1992, to all those aged over 20 years who wish to undertake it. There are no formal entrance requirements. Courses are offered at basic and upper secondary school levels (including vocational programmes), and there are also other supplementary courses. The latter are meant to lead to a new profession or a higher level in the existing profession, and are therefore designed to meet needs which do not exist in youth education.

All courses and leaving certificates are comparable with those in the youth education system. Courses are organised, and certificates awarded, on a modular basis. This means that the student has a great deal of choice in subject combination, evening or daytime, and full- or part-time study, and it is thus relatively easy to combine study with employment, although the traditional part-time evening classes still prevail.

Courses cover a wide range, from short vocational to post-secondary academic and advanced vocational. Many students use this type of education as a means of improving their professional qualifications.

About 160,000 people per week attend formal adult education courses, two-thirds of them women. Just under half are taking basic-level courses, 30 per cent are taking general subjects at upper secondary level and 25 per cent are engaged in vocational training.

For those unable to attend local authority courses due to shiftwork or distance there are two state-run schools offering the same kind of educational opportunities through intensive short courses and distance learning.

A recent government initiative aims to create an extra 100,000 places in the adult education system over the next five years. The measure is particularly aimed at the unemployed with low educational skills – a recent study by the Labour Market Board AMS has shown that 40 per cent of the current long-term unemployed (over two years) have only basic schooling. A special one-year education grant, available from July 1997, provides funds equal to unemployment benefit (currently 75 per cent of previous earnings, but set to rise to 80 per cent in 1998) and available to both the employed and unemployed. Employed claimants must be replaced in the workplace by a long-term unemployed person.

Labour market training (*arbetsmarknadsutbildning*)

The provision of various types of vocational training for the unemployed is an important factor in the active labour market policy which has been traditionally pursued in Sweden.

Participants receive free tuition and a training allowance equal to unemployment benefit. The main qualifications for eligibility are that applicants must be at least 20 years old and registered with the public employment service. Participants enter on course as soon as a vacancy is available; there are no terms. Training is more narrowly focused than the general education system – the main areas are manufacturing industry, the care services, and office work.

Training usually takes the form of courses bought in by the 24 county labour boards (*länsarbetsnämnderna*) in conjunction with the 380 job centres (*arbetsförmedlingar*), and lasts on average 25 to 30 weeks. Applications for training are made to local job centres. There are many training providers: AMU, the state labour market training provider, is a major supplier, but training is also bought from local authorities, companies, universities and private training organisations.

The number of people engaged in this type of training has shot up dramatically in the 1990s as a result of the sharp rise in unemployment. At the beginning of the decade about 100,000 were in receipt of labour market training; by 1995 the number of participants had doubled and the annual cost, including training allowances, had reached Skr 12 billion (£1.1 billion).

Company training

Company training expanded rapidly during the 1980s. By 1993, 25 per cent of the labour force was involved in some sort of employer-paid training, an equivalent of 58,000 employees in education all year. While about 40 per cent received one or two days' training, 30 per cent received three to five days' and another 30 per cent over five days.

Such education is very unevenly distributed within the labour force. Roughly speaking, the proportion of employees receiving training and the extent of the courses are in proportion to existing levels of education and salary, with highly- paid, highly-educated workers receiving more. Public-sector employees are more often involved than those in the private sector, and part-timers less than full-timers. There are also differences according to company size – most education is provided by large concerns in expanding industries – and sector; finance, insurance and other services provide twice as much training as construction, for instance, and the level of provision is generally higher in services than in manufacturing.

Advances in manufacturing technology have meant that, especially in large companies, there is a need for an increased knowledge of IT among shop-floor workers. Several companies have therefore started initiatives to provide portable PCs which employees may use at home for educational purposes, as well as paying for tuition. The tax position on such arrangements is unclear at present.

A possible way around such difficulties is being tried at ball-bearing manufacturers SKF in Gothenburg, where unions have obtained bulk discounts by purchasing about 1,000 PCs and associated software on behalf of their members. The company is paying six days' wages for training purposes, although training is taking place in non-working time. The company has also offered three-year loans to employees purchasing PCs. Initiatives on providing PCs for educational purposes are being considered at ABB, Volvo, the State Post Office and several other companies.

Educational attainment of the population

Level	Percentage of 25–64 age-group
Lower secondary	28
Upper secondary	46
Higher education (non-university)	14
University	12

Source: OECD (1994)

Organisations

Landsorganisationen i Sverige (LO)
(Swedish Confederation of Trade
Unions – blue-collar)
Barnhusgatan 18
S-105 53 Stockholm
Tel. +46 8 796 25 00
Fax +46 8 20 03 58

Tjänstemännens Centralorganisation
(TCO)
(Central Organisation of Salaried
Employees)
Linnégatan 14
S-114 94 Stockholm
Tel. +46 8 782 91 00
Fax +46 8 663 75 20

Sveriges Akademikers Centralorganisation
(SACO)
(Confederation of Professional
Employees)
Lilla Nygatan 14
S 103 15 Stockholm
Tel. +46 8 613 48 00
Fax +46 8 24 77 01

Svenska Arbetsgivarföreningen (SAF)
(Swedish Employers' Federation)
Södra Blasieholmshamnen 4A
S-103 30 Stockholm
Tel. +46 8 762 60 00
Fax +46 8 762 62 90

Arbetsmarknadsdepartementet
(Ministry of Labour)
Drottninggatan 21
S-103 33 Stockholm
Tel. +46 8 763 10 00
Fax +46 8 20 73 69

Dagens Nyheter
Rålambshovsvägen 17
S-105 15 Stockholm
Tel. +46 8 738 1000
Fax +46 8 719 0811

Main sources

CEDEFOP. *Coherence between compulsory education, initial and continuing training and adult education in Sweden.* CEDEFOP, Berlin, 1995.

THE SWEDISH INSTITUTE. *Fact Sheets on Sweden: Primary and secondary education, Upper and secondary education in Sweden, Higher education in Sweden.* The Swedish Institute, Stockholm, 1994/5

ARBETSMÄRKNADSSTYRELSEN. *Arbetsförmedlingens service och arbetssökandeprocessen.* AMS, Stockholm, 1996

ARBETSMARKNADSSTYRELSEN. *Personaluthyrning och icke-offentlig arbetsförmedling.* AMS, Stockholm, 1996

13

Switzerland

Recruitment in Switzerland is largely free of statutory constraints, with a pronounced role for private employment agencies – which account for three-quarters of all hirings effected through placement services. Although Swiss salaries and living costs are the highest in Europe, this is offset by high productivity levels, a long working week, and an effective infrastructure and business culture.

The system of vocational training closely matches that of its neighbours, with the German-speaking cantons characterised by a strong role for workplace-based training, and French-speaking Switzerland tending to pursue initial vocational training through the education system.

The labour market

Overall labour participation, at 74 per cent, is about the European average, and more closely in line with the North European norm. However, this average is achieved by a combination of the highest male participation rate in the OECD – 92 per cent – and a fairly low female participation rate of 57 per cent.

The increase in registered unemployment has been one of the most dramatic changes in recent years. The rate of unemployment rose from 2.5 per cent in 1992 to 4.7 per cent in 1994, and eased back slightly to 4.6 per cent in mid-1996: the level of unemployment for foreign workers, at just over 9 per cent, is nearly three times the rate for Swiss nationals. Although still fairly modest in European comparison, these figures represent a historic shift compared with the levels of below 1 per cent seen as late as 1990. The higher figures reflect the growing population of residential foreign workers, who make up some 16 per cent of the workforce, and who are no longer exported or exportable during downturns. Compared with the 1970s and 1980s, the unemployed are also registering themselves more rapidly and in greater numbers, and are being dismissed more readily by companies during downturns. Companies have been moved to abandon traditional job security policies, but have tended to replace them not by a hire-and-fire culture but through enhancing their workforce's employability: Switzerland is reported to have one of the highest incidences of outplacement provision by companies.

One major outcome of this change has been efforts to reform the public employment service, with greater stringency in the handling of claimants and concentration on returning people to work – with the range of 'acceptable' job offers widened for claimants, and a reorganisation of public placement services to offer more expertise to claimants and be more responsive to the needs of employers.

Rising unemployment and populist fears about the labour market being over-whelmed by foreigners has meant that the labour market occupies a crucial role in domestic economic and fiscal policy and, via negotiations with the EU on various areas of co-operation, with foreign policy.

Recruitment

Work permits

The Swiss government generally practises a restrictive immigration policy: one important factor behind the rejection of membership of the European Union was the fear that the Swiss labour market might be 'swamped' with EU nationals using the right of free movement to take up employment in Switzerland. Ironically, given this stance, Switzerland has the highest proportion of foreign residents – nearly a fifth – of any European country: the vast bulk of these are, or were, migrant workers on short-term contracts in seasonal industries or low-paying jobs, many of whom were subsequently able to move on to higher-category residence permits to live there permanently.

Because Switzerland is not a member of the European Union, there is no right of free movement for EU citizens. However, entry into the country does not require a visa for citizens of most European countries. Individuals who want to work in Switzerland need a residence permit (*Aufenthaltsbewilligung*), which also serves as a work permit and entitles the holder to live in a particular canton and carry out the allowed job for a specified employer. The prospective employer must make the application, and be able to demonstrate why the position cannot be filled by a Swiss national. On arrival in Switzerland, individuals must register with the Aliens Police and undergo a medical examination.

Apart from seasonal work, there are two other types of residence permit. A 'B' permit covers a specific job, is usually valid for one year, and is renewable. A 'C' permit confers the right to work in any occupation (except law and medicine) and is permanent: it can be applied for only by people who have already held a 'B' permit for five to ten years, depending on nationality.

Official notification   There is no obligation to register vacancies with the public employment service. However, the authorities must be notified in advance of any collective redundancies, and informed about ordinary economic dismissals (see Volume 1 in this series, *Contracts and Terms and Conditions of Employment*).

Using part-timers and temps

Part-time work

About 14 to 15 per cent of the Swiss workforce are part-timers, with a gentle but steady increase in part-time work since the early 1970s, following a rapid expansion during the 1960s. Some 80 per cent of part-timers are women.

Part-time contracts are subject to the Code of Obligations, with no specification as to a minimum number of hours to be worked, provided the employment is 'regular'. Moreover, there is also a basic presumption that employees must be treated equally, in the absence of a material reason which would warrant differential treatment. In theory this entitles part-time workers to sick pay, and pro rata pay, holidays, and other benefits.

Collective agreements may make some supplementary provisions. For example, the agreement in the engineering industry excludes part-timers who work fewer than 12 hours a week from all the provisions of the agreement except those detailing terms and conditions of employment: that is, they are not covered by provisions on employee participation and training. In the chocolate industry, the terms of the collective agreement apply only to employees who work for at least 20 hours a week.

'Work on call' is generally regarded as a sub-species of part-time work. The main area of application has been in the retail sector.

Fixed-term contracts

A fixed-term contract may be concluded when both the start and finishing point of the contract are clearly identifiable in advance. This does not necessarily mean that a finishing date has to be agreed: a contract may be agreed for a particular task, provided the time of completion can be estimated during the work in question. In contrast, a contract to deputise for a sick employee until they recover would not meet these criteria, and could be deemed to be open-ended.

Successive fixed-term contracts (known as *Kettenverträge*), intended to restrict the statutory rights of an employee, could, if contested, be held to constitute a permanent contract.

Agency employment

Temporary employment agencies, as with all forms of private placement, are regulated by the 1989 Federal Law on Placement and Employee Hiring (*Arbeitsvermittlungsgesetz*). Much of the pressure for this legislation, which replaced previous statutes, stemmed from a desire to regulate the practice of agency employment, as well as to embrace other recent forms of placement such as executive search.

There are about 750 organisations registered to carry out temporary employment agency activity, of which three-quarters also undertake permanent placement; of this total, some 400 are estimated to be currently operational. Less than 1 per cent of the workforce is engaged in temporary work.

There is a trade organisation, SVUTA (see *Organisations*) which represents both temporary and permanent employment agencies. Its member firms account for 60 to 70 per cent of the total turnover in both spheres, and include the larger service providers. Members are subject to a code of conduct and are also subject to the collective agreement applying to temporary workers concluded between SVUTA and the Swiss Confederation of Salaried Employees (SKV). This agreement does not cover the issue of payment, but does regulate notice periods, overtime supplements, holiday payments, and time-off arrangements.

Organisations engaged in providing temporary employees must register with their cantonal authority, and fulfil criteria of acceptability such as being incorporated in Switzerland, possessing appropriate premises and not being engaged in any other business which might prejudice the interests of either temporary employees or client companies. Those responsible for the management of such organisations must be Swiss – or enjoy permanent residence – guarantee their ability to provide a high-quality service, and be of good reputation. Agencies may provide temporary workers for use outside of Switzerland only if they can demonstrate adequate knowledge of the circumstances in countries in which the activity is to be performed. Agencies must leave a precautionary deposit with the authorities to secure payment of wages of employees; the level depends on the size of the individual company. As with agencies for permanent employment, all registered temporary agencies are listed in an official register produced by the Federal Labour Ministry.

The temporary employment agency remains the employer of the temporary worker, and concludes a contract of employment with him or her – as specified below. The contract with the client company is a commercial arrangement, albeit of a unique kind, and is subject to statutory control – also specified below. The law distinguishes two types of temporary employment: *Leiharbeit* and *Temporärarbeit*. Under *Leiharbeit* – sometimes translated as 'worker leasing' – the employee has a permanent contract with the agency, and is 'lent out' to other employers to work on their premises: as under German law, this system had its origins in mutual help between nearby companies working in the same field, operating out of solidarity rather than for commercial gain as employment intermediaries. Under *Temporärarbeit* there is no permanent contract between the agency and the temporary employee: rather, and typically, the agency concludes a 'framework agreement' (*Rahmenvertrag*) with the employee which regulates the broad terms of the arrangement between the two: once the agency has an assignment for the employee, they conclude an 'assignment contract' (*Einsatzvertrag*) which is a specific contract of employment detailing the terms and conditions for that particular task.

In practice, there is no real difference between *Temporärarbeit* and *Leiharbeit*;

the overwhelming majority of assignments are organised as *Temporärarbeit* – that is, the agency rarely employs the temporary employee on an enduring basis.

All contracts between the agency and employee must be in writing and set out all the details of the employment, including the duration of the engagement and any notice periods, pay and hours, and other salient terms and conditions. If the contract is deficient as regards either its form or content, then a temporary employee is entitled to the locally customary terms and conditions.

The contract with the client company must also be in writing and specify the period for which the engagement will continue, the vocational qualification of the employee, the employee's working hours, and the cost of the engagement to the client, including all social benefits, supplements, expenses and fringe benefits. Any contract that prevents the client company from taking on the employee when the period of temporary engagement is complete, is null and void.

However, an agreement may be concluded which provides for the client company to pay the agency a sum in compensation if the period of engagement has lasted for less than three months and the employee is hired permanently by the client within three months of the engagement's ending: however, the sum may not be greater than the amount which the client would have paid to the agency for administrative costs plus profit during a three-month engagement. Such agreements are quite common. Many agencies also offer 'Try and Hire' with an extended probationary period and a fee arrangement similar to the compensation paid above.

If the engagement is for an unspecified term, it may be terminated by either side giving a minimum of two days' notice in the first three months, and seven days' notice during the first six months.

If the client company is covered by a collective agreement that has been declared generally binding in its industry, then the stipulated terms must be provided.

Anti-discrimination provisions

Sex equality

Federal legislation providing for equal opportunites for men and women (*Bundesgesetz über die Gleichstellung von Frau und Mann*) was passed in 1995, and came into force on 1 July 1996. As yet, therefore, there is no experience of working within such a statutory framework in Switzerland, and many of the issues are new for public officials, employees and employers.

The law prohibits discrimination, both direct and indirect, on grounds of sex, including civil status, family situation or pregnancy. It applies to appointments, allocation of duties, terms and conditions of employment, training, promotion and dismissal. Measures to achieve actual equality will not be regarded as discriminatory.

The law entitles anyone suffering discrimination to apply to the courts or public authorities for an order to prohibit any threatened discrimination, to remove any actual discrimination, to identify any act of discrimination, and to pay any wages owed as a result of discrimination.

It also expressly states that sexual harassment – which includes threats, offering advantages, pressure in order to obtain sexual favours – will be regarded as a form of sexual discrimination. Compensation may be payable if the employer does not take those steps deemed to be necessary to prevent such harassment: such compensation will be based on 'average pay in Switzerland', but may not exceed six months' pay.

In the event of discrimination manifested through a rejection of a candidate for a job (or a discriminatory dismissal), the affected person is entitled only to compensation – not to reinstatement or appointment. The sum, to quote the Act, is to be 'calculated on the basis of the prospective or actual remuneration, in the light of all the circumstances'; however, the sum may not exceed three months' salary in the post (six months' in the case of discriminatory dismissal). This total also applies in the event of a group action on discrimination. A complaint must be made within three months of receipt of a letter of rejection from an employer. Anyone claiming that they have not been appointed on grounds of their sex has the right to demand a written justification from the employer.

There are provisions under the statute for voluntary conciliation procedures, operated at no charge to the parties involved, at canton level to achieve a resolution of differences. The law allows organisations to pursue cases to establish the fact of discrimination, if they have been established to promote sexual equality and have existed for at least two years.

The Act constitutes the existing federal equal-opportunities bureau (*Das Eidgenössiche Büro für die Gleichstellung von Frau und Mann*) as an independent body. Its duties will be to undertake public information activities, advise the authorities and private individuals, carry out investigations and make recommendations, and participate in the formulation of policy and monitor measures to promote equal opportunities.

Finding the applicant

According to a 1995 survey of recruitment approaches (Robert Zaugg, *Personalbeschaffung und -auswahl in schweizerischen Unternehmungen*, Bern, 1996), the following methods were most commonly used for external recruitment activities covering all types of employee.

Method	Frequency (%)
Print-media advertisement	99
Assessment of speculative applications	89
Recruitment via existing employees	77
Contact with schools	75
Temporary work agencies	73

Recruitment consultants	71
Informal contacts	69
Recruitment agencies	67
Official placement service	61
Direct approach	56
Trainee programme	35
Hoarding advertisement	15
Electronic media	9

Methods varied depending on the type of employee involved. For example, advertisements remained the predominant form for managers (86 per cent), but recruitment consultants were the second most-favoured method (66 per cent), followed by informal contacts (57 per cent). There were some sectoral differences in preferred methods: industrial companies tend to use a much broader range of approaches than service or public sector organisations – in part a consequence of their need to take more assertive steps to overcome a perceived image problem.

Filling vacancies by internal recruitment is dominated by informal mechanisms such as direct approach to potential applicants (85 per cent) and personnel development (83 per cent), combined with informal contacts. Formal internal advertising of positions was cited in 70 per cent of cases. Internal job fairs (*Personalbörse*) also play a role in larger companies, especially in banking and finance.

Unemployment has remained comparatively low, especially for Swiss nationals (see above), and companies still regard active policies to recruit skilled staff as an important component of personnel work.

Most companies do not undertake systematic labour market research – only 17 per cent of respondents did so – but some 80 per cent practise manpower planning. Some 40 per cent of companies carry out an analysis of competitors in their field, and 37 per cent conduct image research.

Placement services

In contrast to most other Western European countries', the Swiss labour market has long been characterised by the predominance of private sector placement over the public service: both have co-existed on a non-competitive basis, with complementary rather than overlapping areas of the market, and there is none of the controversy, and sometimes rancour, that has marked out public/private sector relationships elsewhere. Switzerland has never ratified ILO Convention 96 (1949) which called for the phasing-out of for-profit placement agencies. The governing legislation requires co-operation between public and private services, and private agencies can use the official service's databank and network to make placements.

About half of all new hirings are effected through either the public or private placement systems. Private agencies accounted for about four times as many long-term placements as the public service. While the private sector is overwhelmingly involved with people already in employment, the public service has been predominantly concerned with placing the unemployed. The private sector's share of placements grew during the 1980s. The 1990s, and the more difficult economic climate, led to a substantial fall in placements, and pressure on agencies – manifested mostly clearly in much tighter margins and some reorganisation of the sector.

In 1995 there was a total of 2,047 organisations registered to conduct placement, of which 995 were employment agencies only (including executive search), 207 temporary work agencies only, with 540 companies combining both activities. Three hundred companies were engaged in placing models, musicians and performing artistes. (An official listing produced by the Ministry of Labour (BIGA) details all these companies, together with contact addresses and areas of specialism.)

The effect of the economic slackening since the early 1990s has mainly been to lead more companies previously undertaking only permanent placement to add temporary work to their portfolios; the number of agencies carrying out both activities grew from 288 in 1992 to 547 by 1995.

Private and public placement services are regulated by the 1989 Federal Law on Placement and Employee Hiring (*Arbeitsvermittlungsgesetz*) which came into force in 1991. This regulates the various forms of 'brokerage' offered by companies, including executive search and selection, employment agencies, and agencies providing temporary employees. In addition to commercial activities, the law also regulates placement services provided by occupational associations.

The public employment service

As noted above, the public employment service has tended to play a role subordinate to private placement services – at least as far as filling vacancies with people already in employment is concerned.

The public employment service is in the throes of a substantial organisational reform under legislation which came into force on 1 January 1996, following a study of the service by consultants Arthur Andersen and the operation of a number of pilot projects since 1994. The reforms – which were prompted by the difficulties experienced by the service in meeting its responsibilities in the face of rapidly rising unemployment – are centred on the reorganisation of placement services on a regional basis, supplanting some of the services previously provided at communal level, and more stringent conditions on the unemployed. The service, which had been overwhelmed by the increase in unemployment, was obliged to concentrate on paying out unemployment benefits and, as a consequence, was unable to offer effective advice to job seekers or to develop relationships with employers. The new Regional Placement Centres (*Regionale Arbeitsvermittlungszentren*, RAV) will be oriented towards a more active placement role, with counsellors for the unemployed (at a ratio of roughly 1:140) entitled to cold-call on employers in the search for vacancies, combined with a better service for firms looking for staff. If successful, the changes could shift the balance between public and private placement activities. The addresses of the Regional Placement Centres can be obtained from cantonal labour offices, via the local authority, or on Swiss Teletext (pp. 670ff).

Employment incentives   People who fall into the category of the hard-to-place unemployed can be granted job insertion allowances (*Einarbeitungszuschüsse*), paid via the employer, during their induction period, should an employer take them on a permanent contract at a rate of pay which is lower than that usually offered to experienced employees in the field. The allowance bridges the gap between the starter rate and the usual pay for the job. The allowance, worth up to 40 per cent of usual overall salary, is payable for a maximum of 12 months, but more usually six months – and is tapered off by a third after each third of the overall expected induction period is completed.

Employment agencies

Employment agencies undertaking permanent placement are, as noted above, not only permitted but account for the bulk of long-term placements, especially of employees moving from one post to another.

All organisations engaged in placement, either permanent or temporary, must register with the cantonal employment authorities to obtain a licence to operate. The concept of 'placement' is wider than in Germany, for example, and embraces all activities regularly carried out by an organisation that are intended to bring together employers and job seekers with the aim of establishing an employment relationship. Thus, it would generally include 'personnel consultancy' (*Personalberatung*), especially where this is simply a synonym for executive search – although the legal position is not wholly unambiguous. For example, the targets of headhunters are not usually, or initially, job seekers in the narrow sense. A broader consultancy role, or one in which there was some form of contingency fee, might be more borderline. In practice, all the leading executive search companies are registered with the Ministry – but none of the major management consultants.

The law sets criteria which those employed in labour market 'brokerage' must meet – such as local business registration, and possession of appropriate offices – and sets licence fees for the agencies. There is no obligation to leave a precautionary deposit with the authorities for companies engaged in permanent placement. Owners and/or managers must be Swiss nationals or enjoy full right of establishment in Switzerland. Managers must also be able to demonstrate relevant skills in the field; to this end SVUTA, the trade association for the industry, has established a vocational qualification for 'personnel consultancy' which has been developed in conjunction with the relevant public authorities.

There are also statutory provisions and limits on fees chargeable to work seekers: an agency may not charge someone seeking employment more than SFr 30.00 (£15) to register, and 5 per cent of the prospective annual salary once placed, or of the total prospective remuneration if the employment contract is for less than a year. In practice, the registration fee is only rarely charged.

There are no statutory limits on what agencies may charge employers. Fees are usually success-based and in the range of 8 to 16 per cent of annual salary for non-executive appointments.

In practice, many employment agencies and executive search consultants offer a variety of guarantees, including partial repayment of any fees charged to either party if the employee resigns shortly after starting employment, or if the employer feels compelled to dismiss them on grounds of lack of suitability.

Any contract to undertake a placement on behalf on an employee must be in writing, and may not endow the placement agency with the sole right to undertake the placement. The law also forbids placement agencies to practise 'misleading propaganda for emigration'.

Executive recruitment consultants

Executive search is well established in Switzerland, exemplified in the fact that Egon Zehnder, the founder of the largest executive search company in Europe, established his operations in Zurich in 1964. Egon Zehnder remains the largest executive search consultancy in Europe as well as in Switzerland. However, the market is not as strongly developed as in the USA or the UK. In common with other continental European countries, Switzerland has a strong culture of internal promotion. One large bank reported that it has not had recourse to an executive search company to fill a top position for over 20 years. However, the high proportion of highly internationalised companies headquartered in Switerland has provided an opening to wider cultures of employment, including recruitment and promotion. The response of managers to search consultants may turn on their own degree of international experience.

There are thought to be about 40 search consultancies, with a further 200 engaged in various forms of selection, ranging from middle managers to secretarial positions.

Executive search companies are covered by the provisions of the Job Placement Act and must obtain permission from the Ministry of Labour to operate: however, the requirements are not seen as onerous. Most executive search consultants are self-regulating, following typical established international codes of conduct, and tend not to join the trade body for employment agencies, although some may be members.

While some consultants confine themselves exclusively to executive search, a number are also engaged in search and selection (or may have subsidiaries to handle specialised parts of the business). Search and selection might be combined for middle management positions. However, local practitioners noted that the response to advertised vacancies was often not encouraging, and that 'good people don't respond to ads'.

There are cultural differences in the area of executive recruitment between German-speaking Switzerland and the Swiss Romande. It can be difficult to persuade French-speaking managers to move to the German cantons, although movement in the other direction is more common.

Fees for executive search are usually of the order of 20 to 30 per cent of salary, agreed in advance as a fixed fee, which may reflect other aspects of the assignment, and paid in tranches plus expenses. Some consultants also mix fixed and percentage fees. Guarantees are customary. For a selection exercise there is usually a fixed fee plus 12 to 20 per cent of the annual salary associated with the position.

The main selection methods are set out separately below. Graphology is still used extensively for managerial recruitment, and is acceptable for board-level appointments – although it may not necessarily be held in high regard by candidates as a reliable or welcome procedure; in general, graphology is used more for higher-level appointments than for other employees. Search companies tend to use those methods which their clients believe in, even when sceptical about their predictive value themselves.

Assessment centres are well established and used for recruitment, including graduates, and especially for internal development (see below). Group discussion is also more common among managers than for other grades, principally as a result of the increasing value placed on communication competencies.

Professional placement associations

Some professional associations offer placement services to their members: these include the Association of Swiss Commercial Employees (*Schweizerischer Kaufmännischer Verein*, SKV), a placement service for engineers and technicians (*Schweizerische Techniker-Vermittlung*) and a service for musicians (*Schweizerische Facharbeiternachweis für Musiker*).

Application documents

Applications for most positions will consist of a CV, school certificates, other qualifications, and the candidate's employment record (*Arbeitszeugnis*). The employment record is a document which an employee can ask the employer to provide, detailing the type and length of their employment, performance and conduct: under Article 330a of the Law of Obligations, the employee can request that the record merely documents the type and length of employment.

An employment record must be true, may include the employer's assessment of the employee, but may not needlessly obstruct the professional advancement of the employee.

Recruitment media

The press

The main vehicle for job advertisements in the German-speaking part of Switzerland is the daily *Neue Zürcher Zeitung*. The *Tages-Anzeiger* also carries job advertisements three times a week, and is an important vehicle for middle managers. The weekly *Cash* carries job advertisements for the financial sector, as does the weekly Zurich-based *Weltwoche*. On a regional basis, the *Berner Anzeiger* might also be considered.

In French-speaking Switzerland, the main newspapers for job advertisements are *Journal de Genève* and *Tribune de Genève*.

Local papers often carry advertisements for middle managers and specialists. There are a number of free papers which include advertisements for less skilled positions.

There are few trade journals, but this is not an important medium.

Salaries are never quoted in job advertisements, although age limits (upper and lower) are customarily cited. There is a reported swing away from employing young people in senior positions – in part because older managers are now more willing to accept lower salary packages.

It is permitted to use a code number (*Chiffre*) in advertisments, but this is not generally regarded as good practice unless there is a very strong reason for retaining the employer's anonymity.

There is a statutory prohibition on employment agencies' placing fictional advertisements (for example, to collect names or salary indicators), and on anonymous advertisements.

The Internet

A consortium of private employment agencies runs a Web page called the *Schweizer Stellenmarkt* (Swiss Jobs Directory) (http://job.inserat.ch) which takes notices from job seekers and companies free of charge. The site also contains links to the vacancies of the main employment agencies via SwissWebJobs (http://www.swisswebjobs.ch) and other job-related pages, both in Switzerland and elsewhere in Europe.

Selection procedures

Employer's right to ask

There are no statutory provisions regulating the employer's right to ask during an application procedure. However, there is a legal presumption that there are limits on the prospective employer's curiosity covering issues such as religious beliefs, party political affiliation, leisure activities, friendships, and previous criminal convictions unrelated to the nature of the job. Conversely, there is an obligation on the employee to disclose all matters relevant to their ability to carry out the required task, including the state of their health. In practice, employers have been accustomed to ask questions about personal and family life which would, at least formally, be problematic elsewhere in Europe. Any limits which are respected are often set aside in the case of senior management appointments.

This may change to some degree with the new law on equal opportunities (see above) which prohibits discrimination on grounds of sex, family status or pregnancy, and which entitles candidates who are not appointed to a written justification from the employer if they suspect that the failure to appoint them was directly or indirectly discriminatory. The employer may ask a candidate whether she is pregnant, and she must give an honest answer: however, there is no obligation on her to volunteer the information unless it is directly related to her ability to work during pregnancy.

Survey of selection methods

According to a survey of the selection methods and procedures of some 800 organisations carried out in 1995 (Robert Zaugg, *op cit*), personnel departments still play the dominant role in shaping the recruitment and selection process, except for very senior appointments or where highly-specialised knowledge was involved. Personnel departments, for example, were responsible for labour market analysis, shaping the basic search and recruitment approaches, choice of advertising media, conducting pre-selection, and organising references and candidate testing. Line management's task was to assess demand for new employees, carry out induction of new staff, and assess employees after completion of the probationary period (see IDS/IPD, *Contracts and Terms and Conditions of Employment*, pp. 359ff). Both personnel and line managements jointly elaborated the job profile, conducted interviews and made the final decision.

The main selection methods found in the study were as follows: the overwhelming number of organisations (99 per cent) analysed the candidate's CV, formal employment record (*Arbeitszeugnis*) and, where appropriate, school record (*Schulzeugnis*) and application documents. Structured interviews were used by 85 per cent of respondents, and 68 per cent of organisations took up references. Of all selection methods, the structured interview was best regarded by employers.

One continuing Swiss speciality – which it shares with France – is the use of graphology: this was cited by 68 per cent of companies, and was the single most common formal test used. However, external graphological experts were used in less than half of all cases: in 40 per cent of companies, the personnel department itself carried out the graphological analysis – a matter of some concern in specialist recruitment circles, given the uncertainties surrounding the procedure. Despite its prevalence, graphology is not generally well regarded by candidates, and rated as only averagely effective by employers in aggregate. One large financial services company reported that it used graphology as a supplement to the decision-making process, where a decision on other criteria is not clear cut. A graphologist might be asked to focus on particular aspects of the candidate that are cause for concern or are ambiguous.

However, as a method it aroused the strongest differences of opinion over its validity: there were marked divergences of view between those who actually used the technique and those who did not. Using a handwriting sample for a graphological analysis requires the express permission of the applicant: opinion differs as to whether the candidate's access to an employer's request for a hand-written letter to accompany a CV is sufficient.

Use of graphology varies considerably by linguistic region. Whereas 77 per cent of organisations in the German-speaking cantons used this approach, the proportion was only 41 per cent in the Swiss Romande. In general, there is a slight tendency for it to be used more frequently by larger companies than by small or medium-sized enterprises.

Psychological tests were used by a minority of organisations – albeit a substantial one. The most common were personality tests, used by 42 per cent of companies who responded to the survey, and held to have increased in use over the past decade or so. As with graphology, their use increases somewhat with company size, possibly reflecting the availability of personnel specialists to administer and interpret tests.

Intelligence tests were used less frequently, in only some 25 per cent of companies: of all methods used, these were the least accepted by candidates. Declining credibility of these tests for forecasting performance has led to a fall in their use in recent years. However, there were sectoral variations: about half of all organisations in the transport and food industries made use of intelligence tests, for example.

In all, 43 per cent of organisations set applicants practical work tests, with 32 per cent using aptitude tests. Assessment-centre procedures were found to be fairly widespread in the financial services sector.

The extent to which different selection methods were combined was found to vary substantially. Just over a fifth of companies combined a broad range of methods, including evaluation of application documents, references, interviews, testing and a graphological assessment. A further fifth used all these methods plus an assessment centre. Almost 80 per cent of companies used a combination of at least four methods, typically including testing procedures and graphology.

A core of similar methods (CV, employment record and application documents) was used for all employees, including managers and graduates – where, for example, school reports were considered by 60 per cent of organisations. Differences appeared in the use of the range of supplementary methods: graphology and personality tests were used more frequently in the case of higher-skilled and managerial appointments, with much less emphasis at this level on intelligence tests and practical tests.

About two-thirds of companies undertake a subsequent audit of any given recruitment exercise, of which 90 per cent interview new employees towards the end of their probationary period.

Medical examinations

Medical examinations were required by about one-third of companies in the 1995 survey cited above. They are also compulsory for foreigners entering Switzerland to take up employment.

Data protection

Data protection, in the case of employment agencies, is regulated by the 1989 Law on Placement. Information on job seekers and vacancies which serves to identify the individuals or companies concerned may be processed and communicated to other parties outside the agency itself only with the permission of those involved. Information collected by an agency must be of a type needed for them to carry out their activity.

Once an assignment is completed, a placement organisation may not further process or store information without the express permission of the individual concerned.

Appointment of employees

Appointment procedures may be regulated by collective agreement, which also gives some indication of custom and practice in the field. Typically, this includes a requirement that the contract of employment must be in writing. In the banking industry, the collective agreement requires the employer to give new employees a copy of the industry agreement, together with the company rule book and notes (*Reglement*) which form an integral part of the contract of employment.

Rejection of candidates

There is no specific form for the rejection of unsuccessful candidates. However, measures incorporated in the new Act on equal opportunities, which entitle rejected applicants to ask for a written justification of the employer's decision, could alter practice in this area.

Unsuccessful applicants are entitled to have all their application documents returned to them, and to insist that the results of any tests or medical examinations are destroyed. Under data protection legislation, candidates also have a right to inspect such reports.

Education system

One study on education in Switzerland noted that, rather than speaking of the 'Swiss system of education', it would be more appropriate to refer to 'the education system in Switzerland'. Education, with some exceptions at university level, is regulated and administered by the 26 cantons, leading to a diversity of arrangements. Moreover, at canton level different aspects of the education system might be organised by different branches of public administration. However, the cantons co-operate through a Federal-level co-ordinating council as well being subject to some minimum federal requirements. There are also inter-cantonal working groups on specific subject areas.

The Federal government retains competencies in the fields of vocational training and scientific education and research (see below).

Primary and secondary education

Almost all children attend a nursery (*Kindergarten*) or pre-school (*Vorschule*) for one year, and about three-quarters for two years prior to the beginning of compulsory education. Compulsory schooling of nine or ten years then follows, depending on the canton. Primary education generally takes six years, and is usually organised on the same basis in all cantons.

A lower secondary phase of varying duration follows from the age of 11 or 12: this is typically for three years, but may be longer in cantons where primary education is shorter. The organisation of lower secondary education differs by canton, and is selective in most cantons, with the exception of Geneva and the Ticino. Apart from Geneva, there have been no initiatives towards comprehensive education. There are two basic types of lower secondary school: *Realschulen* take the less academically able and normally constitute the route to initial vocational training; *Sekundärschulen* prepare young people for more demanding vocational training or entry to a *Gymnasium*, also termed a '*Maturitätsschule*'. In some cantons, these schools extend backwards and take students of lower secondary age.

There is no specific qualification marking the completion of compulsory education.

In many cases, after completion of an interim year, school students pass into upper secondary education or basic vocational training at the age of 15 or 16. (Initial vocational training under the 'dual system' or in a full-time vocational school is set out below.) Some 70 per cent of school students move into initial vocational training, 15 per cent into a *Gymnasium* which prepares them for the *Matura*, the university entrance certificate which confers university admission, and 5 per cent into other schools (*Diplommittelschulen*) offering either continuing general education – but at a less demanding level than *Gymnasia*, and also including the first stages of teacher training for primary teachers or other education-related professions, such as nursery teachers.

While primary education must be carried out in state schools, in most cases the rest of compulsory schooling is conducted through public institutions. Most general secondary schools – such as *Gymnasia* – are also overwhelmingly in the state sector, although there are some confessional schools run on a private basis.

Five distinct types of *Gymnasium*, each specialising in a different field, are officially recognised: classical and ancient languages, modern languages, modern languages plus Latin, maths and natural science, and economics and commerce. Access is by selection, although the manner in which this is organised can vary from canton to canton. Employers may ask for a *Matura* from a particular type of *Gymnasium* when recruiting people at age 19.

Higher education

Students can enter higher education with a *Matura* – usually without having to meet additional entrance requirements. However, some universities may introduce a requirement for particular marks to be achieved in the *Matura* – the '*numerus clausus*' – in oversubscribed subjects.

There are 10 full university-level institutions. All are organised at canton level, with the exception of the two federal technical universities: the ETH (*Eidgenössische Technische Hochschule*) in Zurich and the EPF (*Ecole polytechnique fédérale*) at Lausanne.

Higher education qualifications   Students must normally study for a minimum of six to eight semesters, or 13 in medicine, before being entitled to take the first academic qualification. In practice, students normally study for longer. There are two recognised main qualifications: the *Doctorat* and the *Lizentiat*, together with a number of specialised diplomas.

In most cases, and in most universities, the first degree is the *Lizentiat*, which requires a dissertation. The federal technical universities confer a diploma in engineering, pharmacy, maths, physics, natural science amd architecture.

Graduate recruitment   Important routes for graduate recruitment are:

- contacts established between companies and academic departments and their professors, possibly involving preparation of case-studies for employers, or work placements for students. Such placements typically last four to six weeks, and students try to organise them after two or three years' study
- recruitment fairs held on campus
- unsolicited applications by university graduates.

Many larger employers also continue to have active 'personnel marketing' strategies to reach graduates, using a variety of media and recruitment forms.

Graduate selection procedures vary considerably: while some firms conduct testing and run assessment centres for graduates, others rely solely on structured interviews.

Traineeships, as offered by larger employers, typically last for one or two years and include a mix of on-the-job and off-the-job training.

University graduates are not prized by all employers – especially smaller firms – because of the difficulties of integrating them into work and giving them meaningful activity at an early stage. Some employers, including one of the largest banks, expressed a preference for graduates from higher vocational schools because of their accumulated work experience as well as more vocationally-tilted academic background.

Because of military service, graduates are normally aged 27+ and can join some trainee schemes up to the age of 30.

Graduates' annual starting salaries in 1996/7 were expected to be in the range SFr 68–79,000 (£34–39,500). Salary is no longer seen as quite the determining factor in a graduate's decision to join a company that it was in the late 1980s and early 1990s.

The graduate recruitment organisation Forum, which publishes recruitment guides, is located in St. Gallen.

Management education

The University of St. Gallen is an important centre for the study of business economics, management and law, and has a unique structure of small specialised semi-autonomous institutes for advanced research. The ETH also offers specific management education.

MBA programmes are offered at two institutions in Switzerland. The University of Lausanne School of Business (*Ecoles des Hautes Etudes Commerciales,* HEC) offers a nine-month course, taught in French, with an associated consultancy project. The HEC also offers other master's degrees in international management, in banking and finance, and in business information systems.

The private International Institute for Management Development (IMD), also located at Lausanne, offers a one-year MBA taught in English – almost exclusively to non-Swiss students. The Institute was established in 1989 by a merger of two former institutions, IMEDE (Lausanne), which was originally set up by Nestlé, and IMI (Geneva), founded by Alcan.

There are also a number of private, corporate and industry-based management training centres. One notable example is GAF (*Gesellschaft für Ausbildung von Führungskräften*), which is jointly run by the national employers' association, the engineering employers' and other industry associations, and the Institute for Business Management at the University of St. Gallen.

Management development features as the most important single means for filling internal vacancies. At present there is a perceived need to turn technical specialists into general business managers through broadening the content of technical education and subsequent learning opportunities.

Initial vocational training system

The predominant form of vocational training is through formal apprenticeship/ traineeship: this can be delivered either through a 'dual system', in which on-the-job training is accompanied by attendance at a vocational school (*Berufschule*), or a 'triad system', in which attendance at a vocational school is supplemented by introductory courses held in off-the-job training centres run by training associations. Such courses have been compulsory since 1980.

Training can also take place in full-time vocational schools (*berufliche Vollzeitschulen*): whereas this option is more common in the French- and Italian-speaking parts of Switzerland, the dual system is most highly developed in the German-speaking cantons – reflecting the training cultures of the contiguous countries.

Training is regulated at Federal level by the 1978 Vocational Training Act (*Berufsbildungsgesetz*). This regulates the Federal government's obligations in the fields of occupational guidance and advice, basic vocational training, further vocational training and research into vocational training.

The practical implementation of training is carried out by co-operation between the Federal Ministry for Industry and Employment (BIGA) and the employer, trade union and professional organisations, to develop training and examination regulations for individual occupations, and the syllabuses for vocational schools. The law is implemented at canton level by canton Offices of Vocational and Technical Education: these are primarily concerned with administering vocational schools (subject to the federal inspectorate), overseeing apprenticehip contracts, and organising final examinations.

Apprenticeships under the dual/triad system

About 75 per cent of young men and 60 per cent of young women proceed to vocational training at age 15 or 16, on completion of nine years of mandatory schooling – relatively early compared with some other systems. Of these, 80 per cent begin an apprenticeship, involving a mixture of on-the-job training with formal theoretical education. Some school students complete an interim year before beginning vocational training. There is also a scheme of elementary vocational training (*Anlehre*) for students with weaker school records: this scheme, established in 1980, offers on-the-job training plus attendance at specially designed courses at vocational schools: it currently covers only about 1 per cent of apprentices. Apprentices train and work under a training contract (*Lehrvertrag*), which is a specific type of employment contract. This is established by the cantonal authorities, which are responsible for the quality of training delivered. Apprentices' pay is not regulated in the contract as such, but may be set by trade associations, by the company, or between the employer and the parents.

Small and medium-sized enterprises are heavily engaged in training, and offer places to about three-quarters of those in the dual/triad system. Large firms –

there are only 73 employing more than 1,000 in Switzerland – do not account for a disproportionally large share of initial training.

Apprenticeships typically last from two to four years. Those entrusted with training on-the-job, the 'vocational tutors' (*Lehrmeister*), must have had at least 40 hours of training on learning techniques, law, and personnel management. Apprentices attend vocational school for one-and-a-half to two days a week.

Especially able apprentices have an opportunity to attend advanced vocational schools (*Berufsmittelschulen*) with a broader and more complex curriculum, creating a basis for participation in more demanding programmes later in the individual's career. These programmes were developed in the late 1960s in an attempt to create a vocational stream able to compete with university entrance. However, the scheme has not yet acquired major significance, although this might change with the restructuring of higher vocational training, for which these schools would offer formal preparation. Apprentices at such schools – some 3 per cent of all apprentices – would normally attend for a half to one day longer per week than in the case of normal apprenticeships. A diploma (*Berufsmaturität*) from an advanced vocational school allows the holder to move into further training at one of the higher vocational schools or specialised vocational colleges (see below).

There are some 300 apprenticeships in all, although a much smaller number account for about 70 per cent of apprentices: these are commerce, banking, and engineering. Health care training at initial, further and continuing levels is delegated to the Swiss Red Cross.

On completion of training and a successful final exam, the apprentice is awarded the 'Federal Certificate of Competence' (*Eidgenössischer Fähigkeitsausweis*), with grades, in their field. They also receive a certificate of employment for their period of on-the-job training.

Full-time vocational schools

Some 20 per cent of those undertaking vocational training attend full-time vocational schools (*école de metiers*), compared with the 80 per cent taking an apprenticeship. As noted above, full-time vocational schooling is much more prevalent in the French- and Italian-speaking cantons. Successful participants receive the same qualification as apprentices.

Trends

There has been a steady decline in participation in the system of initial vocational training since the mid-1980s as increasing numbers of school students have taken the *Matura* in order to pursue tertiary education.

In addition, some organisations take fewer apprentices, and are keener on those extending their education to 18 or 19 but who, for one reason or another, do not go on to tertiary education. In some sectors such individuals may be offered industry-specific on-the-job training, while others move on to take formal apprenticeships: their higher level of general education means that cantons can reduce the length of apprenticeship for such people.

There are skill shortages in the engineering trades, with an overproduction of commercial trainees.

Further and advanced training

Some 40 per cent of the population aged between 20 and 70 participate in some form of continuing education in any one year, of which about half is vocational and half general. Switzerland is also fairly unusual in comparison with other advanced countries in that it has a much higher than average proportion of the population whose highest education level is non-university tertiary education (13 per cent compared with an average 8 per cent) – embracing some of the vocational institutions set out below – and a lower than average proportion with university degrees (8 per cent compared with an average 12 per cent).

Further vocational training is offered through a variety of institutions and courses, including private schools preparing candidates for trade association examinations and schools run by trade associations as well as vocational schools: in fact, there is growing competition between providers because the vocational schools, which traditionally train apprentices, have been begun to offer further training to offset the decline in apprenticeships. A central databank is run by the Federal Office for Industry and Employment. Courses may be financed by the employer, but individuals may also pay for them privately and attend in their own time.

However, all examinations are organised by the relevant trade association – meaning that for every recognised trade, there is a corresponding trade association. The federal authorities vet both examinations and the associations.

Advanced examinations

Advanced trade examinations (*Höhere Fachprüfung*) and Professional Examinations (*Berufsprüfung*) are proposed by trade associations and formally recognised by the Federal government. They include the *Meister* examination, rated as the most advanced of this type. The Professional Examination is a less advanced qualification, and can either be an end in itself or be taken as an admission requirement to pass on to an Advanced Trade Examination. Admission to both levels usually requires a completed apprenticeship together with practical experience.

Higher vocational colleges (*Höhere Fachschulen*), such as engineering colleges and technical colleges, train candidates for the Advanced trade examination (see too below, *Training arrangements in the engineering industry*). Specific examples include Higher Technical Colleges (*Höhere Technische*

Lehranstalt, HTL) and Higher Business and Administration Colleges (*Höhere Wirtschafts- und Verwaltungsschule, HWV*). Full-time courses last two to three years, and part-time courses three or four years, the candidate working in the relevant profession. Qualifications from either can serve as a minimum requirement to join a number of company-specific schemes, and are sometimes accepted as equivalent to a university degree for traineeships. The HTL are the main source of qualified engineers, producing three times as many each year as the two federal technical universities.

Specialised colleges (*Fachhochschulen*)

From 1996/7 some of the higher vocational schools offering three-year programmes will be upgraded to specialised colleges, with a broader curriculum. Initially, around 10 specialised colleges will be created. The main requirement for admission will be a new advanced vocational diploma (*Berufsmaturität*) obtained from one of the advanced vocational schools (see above).

One aim is to broaden the existing curriculum, for example by adding languages. There is also a hope that the new specialised colleges will be able to engage in more research and technology transfer to small and medium-sized companies. Graduates from the specialised schools will also receive a graduate diploma – Dipl. Ing. (FH) – which will qualify them as graduate engineers; such individuals are more likely to be attractive to, and attracted by, small and medium-sized enterprises which are often shy of employing university graduate engineers. These courses would also offer a path into tertiary education for people holding completed apprenticeship qualifications.

Training arrangements in the engineering industry

Training arrangements in the engineering industry offer a useful concrete example of the practice and culture of training and further training. Employers' organisations, and through the industry agreement the trade unions in the industry, play a major role in the organisation and delivery of both basic and further vocational training.

The collective agreement for the industry provides for both individual employee rights (see below under *Agreed training provisions*) and the creation of joint institutions, dealt with here.

The engineering industry agreement commits both sides to support and promote the Swiss system of vocational training, and in particular the retention and upgrading of apprenticeships. About 80 per cent of companies covered by the agreement, and hence about 50 per cent of all firms in the industry, offer apprenticeship training. Both sides also express their support for further training through the creation of joint institutions and the organisation of examinations for various categories of employee, such as skilled foreman, skilled worker and automation specialists. A jointly run structure also exists to train employee representatives.

At the level of basic vocational training, the Association of Swiss Engineering Employers (ASM) is responsible for drawing up training requirements and provisions for apprenticeship schemes with its member-companies, which then go on to the Federal Ministry for Industry and Employment to become the official training regulations (*Reglement*) for these occupations. At present, there are 15 separate apprenticeship schemes in the industry. The ASM wants to reduce the number of schemes to seven 'core occupations' and to extend the content of basic training to include more 'subjective' components, such as learning techniques, creativity and ability to work in teams, as well as craft and technical skills. Although there are pressures to reduce the costs of apprentice training to ensure that firms still offer training places, the ASM is opposed to cutting the length of apprenticeships below the current four years for most engineering trades; it regards this period as key to the proper socialisation of trainees. In fact the ASM is keen for companies to produce an excess supply of engineering apprentices who can then move on to higher vocational colleges (see below) to acquire advanced professional qualifications in engineering disciplines.

Two specific jointly run institutions exist under the terms of the agreement and receive finance from a levy of Sfr 24 per employee, divided equally between the employer and employee. The Working Party for Further Vocational Training (*Arbeitsgemeinschaft für Berufliche Weiterbildung*) is a non-profit-making association charged with the promotion of continuing vocational and professional training. In practical terms, the Working Party establishes training requirements, prepares and organises courses and teaching materials, and provides instructors.

The Swiss Technical School (*Schweizerische Fachschule für Betriebstechnik*), run by the engineering employers and union side in conjunction with the Federal authorities, exists to offer basic and advanced training for specialists in the field of applied business management. Courses provided by the school are open to anyone who meets the admission requirements.

Joint bodies set and organise higher specialised qualifications for various categories of employee, such as industrial technicians, skilled foremen (*Meister*) in mechanical engineering, and automation specialists.

As well as joint initiatives, the Swiss Engineering Employers Federation (*ASM*) also runs its own training centre which offers training for first-line and middle management, training materials for apprentices, and regular seminars. Together with a number of other employers' associations, ASM also operates a centre – GAF – offering short courses for middle and senior management.

Company-based training

Employers may offer company-specific training to people who have completed an apprenticeship or acquired their *Matura* but who do not want to continue into tertiary education.

One example is the Junior Succession Management Scheme (*Junior-Nachwuchsförderung*) run by the Swiss Bank Corporation, SBG. This programme takes young people aged 19–21 with a completed three-year apprenticeship at the bank or an 'All Round Placement': the latter is a two-year programme for school-leavers with matriculation at a trade school or commercial *gymnasium*. The training takes place over three to four years, and is completed when the employee is 24. There are two basic components – both of which are accompanied by practical experience. The 'generalist' phase lasts two to three years and involves acquaintance with basic financial services and customer service, together with a foreign language; trainees are expected to pass through their basic military service (recruitment school and *Beförderungsdienst*) during this period. In a second 'specialisation phase', lasting one to two years, trainees begin to specialise in particular operational/service areas, and possibly add a further language. Trainees have scope to prepare for the Federal higher vocational examination in banking in courses held at independent training institutions, although trainees must contribute to some of their own costs.

Agreed training provisions

Some aspects of training are regulated by collective agreement in a number of industries. Issues affecting individual employee rights include:

- *Levies*: in the engineering industry, the sum of Sfr 24 (£10.35) per year is levied 50/50 on employers and employees and paid into a fund to finance further training; the money can be used for running joint training establishments, providing training materials, and paying for the administration of examinations.
- *Provision of facilities*: the engineering agreement contains a recommendation that employers should promote further training through careers advice, training programmes and access to external providers, and part or entire covering of costs.
- *Time off*: employees in the engineering industry have a right to paid time off to attend further training where this will improve the individual performance and capabilities of the employee, where the employee is prepared to make their own contribution (in time or money), and where the training is of benefit to the employer. If training takes place wholly outside of working hours, employees may apply to have any costs covered. Time off for training should be discussed once annually between the employer and employee representatives.
- *Equal opportunities*: agreements, as in engineering, may contain recommendations on equal access to training, promotion, and re-integration into existing or new professions following career interruptions.

Agreed provisions can also be expanded and regulated in company rulebooks, which in larger firms will typically give employee representatives a right to information and consultation on training and further training measures at the company.

Financing

Vocational schools are financed almost wholly by the public purse – with costs divided between the Federal government, the cantons, and local authorities, the bulk coming from the cantons. Some costs are borne by professional associations. Public money is also available to defray some of the costs of the training centres run by trade associations. In the canton of Geneva there is a levy system on employers which raises funds to cover the costs of centres for the delivery of initial and continuing training. All on-the-job is training is wholly paid for by the employer.

Private trade schools offering tuition in recognised courses are financed by students themselves.

Educational attainment of the population

Level	Percentage of 25–64 age-group
Lower secondary	18
Upper secondary	61
Higher education (non-university)	13
University	7

Source: OECD (1994)

Organisations

Federal Ministry of Industry and Labour
(Bundesamt für Industrie, Gewerbe und
Arbeit, BIGA)
Gurtengasse 3
3003 Bern
Tel. + 41 31 322 2948
Fax + 41 31 322 7831

Federal Social Insurance Department
(Bundesamt für Sozialversicherung)
Effingerstrasse 31
3003 Bern
Tel. +41 31 61 91 11

Central Confederation of Swiss
Employers
(Zentralverband schweizerischer
Arbeitgeber-Organisationen)
Florastrasse 44
8034 Zurich
Tel. + 41 1 383 0758

Confederation of Swiss Trade Unions
(Schweizer Gewerkschaftsbund)
Monbijoustrasse 61
3007 Bern
Tel. +41 31 45 56 66

Federal Equal Opportunities Bureau
(Eidgenössiches Büro für die
Gleichstellung von Frau und Mann)
Eigerplatz 5
Postfach
3000 Bern 6
Tel. + 41 31 61 68 43

Swiss Confederation of Temporary Work
and Employment Agencies
(SVUTA)
Klausstrasse 43
8034 Zurich
Tel. +41 1 383 3511
Fax +41 1 383 7558

Media

Neue Züricher Zeitung
Falkenstrasse 11
Postfach
8021 Zurich
Tel. +41 1 258 1111
Fax +41 1 258 1329

Tages Anzeiger
Werdstrasse 21
Postfach
8021 Zurich
Tel. +41 1 248 4111
Fax +41 1 248 5032

Cash
Hohlstrasse
8040 Zurich
Tel. +41 1 238 2828
Fax +41 1 238 2899

Main sources

BIGA, *Arbeitsvermittlung und Personalverleih*, listing of authorised employment agencies. Bern, 1995
BUCHER, PETER. 'Einführung Regionaler Arbeitsvermittlungszentren (RAV)' in *Die Volkswirtschaft*, April 1995
OECD. *Labour market policies in Switzerland*. Paris, 1996
RITTER, ANDREAS. *Das revidierte Arbeitsvermittlungsgesetz*. Bern, 1994
ZAUGG, ROBERT. *Personalbeschaffung und -auswahl in schweizerischen Unternehmungen*. Arbeitsbericht No. 11, Institut für Organisation und Personal, Bern University. Bern, 1996

14

United Kingdom

The UK's 'voluntarist' tradition of employment regulation has meant that statute law has never played a major role in determining terms and conditions of employment, or employment procedures. The legislative activity of post-1979 Conservative governments has not changed this approach fundamentally: while the qualifying periods for some employment rights were lengthened, for example on unfair dismissal, and union practices affecting recruitment, such as the closed shop, outlawed, there was no large body of legislation imposing constraints on employer prerogatives in the recruitment process offering itself as a target for deregulation. This does offer a point of contrast to Continental European labour markets where issues such as hiring agency employees, concluding fixed-term contracts, official notification of hiring and vacancies, and workforce consultation on recruitment are all subject to varying degrees of statutory regulation.

In some areas, however, largely as a result of European law, individual employment rights, such as the rights of part-time workers, have been extended in the UK. Britain has also long had laws in place which prohibit discrimination on the grounds of sex or race in recruitment, and these have played a major part in shaping approaches to recruitment, testing and promotion. In Northern Ireland there are also laws prohibiting discrimination on religious grounds. Legislation is also in place to protect people with disabilities from discrimination in the employment field.

Although the UK has been widely perceived as having a uniquely flexible labour market, this view is not entirely sustainable on some measures of flexibility: for example, many other EU member states have higher incidences of part-time work and employees on fixed-term contracts, and faster rates of growth in other forms of flexible employment, including innovation on the organisation of working time. However, on a combination of indices, including ease of hiring and dismissal and the absence of legally set minimum conditions, the UK is undoubtedly characterised by a low burden of official regulation.

The overall operation of the UK labour market has been adversely affected by geographical and skill-based mismatches between the supply of and demand for labour, with employers often reporting skill shortages even at the early stages of economic recovery and against the background of a high unemployment count. Although education and training have been dominant themes in political debate in recent years, with a growing awareness of the UK's weaknesses in international comparisons, it has proved consistently difficult to bridge the gap between a faltering training tradition rooted in on-the-job skills acquisition, which has largely failed to produce an adequate supply of qualified workers with transferable skills, and an education system which, in contrast to countries such as France or the Netherlands, is not fully equipped to offer initial vocational education through dedicated secondary schools. The absence of a clearly marked path into high-quality vocational education and training for 16–17-year-olds has also meant that many more of them in the UK have decided to pursue higher and further education – a model more in keeping with the high rates of college graduation seen in the USA than the vocational routes available in Continental Europe. Some commentators have noted that this might in fact be a more appropriate path for the UK, with its service-based industries and their need for social and analytical as well as technical skills.

According to a government audit of workforce skills, Britain continues to exhibit a strong performance in higher education but is lagging behind its principal international competitors on basic skills for the majority of school-leavers. These findings are just the most recent confirmation of training and education weaknesses observed over many years, and documented by comparative research carried out at workplace level notably by the National Institute of Economic and Social Research (see Prais in *Main Sources*). In particular, the NIESR studies have illustrated the comparatively low proportion of British shop-floor workers holding craft-level qualifications.

The labour market

At the end of 1995 the total working population in Britain stood at a little over 25.5 million, with an overall participation rate of 73 per cent – above the European average, and midway between the very high rates seen in the Nordic countries and those of southern Europe. Full-time employment overall is rising slowly, but for men, it has fallen over the past ten years.

Part-time employment, however, had risen from 16 per cent of total employment in 1973 to 24 per cent by 1995 – on the high side in Europe, but exceeded by Switzerland (28 per cent), and the Netherlands (37 per cent). Much of the increase has been accounted for by a growth in the employment of women, reflecting developments in the service sector, exemplified by the lengthening of opening hours in retailing, including Saturday and Sunday.

Whereas the overwhelming majority of women part-timers have chosen part-time work by choice, only a third of men in the same position have opted for part-time work: male part-time working as a proportion of male employment has more than tripled over the past two decades. There has also been a rise in the number of people holding two or more jobs.

Employment for both men and women is growing, but while the disparity between activity rates for men and women is closing, there is still a large difference – 72.5 per cent for men and 54 per cent for women. Compared with ten years ago, total employment has risen by 1.7 million for women and just 317,000 for men.

Manual jobs account for 40 per cent of total employment. Of the non-manual sector, the largest occupational groups are managers and administrators, clerical and secretarial, and craft jobs. The public sector in Britain employs some 23 per cent of the working population.

The self-employed sector, apart from the years of the economic depression of the early 1990s, has risen over the last ten years and now stands at 3.25 million.

The growth in part-time, temporary and self-employed working is seen by some commentators as part of a trend towards greater flexibility in the labour market where, eventually, permanent full-time employment will no longer be the norm. While it is true that these sectors have grown, and may continue to grow, there is a need for some caution before such weighty claims are made about Britain's labour market.

Part-timers, for example, are not necessarily short-term employees; many are permanent staff with the status and benefits of full-time employees. And there is evidence that the number of temporary workers grows after a recession – employees are often wary of recruiting permanent staff after experiencing economic difficulties – and recedes as prosperity returns.

Legislation outlaws the employment of children under 13 years of age, and the employment of children who have not reached the minimum school-leaving age in any industrial undertaking, with some exceptions for family businesses.

Unemployment in Britain is now 2.4 million, a rate of 8.6 per cent, and is falling gradually. The most significant factors behind this fall, apart from the impact of the growth of the economy after the recession of the early 1990s, are the numbers of young people choosing to move into higher education, and demographic trends which have seen a slow-down in the growth of the working-age population. Also of significance has been an increase in early retirement.

Unemployment rates are higher for men than for women, and for short periods of unemployment the young are disproportionately affected. Older age-groups, however, are more affected by long-term unemployment than younger age-groups.

Recruitment

There are no overarching statutory or agreed provisions governing recruitment procedures in general, nor binding codes of conduct. The most important legislative provisions are those covering sex equality and race discrimination, and discrimination against disabled people (see below), with a number of important court judgments in these areas that have shaped policy and practice. Other relevant legislation is that affecting people with a criminal record (Rehabilitation of Offenders Act, 1974) and data protection legislation (Data Protection Act, 1984).

The Institute of Personnel and Development produces a guide to recruitment which offers pointers to best practice in the field of recruitment and selection. The trade association for employment agencies FRES (see below) also has a code of conduct on recruitment which is binding on its member companies.

Work permits

Many categories of people do not need a permit to take up employment in the UK. These include European Economic Area nationals, Gibraltarians, some Commonwealth citizens, the spouses of overseas workers who can lawfully work in the UK, and people with 'settled status'. Settled status or indefinite leave can be granted, on application to the Home Office, to an overseas worker after four continuous years' working in a job or jobs.

There are also a number of occupations – for example, trainee nurses and mid-wives, doctors and dentists, and representatives of overseas newspapers – which do not require permits. Permission to enter the UK is usually limited to a period of 12 months, although this may be extended.

For overseas nationals who need a work permit, this has to be obtained before coming to work in the UK. Applications are made by the prospective employer to the Department for Education and Employment's Overseas Labour Service (OLS). Usually permits are issued only for workers with a professional qualification, degree, or specialised skills. Permits are not issued for jobs at manual, craft, clerical, secretarial or similar levels. Since October 1991, a two-tier system has made it easier to obtain work permits for employees in some high-level positions. These include board-level posts and new posts essential to inward investment to the UK.

Applications for work permits are normally processed within six to eight weeks. A permit may be issued for an initial period of four years, although this is the case only when the OLS states that a clear business case applies. Applications for extensions to permits are made to the OLS as the date of expiry of the permit approaches.

The new Immigration and Asylum Act, 1996 has implications for the recruitment of foreign workers. Under the Act it will become an offence to employ a person who has no immigration entitlement to take work in the UK. This includes illegal immigrants, overstayers and those in breach of immigration procedures.

Official notification

There is no requirement to notify the authorities of vacancies or hirings.

Workforce consultation

There are no statutory requirements to consult with employees or employee representatives. However, larger and unionised workforces may have agreed policies on recruitment covering issues such as early notification of vacancies internally, and equal opportunities programmes.

Employment incentives

Some incentive to employ more workers is included in Britain's system of National Insurance (NI). In the 1995 budget, for example, the government announced that the main rate of employers' NI contributions would be cut by 0.2 per cent to 10 per cent from April 1997.

A year previously the government announced a NI 'holiday' for employers taking on the long-term unemployed. In the 1995 budget, the holiday was extended to cover the employment of trainees. In both cases the work incentive measures came into force in April 1996.

There is no co-ordinated national policy of job creation in Britain, but there are a number of *ad hoc* schemes that seek to promote employment. Within the government's regional industrial development policies, there is some aid available – 'regional selective assistance' – to companies in depressed regions of the country to create or safeguard employment. These areas are known as the 'assisted areas' and cover about 35 per cent of Britain's working population.

The government has attempted to reverse urban decline through the establishment, for limited periods of time, of 'urban development corporations' (UDCs). Since 1981 12 UDCs have attracted public money to regenerate urban areas and to create jobs. The last of the UDCs will be wound up in 1998.

Another scheme – English Partnerships – promotes job creation through the development of vacant, derelict or under-used land and buildings. Similar organisations have been set up to cover Scotland, Wales and Northern Ireland. The Coalfield Areas Fund provides money to create employment opportunities in areas affected by mass colliery closures.

Part-timers, temporary and agency workers

Part-timers   Part-time working has risen significantly over the past decade, and is now among the highest in Europe. About 90 per cent of part-time workers work in the service sector, and generally in lower-grade jobs.

Through the influence of EU-level law and recent judgments in British courts, there has been substantial harmonisation between the rights of full- and part-timers. For example, under EU equality law, British firms can no longer exclude part-timers from occupational pension schemes. And a 1994 House of Lords' ruling found that qualifying thresholds (part-timers working between eight and 16 hours a week had been required to work for five years before becoming able to bring a complaint of unfair dismissal) were in breach of EU law. Consequently, in February 1995, the government introduced new regulations giving these part-time workers entitlement to all the same statutory employment rights as full-time employees.

In some cases employees are retained on 'zero hour' contracts. Under this system, employees are called in at busy times at short notice, with consequent substantial fluctuations in their weekly hours. There are no statutory provisions covering such employees.

There can also be cost savings in employing part-time staff – employers are not liable for National Insurance contributions until part-timers earn more than the lower earnings limit of £61 a week.

Fixed-term and temporary contracts   The use of temporary workers in Britain is not subject to any statutory restrictions. For many years the proportion of temporary workers in the economy remained static at 5 per cent, but since 1993 it has risen and now stands at 7 per cent.

There is, however, little evidence that temporary workers are being used to replace permanent staff. Rather, they are being recruited as a buffer which can be easily dismissed if the recovery founders: if it continues, they may well be offered permanent positions.

Men are more likely to accept temporary work out of necessity, women from choice. Students during holidays, or after completing their degrees, form a significant part of the temporary workforce. Temporary employment forms the highest proportion of the workforce in agriculture, and in fishing (14 per cent or 32,000 workers in the summer of 1994), while the greatest number of workers are to be found in public administration, education and health – all areas in which government policy has had a major impact on previously tenured and permanent positions. Occupationally, the largest number of temporary employees work in professional occupations, as secretaries or in clerical jobs.

The most popular methods for recruiting temporary workers are from agencies, local advertising, job centres and, particularly for larger companies, speculative applications. Many companies also maintain registers of people available for temporary work.

In 1994, half of temporary workers were employed on fixed-term contracts, 21 per cent as casuals, 9 per cent on contracts through agencies and 9 per cent as seasonal labour.

There is no distinction in employment law between temporary and permanent employees. In practice, however, the requirement that an employee has worked for an employer for a certain amount of time before qualifying for various employment rights means many temporaries are excluded from a number of protective provisions. For example, the qualifying period for unfair dismissal and redundancy pay is two years' service. And although temporary staff may often enjoy pay parity with permanent staff, length of service requirements mean they may not enjoy the same work-related benefits such as sick and holiday pay or pension schemes.

There are no statutory provisions governing the form and substance of fixed-term or temporary contracts, except in the field of dismissal. Non-renewal of a fixed-term contract which ends after a specified term normally constitutes a dismissal, whereas a task-related or temporary contract ends when that task is completed and does not involve a dismissal.

Agency employment   Agencies providing temporary employees are also usually engaged in permanent placement (see below). Currently, agencies account for about 10 per cent of the total number of temporary contracts, a proportion that is increasing. Probably the largest part of agency business is providing temporary workers. In contrast to many EU member states, employment agency workers in the UK are not, in general, regarded as being employed by the agency that supplies them to client companies, although many larger agencies offer training and treat employees that they supply to client companies as if they were employed by the agency. Nor are they deemed to be employees of the client. Rather, their contracts are regarded as *sui generis* – a position which can create some legal uncertainty on issues such as termination of employment.

Typically, applicants will fill in an application form with an agency followed by an interview to ascertain their experience and particular skills. Oral or written references are usually required before people are accepted on to an agency register. Once candidates have been interviewed and assessed, they are matched with the current assignments held by the agency.

One major employment agency has about 18,000 applicants currently on its books, of whom it reckons some 15,000 are on the payroll in any one week. For the most highly skilled staff, it can guarantee full-time work. Whereas some people will not want to work full time, others might register with more than one agency and may be selective about the work they accept. The types of jobs they do can be conveniently split into two: commercial, such as secretarial and clerical work; and industrial, such as production-line work.

Typically, agency staff complete a weekly time sheet and are paid by the agency, one week in arrears. The companies they work for are billed for their services at a rate of their salaries plus about 30 per cent. If a person is found permanent work, the employing company is charged between 10 and 30 per cent of the individual's first year salary.

Some agencies offer a package of benefits to their staff, often prompted by the need to retain capable people during boom periods. One leading agency, for example, offers holiday pay and leave and sick pay after a qualifying period.

Anti-discrimination provisions

Equal opportunities issues affecting sex and race have acquired a high profile in the UK, and can constitute an expensive and embarrassing pitfall for employers where cases come to court and are widely reported in the media. Discrimination may occur not only in the immediate recruitment decision but also through inappropriately targeted advertising that militates against applications from certain groups, through the use of some forms of testing that may contain cultural bias, and through inadequate training and preparation of those engaged in selection. Whereas much of southern Europe is characterised by word-of-mouth or family-based recruitment, such approaches could cause – and have caused – problems in the UK if they lead to the effective exclusion of some ethnic groups from employment opportunities.

Recruitment and sex equality

In Britain the legal regulation of employment is primarily made through Acts of Parliament. Although it lacks legal regulation of conditions of employment, there is extensive statute law on unfair dismissal, redundancy, and sex and race discrimination.

Since 1975 it has been unlawful to discriminate on the grounds of sex or marital status, for both men and women. This discrimination can take three forms:

- direct discrimination – where a women is treated less favourably than a man on grounds of sex
- indirect discrimination – where requirements are applied to a group of employees which fewer women can meet
- victimisation – where an employer discriminates against someone for asserting their rights under the Sex Discrimination Act. Employee complaints are taken initially to an industrial tribunal and, if necessary, to the Employment Appeals Tribunal (EAT).

The Equal Opportunities Commission (EOC), which was established by the 1975 Act, issues codes of practice, carries out investigations and helps individuals to bring complaints. The Equal Pay Act, which took effect from 1975, allows a woman (or man) to bring a claim if she is treated less favourably than a comparable man for any term or condition in her contract of employment.

The EOC may also issue non-discrimination notices, requiring an employer to cease discrimination, with employers required both to comply and to allow for monitoring. The legal route for complaints under the Act is via industrial tribunals, and then on points of law to the Employment Appeals Tribunal, with further appeal possible to the Court of Appeal. Under some circumstances, the EOC will also act on its own to seek a judicial review of government decisions of statutes which it considers discriminatory. In an important case dealing with the rights of part-timers in 1994, the House of Lords upheld the EOC's rights in this area.

The main remedies under the Act are:

- a declaration that the complainant's rights have been violated, possibly specifying action that the employer must undertake to rectify the situation
- payment of compensation.

The upper limits for tribunal awards were abolished in 1993. Since the abolition large sums have been awarded in some discrimination cases. Employees can now recover all losses attributable to an act of sex discrimination.

Opportunity 2000 Launched in 1991 with the support of the government, the Opportunity 2000 initiative aims to make a significant difference to the quality and quantity of women's employment opportunities by the year 2000. The campaign has some 300 member organisations, accounting for a quarter of the country's workforce.

The campaign is based firmly on the business case for equal opportunities. On signing up to the campaign, organisations commit themselves to setting challenging goals for improving women's representation at all levels in the workplace. In particular, it attempts to develop and increase the number of women in management.

Opportunity 2000 is self-financing, with members paying an annual fee. Currently this stands at £1,250 for organisations with over 1,000 employees, with lower, negotiable fees for smaller companies.

Equal Opportunities Policies Some companies ask for equal opportunities information on application forms which they use to monitor the ethnic background of their workforce. If these exercises show that they are not recruiting from all parts of the population they may adjust their recruitment process to attract more applicants from the ethnic minorities. This may involve advertising in the black and ethnic minority press, or changing parts of the selection process that are revealed to be discriminatory. Equal opportunity monitoring is most common in the public sector, but some private companies have made moves in this direction.

Some organisations, often local authorities with a strong commitment to equal opportunities, include questions on a person's understanding of the issues in an interview or on an application form.

Recruitment and race discrimination

The UK is one of the few European countries with a developed system of law in the area of race discrimination. Discrimination on grounds of race in the fields of employment, education and housing is prohibited under the Race Relations Act, 1976. The Commission for Racial Equality (CRE) is charged with monitoring the working of the Act, and may issue codes of practice giving practical guidance. The CRE's 1984 Code of Practice on employment makes recommendations in the fields of recruitment, training, terms of employment, discrimination and victimisation. The Code also recommends that companies adopt positive action programmes. Although not binding, the Code may be taken into account by industrial tribunals.

The Act identifies three forms of discrimination: i) direct discrimination – where an employer treats someone less favourably than other persons on racial grounds. Harassment and abuse have been interpreted by the courts to constitute direct discrimination. ii) indirect discrimination – where discrimination results from criteria required of actual or prospective employees which are not essential to the job, which members of some ethnic groups cannot fulfil. Examples include excessive or irrelevant language or qualification requirements. iii) victimisation – where a person receives less favourable treatment because they have sought to assert their statutory rights.

Race discrimination is prohibited in all areas of employment at an establishment in Great Britain, unless the employer can show that membership of a particular racial group is a genuine occupational qualification for the job, if discrimination is practised in fulfilment of a statutory duty, covers employees working outside Great Britain, or is intended as positive discrimination in favour of an underrepresented racial group (for example, setting up a training programme for ethnic minorities or encouraging job applications from particular ethnic groups). Direct discrimination for reasons of positive action during selection for employment is not permitted. A genuine occupational qualification embraces such areas as the theatre, modelling, working in ethnic restaurants, and providing direct personal services to people of a particular ethnic group.

Action against discrimination can be taken both by the employee and the CRE. The burden of proof rests with the applicant. Cases must be taken to an industrial tribunal, with provision for conciliation by ACAS. Applications must be presented within three months of the alleged act of discrimination. Remedies include:

- a '*declaratory order*' that the employer has violated the employee's rights
- a *recommendation* to remove or reduce the effects of discrimination. Failure to comply may lead to an order to pay compensation. Tribunals cannot require an employer to appoint an employee or increase pay levels but may instruct the employer to pay compensation and correct their policies
- *compensation*. From 1994, there is no upper limit on compensation. Payments may reflect both quantifiable losses as well as offer redress for injured feelings, with extra amounts ('aggravated' damages) in serious cases. Complainants must mitigate losses.

Appeals may be made on a point of law to the Employment Appeals Tribunal and, where leave is granted, to the Court of Appeal.

The CRE has powers to enforce application of the law through its rights to investigate cases and can issue a non-discrimination notice that requires an employer to stop the discrimination, inform the CRE about steps taken, and provide the CRE with information to enable it to monitor compliance for up to five years.

Important recent cases have covered the issue of cultural bias in psychometric testing (dealt with below, see page 362), and discrimination in recruitment, where new employees are hired mostly by word of mouth, reinforcing the ethnic composition of the existing workforce.

Recruitment and religious discrimination

Under the Fair Employment (NI) Act 1989, employers in Northern Ireland may not discriminate between employees on religious grounds. Employers must register and monitor their employment practices, ensure that indirect religious discrimination is not practised and take affirmative action to redress imbalances in their work-forces.

Disability

Until recently the government relied largely on voluntary efforts and self-regulation to combat discrimination against disabled people. Under the Disabled Persons (Employment) Act 1944, employers with twenty or more employees had to ensure that 3 per cent of their posts were occupied by people with disabilities. Employers with more than 250 employees had to set out in their annual reports their policies on employing people with disabilities. But although failure to comply with the quota was punishable by a fine, it was rarely enforced.

However, at the end of 1995 after considerable pressure from disability campaigners and many MPs, legislation – the Disability Discrimination Act – was passed. This makes it unlawful to discriminate against people with a disability in relation to employment and in the provision of goods, facilities and services.

The Act provides a two-fold attack against discrimination in employment. There is a statutory right not to be discriminated against on the grounds of disability, together with a duty on employers to make reasonable adjustments to working practices and the working environment to overcome practical barriers to a disabled worker.

The impact of this legislation, which came into force at the end of 1996, could be immense – there are estimated to be 2.4 million disabled people of working age who could benefit from the Act.

The government runs special schemes to help people with disabilities find work. Disability advisers, for example, are employed by Job Centres. Other assistance includes the Access to Work programme, which tries to improve the job prospects of the disabled, and the Supported Employment Programme.

Age discrimination

There are no statutory regulations on age, and job advertisements often include a preferred age of applicant. Legislation, however, already exists in some countries, notably the USA, Canada and Australia, but the evidence on its effectiveness is inconclusive. A voluntary 'Campaign For Older Workers' was inaugurated in 1994, and a number of large employers have made conscious efforts not only to avoid age discrimination but also to change the age profile of their workforce. A number of publications also now refuse to accept job advertisements specifying age limits.

Less than two-thirds of people aged 50 and over are economically active, and the participation of older people in the labour market has been falling for some years, particularly in the case of men.

Finding the applicant

According to official statistics, almost a third of people find jobs through someone already in employment at a workplace, a quarter by responding to an advertisement, a sixth make a direct approach to an employer, and one in ten finds a job through the public employment service.

There is no official monopoly of placement activity, and specialised private agencies and consultancies exist for permanent placement, temporary workers, and executives.

The public employment service

The Employment Service, a part of the Department for Education and Employment, provides a range of recruitment and employment services. It runs over 1,100 unemployment benefit offices and Job Centres, many of which are being integrated to provide a one-stop service to the unemployed.

The most recently available figures show that the Employment Service found jobs for 1.9 million unemployed people in 1994. It also carried out almost nine million interviews to assist people find work or places on training and employment programmes.

On registering with the Job Centre, the unemployed are required to agree to a 'back to work plan'. Subsequently, they have to attend a 'restart' interview every six months. A number of schemes exist to assist the long-term unemployed to return to work, such as 'jobclubs' where the unemployed receive training and advice in finding work.

For companies seeking workers, Job Centres offer a number of advantages: they are free and, because they are based throughout the country, they give access to the national job market. Often, however, their registers are dominated by relatively unskilled people.

Recruiting from government training schemes

Recruiting staff from a training scheme has the advantage for companies that applicants will already have some level of training. Organisations might, for example, recruit people who have completed a Training For Work course run by the local Training and Enterprise Council (TEC), bodies set up to co-ordinate local training initiatives and deliver youth training and other schemes.

In some cases, the expense of recruiting is borne by the state. Employers may, for example, be helped in recruiting by local TECs or by staff from the local Job Centre.

Employment agencies and personnel consultants

Employment agencies typically combine the placement of fixed-term and contract staff as well as of permanent employees with companies.

The main trade body for agencies is the Federation of Recruitment and Employment Services (FRES). Since the licensing of employment agencies was abolished in January 1995 it has the role of regulating employment agencies through its codes of practice and promoting best practice. The FRES 'code of good recruitment practice' is binding on its members. It covers the duties of agencies to their client firms and their duties to their staff, both temporary and permanent. For example, they must provide a full written contract for temporary workers and pay them promptly and efficiently.

There are still some regulations remaining, however. With the exception of entertainment and modelling agencies, for example, employment agencies are not allowed to charge fees to those looking for work. In general, however, the law is less restrictive than in the rest of Europe and does not prescribe the sorts of situations in which temporary workers may, or may not, be employed.

General employment agencies supply temporary workers, fixed-term contract staff and people for permanent positions with companies. They can also provide teams of people to work on long-term projects for clients. These teams may work on a client's site for many years, although they remain the employees of the agency.

Executive search and selection

The middle and late 1980s witnessed a rapid growth in the number and use of recruitment consultants for managerial jobs, a development promoted by the perceived need to bring greater professionalism to bear on the selection process and spurred on too by the contraction of central personnel departments. Indeed, in some areas – accountancy, law and general management positions, for example – it is rare to find any executive jobs advertised in the press by the company itself. And increasingly, job selection above the graduate intake level in these areas is carried out by recruitment consultants.

Senior jobs in the public sector are usually the exception, with local authorities and health service authorities and trusts advertising under their own names. Even in these areas, however, there are some specialist recruitment consultants in areas such as accountancy.

There are two well established methods of selection: advertising a post in the national or trade press and inviting responses which are then dealt with by the consultancy; or direct search by the consultant to draw up a short-list of candidates based on their own research. Consultancies also advise on the best advertising media to use, the terms and conditions for the post and the appropriate wording to use to attract high-quality applicants.

Responses to advertisements are dealt with in the first instance by the consultant. Following interviews, a short-list of candidates is passed on to the client for them to make the final selection. Usually, there is no cost to the client company unless an appointment is made – a contingency arrangement which is not always technically possible in Europe, and which has caused problems when UK companies use foreign headhunters. Fees are usually based on a percentage of the starting salary of the candidate appointed. For advertised posts, the percentage is usually between 15 and 25 per cent; for candidates found from the consultant's database, the fee is higher at about 30 per cent of salary. As well as finding permanent employees, consultants also supply contract staff and interim managers.

By turnover, the largest search consultancies in the UK are Russell Reynolds, Heidrick & Struggles, Amrop, Spencer Stuart, and Norman Broadbent. However, with a large and differentiated market, the UK has also generated a number of tailored consultancies, with highly-developed firms in the financial services sector operating alongside the larger, more generalist, practices.

Recruitment media

The media   Press advertisements remain at the centre of most recruitment strategies, especially for qualified employees. The type of newspaper used depends on the type of staff being recruited and their degree of specialisation and scarcity.

For manual operatives and basic clerical jobs companies tend to use local or regional papers. The higher the level of the job, the more widespread coverage is needed. Management jobs, therefore, tend to be advertised in the national press using one of the quality dailies, *The Times*, *Daily Telegraph*, the *Financial Times*, *The Guardian* and *The Independent*, or their Sunday counterparts – with *The Sunday Times* dominating the market. Some national papers have also specialised in particular areas. *The Guardian*, for example, has cornered the market for jobs in media and marketing, local government and teaching; *The Times* takes most of the legal advertisements; and the *Financial Times* and *Daily Telegraph* preponderate in finance and accountancy.

Many specialist magazines also carry job advertisements. Using the examples from the paragraph above, media jobs might also be advertised in the *UK Press Gazette*, local government vacancies in *Municipal Journal* or *Local Government Chronicle*, education jobs in *The Times Education Supplement* (with vacancies included in its on-line edition) and legal jobs in *Law Society's Gazette*.

Organisations with a strong commitment to equal opportunities also advertise vacancies in Britain's black and ethnic minority press, such as *The Voice*.

Job advertisements must not discriminate against one sex or race, apart from situations where this is an indispensable prerequisite for the job. Age limits are often given, although stating limits in public is gradually becoming frowned on. In contrast to Continental Europe, salaries are frequently stated – although for senior jobs this may be a very broad range indeed.

The Internet The UK has seen a rapid advance in the use of the Internet for recruitment. There are a number of general job-banks, many of which allow job seekers to attach their details free of charge, as well as highly specialised agencies which simply use their Web sites to notify vacancies, often via a structured set of links by sector or type of occupation. As well as the predictable IT employment agencies, there are also a host of agencies on the Web covering such specialisms as financial services in the City of London, graphic design, and nannies. Some of the larger general job-banks also include links to foreign sites, most of which seem to be in the US or Australia. In addition, a number of employers use their own home pages for notifying vacancies, although the majority of these are still in the IT sector.

Only a small number of sites allow job seekers to apply on-line: in most cases, they simply refer to the relevant consultant at the agency – although these can also usually be reached by e-mail.

Some newspapers with on-line editions also include recent job ads.

Recruitment procedures

Selection methods

Application forms and CVs Application forms and CVs are extensively used by companies as the first stop in the recruitment process. Forms are used mostly by the larger companies and organisations, and commonly demand the following information: educational achievements, work experience, interests and hobbies, and an assessment of why applicants believe they are suitable for the position.

CVs should contain similar information on education and work experience, with companies asking for a supporting letter (often hand-written) on why applicants believe they should have the job. It is not customary in the UK to ask for a photograph, nor are candidates required to submit written proof of their qualifications at the initial stage – and often not at all.

The IPD Guide recommends that detailed personal information should not be sought unless it is relevant to the job or selection process. Equal opportunities data should be used only for monitoring, and be kept separate from information on which decisions will be made.

The interview The centrepiece of most recruitment processes remains the interview. Traditional interviews involve a discussion between the candidate and line or personnel managers assessing how well the candidate is suited to the job and how he or she will fit into the company. This form of interview can be taken further with the application of strict criteria-based questions, designed to assess a candidate's skills and qualities and how they meet the job requirements.

Assessment centres In Britain, assessment centres were pioneered by the

Civil Service. They are used by organisations that believe that interviews alone, because they tend to focus on how well candidates perform in their current jobs rather than assessing the skills required to perform a new job, are not always adequate as a basis for recruitment decisions: for this reason they also feature in graduate recruitment.

Assessment centres, which combine interviews with other exercises and tests, may give a better picture of candidates' real aptitudes. Common features of centres include interviews, presentations, group exercises, written tests and psychometric tests. Centres are also used for employee training and development, as well as for recruitment.

In particular, they are proving increasingly popular in recruiting high-fliers and senior managers. In part, however, the high cost of running assessment centres has also restricted their use to more senior appointments.

Testing   Psychometric testing is a technical term that covers both ability tests and personality assessments. Ability tests provide objective data, while personality assessments offer more subjective and controversial evidence. More than 70 per cent of medium- and large-sized companies regularly use ability or personality tests.

The former, which have been used widely for many years, are tests of numerical, verbal and abstract reasoning, which gauge candidates' problem-solving and analytical skills. The Civil Service, for example, puts fast-track candidates through a day of these tests.

Personality assessments are designed to provide evidence of a candidate's motivation and personality. These are commonly used by major companies, especially for graduate and senior appointments, and have been growing in popularity since the late 1970s. Some three-quarters of large companies use personality questionnaires and two- thirds use ability tests – both substantial increases on their prevalence in the mid-1980s.

While their supporters believe personality tests can be a useful selection tool – they can, for example, be used as a quick and cost-effective method of differentiating between applicants – others believe they are not able to predict actual or potential competence in performing a particular job.

Moreover, psychometric testing has acquired a high and controversial profile because of concerns – following a number of industrial tribunal rulings and out-of-court settlements – that they may lead to race discrimination in the recruitment process as a result of cultural bias, despite their intended use as an 'objective' complement to job interviews. These incidents, in some cases involving payment of thousands of pounds in compensation, have prompted many organisations to review their use of tests, to have their existing practice validated, and share best practice. A number of established test providers are also engaged in research into the design of tests. Several unions, and notably the public-sector trade union Unison which brought some of the leading cases, are actively campaigning against the use of all psychometric testing, especially for selection for redundancy. Details of tests and test providers can be obtained from The British Psychological Society.

References, medicals and confidentiality

Providing job references for former employers is standard practice for most employers, although there is no obligation on them to do so.

If a former employee is unable to obtain employment or is dismissed for an unsatisfactory reference drafted with 'malice', he or she can sue for defamation or malicious falsehood. A company that employs someone on the basis of a good reference that subsequently turns out to be inaccurate also has some redress. As well as having grounds for dismissal, it could, in theory, sue for fraudulent misstatement and possibly negligent misstatement.

Doubts about the usefulness and reliability of references are expressed by many British companies. Some feel that referees often pull their punches for fear of facing legal action, others that a company will give almost any member of staff a good reference if it means their leaving.

Despite these fears, references are widely used, and usually taken up after a provisional job offer has been made. However, it is rare for job offers to be withdrawn as a result of a poor reference.

A number of headline cases, in which supposedly medically qualified employees did not in fact possess their required qualifications or had been dismissed for misconduct, has led to a tightening of reference checking, especially in public organisations.

Medical examinations   While it is common for staff to complete a health questionnaire, medical examinations are less common. Managers, especially if they are being offered private health care as a benefit of the job, will usually have a full medical check. Employees in certain occupations – the police, train drivers, pilots – are given thorough medical examinations.

A right of access to information is given to employees by the Access to Medical Reports Act 1988. This allows an individual to have access to any medical reports supplied by a medical practitioner for employment or insurance purposes. Thus, it covers health check-ups with a view to recruitment.

Confidentiality   Once recruited, information that employers hold about employees on computer is subject to statutory control under the Data Protection Act 1984. Employers who hold information on their employees must register under the Act and specify the nature of the data held by them and the purpose for which it is held. Using the data beyond the purposes specified in the registration is a criminal offence under the Act.

Individuals can apply to any data user and require its records to be checked to see whether the individual is the subject of any of the personal data held. If, for example, data are found to be inaccurate, the individual can apply to the courts for compensation for any loss sustained and any distress caused. Protection from the Act does not currently extend to information on paper, although employees will acquire this right for new manual records, subject to some qualification, under the 1995 EU Directive on Data Protection due to be transposed in 1998.

Criminal offences   Ex-offenders are protected in the recruitment process by the Rehabilitation of Offenders Act 1974. This allows certain convictions to drop out of their criminal record once they are 'spent' – that is, after a lapse of time, ranging from five to 10 years, depending on the offence. The Act covers the imposition of fines and imprisonment for up to 30 months: a longer sentence can never become spent. It is unlawful for an employer to ask about spent convictions or let the fact that an applicant has a spent conviction influence a recruitment decision. Nor can the existence of a spent conviction constitute grounds for dismissal.

Offer and rejection

There is no set procedure for making an offer of employment to the selected candidate. But in the overwhelming majority of cases a written job offer will be made. To establish a contract of employment the employer has to have made a job offer and received acceptance from the employee, with both parties indicating that they will be bound by what they have agreed.

There is no legal obligation to put a contract of employment in writing, but there is a statutory obligation to provide written particulars of the contract of employment, not later than eight weeks after the start of employment. These terms (only for employees working at least eight hours a week and for an employment period of at least a month) include pay details, hours of work, sick pay and pension provision, notice periods, job title and brief job description, the place of work and details of any applicable collective agreements.

Rejecting applicants   There is no standard method of informing candidates that they have been unsuccessful in their application. Some companies will acknowledge receipt of all applications and inform all unsuccessful candidates in writing. But with some jobs attracting hundreds or even thousands of candidates, not all employers inform candidates of their unsuccessful application. Job advertisements, for example, might warn candidates that if they hear nothing from the company within a certain period of sending their application, then they can assume they will not be invited to attend an interview.

Military service

There is no compulsory military service in the United Kingdom.

The education system

The Education Act of 1944 introduced a system of universal education in Britain. The school-leaving age was raised to 15, with all children receiving a secondary education to this age at grammar, technical or secondary modern schools, depending on the results of a test – the '11 plus' – taken at the age of 11.

During the 1960s and 1970s, comprehensive schools slowly replaced this selective system of education, although some grammar schools remained. Since 1972 the school-leaving age has been 16. Proposals to raise the amount of selection in the state system, either by reintroducing grammar schools or allowing comprehensive schools to select a larger proportion of their intake, have generated great controversy.

Education is primarily the responsibility of local government, subject to supervision and inspection from central government and its associated educational agencies. However, under reforms pursued since the mid-1980s, schools have been allowed to 'opt out' of local authority control and become independent 'grant-maintained' schools with their funds coming from central government (see below).

Britain's education and employment departments were combined in 1995. Part of the reason behind this decision was the government's wish to 'demolish the false divide between academic and vocational education and training' which it believed had stifled the economy. It was also designed to offer young people a 'single, seamless progression' from education into jobs.

There are significant differences between the education systems of England, Wales, Scotland and Northern Ireland. Indeed, different government ministers are responsible for education in each of these regions.

The Northern Ireland system of education reflects the religious divide – between Catholics and Protestants – in the country. Most Catholic children attend Roman Catholic-run schools, although these are mostly funded by the state and are non-fee paying. Protestants generally attend voluntary grammar schools, which are overwhelmingly funded by the public purse.

There are also a number of integrated grant-maintained schools, wholly funded by central government (see below). However, only about 2 per cent of children attend these. The government has a statutory duty to develop this form of education as a way of breaking down sectarian barriers. Education in Northern Ireland is administered by five education and library boards.

Educational performance in the UK has been a major political issue, with differences between the political parties on the introduction of selection into the state system, and the creation of new types of school and new patterns of school management. Educational standards have also been a matter of persistent concern to employers, who have frequently pointed to the lack of basic skills of school-leavers.

Secondary education

Currently, the secondary state school system in Britain as a whole is made up of 4,246 schools, employing some 218,000 teachers and teaching 3.5 million children.

Comprehensive schools educate about 90 per cent of the state secondary school population in Britain. The balance attend grammar or secondary modern schools after a selection process at the age of 11. While Scotland is almost wholly non-selective, the Northern Ireland system is overwhelmingly selective.

There are also 'voluntary schools' run on denominational lines, with some latitude over their internal organisation. Although formally part of the state sector and nominally non-selective at secondary level, many denominational schools select pupils and in some parts of the country parents seek out such schools – even if they are not religious believers – because they are felt to offer higher academic performance and more stringent rules of conduct.

Parents have some choice over which schools their children attend. National performance tables are produced annually to help parents make their decision. These include information on examination results and absence rates. In addition, schools have to provide parents with a written report on their children's school performance.

Grant-maintained schools   A number of fundamental changes have been made to the education system since the mid-1980s, with the creation of the grant-maintained sector and specialist schools intended to re-introduce elements of selection and greater specialisation into the state system. As a result, the state system has become somewhat fragmented, with access to the new schools – where they exist – via various forms of selection.

There are currently 622 grant-maintained secondary schools in England, ten in Wales and just one in Scotland. A school can achieve grant-maintained status if the parents support the idea in a ballot, and if the government's Education Secretary gives approval. Grant- maintained schools are no longer subject to control and supervision by the local authority, and receive their funding direct from central government. They are run by governing bodies made up of parents, teachers and people from the local community.

Technology Colleges   Another new type of school introduced in the last decade has been the city technology college (CTC). These schools are run independently of local education authorities, with the support of private-sector sponsors, and are non-fee paying. They teach the national curriculum (see below) but place greater emphasis on teaching technology and science. There are 15 city technology colleges in England.

Placing the same emphasis on science and technology are the 153 technology colleges in England. Created under the specialist schools programme, which was launched in 1993, these are secondary schools funded jointly by the state and business sponsors. There are also 16 language colleges which are run on the same lines and specialise in teaching modern foreign languages.

The National Curriculum   In England and Wales pupils follow the National Curriculum between the ages of 5 and 16. The curriculum is made up of 'core' subjects – English, mathematics and science (in Wales, Welsh is a core subject in Welsh-speaking schools) – which are compulsory until age 16. There are also a number of foundation subjects – technology, history, geography, music, art, a modern foreign language and physical education – which are studied at least until the age of 14. Pupils must also receive instruction in religious and sex education.

In Scotland the curriculum is not set by the state but by local education authorities and head teachers. In Northern Ireland there is a common curriculum consisting of English, mathematics, science and technology, the environment and society, creative and expressive studies, language studies and religious education.

In England, Wales and Northern Ireland, children take the General Certificate of Secondary Eduction (GCSE) at the age of 16. In 1995, the proportion of pupils with five or more GCSEs at grades A to C – commonly accepted as passes – was 43.5 per cent.

From September 1996, new GCSE (Short Course) qualifications have been introduced. These take about half the time to complete, and cover modern foreign languages, religious education, design and technology, and information technology.

From September 1995 a new vocational qualification – the Part One General National Vocational Qualification (GNVQ) is being piloted in 115 English and Welsh secondary schools. This qualification is a slimmed-down version of the full GNVQ course (see below, page 368), taking two years to complete and consisting of six units – three core skills in the application of number, communication and information technology and three vocational units in the particular subject of the course. For the first year it will cover business, health and social care, and manufacturing. From September 1996 the pilot has been extended to include art and design, information technology, and leisure and tourism. The new GNVQ broadly equates to a qualification in two GCSE courses.

In Scotland, children take the Scottish Certificate of Education (SCI) at the end of their fourth year – generally around 16 years of age.

Private secondary education   In addition to state-funded schools, Britain has some 2,260 fee-paying independent schools. About 550 of these, including the most prestigious such as Eton and Harrow, are paradoxically termed 'public' schools. Currently about 7 per cent of secondary school children attend fee-paying schools, although there is some regional variation. In common with the state sector, pupils sit GCSE and GCE A-level (see below) examinations.

Through the government's Assisted Places Scheme, financial assistance can be given to parents wanting to send their children to an independent school. Currently, there are 38,000 places offered in England, Scotland and Wales.

Further education

Two-thirds of children remain in education after the age of 16 at school sixth forms, sixth-form colleges and further education colleges. Including sixth forms, there are some 460 further education colleges, teaching 1.9 million pupils. Examinations taken in the sixth form are mainly for entry into higher education and professional training. The GCE A (advanced) level is taken at the age of 18 or 19 after two years' studying, with most students taking three (and sometimes four) A levels as the main route to higher education. Staying-on rates to take A levels increased markedly during the recession of the early 1990s, and have continued. Many school students now take a 'gap' year of work or travel between finishing school and starting higher education.

In contrast to the equivalent examinations taken by school students in mainland Europe – such as the German *Abitur* or French *baccalauréat*, A levels have been criticised for being too narrow in their approach, with no requirement for continuing study of a foreign language or a technical subject, and for being designed to weed out those unlikely to profit from higher education rather than offering a positive curriculum in their own right.

Pupils can take the Advanced Supplementary (AS) examination, which takes half the studying time of an A level and enables pupils to study a wider range of subjects, although there are plans to scrap this qualification.

Pupils can also take the more vocationally based advanced General National Vocational Qualifications (GNVQs). This is effectively a vocational A level and carries similar esteem. There are three levels of GNVQ, which are designed for 16- to 18-year-olds. In addition to the advanced, there are also intermediate and foundation levels. Since their inception in 1992, some 100,000 people have gained full or part-time GNVQs.

Scotland follows a different system; pupils take the Higher Grade Scottish Certificate of Education examination between 16 and 18. Similar to A levels, 'Highers' constitute the entry requirement for higher education. A system of vocational courses, similar to GNVQs – the General Scottish Vocational Qualifications – also operates.

Pupils can continue their education outside of schools at further education colleges after the age of 16. Here they take work-related and vocational qualifications, such as National Vocational Qualifications (NVQs). In Scotland, NVQs are known as Scottish Vocational Qualifications (SVQs). Each NVQ or SVQ in a particular subject has five levels: Level 1 – foundation; Level 2 – basic craft; Level 3 – technician and advanced craft; Level 4 – higher technician and middle management; and Level 5 – middle to higher management. NVQs are explained more fully below, on page 374.

There are almost 600 colleges that take students, often on day-release from their jobs. Much of their work consists in offering the education part of the government's training programmes for young people. Currently, about 3.5 million people are enrolled at further education colleges.

National education and training targets have also been set, and these are discussed in more detail below; however, for education the two most pertinent targets are that by 2000:

- 85 per cent of 19-year-olds should have five GCSEs at grade C or above, an intermediate GNVQ or an NVQ Level 2
- by the age of 21, 60 per cent should have two A-levels, an advanced GNVQ or an NVQ Level 3.

Following the Dearing Review, published in March 1996 and chaired by the government's senior education adviser Sir Ron Dearing, further changes are on the way. He proposed a broader mix of sixth-form courses, with students able to take a combination of A Levels and vocational courses, the vocational GNVQ to be renamed the 'Applied A Level', and the AS Level to be scrapped and replaced by an examination at 17 covering the first half of an A level course.

Younger children – the 14-year-olds who are struggling at school – will be allowed to take vocational courses at college, or workplace training. Finally, all students will have to learn communication and numeracy skills. Sir Ron's proposals have all-party support and are expected to be introduced, regardless of any change of government.

Higher education

Entry to higher education is overwhelmingly via A levels or Highers, with entrance via a national competitive system in which students, who can apply to up to eight universities, are given places conditional on certain grades at A level. Mature students can enter without A levels, but may often be required (or advised) to take a foundation year at a further education college before entering university.

The system of higher education in the UK has undergone both massive growth and organisational transformation in recent years: one in three young people now enters universities or higher education colleges, with the number of students entering university almost doubling since the early 1980s. Many more are now mature students, with a large proportion of students pursuing post-graduate degrees on a part-time basis for professional development. At an institutional level, the number of universities has expanded with the acquisition by polytechnics of university status in 1992. In contrast to the situation in which the 'classical' British universities, which dominated higher education up until the late 1970s, took in overwhelmingly school-leavers with A levels (or equivalent) typically studying away from home on mainstream full-time academic degree courses, institutions are now developing a more local focus, with greater emphasis on vocationalism and with a much more diverse student body.

Rapid expansion has not been without its problems, and organisational and academic resources have often been greatly stretched – with concerns about the maintenance of standards – by the increase in numbers. Difficulties in financing direct support for students through the grant system have also led to an increase in financing via grants and parental support. Whether the large numbers of graduates produced are now really needed, or whether there could be – expensive – under-utilisation of graduates has also become a major issue; certainly, employers have become more sensitive to the quality of graduates and the institutions they come from.

Tuition fees are paid from the public purse. Some maintenance money is paid by local authorities to students who are ordinarily resident in their areas – the mandatory student grant – but students are expected to supplement this with a student loan and, in some cases through a parental contribution. The student loan was introduced in 1990 to provide extra resources to students. Subsequently they have partially replaced grants. The mandatory grant has been pegged to about its 1990 level, leaving students to supplement this grant through a loan.

There are just over 100 universities in Britain, which can be split into four broad groups:

- The ancient universities dating from the Middle Ages: Oxford, Cambridge, Edinburgh, St Andrews, Glasgow and Aberdeen.
- The Victorian 'red brick' universities, such as Leeds and Manchester, and other universities created in first half of the 20th century.
- The 'plate-glass' universities, such as Sussex and Warwick, dating from the expansion of higher education in the 1960s.
- The former polytechnics that acquired university status in 1992 when the university-polytechnic divide was ended.

    In contrast to much of mainland Europe, where non-university tertiary education is being expanded and developed, the UK has ended a dual structure of higher education which prevailed since the 1960s. However, the former polytechnics (now dubbed the 'new universities') still have a higher proportion of vocationally-oriented students, who are often studying sandwich courses in which study and short-term on-the-job placements alternate.

There is a hierarchy of establishments – albeit one in which university departments rather than the whole institution are of immediate relevance to employers; there are official measures of research excellence as well as unofficial rankings of graduate 'employability'. In a survey published by the Performance Indicator Project (see *Main sources* below) in December 1996 Cambridge University was seen by employers as producing the most employable graduates, followed by University of Manchester Institute of Science and Technology (UMIST), Oxford, Imperial College London, Manchester, Bristol, Edinburgh, Warwick, Loughborough and

Nottingham universities. Most of the 'new universities' were not highly ranked, with the highest-placed – Nottingham Trent – rated 36th.

Since 1970 the Open University has also offered degree and other courses, on a non-residential basis, to students of all ages, often those without formal education qualifications. There is also one private university, the University of Buckingham.

In addition to the university system, there is also a network of other further and higher education establishments offering degree qualifications, technical qualifications, and adult education.

Higher education qualifications Most degree courses last for three years, although language courses or business courses may involve an additional year of work or study away from the university. The legacy of small student numbers and restricted enrolment has meant that university curricula are fairly tightly organised, with an intensive timetable.

Drop-out rates in British universities have traditionally been very low – with over 90 per cent of students completing their degrees in the early 1990s: this reflected the stringent entry criteria designed to adjust applicants to the small number of places available. However, the rapid expansion of higher education to include broader ability- and age-groups combined with greater financial pressures on students have combined to raise drop-out rates substantially in recent years.

The standard first degree is the bachelor's degree, taken after three years for the most part, but in some cases four. Scottish first degrees may take four years and conclude with a master's degree (MA), although this title is normally reserved for post-graduate qualifications at English universities. The bachelor's degree may be designated either a BA (Bachelor of Arts) or BSc (Bachelor of Science), with some specialist titles such as LL B (Bachelor of Laws). All Oxford or Cambridge degrees are termed BA irrespective of specialism – and are written as BA (Oxon) or BA (Cantab).

Most bachelor's degrees are termed 'honours' degrees, with corresponding degree qualifications written BA (Hons), although this is often omitted. However, some universities may offer 'ordinary' degrees: in Scotland, this is frequently taken after three years with a full honours degree after four.

Technical qualifications taken at colleges of higher education and ex-polytechnics include the standard Higher National Diploma (HND), awarded after two years' full-time study, or the Higher National Certificate (HNC) after two years of part-time study.

The main post-graduate degree is the master's (MA or MSc), typically requiring one to two years' study and involving a mixture of teaching and research culminating, in some subjects, in a dissertation. Recent years have seen a proliferation in master's qualifications, with ever-greater specialisation – of both an academic and vocational nature – beyond traditional disciplinary boundaries.

Doctorates (PhD or DPhil) are awarded after submission of a research thesis and an oral examination – usually from between three and five years after registration.

Graduate recruitment   As a result of fairly short courses, British graduates tend to enter the labour market at between 21 and 23 years of age: there is no compulsory military service, and effective entry to the labour market can therefore begin at a much earlier age than is customary in mainland Europe.

Since 1994 the demand for graduates has been rising, although recruitment figures have not returned to the levels seen during the boom years of the late 1980s. However, competition for jobs is growing because of the increase in student numbers over the last few years.

As a consequence, there are too few vacancies to ensure that all graduates are able to find a suitable opening. What constitutes a 'graduate job' is being redefined. A recent survey from High Fliers Research shows that graduates are all too aware of this fact. It found that two-fifths of graduates were planning to take post-graduate studies or travel.

The main component of many companies' graduate recruitment activities is the 'milk round', in which companies visit universities in the autumn, followed by first interviews in the following spring.

British universities have their own careers services, which offer advice and placement services and host the 'milk round'. As well as participating in the 'milk round', companies advertise in student papers and national newspapers and may take stalls at recruitment fairs for specific occupations such as law. Graduates can also make speculative applications to companies.

A recent study of 20 leading companies carried out by Cranfield University found that firms are targeting specific universities on the 'milk round', on the basis of perceived graduate quality, the specialisms offered, or research links. Recent IDS research supports these findings. It found that some companies are abandoning or severely reducing their participation in the 'milk round' and in its place are developing links with the university departments considered to produce the best candidates.

Many companies now consider the traditional graduate recruitment process to be time-consuming and unwieldy. Methods introduced to reduce the workload include, shorter assessment courses, self-selection questionnaires and telephone interviews for the first stage of application and the use of agencies to reduce the strain on company personnel and recruitment departments. Some companies have also abandoned the once-a-year recruitment process and now recruit throughout the first year following graduation.

Some companies, particularly those in manufacturing, sponsor students through university. A typical bursary for a sponsored undergraduate is £1,300 a year. Students are normally employed by the company during holidays and some may take a year out of their studies to gain more working experience with the company. The number of sponsored students, however, is falling, with a number of companies abandoning their schemes. In its place, vocationally-oriented sandwich courses, with students spending their third year of study in industry, are becoming more popular.

The Cranfield study also found that once in the job, career development is becoming less rigid, usually involving a series of lateral moves, or specialist/generalist development. But there is no guarantee of rapid progress. The study also found that graduates are expected to 'perform or perish' from day one of the job and to take more initiative in managing their careers.

Parallel to the growing demand for graduates has been an increase in starting salaries, albeit only by about the rate of inflation. Average graduate starting salaries for 1996 were just under £15,000. There is little difference in starting salaries across the industrial sectors, although salaries are slightly lower in the finance sector. Once in the job, graduate salaries increase rapidly – by about 10 per cent a year for the first five years over the normal annual pay rise.

Training

Training provision in Britain is voluntary: there is no compulsion on employers to train their workforces, and – with very few exceptions – no system of levies to finance training, many of which were abolished in the 1980s. Industrial training in the past was centred on the traditional apprenticeship; such apprenticeships went into a decline, especially in the engineering industries, during the 1970s and 1980s – in part reflecting a weakening of craft control at the workplace, allowing semi-skilled employees to take on jobs previously reserved for time-served craftworkers, and in part a contraction in the supply of places. They have, however, continued to play a role in the construction industry, with its traditional occupational differences.

Initial vocational training is provided through a diverse set of pathways and institutions, including apprenticeships and their commercial equivalents (as well as 'Modern Apprenticeships' see below), study for a GNVQ or NVQ (see below) in school or a college of further education, and acquisition of NVQs at the workplace. In addition, there are a number of government-supported schemes, some of which have been attempts to broaden access to vocational training and ensure that 16-year-old school-leavers not in full-time work have an opportunity to develop skills. Higher staying-on rates at school and the guarantee of access to training via the Youth Credits system have lowered the proportion of young people with no qualifications entering the workforce at 16 .

National education and training targets   These targets were originally launched in 1991 by the Confederation of British Industry (CBI) and other organisations, and endorsed by the government. The targets have been updated recently. Their main aim is to improve Britain's competitiveness by raising education and training standards.

Training targets for the whole workforce, to be achieved by 2000, are as follows:

• 60 per cent of the workforce should have an NVQ Level 3, an advanced GNVQ or two GCE A levels

- ●30 per cent should have an academic, management, professional or vocational qualification at NVQ Level 5 or above
- ● 70 per cent of organisations employing over 200 people and 35 per cent of those with over 50 employees should be recognised as Investor in People (see page 376).

On the government's own admission, progress towards these targets has been mixed. While the number of young people attaining an NVQ Level 3 or its equivalent is increasing, the proportion of the employed workforce qualified to this level has remained static. Some sectoral employers' organisations have also scaled down their expectations of workforce attainment, regarding the targets as unrealistic.

Training and Enterprise Councils (TECs)   TECs operate in England, Wales and Northern Ireland (in Scotland, they are similar and termed 'Local Enterprise Companies') and have the role of building skilled workforces in their local areas. They are independent companies run by business people, but accountable to government. They manage training and enterprise programmes, and in England and Wales also have responsibility for work-related further education.

According to recent research, the major role of TECs and LECs is to provide information and assistance with the Investors in People scheme (see below) and National Vocational Qualifications and their Scottish equivalent, SVQs. But doubts about the effectiveness of TECs persist. A recent report from the House of Commons Employment Select Committee reported that they had made only a 'modest' contribution to improving the training of the unemployed and to promoting economic regeneration in their areas.

In addition to the network of TECs and LECs, there are also over 120 Industry Training Organisations, which have the role of ensuring the training and skill needs of their particular industry are met. These bodies, for example, will organise the Modern Apprenticeship scheme (see below, page 375) for their particular industry.

National Vocational Qualifications

National Vocational Qualifications (NVQs) can be studied in colleges and in some schools (see above, page 368), but they are designed mainly for people in work. In Scotland, there is an equivalent qualification called the Scottish Vocational Qualification.

NVQs are based on the measurement of competence in the workplace against pre-determined national standards. Candidates are judged on their abilities to perform work-related activities and their performance is assessed by observation in the workplace. There are five levels of NVQ: Level 1 – foundation; Level 2 – basic craft; Level 3 – technician and advanced craft; Level 4 – higher technician and middle management; and Level 5 – middle to higher management.

NVQs have been available since 1991, but can be deemed only a qualified success. Recent evidence showed that only about three-quarters of employers knew of NVQs, and that half of all employers felt they were of little relevance to their organisation. Their use is heavily biased towards larger employers. The most commonly cited problems are that companies feel employees already have appropriate qualifications, and that NVQs are too bureaucratic and not a credible qualification.

None the less, there have now been over 650,000 NVQs awarded in England, Wales and Northern Ireland, with many companies seeing them as an effective way of measuring abilities and motivating staff. Almost half of these are in business services, including administration, information technology and management.

Youth training

All 16- and 17-year-olds, if they are not in work or full-time education, are guaranteed training through the Youth Training or Modern Apprenticeship schemes.

Youth Training   The YT programme was introduced in 1990 and is delivered at a local level by TECs in England and Wales and by LECs in Scotland. The scheme is designed to raise the number and level of vocational qualifications achieved, and to match training more closely to the needs of the labour market.

Each YT trainee has a personal training plan, which is usually made up of a mixture of on-the-job training, including work experience, and off-the-job training at a college or in a training centre. There is no limit to the training, and no upper age limit, although 16- and 17-year-olds get priority for places. But while all young people of this age are guaranteed an offer of a YT place, they are not guaranteed a job at the end of the training – even if their training has been provided by a company.

Youth Training usually leads to an NVQ Level 2. The minimum training allowance for 16-year-olds is currently £29.50 a week and £35 at 17 – allowances which date from 1988 and 1986 respectively. Employers can top up these allowances, although not all do so. YT trainees must not work more than 40 hours a week and must receive a minimum of 19^{1}/$_2$ days' holiday a year, plus statutory holidays.

Latest official figures reveal that over half of YT leavers had found a job after six months and that 70 per cent were in a job, further training or full-time education.

'Modern Apprenticeships'   Modern Apprenticeships were introduced in September 1995 (after a pilot scheme) to create a pool of well-trained young employees to meet the needs of industry, and to compensate for the decline of traditional apprenticeships. The intention is to train young people to achieve an NVQ Level 3 – a higher level than Youth Training – and to equip them with a range of more general skills to help them adapt to future changes in the workplace. When the initiative is fully established, the aim is to have 150,000 apprentices in training at any one time.

Modern Apprenticeships are work-based, covering over 50 industries, and aimed at 16- and 17-year-olds. To qualify for the apprenticeship, young people generally need to have achieved three or four GCSEs. Funding for the scheme is provided by the network of Training and Enterprise Councils in England and Wales and by Local Enterprise Companies in Scotland. The qualifications were developed by the Industry Training Organisations (ITOs) for each sector, and have tended to flourish where there was pre-existing training infrastructure and culture. Most modern apprentices have the status of an employee with their employer, but their rates of pay vary widely. Currently, pay varies between £30 and £165 a week.

Early indications suggest that the initiative has been more successful than earlier schemes for young people. However, it has still not managed to displace full-time education as an option, and risks becoming a second choice for the less academically able. The overwhelming majority of apprentices under the scheme have been male.

Youth Credits Scheme   Young people can also gain access to Modern Apprenticeships through the Youth Credits Scheme. In effect, this allows young people to purchase their own training by means of vouchers or 'credits'. These have a monetary value and are exchanged for training with an employer or training provider, who in turn redeems the credit from the local TEC. Youth Credits are designed to offer a greater sense of personal responsibility and more individual choice in buying training.

Training for the unemployed

Training for Work   The government's Training for Work programme aims to help long-term unemployed adults find jobs through training and work experience. In 1995/6, about 110,000 places were available in Britain. The most recent official figures show that within six months over a third of people who left Training for Work were in employment. However, many commentators believe this is a poor return for the money spent on the scheme.

The government has also made the first moves, admittedly on a small scale, towards introducing a form of workfare. This is the principle that access to benefits depends on claimants' taking up state-subsidised training places or jobs. The Jobseeker's Allowance, for example, allows unemployed people to earn up to £1,000 for part-time work done while they are out of work.

Other training schemes

Investors in People   Investors in People (IIP) is a national standard which recognises effective investment by employers in the training and development of their employees. To achieve the standard, companies are required to link their training practices to business objectives. Launched in 1991, some 3,000 employers have now achieved IIP recognition. The standard is administered by a business-led body, Investors in People UK, and is promoted locally by TECs and LECs.

There are a number of other government training schemes currently running. These include the National Training Awards, which rewards organisations with good training practice; Small Firms Training Loans, a three-year programme which assists companies with less than 50 employees to train selected key workers to pass on their knowledge and expertise to colleagues; and the Career Development Loan Scheme, which offers loans of between £200 and £800 to help people pay for vocational training of their choice.

Workforce training and development

The amount of workplace-based continuing training carried out in Britain has increased substantially over the last few years. Current figures from the APAC National HR Database reveal that employees receive an average 3.1 days of training a year, with the average higher in the private than the public sector. A little over half of employees receive training, with the figure rising to two-thirds for private sector firms employing over 1,000 employees.

A recent Industrial Society survey found that organisations spend an average of just under 3.7 per cent of their total salary bills on training and development, and that spending on training has increased in all sectors of the economy. The most popular form of training is short in-house courses lasting a day or two.

The latest official training statistics show that women employees are more likely than men to receive job-related training, but of those receiving training, men receive more hours than women. Young employees between 16 and 19 receive more training than other age groups, and those with higher qualifications receive more training than those with low or no qualifications.

The areas where on-the-job training is most widespread are the public sector and professional occupations. The least training is offered in manual occupations, particularly agriculture, and to machine and plant operatives.

Employers pay two-thirds of job-related training fees, and nine out of ten employees receive full pay while training. Over half medium-size and large organisations have a training budget and 80 per cent provide training to at least some of their employees of at least 12 months standing.

Workforce consultation on training

There are no statutory forms of employee representation in the UK, and, as a consequence, no requirement for employers to provide information on training or consult with workforce representatives.

However, training is likely to figure on agendas of meetings between managements and employee representatives where trade unions are recognised, where companies have established their own mechanisms for employee involvement, or where UK employees are included in European Works Councils (EWCs). As yet, almost without exception, UK-based companies that are required to establish EWCs have included their UK workforces, despite the opt-out.

Workforce appraisal and development approaches   Workforce appraisal with a strong link to the training and development of staff is becoming increasingly popular in Britain for white-collar staff. For some companies, particularly where there is no link between appraisal and salary, training and development is the most important function of the appraisal system.

The most popular approach probably involves a yearly appraisal of an employee's performance, which includes the identification of training needs and the implementation of individual development plans. An appraisal will usually be carried out by an employee's line manager, but some companies are now introducing '360-degree feedback'.

This technique provides a fuller picture of an employee's performance by gathering information from a wide variety of sources other than the immediate manager, including senior managers, peers, subordinates and even customers of the business. This approach has so far been used mainly to assess managers' performance, but it is now increasingly becoming an option for other white-collar staff.

In some companies the employee's role in appraisal has been strengthened. Employees, for example, are encouraged to take time to prepare for their appraisal to allow a two-way discussion of performance.

Employee development   Employee development approaches in the UK embrace a wide range of policies. While some are tied fairly narrowly to developing vocational requirements, including social and communication skills, others are more broadly conceived.

Employee development initiatives at a number of large employers, with some notable examples in the car industry, embrace a range of courses, including non-work-related programmes such as language learning; participation is voluntary and activities are often undertaken outside working hours. Employers may, for example, pay for employees to take a course at a local college.

Another recent development – and often part of an employee development initiative – is 'open learning'. Here an employer provides an open learning centre or related training provision, such as study packs, videos and increasingly new technology such as CD-ROM, on a voluntary basis as a contribution to the development of its employees. Recent research indicates, however, that while open learning is often aimed at all employees, it is managers and supervisors who make most use of the facilities. Only about one in ten companies, at most, adapts its open learning facilities for use by manual workers.

Mentoring has also emerged as a tool for employee development since the 1980s, with distinctive schemes typically used for new graduates, for professional development – especially where those being mentored are pursuing a professional or business qualification – and to help disadvantaged groups.

One widespread criticism of employee or personal development initiatives is that they favour employees who already have qualifications. Part-time and older workers are regularly excluded from training opportunities. Furthermore, workers in larger companies are more likely to receive training than those employed by small firms.

For manual workers, the opportunities for training and development are fewer. Performance appraisal, linked to training opportunities, has increased in recent years, but is still confined to a minority of companies.

This also applies to initiatives such as multi-skilling and skill-based pay. Multi-skilling is most commonly used for craftsmen and involves them acquiring additional skills, either in their own discipline or in a skill outside of their own core trade. For example, a mechanical craftsman may be trained in limited electrical skills. Under some schemes, pay increases may be formally linked to the acquisition of formal skills, and in some cases the entire pay structure is skill-based. To assess whether a craft employee is competent in any newly-acquired skill, many employers make use of the national standards provided by the NVQ system in their training programmes.

Competency-based pay, and the focusing of development strategies around the identification and acquisition of competencies, represents an extension of the idea of reward for skill acquisition to those working in supervisory and management positions, where the requirements expected of employees – and the attributes of successful employees – are less easily and formally defined than for manual employees. A number of leading companies have pioneered competency-based pay schemes, usually as a complement to traditional performance-related pay, and in the context of large-scale corporate and cultural change. There is also a wide debate among personnel professionals in the UK about the validity of the competency approach, as well as interest in using competencies to resolve organisational problems. In particular, competency assessment and reward has been associated with the management of expanding roles, either as a result of new customer requirements or following reductions in staff numbers.

The introduction of competency-based pay approaches has been associated with susbstantial increases in training expenditure: in one study, reported to IDS, annual expenditure on training per employee rose from £500 to £1,500 between 1991 and 1996.

Training managers and supervisors

Frequent complaints have been made over the last decade about the quality of Britain's managers and supervisors. The most commonly cited reason for this poverty was the lack of a formal training system. It was also noted that many lacked education to degree level.

Current figures bear this out, but progress has been made. Official training statistics, for example, reveal that just six out of ten people in professional occupations have a degree-level qualification, while only a quarter of associate professional and technical occupations are qualified to this level. Some 70 per cent of this latter group are qualified to NVQ Level 3 or equivalent.

In 1988 the Management Charter Initiative was formed to improve the performance of UK companies by developing the quality of managers. Initially funded by private and public sector organisations, MCI is a non-profit-making organisation that generates income from membership subscriptions and its range of products and services.

The MCI has developed national standards of performance for managers and supervisors. To become a member of the MCI, members have to commit themselves to a management code, which includes a commitment to providing improving management and leadership skills, encouraging continuous development and providing access to training. MCI does not award qualifications itself, but works with awarding bodies to develop NVQs in management and supervision.

Increasing numbers of supervisors and managers are now taking the NVQ qualifications. MCI is also linked with the Investors in People scheme, see above, on page 376.

The MBA grew enormously in popularity during the 1980s as a means of acquiring management skills and a formal transferable managerial qualification, especially against the background of the relative shortness of British degree courses, with most graduates entering the labour market at age 23–25, and the lack of business-related degrees. Older managers have also been prompted by delayering and organisational change to acquire qualifications which would enhance their overall employability.

Although there are concerns about the devaluation of the MBA as a result of the proliferation of courses, with 109 institutions in the UK now offering the degree, an MBA from a good-quality business school is still regarded as the most highly-rated management qualification – despite, or perhaps because of, the high cost and investment of time required. These pressures have led to a shortening of the overall study period, with many business schools now offering one-year full-time courses, implying great intensity of study. Fees for one-year courses range from £12,000 to £17,500.

The Association of MBAs (AMBA) accredits courses from the top business schools, with 31 currently under accreditation, and admits only graduates from these schools into its ranks.

Financing the system

It is estimated that employers currently spend over £20 billion a year on employee training and development in Britain. The greater part of public money spent on training is channelled through the Training and Enterprise Councils (TECs), which have the responsibility for delivering the government's training programmes.

However, there is no general system of levies to promote or finance training, and this approach seems to be ruled out for the foreseeable future. Some industry training boards (ITBs) do have compulsory levies on member companies, the most notable being the Construction Industry Training Board.

The tax system also provides some help in the financing of training provision. Employees, for example, are not liable for tax on the further education and training costs paid for by their employers, providing, if the course is for general education, that the employee is under 21 when it starts; and if it involves vocational training, it must lead to the acquisition of knowledge and skills that are either necessary for the job or will increase an employee's effectiveness at work. Tax relief is available on the following expenses, with some conditions: essential books, additional travel costs and subsistence expenses while away from the normal place of work. If an employer pays for the retraining of a employee who is about to leave employment, or has left within the previous year, the benefit is tax-free, subject to some conditions.

Educational attainment of the population

Level	Percentage of 25–64 age-group
Lower secondary	26
Upper secondary	54
Higher education (non-university)	9
University	12

Source: OECD (1994)

Organisations

Department for Education and
Employment
Sanctuary Buildings
Great Smith Street
London SW1P 3BT
Tel. +44 171 925 5000
Fax +44 171 925 6000

Institute of Personnel and Development
(IPD)
IPD House
Camp Road
Wimbledon
London SW19 4UX
Tel. +44 181 971 9000
Fax +44 181 263 3333

Confederation of British Industry (CBI)
Centre Point
103 New Oxford Street
London WC1A 1DU
Tel. +44 171 379 7400
Fax +44 171 240 1578

Trades Union Congress (TUC)
23–28 Great Russell Street
London WC1B 3LS
Tel. +44 171 636 4030
Fax +44 171 636 0632

Association of Search and Selection
Consultants
(member of FRES)
36–38 Mortimer Street
London W1N 7RB
Tel. +44 171 323 4300
Fax +44 171 255 2878

Association of Graduate Recruiters
(AGR)
Sheraton House
Castle Park
Cambridge CB3 0AX
Tel. +44 1223 356720
Fax +44 1223 324871

Association of MBAs (AMBA)
15 Duncan Terrace
London N1 8BZ
Tel. +44 171 837 3374

The British Psychological Society
St. Andrews House
48 Princess Road East
Leicester LE1 7DR
Tel. +44 116 254 9568
Fax +44 116 247 0787

Media

Daily Telegraph
1 Canada Square
Canary Wharf
London E14 5DT
Tel. +44 171 538 5000
Fax +44 171 538 6242

Financial Times
1 Southwark Bridge
London SE1 9HL
Tel. +44 171 873 3000
Fax +44 171 873 3062

The Guardian
119 Farringdon Road
London EC1R 3ER
Tel. +44 171 278 2332
Fax +44 171 837 2114

The Independent
1 Canada Square
Canary Wharf
London E14 5AP
Tel. +44 171 293 2000
Fax +44 171 293 2435

The Times
The Sunday Times
Virginia Street
London E1 9XT
Tel. +44 171 782 7000
Fax +44 171 488 3242

Main sources

ASSOCIATION OF MBAs. *Guide to business schools*. London, 1996
CONNOR, H. *et.al*. *University challenge: student choices in the 21st century*. Institute for Employment Studies, Brighton, 1996.
INCOMES DATA SERVICES. *Large-scale recruitment*. IDS Study No. 581, 1995
INCOMES DATA SERVICES. *Training strategies*. IDS Study No. 608, August 1996
INCOMES DATA SERVICES. *IDS management pay review*. 'Paying for Competency', Research File 39, August 1996
IPD. *The IPD guide on recruitment*. Institute of Personnel and Development, London, 1996

JENN, NANCY GARRISON. *Executive search in Europe.* Economist Intelligence Unit, London, 1995

NIESR. *Productivity, education and training.* Reprints of studies originally published in the *National Institute Economic Review.* Two volumes, London, 1995

PERFORMANCE INDICATOR PROJECT. *Signposts to employability.* Harlaxton College, Grantham, 1996

PICKARD, JANE. 'The wrong turns to avoid with tests', *People Management,* 8 August 1996

PRAIS, S. J. *Productivity, education and training. An international perspective.* Cambridge, 1995